The Ultimate
DIGITAL
MUSIC
GUIDE

Michael Miller

Funded by
MISSION COLLEGE
Carl D. Perkins Vocational and Technical Education Act Grant

 800 East 96th Street,
Indianapolis, Indiana 46240

The Ultimate Digital Music Guide

ISBN-13: 978-0-7897-4844-7
ISBN-10: 0-7897-4844-4

Library of Congress Cataloging-in-Publication Data is on file.

Printed in the United States of America

First Printing: June 2012

Trademarks

Warning and Disclaimer

Bulk Sales

Que Publishing offers excellent discounts on this book when ordered in quantity for bulk purchases or special sales. For more information, please contact

U.S. Corporate and Government Sales
1-800-382-3419
corpsales@pearsontechgroup.com

For sales outside of the U.S., please contact

International Sales
international@pearsoned.com

Associate Publisher
Greg Wiegand

Acquisitions Editor
Rick Kughen

Development Editor
Rick Kughen

Technical Editor
Karen Weinstein

Managing Editor
Kristy Hart

Project Editor
Anne Goebel

Indexer
Erika Millen

Proofreader
Jess DeGabriele

Publishing Coordinator
Cindy Teeters

Cover Designer
Anne Jones

Compositor
Tricia Bronkella

Contents at a Glance

Table of Contents

Part III: Managing Your Music

About the Author

Michael Miller has written more than 100 nonfiction how-to books over the past 20 years, including *Sams Teach Yourself Spotify in 10 Minutes, How Home Theater and HDTV Work, Creating a Digital Home Entertainment Center with Windows Media Center, The Complete Idiot's Guide to Home Theater Systems, The Complete Idiot's Guide to Music History,* and *Absolute Beginner's Guide to Computer Basics.*

Mr. Miller has established a reputation for clearly explaining technical topics to nontechnical readers, and for offering useful real-world advice about complicated topics. More information can be found at the author's website, located at www.molehillgroup.com.

Dedication

To Sherry, with whom I share all my music.

Acknowledgments

Thanks to all the usual suspects at Que who helped to turn my manuscript into a printed book, including but not limited to Rick Kughen, Anne Goebel, and Greg Wiegand. Thanks also to Karen Weinstein, who served as technical editor for this book and helped to make sure all the technical details are correct.

Most especially, thanks to all my friends who have graciously shared their music with me over the years. You turned me on to a lot of great stuff, and I hope I've returned the favor.

We Want to Hear from You!

As the reader of this book, *you* are our most important critic and commentator. We value your opinion and want to know what we're doing right, what we could do better, what areas you'd like to see us publish in, and any other words of wisdom you're willing to pass our way.

We welcome your comments. You can email or write to let us know what you did or didn't like about this book—as well as what we can do to make our books better.

Please note that we cannot help you with technical problems related to the topic of this book.

When you write, please be sure to include this book's title and author as well as your name and email address. We will carefully review your comments and share them with the author and editors who worked on the book.

Email: feedback@quepublishing.com

Mail: Que Publishing
ATTN: Reader Feedback
800 East 96th Street
Indianapolis, IN 46240 USA

Reader Services

Visit our website and register this book at www.quepublishing.com/register for convenient access to any updates, downloads, or errata that might be available for this book.

Introduction

I am a music lover. Big time. My wife and I try to catch at least one or two major shows a month, and I'm an "A Train" member of and frequent visitor to our local jazz club. (That's the Dakota Jazz Club in Minneapolis, one of the best in the nation.) I have more than 1,700 albums in my music collection, or more than 25,000 individual tracks if you count that way. I listen to jazz and rock and folk and soul, and even the occasional Broadway show tune. I'm fairly sure I know the entire Great American Songbook by heart, and can throw out the names of all the backing musicians on most of the big hits (and a lot of album cuts) pressed during the 1960s and 1970s. I play drums, piano, and a little guitar, and write books about music history and music theory and the like. I may be an expert on certain aspects of music, if that sort of thing matters or impresses you.

I'm guessing that you're a music lover too. Maybe not as extreme as me—or maybe you are—but a music lover, nonetheless. You have your own personal tastes and opinions as to what makes good music, I'm sure, and no doubt have a decent collection of said music in your possession. Your collection might be on compact disc, or it could be on vinyl or audiocassette, but I'm guessing at least part of your collection is digital, coming either from ripped CDs or Internet downloads. Or maybe your collection isn't digital—yet—but you want to go that route.

I have to tell you, moving to an all-digital music library has a lot of benefits—if you do it right. When your music is in digital format, it's a snap to find that one track or album and play it virtually instantly; no more hunting through your entire collection for that song you just can't quite put your fingers on. A digital music library is also easy to organize just about any way you want to, and then reorganize with the click of a button; if you want to play only soul music or only folk, that's a snap, too.

Even better, a digital music library doesn't take up any physical space. You know those shelves and racks of discs and tapes? Pack all those old relics up and put them in the attic, because your new digital collection takes up no more space than a computer hard drive. Make your digital collection as big as you wish, it doesn't expand any physically.

You can also play a digital music library in multiple rooms of your house. You're not limited to that one CD player or turntable in your den or living room; with the right equipment, you can beam your music from a central location to any room you want. You can even listen to different tunes in different rooms at the same time—or the same tune in more than one room. Digital makes that easy.

Plus, when your music library is digital, it's easy to take it—all of it—with you. You can load your music on an iPod or iPhone, or listen to it over the Internet on another computer in another location. And all without carrying a single disc with you.

Of course, there are issues involved with maintaining a completely digital music collection. You have to decide on where to store your collection, which file format(s) to use, which bitrate to rip at, what kind of equipment to hook up in each room, how to organize your library—like I said, a lot of issues and a lot of choices to make. Make the wrong choices, and your easy-to-use digital music library becomes less convenient, if not downright annoying. Make the right choices, and listening becomes a real pleasure.

But which choices are the right ones for you? I'll tell you right now—there are no universal best choices that fit every music lover. Your situation is unique, and requires unique solutions.

I can, however, provide advice and guidance and tons of information that can lead you to the best solutions for you. That's why I wrote this book; *The Ultimate Digital Music Guide* is for music lovers like you and me who want the best possible digital music experience.

What's in This Book

I've tried to make the content of this book reflect its title. That is, *The Ultimate Digital Music Guide* attempts to be the ultimate guide for digital music lovers. As such, it contains all the information you might need to create and maintain a digital music library, and to listen to your digital music. It even contains information on where you can find new music to listen to, and where to purchase and download new music.

That's it in a nutshell—*The Ultimate Digital Music Guide* is a book to enhance your digital collecting and listening experience. But what does that mean?

First, this book is designed to educate you about how digital music works. You need to have a little background before you can get started.

Second, this book is designed to inform you about the various options available. I'm talking both hardware and software options—the various ways you can store and listen to a digital music collection.

Third, this book is designed to show you how to do the things you need to do—how to hook up different types of equipment, how to rip and burn CDs, how to edit file information, and so forth. There's lots of "how to" information in these pages, as you might suspect.

Fourth, this book is designed to show you where to find the things you need. This means finding music to download, software programs to install, album cover art to use in your library, hardware to purchase, even new music to discover. There's a lot of good stuff out on the web, if you know where to look.

Fifth and finally, this book is designed to entertain, just a little bit. I like to think of myself as a somewhat entertaining writer, even when I'm writing about serious topics, and I think music is a fun topic to write about and discuss. Digital music isn't just about the bits and bytes, after all; it's also about the music itself, those songs and artists that mean something to us. Whether you're into the Beatles or the Rolling Stones (and if you're of a certain age you know they're somewhat mutually exclusive), or into Romantic symphonies or classic jazz or the latest hip hop, music matters to you. Well, it matters to me too, and I try to treat it with the respect it deserves, while not taking things too seriously. You'll understand.

Who This Book Is For

This book is for the serious music lover, someone who listens to a lot of music and has a large music collection. You know who you are.

This book is probably not for the casual listener. If you only buy one CD a year (probably a greatest hits collection), or if your music library consists entirely of Justin Bieber tracks, then this book probably isn't up your alley. Not that you wouldn't find some of the information useful, but it's probably not necessary for you. Sorry.

This book is *not* focused exclusively on any particular technological ecosystem. That is, I treat Apple, iTunes, and the iPod as just another option, not the only option available. I'm somewhat agnostic as to ecosystems and formats; I see the good (and the bad) of MP3, AAC, WMA, and FLAC. I hope that lets me present a balanced approach to the topic.

I'm also cognizant that not everyone is a golden-eared audiophile, and not everyone has tens of thousands of dollars to spend on high-end equipment. Some music lovers listen to their tunes on iPhones, and others on expensive home audio systems. I try to treat each situation with the requisite respect.

Finally, I don't expect you to be fully versed on all things digital. If you don't know an MP3 from a FLAC, that's okay—I'll tell you. I try to explain the more technical things in everyday language, so don't feel as if you need to be a Geek Squad member to proceed. Anyone's welcome in this club; all you really have to do is have a love for music.

How This Book Is Organized

There's a lot of information packed into the pages of this book. To make things a little easier to navigate, I've organized things into eight main parts, each focused on a particular aspect of digital music:

■ **Part I, "Understanding Digital Music,"** is a good place to start, especially if you're somewhat unfamiliar with digital music world. We start with a history of how music is distributed, look at all the different ways you listen to music today, explain how digital music works, and then talk about the various digital music file formats, copyright and piracy issues, and this thing called digital rights management. Think of this section as "digital music 101."

- **Part II, "Downloading Music,"** explores probably the most popular way to obtain digital music today—via downloading. That means purchasing music from iTunes, Amazon, and other online music stores, as well as finding free music to download from the web. We'll even examine so-called high definition music downloads which can sound even better than the music you currently listen to on CD.

- **Part III, "Managing Your Music,"** shows you how to organize and manage all the digital music you download. You'll learn the best ways to store your digital music library, how to properly edit the informational tags that accompany each track, how to find and add the best cover art images, and how to create the perfect playlist—if there is such a thing.

- **Part IV, "Streaming Music,"** examines another way to listen to music, digitally—via streaming audio over the Internet. You'll learn how streaming music works, and how to use the most popular streaming music services, such as Spotify. You'll even learn how to upload your own music collection to the cloud (and we'll explain what that cloud thing is, too) so you can listen to your music from any computer or device, anywhere in the world. We'll even discuss this thing called Internet radio—what it is and how it works.

- **Part V, "Playing Your Music—at Home,"** gets into listening to all the digital music you've collected. You'll learn how to rip digital music from CDs, how to play music on your computer (including how to pick a music player program and how to connect your computer to your home audio system), how to choose a home media player for music playback, and how to build a whole house digital audio system. There's a lot of good stuff here.

- **Part VI, "Playing Your Music—On the Go,"** is for everyone with an iPod or iPhone or other portable digital music player. You'll learn the best ways to play music on a portable player, how to listen to streaming music while you're on the go, and how to play music from your portable device in your living room—without earbuds.

- **Part VII, "Sharing Your Music,"** is all about sharing the music you love with friends and family. You'll learn the various ways to share, including physically (by burning CDs), virtually (via email or over a network), and socially (on Facebook and other social networks). What good is finding a great tune if you can't share it?

■ **Part VIII, "Discovering New Music,"** is a fun collection of chapters that shows you the many different ways you can use the Internet to find new music you might like. I'm talking about discovering music on Last.fm and other online music services, in the Amazon and iTunes stores, and on Facebook and other social networks. I'll also give you a list of interesting and useful websites and blogs where lots of music news and reviews can be had.

By the end of the book you should know pretty much all you need to know to build and maintain (and listen to!) a serious digital music collection. Make sure you take notes.

Conventions Used in This Book

I hope that this book is easy enough to figure out on its own without requiring its own instruction manual. As you read through the pages, however, it helps to know precisely how I've presented specific types of information.

As you read through this book you'll note several special elements, presented in what we in the publishing business call *margin notes*. These notes present additional information and advice beyond what you find in the regular text. There are three kinds of margin notes in this book:

> **ULTIMATELY INTERESTING**   This is a note that presents some interesting and useful information, even if it isn't wholly relevant to the discussion in the main text.

> **ULTIMATELY USEFUL**   This is a tip that presents some advice that could be useful in doing whatever it is you're doing at the moment.

> **ULTIMATELY CAUTIOUS**   This is a caution about something tricky or even harmful that you should try to avoid.

In addition to the main text and these little margin notes, I include at the end of each chapter an extended observation, in sidebar format. These sidebars aren't necessarily factual, as the rest of the text is supposed to be; they're more opinion, looking at the world of digital music (or just music in general) from my own personal viewpoint. Remember, I'm a music lover, just like you, and all music lovers have opinions about music. Take 'em or leave 'em—that's up to you.

Let's Get Ready to Rock and Roll

Now that you know how to use this book, it's time to get busy doing just that. But before you do, here are a few words about some more stuff available online.

First, I've created a blog to accompany this book, located at UltimateDigitalMusicGuide.blogspot.com. This blog may contain a little news and information related to the world of digital music, or just my own thoughts on music and such. It all depends on what I'm feeling like that day. I'll try to update it on a regular basis (no promises there; I get busy, some-times), and hope you'll find what's there somewhat interesting.

While you're online, feel free to stop by my personal website, located at www.molehillgroup.com. Here you'll find more information on this book and other books I've written or am about to write. There's always something new.

In addition, know that I love to hear from readers of my books. If you want to contact me, feel free to email me at digitalmusic@molehillgroup.com. I can't promise that I'll answer every message, but I do promise that I'll read each one!

With these preliminaries out of the way, go ahead and turn the page—and start learning more about the wonderful world of digital music.

Understanding Digital Music

The History of Music Distribution—From Piano Rolls to iTunes

Things change. How you get your music today is much different from how I got it when I was a kid, which was much different from how my parents got their music. Mainly, this is due to changing technology; we have much different recording and delivery technology today than in years past.

The more things change, however, the more they remain the same. Music lovers want to collect the music they like—and only that music. We need a way to store the music we own, and to easily retrieve it when we want to listen to it. And we don't like the fact that every new technological advancement seems to make obsolete all the music we've previously collected.

Let's take a tour, then, through the history of music distribution—how music lovers throughout recent history have collected their favorite tunes.

How Do You Collect Music When There's No Music to Collect?

We have it pretty easy today. You discover a tune you like, you find it online, and you download it. Yes, there are the inevitable issues of which site to download from, which file format to download to, and which music player to use to play the darned thing (all of which I address in this book, of course), but in general it's pretty easy to find and collect the music we love.

This wasn't always the case.

Imagine a time before music was digital. (Okay, that doesn't take much imaging; just go back a dozen years or so.) Now imagine a time before music was even recorded—or available in written format.

In other words, imagine life before the 1900s.

> ♩ ULTIMATELY Learn more
> ♪ **INTERESTING** about the history of music in general in another book I wrote, *The Complete Idiot's Guide to Music History* (Michael Miller, Alpha Books, 2008).

Before recording technology existed, before printed sheet music became common, the only way to hear music was to experience it live. Now, that could be a concert performance from your favorite soloist or orchestra, or a more intimate performance from a traveling bard, but it was a live performance, pure and simple.

Live performances started relatively early in human history. Early music was predominantly church music, so music lovers could get their fix by going to church each Sunday. Consider a musician like Johann Sebastian Bach, today regarded as one of the foremost composers in history. In his day (the early 1700s), however, he was just another choirmaster in his church, composing a new piece of music every week for performance at Sunday services. (A conductor I interviewed once joked that this was why J.S. had so many children—to copy all those parts every week.)

This church-centric nature of the music business began to change during the 1600s, however, due to the rise of the patronage system. That is, musicians began to be supported by wealthy patrons, and thus compose and perform music for that patron's court and family. This led to secular music becoming more popular, both among the elite and the masses.

The patronage system died out by the mid-1700s or so, after Bach's heyday and around the time that Wolfgang Amadeus Mozart was making a name for himself. Without wealthy employers paying the bills, composers had to pay their own way, typically by performing. We're talking public concerts here, not the private ones common previously, which led to a greater exposure of the day's popular music to the masses. For example, Ludwig van Beethoven made good money by producing a series of subscription concerts, essentially functioning as his own concert promoter.

Old Ludwig also made money by selling his compositions to music publishing companies. These companies, in turn, sold sheet music of Beethoven's works. Now, sheet music wasn't a huge business back then, as the technology didn't allow for mass printing and distribution; sheet music that was sold typically went to wealthy households, who could afford both the music and a piano to play on. The average Joe got his music fix from going to concerts.

Between the Sheets

Things changed during the late 1800s, due to a shift in technology—actually, in several technologies.

The first technological change was printing-related; the widespread adoption of the modern printing press made mass-produced printed sheet music both affordable and common. This spurred the growth of music publishing companies, which in turn provided opportunities for songwriters to publish their songs to a broader market. For music lovers, this meant that you didn't have to wait for your local chamber orchestra or brass band to learn and play a new piece; you could purchase the sheet music and play it yourself, at pretty much the same time people around the country were doing the same.

By the turn of the century, then, sheet music became the primary way for music to be disseminated. Listeners would hear new songs at department stores and music stores in their home towns, performed by hired song demonstrators. When you heard a tune you liked, you'd purchase the sheet music and go home to play it on piano.

The piano was part of the second technological revolution; musical instruments started to be mass produced. This made pianos, particularly smaller uprights, affordable enough that just about every middle class household had one. The result was that by the early years of the 20th century, pianos were as ubiquitous as iPhones are today.

So if you were a music lover around the turn of the century, you played it yourself on your own piano from sheet music you purchased at your local music store.

Now, this process wasn't quite as immediate as what you get with today's digital distribution; it took longer for a song to become a hit, but hits were made nonetheless. In fact, the most popular sheet music of the day sold millions of copies—not unlike what a hit song sells today. (In fact, with the 21st century decline in music industry sales, a hit piece of sheet music reached more listeners than today's top downloads do.)

And note something about how music was distributed then—on a song-by-song basis. We're not talking albums of multiple songs (although sheet music songbooks did exist); sheet music was a way to distribute individual songs—printed "singles," if you like.

Remember: The original model for music distribution was a singles model.

Going on Record

The next set of technological developments made it possible for music lovers to own not just the notes and lyrics to their favorite songs but also their favorite performances. Both developments were claimed by inventor Thomas Alva Edison.

The first invention, which Edison claimed in 1877 (but may have been developed concurrently by Emile Berliner), was the microphone. The microphone enabled the capture of live sound and thus entire musical performances.

Initially, these performances were captured on primitive wire recorders. But also in 1877, Edison invented the phonograph, and his pioneering wax cylinders and (later) discs proved an effective and efficient way to distribute musical recordings. Records in particular were a hit with music lovers, and the record industry experienced rapid growth; by the 1920s, when discs overtook cylinders in the marketplace, more than 150 companies, such as Columbia, Decca, and RCA Victor, were making records or record players. (Figure 1.1 shows an early Edison model phonograph.)

> **ULTIMATELY INTERESTING** The development of the microphone also affected singing styles. Before the invention of the microphone, a singer needed a "big" voice to project over the backing orchestra; this favored operatic-type voices like Enrico Caruso or, in the popular vein, belters like Al Jolson. With the invention of the microphone, however, singers could now get soft and intimate, wrapping their voices around a tune without having to worry about reaching the back row of the theater; this new generation of singers, including Bing Crosby, Perry Como, and Frank Sinatra, tended to have light and intimate voices that would have been wholly out of place just fifty years earlier. This led to the more personal styles of singing that we're used to today.

FIGURE 1.1

An early Edison phonograph. (Photo by Gregory Moine via the Creative Commons 2.0 license, http://creativecommons.org/licenses/by/2.0/legalcode.)

These early records were a bit different from the classic vinyl that's popular today. For one, the records weren't made of vinyl, they were made of a hard shellac compound, which made them easily breakable; they also had considerable surface noise. The discs themselves came in several sizes, the most common being 7 inches in diameter, and were played at a speed of 78 revolutions per minute (RPM). As such, each side could only hold about three minutes of recording.

That meant that each side of a 78 RPM record could hold one song. That's right, the era of 78 RPM recordings was a *singles* market. (Seeing a trend here?)

The Rise of Radio

Shortly after the development of the record industry, in the early 1920s, the world's airwaves crackled to life with the advent of commercial radio broadcasts.

Early radio programming consisted of a lot of staged dramas and comedies along with a plethora of live music shows. The radio stations and networks eventually supplemented their live programming with the playing of recorded music—literally playing records over the air.

Now, this was a good thing for both the music industry and music lovers. Radio offered the music industry considerable promotion for their latest records, and thus helped to spur record sales. Music lovers got to hear both new music and old favorites on regular basis (and for free), and thus determine which new records to purchase.

> ♪ **ULTIMATELY INTERESTING** Then as now, radio stations played music for free. That is, they don't have to pay performance royalties when they play music over the air. (They do, however, have to pay songwriting royalties.) This calls into question today's music industry claims of not wanting to give away their music over the Internet; they've been giving it away for almost a century over the airwaves!

And, not to belabor a point, radio stations played individual songs. This was evident in the rise of lists and countdowns, in the form of the Hit Parade and Top Forty formats. Long-form programming did exist, but radio has always been a singles-based medium.

It's a Long-Playing World

So radio helped promote the recording industry, and the recording industry powered radio. It was a nice symbiotic relationship.

As could be expected, of course, the record industry evolved over time, always due to technological developments. The next big change happened in the late 1940s and early 1950s, when the original 78 RPM discs gave way to long playing (LP) records.

Originally developed by Columbia Records in 1948, LPs let music labels put more music on a disc. LPs were larger than 78s (12 inches vs. 7 inches) and spun at a slower speed (33 1/3 RPM). All this, combined with newer technology that enabled more densely-packed grooves, let labels put up to 25 minutes per side, or 50 minutes per album. That's a lot of space to fill, and resorted not just in the recording of more individual songs, but also a creative renaissance on the part of musicians. (Figure 1.2 shows a typical LP in use.)

FIGURE 1.2

Playing a vinyl LP. (Photo by Olle Svensson via the Creative Commons 2.0 license, http://creativecommons.org/licenses/by/2.0/legalcode.)

The first wave of long-form creativity hit in 1955, when Frank Sinatra had the idea of recording a concept album about lost love. That album was *In the Wee Small Hours*, and it was a huge hit—and led to a series of similar concept albums from Sinatra and other singers in the following years.

Further innovation hit in the 1960s, when rock artists like the Beatles (*Sgt. Pepper's Lonely Hearts Club Band*) and the Beach Boys (*Pet Sounds*) used the album format like a musical canvas to create unified musical experiences from the first to the last track. We're talking albums where one track bleeds into another, and where the whole musical experience is much more than the sum of the individual parts.

Music lovers ate it up. I'm old enough to remember the heyday of the LP, where you'd invite friends over to listen—really, *listen*—to a new album. The physical format was appealing in both a visual and tactile fashion; that big ol' album cover and inner sleeve held a lot of great artwork, lyrics, photos, and other information. It was a gas, and I treasure those albums yet today.

This shift to a long-playing musical experience stands as a unique era in the history of music collecting, however. From the advent of the commercial music industry, people bought individual songs, either in sheet music or record formats. Purchasing multiple songs on a single album was something new—and, as we're now seeing, something that wouldn't last.

> 🎼 **ULTIMATELY INTERESTING** Stereo recordings also helped promote interest in long-playing albums. The first stereo recordings were released in 1958, and really took off in the early 1960s—the same time the LP market exploded.

The Singles Life

Simultaneous with the rise of the long-playing album was a market boom for "singles." We're talking 7 inch vinyl discs (same size as the old 78s), but with a large center hole, that revolved at 45 RPM. These 45s were perfect for distributing hit songs, one per side; a 45 could hold up to about five minutes per side—a little longer than a 78 but with much higher fidelity. (Figure 1.3 shows a typical 45 RPM single.)

FIGURE 1.3

A 45 RPM single. (Photo by David Salafia via the Creative Commons 2.0 license, http://creativecommons.org/licenses/by/2.0/legalcode.)

These 45 RPM singles first came to prominence in the mid-1950s, and helped fuel (or were fueled by; it's a bit synergistic) the Top Forty rock 'n' roll era. At less than a buck a disc, teenagers could afford to buy several singles a week— and did. With the invasion of the Beatles in 1964, the singles market literally exploded, with the top singles selling in excess of 5 million units each.

The market for singles stayed strong throughout the vinyl era, but suffered with the shift to compact disc (CD) in the 1980s. (Even though so-called CD singles existed, it cost the same to press a one-track CD as it did to press a full album's worth of tracks.) During its heyday, from the mid-1950s to the mid-1970s, singles were *the* way that most consumers collected their favorite music.

The Tale of the Tape

While we're discussing how music was distributed, I can't avoid talking a little bit about magnetic tape, in a plethora of formats.

Magnetic tape has been used to *record* music since 1947, when singer Bing Crosby championed the use of 1/4-inch reel-to-reel recording (and personally invested in the Ampex company, the manufacturer of the first tape recorders). These first tape recorders were used to prerecord radio shows for later broadcast, but quickly found their way into the music recording booth.

Reel-to-reel tape recorders hit the consumer market in the mid-1950s, along with prerecorded tapes. Music on tape had a higher fidelity than the 78 RPM discs and LPs of the time, and thus appealed to audiophiles. However, they never really caught on in the mass market, and remained a niche market through the mid-1970s.

More popular was the compact audiocassette, developed by Philips in 1963. With its 0.15-inch tape enclosed in a plastic case, there was no threading or winding to do, which made it a lot easier for the average consumer to use. By 1968 the audiocassette represented a $150 million market worldwide; audiocassette machines were commonly used for both recording and playback of prerecorded music. The format had a good run in the late 1970s with the advent of Sony's Walkman portable players, but ultimately got replaced by compact discs by the mid-1980s. (Figure 1.4 shows a tape being inserted into a cassette player.)

FIGURE 1.4

Playing an audiocassette. (Photo by Falk Lademann via the Creative Commons 2.0 license.)

Then there was that groovy product called the 8-track tape. This was a magnetic tape in an endless-loop cartridge, consisting of four stereo tracks (4 x 2 = 8) played one after another. The 8-track was especially popular in the automotive market; it was easy to pop an 8-track in the slot and go cruising—even though playback was frequently interrupted mid-song as the player changed tracks. Prerecorded 8-track tapes were popular from the mid-1960s through the mid-1970s, but ultimately were the victim of an unwieldy form factor (bigger than audiocassettes), relatively low fidelity, and unreliable operation. Few remember them fondly.

ULTIMATELY INTERESTING One interesting trend is that music has become more portable over time. During the first part of the 20th century, most people listened to music in their homes, either on their own pianos, on phonograph records, or over the radio. In the second half of the century, however, new technology enabled people to listen to music in their cars, on portable transistor radios, and on their Sony Walkman portable audio cassette players—and today, on their iPods and iPhones.

Say Hello to My Little Friend, the Compact Disc

All of these old formats were eventually supplanted by the new compact disc (CD) format. Introduced in 1982, the CD is an optical disc, read by a laser, which stores music and other data digitally. Standard CDs have a diameter of just 4.7 inches and can hold up to 80 minutes of music—much longer than a vinyl LP or audiocassette. (Figure 1.5 shows a typical compact disc.)

FIGURE 1.5

A digital compact disc.

The CD's digital storage technology did away with all the pops and hisses of older analog formats—although some claimed (and continue to claim) that CDs sounded cold and sterile compared to vinyl's "warmer" sound. That said, the CD format was revolutionary in presenting such high-fidelity music at an affordable price. The CD was enthusiastically received, first in the classical music community and later, when CD player prices inevitably dropped, in the mass market. Everybody switched from vinyl and tape to those little digital discs.

The CD revolution also led to a bit of artistic excess, as more and more artists felt obligated to fill up as much of those 80 minutes as possible. (Honestly, how many performers really have the equivalent of a double-LP's worth of

1

good material in them? I miss the days of 35-minute albums where every song was a keeper...) And that eventually led to a bit of backlash from consumers, who really only wanted the one or two good songs on an album, not the 15 other filler tracks.

All in all, however, the CD era was a good one for all concerned—recording artists, record labels, and music lovers. The switch to CDs spurred music sales to record highs, with many record collectors replacing their analog collections with new digital copies. By 1988, CD sales had surpassed sales of vinyl records, peaking in 2000 at close to 950 million units.

Going Digital

Since the turn of the millennium, however, CD sales have gone downhill. That's due to a number of factors, including a dearth of talent and an increasing fragmentation of genres. But probably the most significant reason for the slide in sales of physical music product is the shift to virtual products—digital music downloaded from the Internet.

With the rise of the Internet in the late 1990s, music lovers found they could download the songs they wanted from a variety of legitimate and illegitimate websites. The original Napster was one of the first of the free file-sharing websites, encouraging listeners to rip music from their compact discs and upload the tracks to the web, where they could then be downloaded (for free) by others. Napster was eventually shut down for illegal file sharing, but the public developed a taste for downloading single tracks (not complete albums) over the Internet in MP3 format.

This digital music boom got a big boost when Apple released its iPod portable music player, which rode the dual trends of digital and portable music (see Figure 1.6). There were other digital music players before the iPod, but Apple got everything right and encouraged a new generation of listeners to take their music with them, in digital format.

The iPod was to the 2000s as the Sony Walkman was to the 1980s and the transistor radio was to the 1960s—but with even fewer limitations on use. The transistor radio freed music from the confines of the power outlet, but limited listeners to the restricted playlists beamed from AM radio stations. The Walkman let listeners play their own music on the go, but limited playback to the 90 minutes or so of music that would fit on an audiocassette. The iPod removed all those restrictions; not only did it offer music on the go, it let users take with them a seemingly limitless number of songs. It was nirvana for mobile music lovers.

FIGURE 1.6

An Apple iPod. (Photo courtesy of Apple.)

Even better, the iPod was supported by Apple's iTunes Store, which legitimized music downloads. At an initial cost of just 99 cents per track, iTunes enabled listeners to load their iPods with all their favorite songs—and effectively contributed to the death of the $20 CD album. Why purchase an entire album (at a high price) when you can get just the songs you like (for a low price)?

This per-song thinking brings the music industry back full circle to where it started, with consumers purchasing one song at a time. It's a singles world again, just as it was in the days of sheet music, 78 RPM discs, and 45 RPM singles. The album era proved to be an anomaly of the past, not the future of the music business.

Of course, Apple doesn't have a monopoly on digital music. As we'll examine throughout this book, there are a lot of other ways to listen to digital music, including the following:

- Other online music stores, such as the Amazon MP3 Music Store and HDtracks (for high-resolution downloads)

- Free downloads from a variety of sites, including those run by individual artists
- Illegal downloads from various file-sharing sites
- Internet radio stations
- Streaming music services, which serve up all the music you can listen to for a flat monthly charge
- Cloud music services, which upload your personal music collection to the Internet and stream it back to you on any type of Internet-connected device

As you can see, choices abound in this digital era.

> ♪ **ULTIMATELY INTERESTING**   Digital music affects more than just the way consumers purchase their favorite tunes; it also affects how music is recorded. Digital recording made its way into studios in the 1990s, replacing older analog tape recorders, and thus changing the whole nature of the recording industry. Today, virtually any musician can create high-quality recordings in the comfort of their own home studios without racking up huge studio bills; this, as much as anything, has led to the rise of the indie music movement—and the decline in major recording labels.

What's Next

Today we're living in the digital world, and music lovers are foraging through a variety of options available for finding, storing, and listening to their favorite music. That's why you bought this book, of course, to learn more about what's available and maybe even make some decisions about which way to go.

But where is the music industry going tomorrow? That's a tough question to answer, other than things are likely to be even more different in the future.

That said, I can make a few easy predictions. First: The adoption of digital distribution will continue apace. That's just a continuation of trends, of course; physical CD sales continue to decline while digital downloads continue to rise. In fact, it's possible that physical music distribution will fade away completely at some point—maybe not next year, but possibly within a decade.

Today, most online music is sold on a per-track basis by online music stores. But that model is itself changing, especially as more and more listeners want their music on the go—which doesn't necessarily mean from iPods and other portable music players.

To that end, I'm placing my bets on music delivered over smartphones, such as the iPhone and Android phones. Not that these devices will have tons of digital files stored locally—they don't have the capacity for that. Instead, it's more likely that music will be streamed in real time over the accompanying cellular phone network.

I can envision a scenario where you speak into your phone, "Play the Beatles' *White Album*" or "Play 'Louie, Louie'," and the requested music will be sent over the cell network to your phone. It's not that farfetched; you can pretty much do that today (without the voice command, anyway) with streaming services such as Spotify and Pandora, or cloud services from Amazon and Google. You don't have to look too much into the future to envision the day when every track ever recorded is available for immediate streaming to anyone's cell phone, the entirety of music history just a voice command away.

With this in mind, how do you prepare for this streaming digital music future? At this point, it's difficult to say. You'll definitely need to have all your music in digital format, of course, although it's unclear which file format will eventually become the standard. Then we're faced with the issue of who (or rather, which entity) runs the music streaming service. Will it be an existing player, such as Apple or Amazon? Or some new player, like Spotify or someone we haven't even heard of yet? Or will you control your own streaming, from your own home server?

I don't know how it all ends up—nobody does. In a sense, we're all along for the ride, and we all hope we don't have to purchase our entire collection yet again in another new format. About the only thing I'm sure of is that we're solidly in the digital world—and that the future is bright, with more higher-quality music being available on whatever device we choose to listen to, either in the home or on the go.

FRAGMENTING AND PERSONALIZING

Digital aside, the music industry is a lot less monolithic than it used to be, and a lot more fragmented. Some of this results from the continuing decline of the major record labels; with the rise of smaller independent labels, the big companies have less control over what radio stations play and what music lovers listen to.

But there's more than that; the industry itself has changed. Back in the heyday of Top 40 radio, radio stations played pretty much everything from everybody; radio was truly cross genre. A single station would play a little British Invasion rock mixed with Brill Building pop, beach music, sounds, Motown, country, even the occasional Frank Sinatra tune. That kind of variety helped promote all musical genres; everybody heard a little bit of everything.

All you have to do is scan up or down the dial to know that that's not the way it works today. Over the past several decades, radio programming has become much more segmented. Instead of a radio station playing music from different types of artists, stations today have relatively narrow playlists. A station might play only hip hop, heavy metal, or alternative rock—and nothing else. There's no cross-pollination between genres. You pick your station of choice and then never get exposed to anything else.

This blinders-on programming is even worse in the worlds of satellite and Internet radio, where segments get further sub-segmented. You want a station that plays only gangster rap? You got it. How about an outlaw country-only station? It's there. What about a station that plays only Elvis Presley tunes? Yep, there's one of those, too. (Although you can't yet discriminate between early "good Elvis" and later "Vegas Elvis" tunes.)

Then there's the fact that most music lovers today program their own music through personalized playlists on their iPods or streaming music services. When you can program your own music, you need never be exposed to anything new, let alone anything different. How do you hear the latest breaking artists when all you have playlisted is a bunch of New Wave bands from the early 1980s? We're all listening to our own private stations, everything else be damned.

Now, that may sound fine if you're a discriminate music lover; you know what you like and that's that. But this fragmentation and personalization of the market has many ill effects, not the least of which is that we no longer have common musical experiences.

Let's face it, in today's digital world, there's no such thing as a big act any more. In the old days, a hit single could sell tens of millions of copies, because people from all walks of life were exposed to it. Not the case today, where a "big" single only sells a hundred thousand copies or so, and isn't even recognizable by most listeners—who happen not to listen to that particular format.

1

There are exceptions, of course; Brit singer Adele did a good job of bridging genres in 2011, due in no small part to the universal nature of her music and her all-around talent. But for every Adele there are a hundred Arcade Fires. Remember when Arcade Fire won the Best Album Grammy in 2011 (for *The Suburbs*) and the general chorus was "What is an Arcade Fire?" As talented as the group is and as great as that album was, it hit only a small segment of the listening audience. Aside from their small but dedicated fan base, nobody else had heard of them; everybody else was too busy listening to their own personalized and fragmented playlists, and missed out on a great album.

The challenge, then, is to move beyond the music you're comfortable with and discover something new. That used to be as easy as tuning your radio to the AM dial (which is now filled with right-wing airbags); today, you have to try harder.

Exploring the Different Ways to Listen to Music Today

Now that you know how we used to find music to collect, let's take a look at all the various options available today. Today's digital world has created a veritable music lover's paradise; just about everything you could want is available to you, one way or another.

Going Old School with Compact Discs

Let's start with what is rapidly become an old school way to collect music, that very first digital format we all know and love, the compact disc (CD). Old school or not, the CD format is still one of the highest-fidelity formats available today.

If you're like me, you've been collecting CDs for almost three decades. (Or, if you're a younger music lover, all your life.) That's pretty much an average lifespan for recorded music formats; the 78 lasted about as long, as did the LP. And the CD remains viable, if diminished somewhat from its peak a decade or so ago; the music industry still sold 223 million CDs in 2011, which ain't chicken feed, folks.

2

Most long-time music lovers have amassed massive CD collections. I happen to own more than 1,600 of the things myself, and continue to buy another half-dozen or so each month. About the only thing that's changed about my CD purchasing habits is where I buy them; with the virtual death of the local music store, I now buy most of my CDs online, from Amazon, CD Baby, and other sources. But wherever I buy them, I still buy them.

Why do CDs remain viable? I think there are a few reasons:

- First is the audio quality. Most digital downloads are in some sort of compressed audio format, which means that there is some loss of fidelity. Whether you download from iTunes or Amazon, you're getting files at a bitrate that is a subset of the original uncompressed recording. A compact disc, however, represents the fullest audio fidelity, and exhibits none of the compression artifacts you get with MP3 and other digital files. It's a sound thing, in other words.

- Next is the physical nature of ownership. When I purchase a CD, I can hold it in my hands and put in on a shelf and look at it whenever I want to. I know it exists, I know it's mine. You just don't get that sort of physical satisfaction when you purchase a digital file.

- Having a physical product in hand also gives you all the printed material that comes with it—cover art, liner notes, song credits, lyrics, and so forth. You typically don't get any of this (aside from a small cover art thumbnail) when you download a digital product. For many serious music lovers, this ancillary information is almost as important as the music itself.

- Then there's the matter of legal ownership. When you purchase a CD you legally own it and can use it however you like—including reselling it. Many of the sites you download digital music from apply all sorts of legalese that limit how you can use the music you just purchased—how many devices you can listen to it on, and that sort of thing. And forget about reselling it; you're really just licensing the content, and do not have full rights to resell it to someone else.

> **♪ ULTIMATELY INTERESTING** The legal issues with digital music are mind boggling and discussed in much depth in Chapter 5, "Understanding Copyright, Piracy, and Other Legal Issues." I discuss DRM in Chapter 6, "Understanding DRM."

For all these reasons and more (including habit, to be honest), CDs remain an important part of the mix for music lovers today. But they're becoming less important as pure digital distribution, in its many forms, gains prominence. And that may not be a bad thing; if you can achieve the same level of fidelity at a similar cost, moving from CD to pure digital will save you a lot of physical space.

Ripping Digital Tracks from CD

Of course, just because you physically collect compact discs doesn't mean that that's the way you have to listen to them. That is, you're not limited to sticking a CD into a player and giving it a spin; you can also copy (or *rip*) the music from a CD to store as digital audio files.

This is how most audiophiles do it today. If you choose your audio formats carefully, you can store your entire CD collection in digital format with fidelity identical to or close to the original. You can then pack up all your old CDs and store them in boxes in your basement, which frees up lots of shelf space to store your Doctor Who figurines. (Or whatever.)

There are, however, many choices required when you decide to rip your CDs to digital format—not the least of which is *which* digital format to rip to. There are a half-dozen different file formats to choose from, then there's the whole issue of bitrate, which determines the final quality of the audio file. As you'll learn, there are no universal answers here; you need to forge some sort of compromise between sound quality and file size (which affects storage space—as well as the ability to play tracks on a portable music device, such as an iPod or iPhone).

> **ULTIMATELY INTERESTING** Some folks, after ripping their music to digital format, try to make back some of their investment by selling their old CDs on eBay. That's fine unless you're a belt-and-suspenders person, like me; I prefer to store all my old CDs as a backup, or in case I need to re-rip everything to a different file format in the future.

Ripping all your CDs is also a time-consuming process, especially if you have a large music collection and are starting from scratch. I did it back when I had (only) about 1,200 CDs, and it took me a few months, working a few hours a day. There are services that will do this for you, however, which may be worth considering if you have a massive collection and not much free time.

> **ULTIMATELY INTERESTING** Learn more about ripping CDs to digital format in Chapter 23, "Ripping Your Physical Music Collection."

2

That said, once you have your collection ripped, you're in a good position. You can take those digital files and do just about anything you want with them—listen to them on your computer, play them through your main audio system, pipe them to a whole house system, download them to your iPod or other portable device, even upload them to the Internet cloud to then stream to other devices for when you're on the go. It's really the ultimate in versatility.

As you can probably tell, this is the digital solution that I personally opt for. I view ripping your CDs to a library kind of a digital music hat trick—you get excellent audio fidelity, optimal flexibility among multiple devices and locations, and no physical storage and retrieval issues. What's not to like?

Downloading Digital Tracks—Legally

Well, what some people don't like about ripping from CDs is having to buy the entire compact disc in the first place—and then dispose of it when the ripping is done. It's not just a matter of waste; it's also an issue of being forced to purchase all those tracks you don't want in order to get the few you do.

This is one of the reasons why purchasing digital music online has really taken off. You can buy just those tracks you want and skip the rest of the album filler. This helps keep your costs down (spending 99 cents for one track is better than $9.99 or more for an entire album's worth) and reduces the amount of storage space necessary for your digital collection. It also helps focus your digital library; you don't have to shuffle past all those unwanted tracks to get to your favorites.

When it comes to downloading digital music, you have a lot of choices. You can purchase individual tracks (or albums, if you like) from an online music store, such as Apple's iTunes Store or the Amazon MP3 Music Store, or purchase tracks directly from an artist or label website. Some artist sites will offer a limited number of tracks available for free download, as well, which is always nice. There are also some (legal) sites out there that offer a smattering of tracks available for free download, although if you're a serious downloader, a much larger selection is available from the online retailer sites.

That's not the last of your choices, however. You need to decide which audio file format you want to wed yourself to—MP3 (somewhat universal), AAC (Apple's chosen format), WMA (Microsoft's chosen format), FLAC (the format for fanatical audiophiles), or something else entirely. This choice is important because most online download sites offer files only in a single format. The iTunes Store, for example, offers only AAC files; the Amazon MP3 Music Store offers only MP3 files (not surprisingly).

Then there's the issue of bitrate. The higher the bitrate, the better the sound—but also the larger the file sizes. Download at a high bitrate for better fidelity, and the files may be too large to store comfortably on a portable music player. And, again, most online music stores offer only a single bitrate—and one not often high enough to please true audiophiles.

Decisions, decisions, decisions—and we haven't even discussed price, yet. Most online music stores are in the same price range, with single tracks running from 69 cents to $1.29, and complete albums in the $10 range, more or less. If you're looking to recreate your entire collection from scratch, this can get a little pricey.

Availability becomes an issue, as well. The iTunes Store offers more than 20 million tracks for download, while the Amazon MP3 Music Store boasts of more than 18 million tracks. Not everything you want or currently own is available for download at every online store, however; you may need to shop between stores to find the tracks you want. And some tracks from some artists aren't available for (legal) download at all, so it's likely that you won't be able to fully replicate your physical music collection from digital downloads.

Assuming you can find an online music store, file format, and bitrate you can live with, purchasing digital downloads is a good way to add new music to your collection—if you can afford it, of course.

ULTIMATELY CAUTIOUS Going the standard download route, via iTunes or Amazon, may not result in acceptable fidelity, especially if you're listening on a high-quality home audio system. While high-fidelity download stores do exist (we'll talk about HDtracks and others in Chapter 10, "Downloading Music from Other Online Music Stores"), you'll pay more for quality—and have less of a selection, to boot.

ULTIMATELY INTERESTING Availability is a particular issue among older and more obscure releases. Just as some LPs never got released on CD, those same LPs (and additional CDs) probably haven't made it to digital download just yet.

ULTIMATELY INTERESTING Learn more about downloading music in Chapter 7, "Understanding Music Downloading," as well as the other chapters in Part II, "Downloading Music."

Downloading Digital Tracks—Not So Legally

There's a less expensive way to download music from the Internet, but it's also somewhat less legal. I'm talking about downloading tracks from peer-to-peer (P2P) file sharing and bit torrent sites—both of which involve the illegal downloading of copyrighted music.

While I can't personally recommend downloading from these less-than-legal sites, I know a lot of people do—especially younger listeners. It's certainly a lot more affordable for budget-conscious music lovers, but it's also more dangerous.

What's good about downloading from file-sharing and bit torrent sites? The cost, first and foremost. You get to download a lot of stuff for free, which has its appeal. In addition, you can often find tracks on these sites that are not officially available for legal download. You can get more stuff for less cost. I understand that appeal.

Unfortunately, when you download from the unauthorized sites, you're breaking the law. In effect, you're stealing music from the people (well, the companies) that own that music. The music industry takes a dim view of such activities, and has been known to file the occasional lawsuit against illegal downloaders. At a possible fine of $250,000 per track, this is probably something you want to avoid—or at least avoid being caught doing.

It's also an iffy proposition, content and quality wise. The tracks you download from these sites are uploaded (also illegally) from other users, who probably ripped them from their own CDs. You don't know what bit rate these rips were made at, but it's a good guess that they're not the highest possible fidelity. In fact, you may not even be getting the tracks as advertised; you have to rely on the best nature of your fellow miscreants to provide the actual content they say they're providing. Not always a good bet.

In fact, in many instances what is advertised as a specific digital audio file turns out to be a malware file—a computer virus or piece of spyware. This is actually quite common, and a major source of malware infection for a lot of younger computer users. The result is seldom pretty.

Bottom line, downloading from illegal file sharing sites is a risky proposition. I don't do it, and don't think you should either. Still, that option is available if you choose to go that route.

> ♪ ULTIMATELY **INTERESTING** Learn more about illegal downloading in Chapter 12, "Downloading Music from P2P File-Sharing Sites."

Getting All You Can Eat from a Subscription Service

All the previous approaches to collecting music were based on the premise of actually owning your own collections. There's another approach, however—"renting" your music on a month-by-month basis. Such is the nature of subscription music services, such as Spotify and Rhapsody. These are "all you can eat" (or, more accurately, "all you can listen to") services; you pay one flat monthly fee and can then listen to all the music you want. You don't have to own any of it, and in fact don't; it all comes streaming to you over the Internet.

> **♪ ULTIMATELY INTERESTING**   Spotify goes a step further and blends subscription streaming with music you've downloaded or ripped elsewhere. Learn more in Chapter 18, "Listening to Music with Spotify."

You can see the appeal. For $5 or $10 a month, you get access to tens of millions of tracks—if not quite all the music in the world, certainly a fairly large selection. You can listen to this music on any device connected to the Internet—your computer, of course, but also your iPod or iPhone or iPad. There's a certain value to that.

What you get with a music subscription service, then, is access to a large amount of music at a fairly low price. What you don't get is outright ownership. You're in effect renting the music you listen to; if and when you close your subscription, you don't have access to any of that music anymore.

Now, that might not bother you; why own when you can rent? What might be bothersome, however, is the audio quality of the music you rent. Don't expect most subscription services to offer the highest fidelity music; in fact, most offer tracks ripped at a fairly low bitrate. Also don't expect a perfectly smooth listening experience, especially if your Internet connection is slow or spotty.

Even worse, don't expect to listen to your music if you don't have an Internet connection—like if you're driving in your car or flying on an airplane. None of the music resides on your computer or device, which means you have to have an Internet connection to hear anything. Nix the connection and you don't get any music. It's as simple as that.

All those negatives aside, streaming music services are gaining momentum, and could represent the future of digital music delivery. For music lovers, that may be both good (more songs to listen to) and bad (lower audio quality). Still, it's an interesting development and one worth checking out—especially if you do a lot of listening on your phone and other portable devices.

> **♪ ULTIMATELY INTERESTING**   Learn more about subscription music services in Chapter 17, "Understanding Streaming Music," as well as all the other chapters in Part IV, "Streaming Music."

2

Listening Anywhere on Any Device from the Cloud

Here's another interesting option. Take the music you own and make it available out in the "cloud" that is the Internet, and thus be able to access it from any Internet-connected device. I'm not talking about listening to someone else's library, as you get with a subscription service; I'm talking about listening to your digital music library from any computer or device you own.

Thus is the nature of what we're calling cloud-based music services. These services, such as iTunes Match, Google Music, and Amazon Cloud Player, either upload the tracks you own or point to the same tracks in the service's master database. You then access the cloud service from any computer or device connected to the Internet, and stream your own music from the cloud to your device, wherever you and it may happen to be. This makes your own digital music collection available to you anytime, anywhere.

Sounds great, but there's a bit of magic behind the illusion. First off, you seldom get to hear the *exact* files you have stored in your library. That's because even if you upload those files to the cloud service, they're typically converted to a lower bitrate format that is easier to stream over the Internet. So if you spent months ripping your entire CD collection at a high bitrate, you get it streamed back to you at a low bitrate. That's necessary for efficient streaming over today's less-than-speedy Internet connections, but still, it's not really listening to your actual music library.

Some cloud services don't even bother to upload your own music to the cloud. iTunes Match, for example, will "match" (hence the name) the tracks in your library with the same tracks in iTunes' library, and thus stream back to you iTunes' tracks, not yours. (The thinking is that one version of The Beatles' *Maxwell's Silver Hammer* is the same as the next, I suppose.) The only tracks that actually get uploaded are those you own that aren't in the iTunes master library.

Still, cloud music is an interesting concept, and could take off in the future. There are also some variations on the premise, such as Audiogalaxy and Subsonic, which turn your own home computer into a cloud music server, so that you really do stream your own files, at their original fidelity. Like I said, something worth considering.

> ♪ **ULTIMATELY** **INTERESTING** Learn more about cloud-based music services in Chapter 20, "Accessing Your Music in the Cloud."

Listening to Internet Radio

Finally, a few quick words about another digital listening option, Internet radio. These are "radio stations" broadcast over the Internet, the equivalent of listening to FM or XM radio but on your computer.

The nice thing about Internet radio is the variety available. With virtually unlimited bandwidth at hand, you can find Internet radio stations for just about any musical genre you can imagine, no matter how narrow. And most of them are free too.

The problems with Internet radio are pretty much the same as with terrestrial radio. First, you don't control the playlist; you have to listen to whatever the radio station plays. Second, you don't own the music; again, you're listening to someone else's music. And finally, the audio quality leaves a lot to be desired—often much lower than what you find with subscription streaming services.

So for most music lovers, Internet radio isn't a viable listening option—or at least not the sole option. Internet radio is good to listen to occasionally, and to help discover new music you might not hear otherwise. But as the sole source of listening, the other options are better.

> ♪ ULTIMATELY **INTERESTING** Learn more about Internet radio in Chapter 21, "Listening to Internet Radio."

WHAT ABOUT VINYL?

In this chapter, I focused on the various ways to collect music digitally. That, by definition, excludes vinyl, which is an analog medium. Still, I know there is a healthy subset of the collector's market that continues to embrace vinyl records, so let's talk about them a bit.

Given the inherent benefits of digital music, why would anyone still be interested in collecting scratchy, hard-to-handle vinyl LPs? There are lots of reasons—but first, let's recognize that this isn't all about old, collectible LPs. Indeed, many new artists make their latest releases available in vinyl format. So it isn't solely, or even primarily, a collectible thing; vinyl is just another option available to today's music lovers.

Why, then, do some music lovers love vinyl so much? Part of it is the nostalgia factor, no doubt, especially among baby boomers. (Although there's much less nostalgia for other formats from our youth, like the ill-

2

regarded 8-track tapes.) For younger listeners, the nostalgia factor is replaced by a coolness factor; there's a kind of retro charm that appeals to a certain class of quirky hipsters.

Of course, some of vinyl's appeal has to do with the artwork more than the music. Let's face it, the 12-inch format allows for much larger and more impressive artwork than what you get on a dinky little CD—or not at all if you download a digital file.

But most of the appeal for vinyl lovers is sonic. A vinyl record is certainly better sounding than the typical MP3 download, which is compressed to high heaven and grates on any audiophile's ears. But there's also a subtle warmth and nuance in the sound of vinyl that remains lacking, at least to some ears, in any digital format, even the higher-quality compact disc. If you can live with the hiss and scratches, the music underneath has a certain quality unique to the format.

(And it's all about the storage format, not the way the tracks were recorded; most new vinyl LPs were actually recorded digitally, then transferred to the older analog format.)

In any case, if you're a music lover who's into vinyl, you're tasked with integrating your record collection into your digital library. You may want to keep your analog and digital collections separate, or you may want to rip your LPs to digital format. (The highest-resolution digital format available, of course.) If you do want to merge everything onto digital, skip ahead to Chapter 23 for some specific advice. Otherwise, enjoy your albums—along with that terrific large-format artwork!

How Digital Music Works

From Edison's first crude recordings, musicians and engineers have strived to accurately reproduce musical performances, using whatever technology was state-of-the-art at the time. Technology today has progressed to the point that we can create an exact digital copy of the original performance, which Edison could only dream of.

The journey from tin-foil and wax recordings to streaming a series of digital 1s and 0s over the Internet is an interesting one, and one that's important to the understanding of how digital music works today.

The Way We Were: Remembering Analog Audio

In the real world, nothing is digital. All the sounds you hear—music, words, noises, you name it—come to your ears in what is called an *analog* format. Analog simply means that sounds are created continuously, without any breaks. In fact, if you look at a typical sound, of any type, using an oscilloscope, you see an unbroken wave, like that in Figure 3.1.

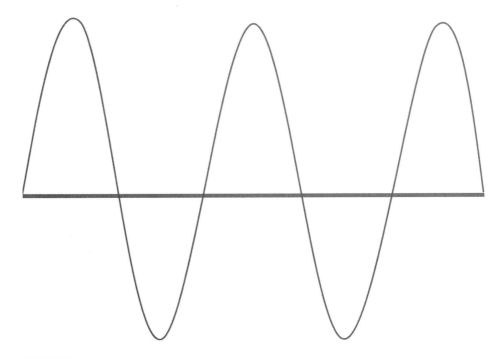

FIGURE 3.1

An analog waveform; the sound is captured as a continuous curve.

The first century of recorded sound attempted to capture analog sound in an analog fashion—to mirror the original sound as accurately as possible, capturing all the subtleties and nuances of the original. For example, Edison's first recording machines used a sound-collecting horn attached to a sharp needle; sounds were collected in the horn, which vibrated the needle, which scratched a path onto a rotating tin-foil cylinder. The needle moved up and down according to the pitch and volume (amplitude) of the sound, approximating the kind of wave shown in Figure 3.1.

To play back Edison's original recording, this same process was done in reverse. Another needle (though not as sharp!) was inserted into the groove that had been cut into the foil cylinder. This second needle was connected to another horn, this one used to amplify the vibrations of the needle. As the needle rode through the grooves, it reproduced the sounds that had been cut into the cylinder.

Wax and vinyl records worked in much the same fashion. At the record-cutting plant, a vibrating needle cut patterns into a master disc, which was then used to stamp out millions of replicas—the records you or your parents (or grandparents!) bought at the local record shops. The records were played back on phonographs equipped with their own needles; special circuitry translated the needle's vibrations into electronic signals that could be amplified and sent through one or more speakers or headphones.

That's how analog recording works, and it works just fine—as far as it goes. The big problem with analog is that, no matter how thin the needle or involved the process, it can't *exactly* reproduce the original music. The waveform associated with live music is rather complex and has a large *dynamic range*—the difference between the loudest and softest passages. This means that even the best analog recording equipment can't make an exact reproduction of the original.

In addition, analog recording introduces extraneous noise and distortion into the process—especially when copies are made. This means that playback is often plagued by the annoying hiss and pops produced when the needle passes over the vinyl groove.

Finally, analog recordings can only be stored physically. You can't transfer an analog recording to a computer for storage without first converting that analog recording into a digital file. That's because all computer data is digital; it's the only way to store files on a hard disk or flash drive.

Taking all these factors into consideration, it's clear that analog is not the best approach for recording, listening to, or storing music.

The New Wave: Understanding Digital Audio

Digital audio takes a much different approach than analog reproduction. Instead of trying to produce an exact image of an analog sound, digital audio uses small bursts of information—digital *bits* in the form of 1s and 0s—to represent pieces of the analog sound wave. When the bits of digital information are small enough, and when there are enough of them, an extremely accurate picture of the original sound emerges.

Making a Digital Recording

When making an analog recording, you attempt to mimic the original waveform on some sort of physical medium—wax cylinder, vinyl disc, magnetic tape, or whatever. Digital recording works much differently.

All digital recordings—starting in the recording studio—are made by creating digital samples of the original sound. An *analog-to-digital converter* (ADC) "listens" to the original analog signal and takes a digital snapshot of the music at a particular point in time. This process is called *sampling* and you can see how it works in Figure 3.2; each digital "snapshot" captures a specific section of the original sound.

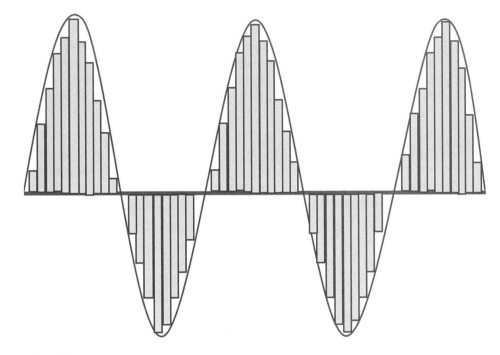

FIGURE 3.2

Digital sampling of an analog sound; the original waveform is captured as a series of discrete segments.

The quality of the digital recording is dependent on how many samples are taken per second. The more samples taken (the higher the sampling rate), the more accurate the snapshot of the original sound. That's because each individual sample captures a shorter segment of the original sound and doesn't have to average out any changes in pitch or volume.

The other quality factor is the length of the sample taken, measured in *bits*. The smaller the sample size, the more accurate the recording.

> **ULTIMATELY INTERESTING** Audio CDs sample music at a 44.1kHz rate—in other words, the music is sampled, digitally, 44,100 times per second. (This is called the *sampling rate*.) Each sample is 16 bits long. When you multiply the sampling rate by the sample size and the number of channels (two for stereo), you end up with a *bitrate*. For CDs, you multiply 44,100 X 16 X 2, and end up with 1,400,000 bits per second—or 1,400Kbps.

Storing and Playing Digital Audio

Once a song has been sampled, it exists as a series of bytes in a data file—the same type of file used by personal computers. That file can be stored on a traditional audio CD or on a computer's hard disk, where you can do anything with the audio file you can do with any other computer file. You can copy it, edit it, delete it, even use your computer to download the file from the Internet or send it from your computer to another electronic device.

And, of course, you can play that file to listen to what was recorded. When you play back a digital recording, the digital audio file is converted back into analog format by a *digital-to-analog converter* (DAC). DACs are found in CD players, A/V receivers, portable music players, and the sound card in your computer. The higher quality the DAC, the more accurate the playback.

Dealing with Digital Compression

One of the issues with digital audio is that the higher the sampling rate, the larger the resulting digital file. For example, a typical three-minute song with CD-quality audio takes up close to 32MB of disk space. While there's more than enough room on a compact disc to hold an album's worth of songs (CD storage capacity is 700MB), files of that size are simply too big to download from the Internet or to store on a portable music player (which has a lot less storage capacity than a computer). Heck, these file sizes can even cause problems when storing on a computer with a terabyte's worth of hard disk storage, especially if you have a large music collection—which you probably do.

Fortunately, there's a way to make these digital audio files smaller, while still retaining much of the fidelity of the source material. This process is called *compression*, and it works by removing slices from the digital file in an attempt to reduce the file size. Ideally, less-important pieces of the recording are lost; a digital audio encoder uses complex algorithms to determine what sounds a human is able to hear, based on accepted psychoacoustic models, and chops off those sounds outside this range. The result is a much smaller file size; for example, the popular MP3 digital audio format reduces the size of digital audio files by a 12:1 ratio, resulting in a file that's only 3MB in size.

Different audio file formats use different types of compression. Naturally, the best audio fidelity comes from using a non-compressed file format, such as WAV or AIF. But when you need smaller file sizes, you can choose from two different types of compression—*lossy* or *lossless*.

Lossy compression is so named because some of the original data is lost in the process. This type of compression works by sampling the original file and removing those ranges of sounds that the average listener can't hear, based on accepted psychoacoustic models. You control the sound quality and the size of the resulting file by selecting different sampling rates for the data. The lower the sampling rate, the smaller the file size—and the lower the sound quality. Popular file formats that use lossy compression include MP3, AAC, and WMA.

If you want to create a high fidelity digital archive, a better solution is to use a lossless compression format. These formats work similar to the ZIP compression used for other types of computer data; redundant bits are taken out to create the compressed file, which is then uncompressed for playback. The resulting file has exact fidelity to the original, while still being stored in a smaller-sized file. Popular lossless file formats include WMA Lossless, ALAC (aka Apple Lossless), and FLAC.

The average listener today seemingly has little problem with the reduced sound quality induced by lossy compression. This is apparently the price we pay to get easily manageable files that can be stored on a pocket-sized playback device. Remember, it's not always the best format that wins the consumers' loyalty; the mass market is quick to accept "good enough" quality.

> **♪ ULTIMATELY INTERESTING** Another way that digital audio encoders reduce file size is by using lower sampling rates; the less sampling taking place, the smaller the file size. Of course, reducing the sampling rate also reduces the sound quality, so it's a bit of a tradeoff. That's why most digital audio encoders let you choose from several different sampling rates, so you can make the right compromise between file size and sound quality.

Audiophiles, however, demand higher fidelity, which means going with less (or no) compression and a higher sampling rate, and somehow dealing with the resulting increase in file size. It's a matter of where you want to make your compromises—in playback quality or storage capacity.

The Benefits of Digital Music

The movement to digital recording, then, provides all sorts of benefits. Not only do you, the listener, get potentially better sounding recordings (compare a song on CD vs. the same song on vinyl), you also get your music in a format that provides a lot of versatility—especially when used in conjunction with your personal computer and portable music player.

Quality

One of the great things about digital recordings is that they don't deteriorate. Remember how those old LPs would start to hiss and crackle after several playings? Not so with digital media. Those 1s and 0s remain 1s and 0s throughout the entire process.

Physically, this means that the music on a CD sounds exactly the same after a thousand playings as it did first out of the jewel case. It's the same with digital downloads; the thousandth digital copy of a song will sound identical to the original.

In addition, if you choose a higher sampling rate with less (or no) compression, a digital recording can come extremely close to accurately mirroring the original sound. Analog recordings can also be very accurate, but are more often than not plagued by a low *signal-to-noise ratio* because of high background noise. Digital recordings have a very high signal-to-noise ratio, with very little background noise or distortion.

The bottom line: digital affords the opportunity for the highest possible audio fidelity, no matter how many times a song is played.

Easier Storage

Digital music differs from analog music in that you don't have to deal with physical storage. (Well, you do if you're listening to CDs, but even they are a lot smaller than LPs.) Digital storage means transferring your music to a computer's hard drive or flash memory, which is relatively cheap.

Even better, you can conserve on electronic storage space by intelligently compressing your digital music files. Depending on the type of compression you choose, file size can be dramatically reduced without noticeable degradation in sound quality. Those smaller files then open the door for all sorts of new uses for the original music, including downloading off the Internet and playback in portable audio devices.

Easier Organization

With a physical CD or album collection, you can only organize things one way. Maybe you sort your CDs by title, by artist, or even (if your mind works in mysterious ways) by date purchased. But once you have them organized in this fashion, there's no way to go back and pull out discs based on another criteria—without re-sorting your entire collection, that is.

Digital music, on the other hand, can be easily organized and categorized in multiple ways, simultaneously. Each track in your collection is tagged with metadata that defines the track's artist, album, genre—you name it. You can then quite easily display your collection, in real time, by any of these criteria. You can even apply multiple sorting criteria, to display only those tracks in the jazz genre that were released in 1955. You just can't do that with a physical collection.

You also have the ability to quickly search your collection for a single track or album. You want to play "I Can't Help Myself (Sugar Pie Honeybunch)" by the Four Tops? With CDs or albums you have to first pull out all the albums by the Tops, and then read through each album's track listings to find the song you want. With a digital collection, all you have to do is enter the name of the song and start searching. Easy as (sugar) pie.

Streaming

There's one more benefit to digital music that we haven't discussed yet—the ability to *stream* the audio over the Internet, in real-time. Streaming audio lets you listen to a file in real time without actually downloading and storing the complete file on your computer. Streaming audio is also ideal for listening to live concerts, news reports, and sporting events.

So whether you're playing back music from a CD, downloading a file from an online music store, or streaming a track over the Internet, digital is the way to go. Better quality in less space with more listening options—what's not to like?

THE DIGITAL RECORDING REVOLUTION

Digital technology has not only changed the way we listen to music, it's revolutionized the way music is recorded. I know this book isn't about music recording, but it's worth a quick peek at how technology has affected things on the other side of the microphone.

In the old days (pre-digital technology), performances were recorded to magnetic tape. Depending on the era, a tape machine might record 1, 2, 8, 16, or 32 separate tracks. If you had more instruments or vocals than you had tracks, you either had to double up multiple performers on the same track or "bounce" two or more recorded tracks to a single track. In either case, there were many compromises to be made, and recording quality ultimately suffered.

Editing was also a challenge. If you wanted to use a guitar solo from one take and a drum track from another, you had to literally splice different tape segments together. Not easy and not always doable.

Digital recording, however, has eliminated all these constraints. Since you're now recording digitally to a hard disk, there are no limitations on the number of tracks you can use. Want to construct a recording from 500 different instrumental and vocal tracks? You can do it.

Digital technologies also simplify the editing process. Inserting a single track from one take into a different take is as easy as cutting and pasting a sentence in Microsoft Word; you can easily cut a few measures from a guitar solo on pass 22 and paste into the master recording, to create the perfect solo. It's just digital bits, and they're easily manipulated.

The result is that making a great-sounding recording is now much easier and costs much less than it used to. Musicians no longer have to rent expensive recording studios; most recordings today are done in someone's bedroom or garage using off-the-shelf personal computers and specialized recording software. The investment is minimal and just about anybody can achieve professional results.

The only thing bad about this is that it's almost too easy. Many of the old disciplines have been forgotten, with the result that too many recordings today have a similar sound. In addition, because software programs like Pro Tools can correct a lot of mistakes, making even an average musician sound good, the magic of a live performance by top-shelf musicians is lost. It all sounds good, but none of it sounds special.

These are my personal grumblings, in any case. I happen to be a big fan of the golden days of studio recording, when a talented producer would bring a team of experienced musicians into a big studio, rehearse them until things were just right, then roll the tape and capture the magic of all those musicians playing together in a single stellar performance. Alas, those days are long gone, replaced by anybody and their brother laying down one track at a time in somebody's basement studio, using Pro Tools to smooth over missed notes and bad pitch.

I suppose this digital recording technology is good for today's musicians, who can make decent-enough recordings with minimal investment; they're certainly less reliant on the big music labels to finance their recording time. But the sound just ain't the same to my ears, sorry to say. Farewell, Phil Spector; we miss that wall of sound.

3

Understanding Digital Audio File Formats

When you download or rip a music track, that track is stored in a digital data file of a given format. There are many different file formats that can be used to store digital audio; some sound better or worse than others, some are larger or smaller than others, and some are more or less common than others.

Which file format you choose will affect just about everything you do as a digital music collector. The file format you centralize on determines which music player programs you can use, which portable music players you can work with, even which online music stores you can buy from. That's because these are not universal file formats; some formats are not compatible with some software and music players, and each online music store specializes in just one format.

In other words, choosing the file format you use for your digital music is both important and complicated. That's why you need to learn the ins and outs of all available formats—and then make an informed decision.

Evaluating File Formats

There are more than a dozen different audio file formats available today. They differ in terms of compatibility, sound quality, file size, and the like.

My preferred approach is to divide the file formats in terms of compression used. As you might remember from Chapter 3, "How Digital Music Works," audio files can use any of the three general types of compression in order to reduce file size:

- **No compression.** An uncompressed file offers the best audio quality but at very large file sizes.

- **Lossless compression.** This is a good compromise in terms of audio quality vs. file size. Lossless compression preserves the original audio quality while still decreasing the file size—but not quite as small as what you get with lossy compression.

- **Lossy compression.** This approach creates the smallest sized files, but at some degradation of audio quality. The amount of degradation depends on the type of compression used, the amount of compression used, and the bitrate at which the audio file was recorded.

If you have all the disk space in the world (which you don't—especially on your iPhone or other portable device), going the uncompressed route obviously yields the best results. If disk space is at a premium, however, you want to go with some sort of lossy compression and accept the lower audio quality. And if you care about both sound quality and file size, consider some sort of lossless compression.

It's all about the trade-offs.

Uncompressed Formats

If you want the best possible audio quality—that is, if you want to replicate exactly the music recorded on the original compact disc—then you want to go with some sort of uncompressed file format. These file formats have a lot of space between bits, which results in very large file sizes, but the reward is being able to archive your music in its original unaltered form.

There are five uncompressed digital audio formats you may run into:

- **AU.** A file format (abbreviation for "audio") that originated on the Sun and NeXT computer systems in the 1990s. Not widely used today.

- **Audio Interchange Format (AIF, AIFF).** The file format for Macintosh system sounds, similar to Windows' WAV format.

- **Compact Disc Digital Audio (CDA).** This is format used for encoding music on all commercial compact discs. If you buy a CD from a store, the music on that CD is stored in CDA format. Unfortunately, your computer can't store files in CDA format, so you still have to convert CDA files to another format to store on your hard disk.

- **SND.** Another file format (abbreviation for "sound") similar to the AU format and used primarily for Macintosh system sounds.

- **Waveform Sound Files (WAV).** This format (pronounced "wave") produces an exact copy of the original recording, with zero compression. The result is perfect fidelity but with very large file sizes—the same size as the original, in fact. It's not a good choice for portable use, because it takes up too much storage space, but it's the preferred format for uncompressed archiving.

Of these formats, the most common (especially in the Windows world) is the WAV format. It's a viable alternative for storing a master digital music archive—assuming you have terabytes and terabytes of hard disk space.

Unfortunately, none of these file formats is viable for storing music on portable devices, which have limited storage capacity. In addition, uncompressed files are simply too large to efficiently download or stream over the Internet.

Lossy Compressed Formats

If you don't have all the hard disk storage in the world, or if you want to listen to your music on an iPhone or iPod or other portable music player, then you have to choose some sort of compressed file format. The most common type of compression in use today is lossy compression.

Lossy compression works by sampling the original audio file and removing those ranges of sounds that the average listener can't hear. A lossless encoder uses complex algorithms to determine what sounds a human is able to hear, based on accepted psychoacoustic models, and chops off those sounds outside this range.

You can control the sound quality and the size of the resulting file by selecting different sampling rates for the data. The less sampling going on, the smaller the file size—and the lower the sound quality. Choose a higher sampling rate and you get better sound—and larger files.

The problem with shrinking files to a large degree, of course, is that by making a smaller file, you've dramatically reduced the sampling rate of the music.

This results in music that *sounds* compressed; it won't have the high-frequency response or the dynamic range (the difference between soft and loud passages) of the original recording. To many users, the sound of the compressed file will be acceptable, much like listening to an FM radio station. To other users, however, the compression presents an unacceptable alternative to high-fidelity reproduction.

The most popular lossy compressed format today is the MP3 format, although there are lots of other formats that work in the same fashion. Here's a list of available lossy formats:

- **Advanced Audio Coding** (AAC, .MP4, .M4A, .M4P). Also known as MPEG-4 AAC, this is the proprietary audio format used by Apple for its iPod and iPhone devices, and for the tracks sold in the iTunes Store. AAC offers slightly better sound quality than similar-bitrate MP3 files. Unfortunately, not all non-Apple music players can play AAC-format songs—but if you're invested in the Apple ecosystem (that is, if you use an iPhone or iPod), this is the format you'll be using.

> **ULTIMATELY INTERESTING** .M4P files were DRM-protected files Apple used to provide from the iTunes Store. (Think of an .M4P file as a protected version of an .M4A file.) Apple no longer uses DRM for the tracks it sells, so the .M4P extension has fallen into disuse. If you have older .M4P files, you can convert them to non-DRM .MPA files using one of the DRM removal programs discussed in Chapter 6, "Understanding DRM."

- **Liquid Audio** (LAT, LQT, LSL). This is an MP3 competitor from Liquid Audio, somewhat popular in the late 1990s but not widely used today.

- **MPEG-1 Layer III** (MP3). The MP3 format is the most widely-used digital audio format today, with a decent compromise between small file size and sound quality. The primary advantage of MP3 is its universality; unlike most other file formats, just about every digital music player and player program can handle MP3-format music.

- **mp3PRO** (MP3). This is an improved version of the original MP3 format, introduced in 2001 but still not widely adopted. mp3PRO files use the same file extension as regular MP3 files, but cannot be played in all music player software.

- **OGG Vorbis** (OGG). An open-source encoding technology originally known as "Squish," OGG Vorbis was designed as a substitute for MP3 and WMA. It uses variable bitrate compression, which encodes different parts of a song with higher or lower compression, to produce better quality when needed.

4

- **RealAudio Media** (RA, RM, RMA). Proprietary format used by Real Networks, designed particularly for real-time streaming audio feeds. Not a real option for ripping or downloading.

- **Windows Media Audio** (WMA). This is Microsoft's digital audio format, promoted as an MP3 alternative with similar audio quality at smaller file sizes—or better sound quality at similar file sizes. Microsoft tends to exaggerate the quality/size difference a bit, but WMA does typically offer a slightly better compromise between compression and quality than you find with MP3 files.

Of these lossy formats, only three are viable choices today—AAC, MP3, and WMA. Which option you choose depends more on the ecosystem you adopt (or are wedded to) than anything else—which we'll discuss later in this chapter.

Lossless Compressed Formats

If you care about audio fidelity, lossy compression just doesn't cut it. No matter how high the sampling rate or how good the compression algorithm, lossy files don't sound quite as good as the originals. (Remember that word "lossy"—you lose something in the translation!)

If you want to create a high-fidelity digital archive and listen to your music on quality audio playback equipment, a better solution is to use a lossless compression format. These formats work more or less like ZIP compression for computer data files; redundant bits are taken out to create the compressed file, which is then uncompressed for playback. So what you hear has exact fidelity to the original, while still being stored in a smaller-sized file.

Of course, a lossless compressed file isn't nearly as small as a file with lossy compression. While an MP3 file might be 10% the size of the original, uncompressed file, a file with lossless compression is typically about 50% the original's size. This is why lossless compression isn't recommended for portable music players, where storage space is limited. If you're storing your CD collection on hard disk, however, it works just fine—especially with today's cheap hard disk prices. You can easily store 1,000 CDs on a 300GB hard disk using any lossless compression format.

What formats can you choose from? The list isn't quite as long as with lossy compression, nor or the formats quite as well known. Here's a short list:

- **Apple Lossless** (M4A). The lossless version of Apple's AAC format, compatible with Apple's iTunes and iPod, as well as any Apple-compatible device.

- **Free Lossless Codec (FLAC).** An open-source lossless format, embraced by many consumer electronics manufacturers and usable with all major operating systems, including both Windows and Linux. This is a popular format among audiophiles, and can actually reproduce music at higher-than-CD fidelity—so-called *high definition audio.*

- **Monkey's Audio (APE).** A free lossless format, not widely used.

- **Windows Media Audio Lossless** (WMA), Microsoft's lossless compression format. This is a good option for lossless compression, especially if you're wedded to the world of the Windows ecosystem. WMA Lossless uses the same WMA file extension as normal Windows Media Audio files, and plays on any player compatible with the WMA format.

- **WavPack (WV, WVC).** An open-source lossless format, similar to FLAC, not yet widely used.

Of these lossless formats, the most popular are AAC Lossless (if you're in the Apple world), WMA Lossless (if you're in the Windows world), and FLAC (if you're independent-minded).

> ♪ **ULTIMATELY** Both Apple
> **INTERESTING** and Microsoft
> use the same file extensions for
> lossy and lossless encoding. So
> an .MP4A file could be either
> lossy or lossless—same with a
> file with a .WMA extension.

Comparing Formats, in a Nutshell

If you want a quick cheat sheet to these digital audio file formats, peruse the data in Table 4.1. This will give you a quick overview of what's what.

Table 4.1   Digital Audio File Formats

Format	Compression	File Extension(s)
Advanced Audio Coding	Lossy	.AAC, .MP4, .MPA, .M4P
Apple Lossless	Lossless	.M4A
Audio Interchange File Format	Uncompressed	.AIF, .AIFC, .AIFF
CD Audio Track	Uncompressed	.CDA
Free Lossless Codec	Lossless	.FLAC
Liquid Audio	Lossy	.LAT, .LQT, .LSL
Macintosh Sound Files	Uncompressed	.SND
Monkey's Audio	Lossless	.APE
mp3PRO	Lossy	.MP3
MPEG-1 Layer III	Lossy	.MP3

Format	Compression	File Extension(s)
OGG Vorbis	Lossy	.OGG
RealAudio Media	Lossy	.RA, .RM, .RMA
UNIX (Sun Microsystems and NeXT) Sound Files	Uncompressed	.AU
WavPack	Lossless	.WV, .WVC
Windows Audio	Uncompressed	.WAV
Windows Media Audio	Lossy	.WMA
Windows Media Lossless	Lossless	.WMA

Considering Bitrate

The type of compression used obviously affects audio quality, but so does the amount of compression. This is measured in terms of *bitrate*; the higher the bitrate, the more bits are included in the digital file, and the better the sound quality. Of course, the more bits in a file, the larger that file is. So a higher bitrate recording is going to take up more storage space than one at a lower bitrate.

All of the major lossy compression formats enable encoding at different bitrates. You can select the bitrate used when ripping music from CD. For example, a file ripped at 192Kbps will sound better than one ripped at 128 Kbps.

In addition, different digital download and streaming sites offer tracks at different bitrates. The iTunes Store, for example, offers its tracks at 256Kbps, as does the Amazon MP3 Music Store, while Google Music on the Android Market sells 320Kbps tracks. Similarly, the free version of the Spotify music service streams audio at 160Kbps, while Spotify's paid Premium version streams at least some files at 320Kbps.

And, in case you weren't totally confused yet, there's the issue of *variable bitrate* encoding. In contrast to standard compression, which uses a constant bitrate from start to finish, variable bitrate compression varies the amount of

> **ULTIMATELY INTERESTING** There's one last digital audio format that you should be aware of, even though it's not used for ripping or downloading music. The MIDI format, short for Musical Instrument Digital Interface, is used by professional musicians to reproduce instrumental music in very compact files. MIDI doesn't record an actual performance; instead, it creates a kind of roadmap for frequencies and rhythms that can be fed to synthesizers and other musical instruments for playback. It's sometimes used to create background music on web pages (with .MID format files), and to record musical "sequences" for various home- and studio-based recordings.

4

data encoded throughout the course of a recording, using a lower bitrate when there's less complex audio content and a higher bitrate with the content is more complex. The result is, theoretically at least, a better sounding recording that takes up slightly more space than one with constant bitrate encoding, but still less than with a comparable lossless format.

When choosing a file format, then, you need to consider both compression and bitrate. For better sounding playback, go with a higher bitrate; to conserve on storage space, choose a lower bitrate.

Comparing the Major Digital Music Ecosystems

Lossy, lossless, or uncompressed files, at a lower or higher or variable bitrate. That's a lot of factors to consider, but there's one more that bears attention—the ecosystem or "family environment" built around the most popular formats. I'm talking about the fact that certain formats work best with certain music player programs and hardware devices; if you're already wedded to a given ecosystem (based on the equipment and software you use), your choice in terms of audio format may be limited.

Let us look, then, at the three major format ecosystems for digital audio today—MP3, Apple, and Windows. Chances are you're invested in at least one of these.

The MP3 Ecosystem

Of all the available digital audio file formats, the one that has enjoyed almost universal popularity is the MP3 format. That's because MP3 was the first widely accepted format that combined good quality sound with reasonably small files.

As you know, MP3 is a digital audio file format that uses lossy compression. Developed (and patented) by Thomson Multimedia and the Fraunhofer Institute, the MP3 digital audio format is an extension of Motion Picture Experts Group (MPEG) technology. (The MP3 file extension is short for MPEG-1 Audio Layer III.) MP3 and other MPEG formats store music digitally, and in the process compress the original data to take up less space than it did originally. MP3's data compression reduces digital sound files by about a 12:1 ratio.

Naturally, the MP3 format allows for sampling at various bitrates. Table 4.2 details some of the more popular bitrates for MP3 files, and describes the sound quality of each.

Table 4.2	Popular MP3 Bitrates
MP3 Bitrate	**Sound Quality**
128Kbps	Soft attacks, slightly compressed sound. Similar to normal FM radio, but still sub-CD quality.
192Kbps	Sounds similar to the original, but with less presence and somewhat restricted dynamic range.
256Kbps	Quality is getting closer to that of the original, but still has a slightly compressed sound.
320Kbps	Approaching CD-quality, but not quite there. This is the highest bitrate possible with the current MP3 standard.

If you're encoding MP3 files for use at your computer or with a portable audio player, the 128Kbps rate is probably good enough quality. If you're encoding MP3 files for playback on a high-fidelity audio system, you'll probably want to move up to at least the 256Kbps bit rate, and 320Kbps is even better.

> ♪ ULTIMATELY **INTERESTING** Sound quality is highly subjective, as you can imagine—some audiophiles (like me) find it difficult to listen to any audio files created with lossy compression—no matter what the bit rate.

Unfortunately, there is no lossless compression version of MP3 files, so ultimate audio quality will never be equal to an original recording. You can, however, rip MP3 files at a variable bitrate, which will improve sound quality somewhat. Still, if you want the highest audio fidelity, MP3 is not your format of choice.

All that said, what makes the MP3 format so popular is the fact that it is relatively universal. That is, it's not a format designed by Apple or Microsoft, so neither of those two camps are inherently biased for or against it. Practically, this means that MP3 files are compatible with virtually every music player program out there, and can be played on just about every portable music player and hardware device available.

So, if you want to be sure that your digital music library is pretty much format- and future-proof, MP3 is the way to go. If you want ultimate audio quality for playback on a good home audio system, however, look elsewhere.

The Apple Ecosystem

Then we have Apple's audio ecosystem, which is formidable. This is due to the unprecedented success (and monopoly position) of Apple's iPod, iPhone, and iPad devices.

Let's face it, Apple and its iPod changed the way we listen to music—and as a result, Apple completely dominates the digital music space. Since its initial release, Apple has sold more than 300 million iPods, which makes Apple's market share more than 70%.

In recent years iPod sales have started to slip, as more and more consumers switch from iPods to iPhones. (An iPhone is really just an iPod that makes phone calls, after all.) To date, Apple has sold more than 140 million iPhones, and you gotta figure a lot of those folks are listening to music as well as calling or texting their friends.

Bottom line, Apple has sold a lot of devices (including more than 20 million iPad tablets) that play Apple-format digital audio files.

Of course, if you have an iPod, iPhone, or iPad, you download your music from Apple's iTunes Store, which is the dominant online music store today, with an 85% or so share of the legal download market. The iTunes Store has sold more than 16 billion tracks, which puts a lot of AAC-format music out there in the real world. And that's not counting all the CDs ripped in AAC format using Apple's iTunes software. That makes AAC a dominant digital audio format, and Apple's ecosystem one that sucks in a lot of users.

Fortunately, AAC is a fairly versatile format. AAC files can be encoded at a variety of bitrates. You also have the option of variable bitrate and lossless encoding. And, because of its dominant position, AAC files can be played on a majority of software and hardware platforms; even Microsoft's Windows Media Player (in Windows 7, anyway) is compatible with the AAC format.

All this makes the Apple ecosystem a decent alternative to the MP3 ecosystem; near-universal acceptance with better potential sound quality, at least on the high end. Of course, it isn't an apples-to-Apple comparison, as the MP3 and AAC compression schemes work slightly differently. Table 4.3 attempts to make the comparison.

Table 4.3   Comparing Compression Quality Between MP3 and AAC Audio Formats

AAC Bitrate	Comparable MP3 Bitrate	Sound Quality
48Kbps	64Kbps	Suitable for voice only
64Kbps	96Kbps	Suitable for voice or low quality music only; very noticeable compression
96Kbps	128Kbps	Similar to FM radio, with soft attacks and still-noticeable compression
128Kbps	192Kbps	Similar to the original but with restricted dynamic range
160Kbps	256Kbps	Approaching original quality, but still slightly compressed
192Kbps	320Kbps	Equal to the best of the MP3 format; good choice for portable use
224Kbps	NA	Quite good; better than anything you can get with MP3 compression
320Kbps	NA	Near-CD quality; highest bit-rate possible without moving to lossless format

The Windows Media Ecosystem

Microsoft's entrée in the digital audio format marketplace is Windows Media Audio (WMA for short). Like the standard MP3 and AAC formats, WMA uses lossy compression. Sound quality is better than MP3 with smaller file sizes, much like Apple's AAC format.

As with the AAC format, WMA offers a variety of bitrates, including variable bitrate and lossless options. Table 4.4 compares WMA and MP3 bitrates.

Table 4.4   Comparing Compression Quality Between WMA and AAC Audio Formats

WMA Bitrate	Comparable MP3 Bitrate	Sound Quality
48Kbps	64Kbps	Suitable for voice only
64Kbps	96Kbps	Suitable for voice or low quality music only; very noticeable compression
96Kbps	128Kbps	Similar to FM radio, with soft attacks and still-noticeable compression
128Kbps	192Kbps	Similar to the original but with restricted dynamic range
160Kbps	256Kbps	Approaching original quality, but still slightly compressed
192Kbps	320Kbps	Near-CD quality; highest bit-rate possible without moving to WMA Lossless format

As with the other formats, you can really hear the difference between the different WMA bitrates. A 48Kbps recording sounds a lot like AM radio, while a 192Kbps recording is close to CD quality. Pick something in the middle, like 128Kbps, and you get a recording that sounds like decent FM radio.

In terms of the Windows Media ecosystem, it isn't as widely supported as either the MP3 or Apple formats. Don't expect the iTunes player or your iPod or iPhone to play back WMA files (they will play MP3 files, however), and don't expect to find WMA files available from too many online music stores. It's not an orphan format, by any means, but your choices are more limited.

That said, I personally like the WMA format (specifically WMA Lossless) for home audio playback, especially if you buy into the whole home theater PC/Windows Media Center thing. It's certainly one of the top contenders.

Choosing the Right File Format

Now that you know a little bit about a lot of different audio file formats, how do you decide which format works best for you? There's no one right answer, unfortunately.

What Works with What

For many users, which audio format you choose is decided by the hardware or software you're already using. If you use an Apple iPod or iPhone, for example, and have downloaded a ton of tracks from the iTunes Store, you're pretty much wedded to the Apple ecosystem. Not much you can do about that.

With that in mind, Table 4.5 shows you which ecosystems are compatible with popular music player programs and playback devices.

Table 4.5   Hardware and Software Compatibility

Device/Software/Service	MP3 Compatibility	Apple (AAC) Compatibility	Windows (WMA) Compatibility	FLAC Compatibility
Amazon Cloud Player (service)	Yes	Yes (ripped only, not purchased)	No	No
Amazon MP3 Music Store (downloads)	Yes	No	No	No
Apple iCloud Match (service)	Yes	Yes	No	No
Apple iPod/iPhone/iPad (hardware)	Yes	Yes	No	No
Apple iTunes Player (software)	Yes	Yes	No	No
Apple iTunes Store (downloads)	No	Yes	No	No
Google Music (service)	Yes	Yes	Yes	Yes (but not lossless)
HDtracks (downloads)	Yes	No	No	Yes
MediaMonkey (software)	Yes	Yes	Yes	Yes
Spotify (service)	Yes	Yes	No	No
WinAmp (software)	Yes	Yes (ripped only, not purchased)	Yes	Yes
Windows Media Player/Windows Media Center (software)	Yes	Yes (Windows 7 and later; ripped only, not purchased)	Yes	No

As you can see, MP3 has pretty much universal compatibility, with Apple's AAC format close behind. Note however, that not all players will play AAC files purchased from the Apple store, because of digital rights management concerns; in addition, the only online store that offers AAC files for download is Apple's iTunes Store.

> **ULTIMATELY USEFUL** While Windows Media Player does not support the FLAC format natively, you can install a FLAC codec that enables playback of FLAC files. You can download the codec, for free, from www.xiph.org/dshow/.

Notice that I included the FLAC format in this comparison. That's because FLAC is a popular alternative among audiophiles who don't want to be locked into the Apple or Windows ecosystems. It's an open source format and delivers superb audio quality with its lossless encoding. That said, you have to really move outside the mainstream to find hardware and software support, or at least perform some gyrations in terms of installing additional codecs, but it's doable if you put the effort into it.

Choosing an Ecosystem

So let's consider which ecosystem is best for your personal use.

Like I said, you may have this already decided for you. If you have an iPod or iPhone and lots of AAC files downloaded from the iTunes Store, you're a slave to the Apple ecosystem. If you've ripped a thousand CDs to WMA Lossless format, you've obviously bought into the Windows ecosystem. If you're so subjugated, there's no point even thinking about changing.

However, if you're new to the digital game, or not too beholden (yet) to a given format, there's value in examining the options and choosing an ecosystem from scratch.

For ultimate flexibility, MP3 is the universal constant; every music player program and portable audio player in the world, including the Apple iPod and iTunes player, can play back MP3 files. So when you want universal compatibility, MP3 is the format to use.

That said, Apple's AAC format has become almost as universal as MP3, and offers better sound quality, to boot—especially if you go with higher bitrate or lossless files. I don't think you'll run into too many problems drinking the Apple Kool-Aid.

Microsoft's WMA format isn't a bad choice, if you can live with a few limitations—such as never using an Apple iPod or iPhone to play your music. For a home-based system, however, the Windows ecosystem works pretty well.

Then there's FLAC. This is a hard one to recommend for the casual user, as there's not a lot of compatibility with popular hardware and software, nor do the most popular online music stores offer FLAC-format files. Still, for die-hard audiophiles focusing on a home system, FLAC has some appeal. Just don't expect to play your FLAC files on a portable music player—the files are just too large.

> **ULTIMATELY USEFUL** If you have an Android phone, the default music player doesn't play WMA files. That said, you can install the PowerAmp music player app, which is fully compatible with WMA audio files.

Choosing a Bitrate

Speaking of portable music players, the next choice you have to make is what bitrate you support for your digital music files—in particular, those files you rip from CD. Here's where the worlds of optimal home audio and portable music collide.

If your focus is on the best music reproduction on a quality home audio system, then you want to go with a high-bitrate solution. To be specific, my recommendation is to go with any of the main lossless compression formats—AAC Lossless for the Apple crowd, WMA Lossless for Windows converts, and FLAC for the die-hard audiophiles. With today's hard disk prices hitting rock bottom, you can easily afford a 1 terabyte disk to hold a few thousand albums in lossless format.

There's no way, however, that you're going to pipe lossless files to your iPod or other portable music player; the files are just too large. When you're talking about the best bitrate for portable music, you're looking at something in the 128Kbps to 192Kbps range. Anything higher is wasted effort, as you won't be able to hear the difference on what is essentially a mid-fi device (using middling-quality earplugs, to boot). Anything lower, you'll probably notice. Going in the midrange, bitrate-wise, creates file sizes that fit a lot of music on a typical device.

And here you see the problem. If you rip your files at 128Kbps or even 192Kbps for best portable use, you get audio quality that is decidedly subpar when played back on your home audio system. If you rip at a higher bitrate or using a lossless format for best home audio playback, you end up with files too large to put too many on a portable device.

It's the Kobayashi Maru scenario, in real life; there's no winning solution.

What you may be forced to do is to rip your music twice. Once, in a lossless format, for your home listening library. And a second time, at 128-192Kbps, for portable use. It's a less than ideal solution, but the two scenarios are at definite odds. There's no good compromise.

> **ULTIMATELY USEFUL** If your focus is home playback quality but you still want to listen to your library on a portable device, consider streaming your home library over the Internet. You can do this with some cloud streaming services, such as Google Music or iCloud Match, if the service matches your chosen ecosystem. Even better (but slightly more complicated), Audiogalaxy and Subsonic can stream music directly to portable devices from your home server. Learn more in Chapter 17, "Understanding Streaming Music."

WHITHER FLAC?

Throughout this chapter I've focused primarily on the big three digital audio solutions—MP3, Apple (AAC), and Windows (WMA). The fourth option, FLAC, isn't a wildly popular one, at least among the general populace, but it's one you might want to consider.

Here's the deal with FLAC: It's an open source project, which means anybody can use it without paying any fees. It's not overly supported by any of the major players, but there's surprising support among enthusiasts and in the custom installation market. It'll do what you need it to do, at least in the home—if you do your homework and make the right choices for supporting equipment and software.

In practical terms, FLAC lossless has identical fidelity to any lossless format. There is the option, though, of getting even better sound quality by downloading so-called high-definition audio from a source such as HDtracks; this is music encoded at 96Khz instead of the normal 44.1Khz used with compact discs. (I cover this more in Chapter 10, "Downloading Music from Other Online Music Stores.") Suffice to say, there's not a lot of high-definition tracks available to download, and you can't play them on standard music player software. Still, the option is available if you go the FLAC route.

I think that some of the appeal of the FLAC format is that it isn't from Apple or Microsoft; it's the little format that works outside the system. Some audiophiles are just natural contrarians, I've found.

It helps, of course, that FLAC delivers outstanding results (but no better than competing lossless formats), while consuming minimal resources. But to be honest, I find that the hassles of supporting FLAC diminish its appeal. If you're interested in CD-quality playback, you can get the same results from within the Apple (AAC Lossless) or Windows (WMA Lossless) ecosystems, and encounter a lot fewer issues along the way.

Still, FLAC has its (quite vocal) adherents, which is why I include it in this chapter and throughout the book. It's a viable option, after all, even if it's a bit outside the mainstream.

4

Understanding Copyright, Piracy, and Other Legal Issues

People have always copied music illegally. I'm sure that back in the Tin Pan Alley days that illicit scribes were out there hand copying the sheet music of the day. With the advent of tape recording machines in the late 1950s, there were folks who held a microphone in front of their radio consoles to record music from the airwaves. In the 1960s and 1970s, low-priced audiocassette recorders led to lots of LPs being copied to cassette tape. And today, of course, the youngsters download music for free from file-sharing and BitTorrent sites.

Now, I'm not condoning this behavior, just acknowledging that it exists today, has always existed, and will probably always exist. That doesn't make it right, and in fact it is somewhat harmful to the artists who work hard to create that music. For that reason, it helps to have a little background in copyright law—what's legal and what's not—so you can make up your own mind about the issue.

Understanding Copyright and Royalties

Musicians get paid when their music is sold or performed. It's how they make their living, and any attempt to sell or perform music without paying for it is theft; it's literally taking money out of the mouths of the artists. (It also takes money away from the artists' record labels and music publishing companies, which, while also wrong, you may or may not feel quite as bad about.)

How Copyright Works

Let's start with the concept of *copyright*, which is the right given by law to the creator of a work to determine who may publish, copy, and distribute that work. Every music track you find online is a piece of intellectual property that is protected by one or more forms of copyright.

> **ULTIMATELY INTERESTING** Copyright law differs significantly from country to country. I'll be discussing U.S. copyright law specifically in this book, but the same general principles apply in most other countries.

First, the song itself is copyrighted by the songwriter. In addition, there's the recorded performance of the song, which is copyrighted separately by the recording artist. In the U.S., a song is copyrighted as soon as it's written, and a recording is copyrighted as soon as it's recorded.

Put simply: Copyright identifies the legal owner of a particular work. The writer of a song owns the song itself, while the recording artist (or, in many instances, the artist's record label) owns the specific recording of the song. The song and the recording are property owned by these entities, as specified by copyright law.

Calculating Royalties

These two copyright owners are legally entitled for compensation, in the form of royalties, under specific circumstances of use. The U.S. Copyright Act of 1976 provides for six different types of rights; which rights a copyright owner has depends on the type of work involved. Without going into all the options, most of which aren't relevant to this conversation, know that when a recording is distributed, either

> **ULTIMATELY INTERESTING** Performance rights for digital audio transmissions (Internet, cable, and satellite) were created in 1995, via the Digital Performance Right in Sound Recordings Act. Before this act was passed, recordings could be played on the Internet (and on satellite and cable radio) with no royalties due.

physically or digitally, both the songwriter and the recording artist are legally due royalties. That's the law.

How much money are we talking about? In the case of songwriters (and their publishing companies), the royalties are dictated by the details of the underlying *mechanical license*. A mechanical license gives a record company, musician, or other party the right to reproduce a song on a record, CD, digital download, or other media. The entity doing the recording actually pays the royalties to the songwriter, based on the number of copies sold or distributed.

The rate paid for recording a song is a set fee, called the *statutory rate*, set by the U.S. Copyright Office. As of 2009 the base mechanical royalty rate is 9.1 cents per song for each CD, tape, download, or other recording sold. If the recording is more than five minutes long, the rate is 1.75 cents per minute per recording. So if someone makes a four-minute recording of a song, the songwriter gets 9.1 cents for each copy sold or distributed; if another artist makes a six-minute recording of the same song, the songwriter get 10.5 cents per copy (that's 1.75 cents times 6 minutes).

Note that these mechanical royalties are the same for the sale of music in any format. It doesn't matter whether a consumer buys a CD, vinyl record, or whether he downloads a song from iTunes or some other online store, the same 9.1 cent royalty is due.

Royalties due the recording artist are negotiated between the artist and the record label. The artist's contract details that the label will pay the artist a certain percentage of all monies it makes from selling physical recordings (CDs) and digital recordings. As I said this is a negotiable rate, typically between 6% and 10%, based on the list price of the final product.

For example, if an artist negotiates a deal to earn 10% royalties on a $14.99 CD, the artist is due $1.49 for each CD sold. Rates for digital distribution are often different from the rates for physical sales; an artist might be entitled to 50% of all digital revenues.

Now, all these royalties don't seem like a lot of money, but they add up. That 9.1 cent royalty per song adds up to $91,000 on a million-copy selling hit, which is a nice income for the lucky songwriter. If some portion of a song's sales are pirated, that's real money that the songwriter doesn't earn.

Royalties on Online Performances

There's another kind of royalty that factors into digital distribution. A songwriter earns *performance royalties* when their songs are performed publicly, either live or over the radio or the Internet.

As such, any location (such as a nightclub) that plays music must obtain a performing rights license for the songs played on premises. In addition, radio stations, television stations, and—here we go—Internet radio stations must also obtain performing rights licenses and pay royalties to the copyright owners of the songs they play.

Note that this royalty applies only to songwriters, not to the recording artists—with the exception of Internet, satellite, and cable play. When a recording is played on a traditional radio station, the songwriter earns a performance royalty, but the recording artist doesn't. For digital reproduction, however, royalties are also paid to the musicians performing on the recording.

The Dark Side of Downloading: Online Piracy

The Internet has brought a lot of positive changes to the world of music. But there are also negative effects, in particular the significant rise in music piracy, enabled by illegal music downloads.

The Spread of Piracy

The term "music piracy" is shorthand for copyright infringement, in particularly the illegal copying or sharing of digital music. Pirated music has been copied without the authorization of the copyright owner, who has received no royalties for this illegal use of the work.

Music piracy, of course, has been around forever. Back in the 1970s, for example, I did my share of illegal copying. I wasn't able to download illegal tracks, of course, since the Internet didn't exist then. Instead, one guy in our dorm would buy an album and the rest of us would make illegal copies on cassette tapes. Still, that was piracy, just like the type we have today.

Today's music piracy, however, is more widespread, in part because it's easier to do. One person somewhere in the world buys a copy of a compact disc and then rips that CD to his computer's hard drive. He then uploads the digital tracks to a file sharing service, and anyone anywhere in the world can now download a perfect (or near-perfect) digital copy of that album for free. One legal purchase results in tens of thousands of illegal downloads, all thanks to the Internet.

The recording industry has tried to crack down on this illegal downloading, of course, through various scare campaigns and legal actions. Many illegal download sites have been shut down, but new ones have just as quickly arisen. The result is that illegal downloading continues to thrive, particularly among cash-strapped high school and college students, to the detriment of the big music labels and the musicians who wrote and performed the downloaded songs.

The Impact of Illegal Downloading

The financial impact of this illegal downloading is difficult to ascertain. The RIAA contends that illegal downloading is the cause of the sharp decline in physical CD sales over the past decade, and has released various studies that purport to prove this. Several independent researchers, however, have released competing studies that show just the opposite.

Look, for example, at a 2004 report from researchers Felix Oberholzer-Gee of the Harvard Business School and Koleman S. Strumpf of the University of North Carolina at Chapel Hill. That report, "The Effect of File Sharing on Record Sales: An Empirical Analysis," showed that illegal downloads essentially have zero impact on record sales. According to their analysis, it would take close to 5,000 individual downloads to reduce the sales of an album by a single copy. Why? Because most illegal downloaders are individuals who would not have bought the album in the absence of downloading; in other words, pirated tracks are in addition to those that would have been purchased normally.

The RIAA, in response, noted that total sales of the top ten albums each year, according to SoundScan data, declined from 60 million units in 2000 to 33 million units in 2003. (It's dropped even more since then.) The RIAA contended this sales decline is due primarily to illegal downloads—but without any research to prove that contention. In other words, the RIAA *speculates* that piracy reduces CD sales, but doesn't prove it.

Of course, there can be other factors for the decline of CDs; maybe popular music isn't as good or as popular as it used to be, or maybe consumers are spending their money elsewhere (on video games, for example). The RIAA only speculated, without offering any empirical evidence to support their point.

> **ULTIMATELY INTERESTING** Not surprisingly, the record industry has always been focused on the piracy problem. Back in the 1970s, for example, a slide in album sales led the Recording Industry Association of America (RIAA) to campaign for a tax on blank audio cassette tapes, essentially to fund a de facto royalty that would compensate record companies for claimed lost sales due to illegal recording. They didn't win that particular campaign, but in 1992 prevailed with the Home Audio Recording Act, which levied a 3% tax on blank digital media.

> **ULTIMATELY INTERESTING** Personally, I think the decline in physical CD sales is due more to a combination of the convenience of the digital format and the fragmentation of the music industry as a whole, which makes it difficult for recordings to break out to a mass audience. My reading of the data indicates that piracy is only a small contributor to lost sales.

5

That said, I think we have to face up to the fact that illegal downloading is an issue, at least to some degree. While there is every indication that illegal downloading is this generation's way of sharing music on the cheap, and in fact may help expose more potential purchasers to one's music, sales lost to piracy do affect musicians' income. And digital piracy has probably contributed in some way to the decline in CD sales.

More important, stealing somebody else's property is wrong, and recorded music (as dictated by copyright law) is definitely somebody else's property. You just shouldn't do it.

What's Legal—and What's Not

As you can see, the legality of pirating someone else's copyrighted intellectual property is one of the most important issues in the world of digital music. But what exactly can you copy—and what can you do with the music you purchase?

Some will talk about something called the First Sale Doctrine, which is a neat little loophole in the copyright law that says the purchaser of an item has the right to transfer (either by selling or giving away) a copyrighted work, without needing the permission or having to pay the copyright owner. This doctrine has its limitations, however, especially in regards to what constitutes the original item. Not to get too technical, but you can only resell or give away a physical item from which no new copy has been made. This means you can resell a CD you've purchased, but you can't sell or give away copies of that CD you might have made. So the First Sale Doctrine really doesn't apply when it comes to digital music.

If you want to know what you can or cannot legally do in the world of digital music, consult Table 5.1. Note, however, that some activities exist in a legal gray area.

Table 5.1   Legality of Copying and Downloading Digital Music

Activity	Legal?	Risk of Prosecution
Downloading digital music files from a legitimate online music store	Yes	None
Copying purchased digital music to another device for your own personal use	Yes	None
Copying music from a CD or digital file to another medium for your own personal use	No	Low
Downloading digital music files from an unauthorized file-sharing site	No	Low to Medium
Copying music from a CD to another medium for business or professional use	No	Medium
Making copyrighted digital music available to an unauthorized file-sharing service	No	Medium to High

Let's try to make this easy. It's perfectly legal to download digital music from an authorized source, such as the iTunes Store or Amazon MP3 Music Store. It's also legal to play those downloaded tracks on a number of different devices, as specified by the purchase agreement offered by the specific download site. (Some sites may limit playback to a set number of devices; most will specify that you can only play back the files on devices you personally own, not on friends' devices.)

It is less legal to rip music from a CD to play back on your personal computer, iPod, or home audio system. But it's also something that the recording industry has never explicitly pursued, so there's a tacit permission that this activity is allowed. In other words, feel free to rip away to your heart's content—for your own personal use only.

Where you start running into trouble is downloading music from an unauthorized site—a P2P file-sharing network or a BitTorrent site. This is both illegal and dangerous, in that the RIAA has been known to track down illicit downloaders and prosecute them. Really. The RIAA has gone after tens of thousands of kids, college students, housewives, and even grandmothers, suing them for upwards of $250,000 for each track illegally downloaded. This is serious stuff, folks. And even though the recording industry has backed off from these lawsuits in recent years, and no matter what you might think about such strong-arm tactics, you really don't want to be on the receiving end of a subpoena from the RIAA.

The worst thing you can do, however, is illegally distribute tracks you've ripped from CD or downloaded from another site. That means uploading tracks to a file-sharing or BitTorrent site is a big no-no. If you're found out, you will be subject to legal action. Now, one can debate the odds of being discovered and targeted, but still—it's a big risk. Don't do it.

> **ULTIMATELY CAUTIOUS** Don't kid yourself. Downloading music from an unauthorized site is against the law. Just say no to illegal downloads.

IT ALL STARTED WITH NAPSTER

While music piracy has been around pretty much as long as the music industry itself, digital music piracy was born with the rise of the Internet in the late 1990s. Listeners back then soon discovered that they could download the songs they wanted from a variety of legitimate and illegitimate websites.

One of the first of these file-sharing sites was the original Napster. (This is not to be confused with the later revival of the brand as a legitimate download service—which has since been absorbed into the Rhapsody service.) Launched in 1999 by 18 year-old college dropout Shawn Fanning, Napster was a service, driven by proprietary software, which facilitated the direct connection of two PCs over the Internet.

Napster's software enabled users to search the Napster network for specific files, which could then be downloaded directly to the users' computers. Even more insidious, while a user was connected to the Napster network, other Napster users could search for files on that user's PC, and download those files to their computers.

Given the profusion of MP3 files on user's PCs (most of which were ripped semi-legally from copyrighted CDs), Napster's ability to track down specific files and enable PC-to-PC file sharing hit a nerve. At its height, Napster served more than 25 million individual users; many users stayed connected to the Napster network 24/7, sharing their MP3 files with users around the world.

The problem with all this, as you can no doubt surmise, is that it's illegal to make copies of copyrighted material without the creators' permission—and not too many artists or record labels gave permission for this free distribution of their works. So even though Napster was extraordinarily popular among music lovers, it was not at all popular within the music industry.

As you might suspect, the music industry didn't take the Napster phenomenon lying down. It's initial response was to pressure various colleges and universities to shut down their students' access to Napster. (Many colleges were receptive to this proposal, as Napster connections were eating up a significant amount of their Internet bandwidth; college students download a lot of music!) This had an immediate impact.

The industry's next step was to take Napster to court. Ignoring Napster's last-ditch attempts to negotiate "pay for play" licensing plans with the major record labels, the lawsuit against Napster proceeded in Federal court, with the ultimate ruling (on March 6, 2000) that Napster was in violation of various copyright laws. As a result, the company was ordered to block access to all copyrighted material on its network.

Napster tried to make the best of a bad situation, first by blocking copyrighted files from their site, then by turning the site into a subscription service, but neither approach stuck. The Napster site was eventually shut down and the company went bankrupt in 2002.

Still, Napster had a huge impact on the world of online music. Napster essentially jumpstarted the whole digital downloading craze, and exposed legions of music lovers to a new way of finding, storing, and listening to their favorite tunes. Napster also created the blueprint for today's illegal file-sharing sites, and legitimized (to some extent) digital music piracy. That's an important legacy, both good and bad.

5

Understanding DRM

As you've learned, piracy is a significant issue in the world of digital music. The folks who create and own the music want to keep folks from downloading their property with proper authorization and payment, and one way to do that is to enlist technology. Specifically, we're talking about something called digital rights management, or DRM—technology that limits how a digital file can be downloaded and used.

The problem with DRM is that it can also inhibit how regular listeners use the files they've legally downloaded. In trying to stop the criminals, DRM often makes life more difficult for us law-abiding citizens, too.

If you're an avid collector of digital music, chances are you'll run into DRM at some point or another. Which means it's good to become familiar with what the technology attempts to do, and how it tries to do it.

What DRM Is and What it Does

Digital rights management (DRM) refers to any technology used to enforce copy or playback restrictions on any form of digital data. This includes digital music files, of course, but also DVDs and digital videos, e-books, computer software, and the like.

To the consumer, DRM is synonymous with copy protection. Indeed, DRM was designed to protect copyright owners from unlawful distribution, copying, and sharing of their music.

The problem is, if a track you downloaded is protected with DRM, you're limited as to how you can copy and listen to that song. You might not be able to burn a CD from DRM-protected music files, or copy DRM-protected tracks to your portable music player. Yes, DRM helps to stop illegal copying, but can also put the brakes on *legal* copying.

There are many different DRM technologies in use, but they all work in pretty much the same fashion, by encoding the original digital audio file in a type of wrapper file format. This wrapper file includes a user key, which is used to decode and play the track—under specified conditions. For example, a DRM license might dictate how many different PCs or portable music players the track can be copied to, whether it can be burned to CD, and so on. If you try to use the song in a way not permitted by the license, the DRM protection keeps it from playing or being copied.

DRM technology can be applied to audio files in the AAC and WMA formats; it cannot be applied to MP3 or FLAC files. This is why many concerned music lovers prefer the MP3 and FLAC formats to those from Apple and Microsoft; it eliminates DRM as an issue.

The State of DRM Today

In the world of digital music, DRM isn't as big an issue at it used to be. That's because the major online music stores have moved away from encoding their music with DRM to selling DRM-free tracks.

The benefit to DRM-free music is that once you purchase it, you can use it however you wish. You can play it on any number of PCs or portable music players and burn it onto an unlimited number of custom CDs. It's a much more listener-friendly solution, which is why many online music stores are now offering DRM-free music.

These DRM-free downloads are often in the MP3 format, although Apple sells DRM-free music in its own AAC format. In fact, it's interesting to examine

6

Apple's evolving stance on DRM—because they used to be big adherents.

From day one, Apple sold only DRM-encoded tracks in its popular iTunes Store, using its own proprietary FairPlay technology. But when the public tide began to turn against DRM, Apple rethought its position and in 2007 began selling DRM-free tracks in the iTunes Store. Apple called these new tracks iTunes Plus, and offered them at a higher bitrate (256Kbps) and higher price ($1.29) than its DRM-encoded product.

Within two years (April, 2009) Apple converted to all DRM-free downloads and lowered the price back to the store's original 99-cent average level. (Videos sold and rented through the iTunes Store, however, continue to use Apple's FairPlay DRM technology.)

Most other online music stores have also moved away from DRM encoding—at least on pure downloads. Many music services that offer a monthly subscription plan still encode their tracks with DRM. While a customer subscribes, the DRM-encoded tracks are allowed to playback with minimal restrictions. But when the user's subscription expires, the DRM technology disables playback of all downloaded tracks. It's a way of facilitating music rentals, as opposed to outright purchase. (This scenario does not apply to streaming music subscription services, such as Spotify, which stream music to users in real-time without any permanent downloads.)

> **♪ ULTIMATELY INTERESTING** Even though tracks downloaded from the iTunes Store don't employ obvious DRM, they are embedded with each user's specific account information. This type of digital watermarking makes it relatively easy for Apple to identify the source of any purchased tracks that have been uploaded to illegal file sharing sites.

Problems with DRM

Here's the thing about the DRM-encoded music—you don't actually own it. What you purchase is a license to use the music, in a manner prescribed by the copyright holder or online music service. That means what you can do with the music you download is limited, to some degree, by some form of copy protection.

To that end, DRM often causes more problems than it solves. Let's look at some of the major drawbacks.

First, there's the issue of limiting what you can do with the music you purchase. Many DRM schemes limit playback to a set number of computers and portable devices. What happens, then, when you want to copy that track you

6

purchased to a third computer in your home when DRM limits playback to just two machines? Most music lovers want to be able to do whatever they want, within legal reason, with the music they purchase. DRM limits that flexibility.

There's also the issue that the technology doesn't always work as advertised. (What technology does, 100 percent?) It's not uncommon to find a user with a DRM-encoded track that won't play on a given device, even though it should; it's the encoding technology getting in the way, for whatever reason.

More serious is the issue of technological obsolescence. When standards and formats change—when new types of devices are introduced—older DRM-encoded tracks may not be playable on the newer devices. Just because you purchased a track five years ago doesn't mean you don't listen to it today; unfortunately, that older track may not be playable on a computer with a newer operating system, or on your new state-of-the-art smartphone. That shouldn't be.

Finally, there's the issue of what happens when the store or service that sold you the DRM-encoded track closes its doors. Many DRM technologies require the track to "call back" to the mother ship in order to authorize playback. When the mother ship shuts down, however, there's no place for the DRM-encoded tracks to call back to. Which means, of course, that the tracks become permanently disabled; the music you purchased is now unplayable.

Think this is an unlikely scenario? Think again. There have been several notable instances of online music services closing down and making all the tracks they sold unusable. For example, Microsoft used to run an online music store dubbed MSN Music; all the tracks sold by MSN Music were encoded with DRM technology. Unfortunately, Microsoft shut down MSN Music in August, 2008. All tracks downloaded from the store could still be played on the original download computer, but would no longer play back when copied to another computer. This severely limited the functionality of music legally purchased from Microsoft.

Something similar happened the same year when Yahoo! shut down its Yahoo! Music Store and took offline the servers used to authorize the DRM license keys for the tracks it had sold. This left hundreds of thousands of users in the lurch.

> **ULTIMATELY INTERESTING** This book's editor noted to me that he had this very thing happen to him. He had downloaded several hundred tracks from the now-defunct MusicMatch service before switching his allegiance to iTunes. All those tracks (in DRM-protected WMA format) are now unplayable. Live and learn.

6

Want another example? Wal-Mart used to sell DRM-encoded tracks in its Wal-Mart Music Downloads online music store. In 2008, however, the company switched to a DRM-free model, and shut down its DRM authorization servers. This rendered all tracks sold previously unplayable. Good customer relations, that.

You see the problem—or, rather, problems. DRM is not a consumer-friendly technology. It exists solely to protect the rights of copyright holders, even if enforcing those rights interfere with the rights of customers who legally purchased the music in question.

The ultimate problem with DRM, then, is that users hate it. It gets in the way of doing perfectly legal stuff, such as making backup copies and transferring music from one computer to another. In fact, users hate DRM so much that most of the online music stores no longer sell DRM-protected tracks. So there.

Dealing with DRM

So what do you do if you want to play a DRM-encoded track in a manner not explicitly allowed under the music's purchase agreement? While such actions may be technically prohibited, there is a workaround.

Essentially, what you have to do is burn the protected track to CD, and then rip it back to your PC (in a format other than the original). When you burn the track to CD, the encrypted wrapper is removed as the file is converted from the DRM-encoded format to CD Audio format. Then when you rip the track from CD back to your hard drive, there's no DRM encryption to worry about; the process of burning-and-ripping removes the DRM wrapper and creates a new track without any playback or burning restrictions.

Another approach is to use a software program designed to intercept the decrypted data stream when a DRM-encoded file is played, and uses this data to construct a new DRM-free file. There are a number of such DRM-removal tools available, including the following:

- Aimersoft Music Converter (www.aimersoft.com/drm-music-converter.html)
- freeTunes (www.engelmann.com/eng/freetunes.php)
- Protected Music Converter (www.wma-mp3.com/protected-music-converter.html)
- SoundTaxi (www.soundtaxi.info)
- Tunebite (www.audials.com/en/tunebite/)

6

These programs require a decryption key to do their job, and in fact employ the user's own key. Because of this, they can only process files that you've legally acquired under your own account.

> ♪ **ULTIMATELY INTERESTING** Most of these programs will remove DRM from all types of encoded files, including videos and DVDs.

DOES DRM PREVENT PIRACY?

The companies that create and distribute content—music, movies, even books—are obsessed with stopping piracy. They feel that every pirated copy is a lost sale, and naturally want to protect their bottom line.

Now, one can argue whether all piracy replaces legitimate sales (I tend not to think so) but also understand the thinking that leads to the embrace of DRM solutions. The question is, does DRM really prevent illegal distribution of digital content? The answer is: Not a lot.

Yes, DRM can prevent the redistribution of downloaded digital files, to a degree. While the average consumer will be stymied by the DRM protection, experienced hackers take it all with stride; there's not a single encryption scheme that hasn't been decrypted, with the solution then posted all over the Dark Web where serious pirates live. Where there's a will, there's a way.

In addition, there's really no effective way to keep users from ripping music from normal store-bought CDs and posting those tracks to file-sharing sites. The RIAA does its best to take legal action against these illegal networks, of course, but as soon as they swat one down another pops up in its place. As you learned in Chapter 5, "Understanding Copyright, Piracy, and Other Legal Issues," there was even a campaign to sue individual users who uploaded tracks illegally to file-sharing networks, but that proved relatively pointless and a huge public relations nightmare; there's nothing like suing poor kids and grandmothers to alienate your entire customer base.

So what can the music industry do to stop illegal downloading? As I said, not much. The best thing everyone involved can do is learn to live with some base level of piracy—and find ways to encourage average consumers to download their products legally, instead.

6

Downloading Music

Understanding Music Downloading

To many music lovers, digital music is all about the downloading. That is, you find the music you want somewhere on the web, and then you download a digital copy of that track or album to your computer, for future listening.

Music downloading is actually a fairly simple process, once you make a few basic decisions, get everything configured properly, and—oh, yeah—find a good site to download from. There are sites that let you download music for free and others that function like web-based versions of those old school record stores you might remember from your youth.

What is this music downloading thing all about, then? Read on to learn more about downloading music from the Internet—how it works, why you might want to do it, and where you can find music to download.

How Music Downloading Works

It doesn't take a lot of skill to download digital music from the web. In most instances, it's a matter of clicking your mouse and saving a file.

Downloading a digital music file is just like downloading any other type of file to your computer. You find the file online somewhere, go through the gyrations to save the file to your hard disk, and then let your computer do the rest of the work. The bits and bytes of the digital file are sent over the Internet from the host site to your computer, and then reassembled into a copy of the original file on your hard disk.

You can then do whatever you like with the downloaded file—play it (that is, listen to the music), copy it to your iPod or other portable music player, copy it to other computers in your home, or share it via your home network. It's really quite easy.

Requirements for Downloading Music

What do you need to download digital music? Probably nothing more than you already have:

- A computer (any make or speed will do—although a big hard disk is nice if you'll be downloading a lot of music files). You can also download music to other devices, such as tablets and smartphones, as long as they have sufficient storage capacity.

- A high-speed Internet connection (downloading big audio files on a dial-up connection will sorely test your patience).

That's it, really. Now, to play back the files you download to your PC, you need to have a sound card and external speakers (or headphones) installed, which it no doubt does. You'll also need some sort of music player software program; there are lots of these available, most for free.

You can also play back your downloaded digital music on other devices. You can play downloaded tracks on your iPod, iPhone, or other portable music player, of course, or on a digital media player connected to your home audio system. Download once, play back on multiple devices; that's one of the benefits of downloading digital music (although some online music stores limit the number of devices on which you can listen to their tracks).

> ♪ ULTIMATELY **INTERESTING** The better quality your computer's sound card and speakers, the better your digital tracks will sound when played back. Learn more about optimizing playback on your PC in Chapter 24, "Playing Digital Music on Your Computer."

7

How to Download Music to Your Computer

To download digital music to your computer, all you have to do is connect your computer to the Internet and follow these general steps:

1. Use your web browser to navigate to an online music store or other digital music site.

2. Search the site to find the song you want to download, and then click the "download now" link.

3. Specify where on your hard disk you want to store the downloaded file (on a Windows PC, typically in your My Music folder), then proceed with the download.

If you're on a broadband connection, downloading a typical track will only take a minute or two. If you're on a dial-up connection, expect to spend 10 to 15 minutes per track. (Time to order a pizza!)

Where to Download From

There are hundreds and thousands of websites that offer digital audio files for downloading. Some of these are legitimate sites, many aren't.

Focusing on the legitimate sites first, we have to start with the big online music stores—those sites where you pay a buck or so per track to download high-quality digital files. Then there are sites run by record labels and individual artists, which sometimes sell tracks to download, and sometimes offer free tracks to fans. All legitimate sites, all offering authorized versions of the music in question.

On the less legitimate side of things we have file-sharing and BitTorrent sites. These sites offer tracks obtained unofficially and offered without authorization from, or payment to, the legal copyright holders. You don't have to pay for the tracks you download from these sites, at least explicitly; you may pay later, in the form of unwanted malware added to your downloads, lawsuits brought by the major record labels, or just general shame from doing something illegal.

Let's look, then, at the different types of sites offering digital music downloads.

Online Music Stores

The most popular sites for downloading music are those where you pay for it. I'm talking about online music stores—websites that offer individual tracks and entire digital albums for purchase and download to your computer.

7

There are a handful of big online music stores, all with their own pros and cons. With the exception of Apple's iTunes Store, which is tied to Apple's ecosystem and offers tracks in Apple's proprietary AAC format, most other stores offer tracks in the more universal MP3 format. Some stores also offer higher-quality tracks in the FLAC format.

> ♪ **ULTIMATELY USEFUL** Bitrate differs from store to store. Variable bitrate files will sound better than those at a lower fixed bitrate. If you have a choice, always go with a higher bitrate for your downloads for best fidelity.

Most of these online stores work in pretty much the same fashion. You establish an account (and, in most cases, provide your credit card information ahead of time), then browse or search the store for the music you want to download. The big online music stores have tens of millions of individual tracks available for purchase, typically at prices of a buck or so per track. (Entire albums typically go for ten to fifteen bucks.)

Once you find a track or album you want to buy, all you have to do is click the requisite purchase button. After payment is made (you may have to check out first), the digital file is downloaded to your computer, where you can play it back to your heart's content.

Most online music stores today offer DRM-free downloads; this is a big contrast to just a few years back, when most legal downloads were DRM encoded. Even without DRM encoding, you're getting the real deal when you make a purchase from one of these sites—the tracks are official recordings provided by the record label or artist.

The quality of these digital tracks are often quite good—typically better than what you'll find on a file-sharing network. You'll need to check out the store, however, since some stores offer higher-quality (that is, higher bitrate) tracks than others do. (In fact, some stores specialize in higher-fidelity downloads—for a price, of course.)

In terms of what file format to expect, it depends on the store. The Apple iTunes Store, not unexpectedly, offers tracks in Apple's own AAC format. Other stores standardize on other formats.

What are the most popular online music stores? Table 7.1 details the major stores, along with information you might find pertinent.

7

Table 7.1   Major Online Music Stores

Store	URL	Pricing	Selection	File Format	Bitrate	DRM?	Description
Amazon MP3 Music Store	www.amazon.com/mp3/	$0.99–$1.29/track	18 million tracks	MP3	Variable	No	Largest non-Apple online music store
Bandcamp	www.bandcamp.com	Prices set by individual artists	3.3 million tracks	AAC, AAC Lossless, FLAC, MP3, Ogg Vorbis	Varies by format	No	Marketplace for independent artists to sell directly to fans
CD Baby	www.cdbaby.com	$0.99/track	3 million tracks	MP3	Variable	No	Features independent artists
Classical Archives	www.classicalarchives.com	$0.49–$3.99/track	645,000 tracks	MP3	320Kbps	No	Classical albums; also offers streaming audio service
eMusic	www.emusic.com	$0.49/track and up	13 million tracks	MP3	Variable	No	Offers a subscription plan with additional discounts to members
Google Play Music	play.google.com/store/music/	$0.49–$1.29/track	13 million tracks	MP3	320Kbps	No	Google's competitor to Apple's iTunes; successor to the Android Market
HDtracks	www.hdtracks.com	$2.49/track; $17.98/album and up	N/A	AIFF, FLAC, MP3	Uncompressed (MP3 files at 320Kbps)	No	High-resolution audiophile downloads; most downloads album only
iTunes Store	www.apple.com/itunes/	$0.69/$0.99/$1.29/track	20 million tracks	AAC	Variable	No	Official store for Apple iPod, iPhone, and iPad; Internet's largest online music store
Zune Marketplace	www.zune.net	$0.99–$1.24/track	14 million tracks	MP3, WMA	256/320Kbps MP3; 192Kbps WMA	No (MP3 files only; WMA files are DRM-encoded)	Payment is in Microsoft Points currency; also offers Zune Music Pass subscription service; tied into Xbox game console

7

The most popular of these stores are the iTunes Store and the Amazon MP3 Music Store. We'll cover both of these stores in separate chapters (8 and 9), and the other stores in Chapter 10, "Downloading Music from Other Online Music Stores."

Subscription Download Services

Some music downloads are rentals instead of outright purchases. That is, you pay a monthly subscription fee and can then download as many tracks as you want. You retain access to the downloaded music as long as you keep up your subscription. If you stop the subscription, you can't play those downloaded tracks any more.

This scenario describes how a *subscription download service* works. You pay a monthly fee and can download as many tracks as you can listen to—what some describe as "all you can eat" plans.

Subscription download services aren't as popular as online music stores, at least not anymore, and especially among hardcore music lovers. That's probably because you don't own the music you download, so you never really build up a music collection. Downloaded tracks are all protected by DRM, of course, so you're limited as to what you can do with the music you download. Still, subscription services are a great way to listen to a lot of different music without spending big bucks.

There are only a handful of download subscription services still in operation today. Actually, less than a handful—just two big ones:

- **iMesh** (www.imesh.com). For $9.95/month you get your choice of over 15 million tracks in WMA 128Kbps format.
- **Zune Music Pass** (www.zune.com). This is the subscription arm of Microsoft's Zune Music Store. For $9.99/month you get your choice of more than 14 million tracks in WMA 192Kbps format.

Both of these services offer 14-day free trials, as well as longer (6- or 12-month) subscriptions at a bit of a discount.

That said, download subscription services have pretty much been supplanted by streaming download services. These services stream music to you in real time, to any device (including smartphones) connected to the Internet. It's really a better solution if you want all the music you can listen to at a flat monthly fee, as you don't have to wait on downloads or devote lots of disk space to DRM-restricted files.

> ♪ ULTIMATELY
> **INTERESTING** Learn more about subscription streaming services in Chapter 17, "Understanding Streaming Music."

Free Download Sites

Before the rise of iTunes, there used to be tons of websites that offered free MP3 files for download. Well, there's less than a ton of them still out there, but you can still find sites that offer music downloads for free.

Most of these sites, such as MP3.com, offer tunes from independent artists looking for a little online promotion. Most of these sites are totally legit; they just offer music that artists or labels have opted to put in the public domain, for whatever reason.

> ♪ **ULTIMATELY INTERESTING** Learn more about these free download sites in Chapter 11, "Finding Free Music to Download."

File-Sharing Sites

Then there are those sites that offer digital music files for download for free—but outside the legal system. I'm talking so-called file-sharing and BitTorrent sites, where unscrupulous users upload pirated tracks for other unscrupulous users to download without paying for them.

Obviously, I can't recommend you avail yourself of these illegal sources of free music. That said, unauthorized file-sharing remains popular, especially among cash-starved students. It's impossible to ignore, although not a good source of music for the serious music collector.

> ♪ **ULTIMATELY INTERESTING** Learn more about illegal download sites in Chapter 12, "Downloading Music from P2P File-Sharing Sites."

Choosing the Right File Format

To some degree, the sites you choose to download from will either dictate the audio file format you adopt or the file format you've adopted will dictate which download sites you use. In other words, you need to select your file format ecosystem and find a download site to match.

> ♪ **ULTIMATELY INTERESTING** Learn more about file formats in Chapter 4, "Understanding Digital Audio File Formats."

Most online music stores offer their tracks in MP3 format. The big exception is Apple's iTunes Store, which offers its tracks in the AAC format. As you might recall, the MP3 format is somewhat universal, meaning MP3 files will play on just about any music player software or hardware. The AAC format is less universal, being wedded to Apple's iPod/iPhone/iPad/iTunes ecosystem, but is

7

increasingly compatible with other music player programs and devices. When in doubt, go with MP3—or check to make sure your program or device will play AA3 files.

Whether you go with the MP3 or AAC format for your downloads, you should choose a site that offers the highest quality downloads; that is, not all MP3 files are created equal. Variable-bitrate files will typically have the best fidelity, although high bitrate tracks (192Kbps or higher, let's say) will also sound remarkably good. Not CD-quality good, mind you, but much better than lower-bitrate tracks.

A handful of online music stores, such as HDtracks offer higher-quality downloads, typically in lossless FLAC format. These so-called "high definition" downloads *are* CD quality or even better, if you have software that supports the FLAC format and hardware that's up to the audio challenge. If the best possible sound is what you're looking for, go this route.

Why Downloading Makes Sense

When it comes to obtaining digital music online, you really have two practical choices. You can download music files or you can stream music from a subscription service. While music streaming makes sense in certain circumstances, I think downloading is the activity of choice for serious music collectors. (Emphasis here on the word "collector.") Let me explain why.

Streaming services are aptly called "all you can eat" services, because you get to listen to all the music they have for one low monthly subscription price. (And that price can be zero, for some basic plans.) Now, if all you want to do is listen to a lot of music, or if you want to discover new music without making a big investment, then this is a good way to go. I happen to listen to several of these streaming services myself, both to check out new artists and albums and to listen to favorite tunes on my iPhone and notebook PC when I'm out of the house.

However, if you're interesting in building your own personal music collection, you have to own the music you love. You just have to. Since you don't own (or even physically have possession of) the music you listen to on a streaming service, downloading is the way to go.

When you download an album or a track, you have that specific digital audio file in your possession, stored on your computer's hard drive. You can then

7

copy the audio file to another computer, beam it to a portable music player for listening on-the-go, or use it in whatever fashion you want. It's yours.

In addition, when you download a music file (at least a legal one from an authorized site), it comes with information about the track. The metadata built into the file typically includes the track name, artist name, genre, composer, year recorded, and so forth—everything a collector needs to know to organize his or her collection. (That typically includes an image file of the album cover, too.) That's a nice plus.

> ♪ ULTIMATELY **USEFUL** Digital music files are also yours to back up. For safety's sake, you should make regular backups of your digital music collection, either to another hard drive, network server, or online backup service. Learn more about backing up your music in Chapter 13, "Storing Your Digital Music."

I guess the big difference between streaming and downloading is that streaming is transitory, where downloading is permanent. Think of a streaming music service as the 21st century equivalent of an old school radio station, albeit one you can program yourself. There's certainly a place for music pushed to you in the moment, but serious music lovers want to build their own personal collections of music they own. All the audio files you download (and rip too, of course) comprise your digital music collection. That's why serious music lovers learn to download—for at least part of their music needs.

DOWNLOADING VERSUS RIPPING: WHAT'S THE BEST APPROACH?

I know, you're saying: What about ripping music from compact disc? Isn't that a better way to build a high fidelity music collection?

Well, yes, it is. But that's only because the majority of online music stores and other download sites provide audio files at less-than-high fidelity quality. It's a file size vs. sound quality compromise thing, as well as explicit catering to the portable music crowd. They have to keep the file sizes small enough for easy downloading and efficient storage on limited-capacity devices, such as iPhones and iPods. That means reducing the bitrate, which reduces the audio quality.

The choice of file formats also enters into it. With the notable exception of Apple's iTunes Store, most online music services offer files in the MP3 format, for near-universal compatibility. Unfortunately, the MP3 format is showing its age; it has the heaviest compression and the

7

worst sound of all modern digital audio formats. AAC and WMA files sound much better, but that's not what you get.

As I've hinted throughout this chapter, there are some interesting exceptions in the form of HDtracks and a small number of other online stores offering high resolution music downloads, often in the lossless FLAC format. These downloads offer CD-quality (if not better) sound, but cost more and are much bigger files; they take longer to download and there's no way you want to transfer them to your iPhone or iPod, even if those devices could play the files. (They probably can't.)

Aside from the few high resolution download services, then, you get better audio quality when you rip your own tracks from CD using lossless compression. Now, if you do all your listening on a portable device through a set of standard ear buds, you probably won't notice the difference. But if you play your music through a decent home audio system, the difference is noticeable, to say the least. I can't stand to listen to MP3 files on my living room system, the sound is definitely not audiophile quality. I can tell when I'm playing a track downloaded from iTunes or Amazon, as opposed to the majority of my collection that was ripped from CD in lossless format.

There are disadvantages to ripping your own music, of course. First, it takes time. You have to purchase the CD and then physically rip the tracks, which also takes a bit of effort. The cost of the CD is probably going to be a little higher than if you purchased the album for download; the cost is even more of a factor if you really only wanted to purchase a few tracks instead of the entire album. And then there are all those physical CDs to deal with—where do you store the darned things?

Still, my preference is to rip as much music as possible at the highest possible quality, then supplement my base library with targeted downloads. And, when I download, to choose the highest-bitrate files available, which sometimes means shopping between different online stores. It's more expensive and more time consuming, but to me the sound is all that matters.

If your ears aren't quite as golden, or if you do most of your listening on portable devices or lower-end home audio equipment, doing the download route may be a better choice for you. As I continue to note throughout this book, when you're dealing with digital music there is no such thing as one single right solution; it's different for everyone.

7

Downloading Music from the iTunes Store

The most popular online music store today is Apple's iTunes Store. The iTunes Store is the largest in terms of total customers (more than 160 million), total tracks downloaded (more than 10 billion), and total tracks available for downloading (more than 20 million). It's a much bigger store than any local music store you've ever frequented.

If you have an iPod, iPhone, or iPad, chances are you've visited and probably purchased something from the iTunes Store. Even if you're not a slave to the Apple empire, the iTunes Store is still a pretty good place to shop for music for your digital music collection. You won't find a bigger selection of tunes anywhere else online.

8

iTunes Over the Years: A Musical History Tour

It all started with the iTunes music player.

Apple originally conceived iTunes as a music player program for its Macintosh computers, to compete with similar music players on the Windows platform. As such, Apple launched the iTunes music player software at Macworld Expo in January of 2001. (A Windows version would be released in 2003.)

Simultaneous with the launch of the iTunes software, another group within Apple was looking at opportunities revolving around digital devices for the mass market. This led to the development of the iPod portable music player, which was officially introduced in October of 2001.

Initial iPod sales were good but not earth shattering—just 125,000 units for the 2001 holiday season. Sales picked up a tad in 2002, to 470,000 units, but the iPod remained a playback device for music ripped from CDs.

That changed on April 28, 2003, when Apple announced what was then called the iTunes Music Store. At launch, the store offered 200,000 songs at 99-cents apiece, licensed from the five largest record labels at the time—BMG, EMI, Sony Music Entertainment, Universal, and Warner Brothers.

> **ULTIMATELY INTERESTING** iTunes' major-label offerings were later augmented with music by more than 600 independent artists. The first independent artist added to the store (in July, 2003) was Moby.

The iTunes Music Store was an immediate success, selling 275,000 tracks in its first 18 hours and more than a million tracks in its first five days. By the end of the year, the iTunes Music Store had sold more than 25 million songs; this led to a corresponding explosion in the sale of iPods.

The iTunes Music Store catalog reached one million tracks on August 10th, 2004. By September 1st of that year, the number of songs downloaded from the store hit 125 million; the 150 million level was hit on October 12th. By this point in time, the iTunes Music Store was registering more than 4 million downloads per week.

In October of 2005 (and to coincide with the launch of iPods with video playback capability), Apple added video downloads to the iTunes Music Store. Initially, 2,000 music videos and episodes from five television shows were available for sale at $1.99 apiece. By the end of October, the store had sold more than a million videos; by the end of the year, more than three million videos were sold.

8

Apple sold its 1 billionth music download on February 22, 2006. In September of that year, Apple added full-length movies to what the now-renamed iTunes Store, priced from $9.99 to $14.99. (Apple dropped the word "music" from the title.) At the same time, Apple added iPod games to the store, priced at $4.99 per title.

The iTunes Store got even busier in January of 2007 when Apple introduced the first iPhone. At the same time, Apple announced that music downloads topped the two billion level, along with 50 million TV episodes and 1.3 million feature-length films. The three billion download level was reached in July of that year; the iTunes Store hit the five billion level less than a year later, in June of 2008.

In April 2009, Apple announced that all tracks in the iTunes Store were now DRM-free. (Previously, Apple applied its proprietary FairPlay DRM encoding to all tracks.) In February 2010, downloads hit the 10 billion level, and by October 2011, downloads were at 16 billion.

Getting to Know the iTunes Store

The iTunes Store is the dominant player in digital music today. It offers more than 20 million tracks for purchase and download, at prices ranging from 69 cents to $1.29 each. (It also offers complete albums for download, too.) All tracks are in Apple's somewhat-proprietary AAC file format, not in the universal MP3 format. Apple uses variable bitrate encoding for what amounts to pretty good audio quality—although not as good as what you get from lossless ripping from CD.

The tracks you download from the iTunes Store are playable on all Apple devices, of course, but also in many other hardware and software music players. (Over the years, Apple has become so dominant that other companies have added AAC compatibility to their offerings.) While iTunes tracks are not DRM encoded, they are watermarked (to identify any illegal use) and come with notable restrictions in terms of how many devices on which a given track can be played.

The iTunes Store offers more than just music for download, of course. iTunes also sells movies, TV shows, music videos, podcasts, audiobooks, and ebooks. You even get access to iTunes U, which offers all manner of textbooks, courses, and educational materials, and Apple's App Store for the iPhone and iPad.

Installing the iTunes Software

To access the iTunes Store, you must download and install Apple's iTunes software. That is, you can't access the iTunes Store from your web browser, only from the iTunes software. That's a minor inconvenience.

Fortunately, the iTunes software is free; you download it from Apple's website (www.apple.com/itunes/download/). Separate versions are available for both Windows and Macintosh computers.

The current version of the iTunes software, as of this writing, is iTunes 10.5.3. If you're using an older version of the program, you should go to Apple's website to download the latest version.

iTunes Store Pricing

How much does it cost to purchase items from the iTunes Store? Table 8.1 details the pricing for available products:

Table 8.1   iTunes Store Pricing

Product	Price
Music (single track)	69 cents, 99 cents, or $1.29
Music (complete album)	$3.96 to $17.99
Music videos	$1.99
TV shows (single episode)	$1.99 (standard definition), $2.99 (HD)
TV shows (full-season pass)	$29.99 to $49.99
Movies (rent)	$2.99 to $4.99
Movies (purchase)	$9.99 to $19.99
Audiobooks	$4.95 to $31.95
eBooks	$6.99 to $19.99
Podcasts	Free
Ringtones	$1.29 (99 cents for alert tones)

Naturally, all prices are subject to change. These are prices in the U.S. store, by the way; pricing varies from country to country.

Navigating the iTunes Store

You access the iTunes Store by first launching the iTunes software. You then click iTunes Store in the navigation sidebar to open the store.

As you can see in Figure 8.1, the main page of the iTunes Store offers access to just about everything offered. Main sections of the home page include the following:

Navigation Bar   Quick Links

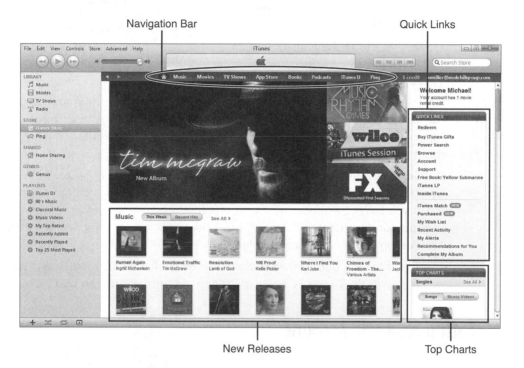

New Releases   Top Charts

FIGURE 8.1

The home page of the iTunes Store.

■ **Navigation Bar** with links to Home, Music, Movies, TV Shows, App Store, Books, Podcasts, iTunes U, and Ping (iTunes' social network for sharing music).

■ **New Releases** by category—Music, Movies, TV Shows, and selected categories. Click the See All link to view all new releases, or scroll to the bottom of the page to see tracks that are Free on iTunes this week.

■ **Quick Links** to key operations—Redeem (gift cards), Buy iTunes Gifts, Power Search, Browse, Account, Support, Free Book, iTunes LP (big album art for selected items), Inside iTunes (blog), iTunes Match, Purchased, My Wish List, Recent Activity, My Alerts, Recommendations For You, and Complete My Album (purchase additional tracks from an album from which you've purchased single tracks).

- **Top Charts** for Singles, Movies, and TV Shows.

> ♪ ULTIMATELY **USEFUL** Different versions of the iTunes Store are available for different countries. Go to the bottom of the home page, click **Change Country**, and then select a country from the list. Apple offers more than a hundred different country-specific versions of the iTunes Store—although it only lets you purchase from your own country's store.

There are three navigational buttons at the left side of the iTunes Store navigation bar. Click the **Back** button to return to the previous store page, click the **Forward** button to go to the next store page (after you've clicked the **Back** button), and click the **Home** button to return to the store's home page.

In addition, your user name (email address) appears at the right side of the navigation bar. Click the **down arrow** next to your name, which appears when you hover the mouse over your email address, to access your account information (Account), redeem gift cards (Redeem), access your wish list (Wish List), or log out of your account (Sign Out).

Finally, at the top right corner of the iTunes window itself is a search box. Use this to search the iTunes Store for specific tracks, artists, albums, and such.

Creating an Apple Account

Before you can purchase items from the iTunes Store, you have to create an Apple account. You may be prompted to do this the first time you click to purchase, or you can create your account manually at any time.

> ♪ ULTIMATELY **CAUTIOUS** You also need an Apple account before the iTunes software can download album art from the iTunes Store.

To create an Apple account, click the **Sign In** button at the top right of the iTunes window. When prompted by the dialog box shown in Figure 8.2, click the **Create New Account** button. (If you already have an Apple account, you should enter your account ID and password instead.)

FIGURE 8.2

Signing into or signing up for an Apple account.

There are three steps to creating an Apple account:

1. Agree to the iTunes Store terms of service.

2. Enter your email address, desired password, security question and answer, and month and date of birth, as shown in Figure 8.3. (And choose whether you want to receive Apple's email promos, of course.)

3. Enter your credit card information—which is how you'll be billed for your iTunes Store purchases.

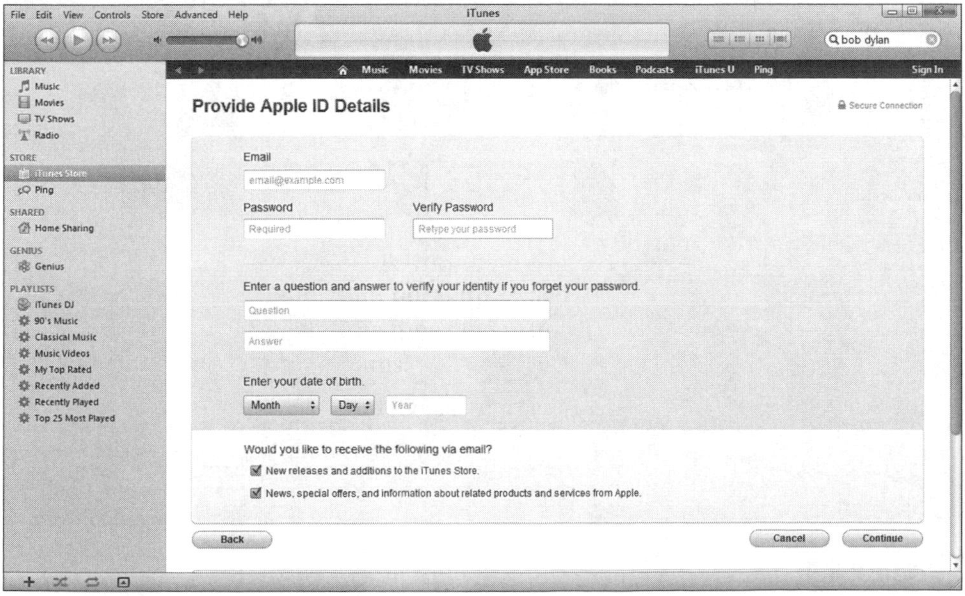

FIGURE 8.3

Creating an Apple account—necessary to use the iTunes Store.

8

There is no cost to create your Apple account. The only charges billed to your credit card come when you make purchases from the iTunes Store.

To manage your Apple account, click the **Account** link in the Quick Links box on the iTunes Store home page. From here, you can change your method of payment, nickname, and so forth; you can also use the Apple Account Information page to view your purchase history from the iTunes Store.

Searching the iTunes Store

To find items for download, you can either browse through the categories presented when you click the **down arrow** next to Music in the navigation bar, or you can search for specific items. Given the tens of millions of items available in the iTunes Store, searching is often the most efficient method.

The easiest way to search the iTunes Store is to use the search box in the top right corner of the iTunes software window. Just enter one or more keywords (such as a song or artist name) and press enter. If you're searching for music, songs that match your query are displayed in the bottom half of the main iTunes window, with albums and other media by that artist in the top half of the window, as shown in Figure 8.4.

FIGURE 8.4

The results of an iTunes search by artist.

More sophisticated searching can be had by clicking the **Power Search** link in the Quick Links section, on the right of the iTunes Store home page. This displays the search page screen shown in Figure 8.5, where you can search by song, album name, or artist. Enter the appropriate keywords into the desired boxes, then click the **Search** button.

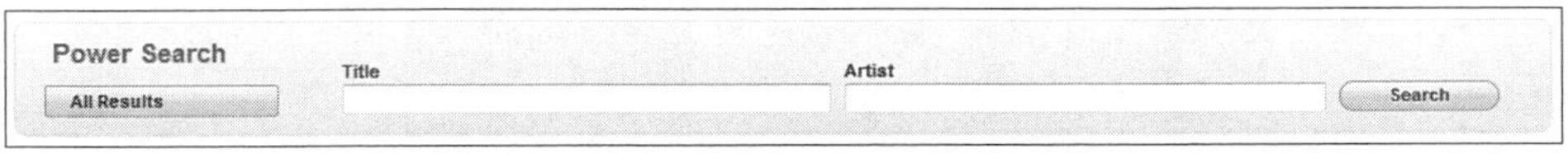

FIGURE 8.5
iTunes' Power Search screen.

You can use the Power Search screen to find songs recorded by specific artists. Consider the song "Walk on By," which has been recorded by hundreds of artists—as you'll find if you just search for the song title. But when you use the Power Search screen, you can search for the song (**walk on by**) and a specific artist, such as Isaac Hayes (search for **isaac hayes**). iTunes will return the recording of this song from Hayes' classic *Hot Buttered Soul* album.

Browsing the iTunes Store

Some days you feel more like browsing than searching. Fortunately, the iTunes Store can accommodate your different moods.

There are two ways to browse the store. You can click the down arrow next to Music on the navigation bar and then select a genre. Or you can click Browse in the Quick Links box on the home page.

If you do the former, you see a page devoted to the selected genre, like the one shown in Figure 8.6. You can now browse the hottest albums in that genre (What's Hot), view the genre's top-selling albums (Top Chart), or use the Quick Links to go directly to an advanced genre search, new releases, and the like.

If you do the latter, you see the browse screen shown in Figure 8.7. From here, it's a matter of narrowing down your browsing. Start by selecting Music in the first column, then select a genre from the second column. You're now faced with additional choices—subgenre, artist, and album. Keep narrowing down your choices until you see a track list on the bottom half of the screen.

> **ULTIMATELY USEFUL** You can preview most items in the iTunes Store by double-clicking that item in any track list. For example, most songs have a short (30-second) preview that plays via the iTunes player software.

FIGURE 8.6

Viewing a genre page (Jazz) in the iTunes Store.

FIGURE 8.7

Browsing for items in the iTunes Store.

Purchasing Items from the iTunes Store

The primary reason to visit the iTunes Store, of course, is to purchase digital music. Apple makes this very easy to do.

Whether you search or browse for music, you eventually end up with either a track list or an artist page, like the one shown in Figure 8.8. The artist page is particularly useful, as this page enables you to purchase complete albums. To view information about an album, click the **album title** or **cover thumbnail**; to purchase the album, click the **Buy Album** button. When you select an album, iTunes displays all the tracks for that album in a track list.

> ♪ ULTIMATELY **USEFUL** Many items in the iTunes Store can be purchased as gifts for other users. Click the **down arrow** next to the Buy button and select Gift This Song to send a link to the gift purchase to the intended recipient.

FIGURE 8.8

An artist page in the iTunes Store.

Alternately, you can display all tracks for an artist by clicking the **See All** link in the Songs section of the artist page. You can then purchase individual tracks; just click the **Buy** button next to the desired track.

8

Once you choose to purchase a track or album, you're prompted as to whether you really want to make the purchase. (This ensures you don't click the Buy button by mistake.) When you confirm your intention, iTunes automatically charges your credit card and begins downloading the purchased music.

All items you purchase from the iTunes Store (music and other items) are listed when you click **Purchased in the Quick Links** section of the iTunes Store home page. As you can see in Figure 8.9, the Purchased page is organized by type of item purchased (Music, TV Shows, Apps, and Books), and then by artist. To redownload a purchased item (or your entire library, if you lose it in some disaster), click the **cloud** button to the right of a track.

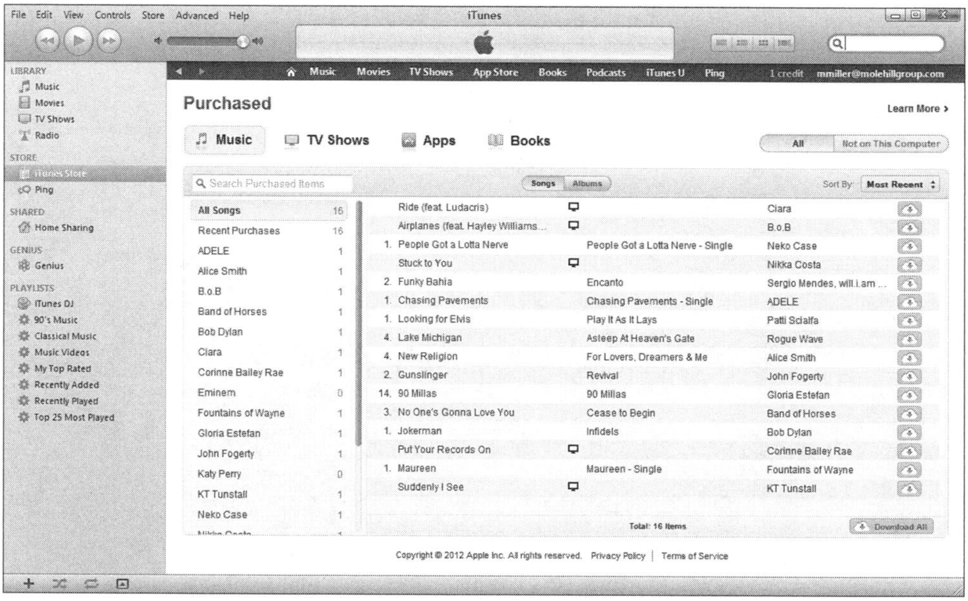

FIGURE 8.9
Viewing a list of all items purchased from the iTunes Store.

Introducing iTunes in the Cloud

Apple recently added a new feature to the iTunes Store, dubbed iTunes in the Cloud. This feature merges traditional store features with cloud-based storage to provide the songs you purchase to any Internet-connected device.

There are several useful features to iTunes in the Cloud. First off, any songs you purchase from the iTunes Store are automatically uploaded to Apple's iCloud cloud storage servers. In addition, any songs you purchase are automatically downloaded to all the devices you have registered to your Apple account. This means if you purchase a track on your home computer, it's automatically downloaded to your notebook PC, iPhone, and iPad (if you have such devices, of course). This applies for new purchases as well as older purchase you've made in the past.

Best of all, iTunes in the Cloud is completely free. You do need to set up iCloud on your devices first, however.

Apple also offers the iTunes Match service, which takes this cloud-based scenario one step further. When you subscribe to iTunes Match ($24.99/year), all the music you've purchased from the iTunes Store, as well as those tracks you've ripped from CDs, can be streamed from the cloud to any Internet-connected device. It's cloud-based streaming, rooted in the Apple iTunes ecosystem, and it's the latest big thing; it essentially makes your entire digital music collection available to you anywhere you go, on almost any device you use.

> ♪ **ULTIMATELY INTERESTING**   Learn more about Apple's iCloud and iTunes Match services in Chapter 20, "Accessing Your Music in the Cloud."

WHY IS THE iTUNES STORE SO POPULAR?

The iTunes Store dominates the online music store space, accounting for 70% of all legal downloads; the Amazon MP3 Music Store is a distant second, with a 12% share. In fact, the iTunes Store is the single largest music retailer in the United States, ahead of Best Buy, Wal-Mart, and everybody else.

What, then, makes the iTunes Store so popular?

Some will say that the iTunes Store owes its success to the popularity of Apple's iPod and iPhone. Fair enough; Apple has sold hundreds of millions of these devices that are strongly tethered to Apple's online music store.

Others will note (correctly) that it's the iTunes Store that led to the success of the iPod. Those of you with long enough memories will remember that the iPod was a moderate success as a standalone device, but

8

really took off when Apple introduced iTunes and legitimized the concept of legally purchasing music online. (Success also coincided with adding Windows compatibility to the iPod; it initially launched as a Mac-only device.)

What's more important, I think, is that Apple really does it right. Using the iTunes Store is a snap; it's easy to find what you want, and even easier to purchase it. It's a truly seamless shopping and buying experience.

The iTunes Store also benefits from an incredible selection of music, much more than your local music store had when you still had a local music store. Apple has also been aggressive about getting artists and labels to release their music digitally; witness the launch of the complete Beatles catalog to iTunes in 2010.

Let's also remember that Apple defined the concept of the online music store, and pretty much dictates terms. It was Apple that set 99 cents as the de facto pricing standard for individual tracks; it essentially created the so-called "agency model" for compensating artists and labels, where Apple takes 30% of the sales price and the balance reverts back to the label or artist. In other words, the iTunes Store is playing by those rules that Apple itself devised, and doing very well by them, thank you.

But what's really important is that the iTunes Store wouldn't be doing so well if it didn't offer a strong selection, good bargains, and an excellent consumer experience. That's what makes any retailer successful, and that's the model that Apple is following with the iTunes Store. It's successful because it's good at what it does. As an avid music collector, it's certainly worth your time to check it out.

Downloading Music from the Amazon MP3 Store

Apple's iTunes Store is the number-one source for legal music downloads. In second place, and gaining ground, is the Amazon MP3 Store. Amazon's a good choice because of its selection (close to that of iTunes) and the fact that its downloads are in the somewhat universal MP3 format, instead of a proprietary format (like you find in the iTunes Store).

In addition, chances are you already have an Amazon account and do some shopping there from time to time, so you're familiar with the way Amazon works. Let's face it, Amazon has become a major player in the retail space because it does a lot of things right—from selection and price, to shipping and customer service.

Amazon.com—From Books to Tunes

You've probably heard of Amazon.com, especially if you do any shopping online. Amazon is, quite simply, the world's largest online retailer. Yes, Amazon sells MP3 music for download, but it also sells physical CDs—and CD players and portable music players and iPods and books and clothing and tools and lawn chairs and toys and just about anything you might want to buy.

Amazon opened its online doors in 1995 as an online bookstore, nothing more and nothing less. Having proven successful at bookselling, Amazon then expanded its offerings to include music, movies, video games, and other soft goods; it later diversified into all manner of hard goods, as well.

The Amazon MP3 Store was launched a dozen years after the online bookstore. At the September, 2007 launch, the MP3 Store offered more than 2 million tracks from more than 180,000 artists, from all the major labels and leading indies.

Within four months of the initial launch (in January of 2008), Amazon had adapted its offerings to include only DRM-free tracks—the first online music store to do so. (Some current tracks are digitally watermarked for third-party identification, but remain DRM-free.)

Since licensing agreements with the major record labels restrict the countries in which music can be sold, Amazon offers separate MP3 stores in different countries. For example, the main Amazon.com site sells only to U.S. customers, while Amazon.co.uk sells to customers in the United Kingdom. (There are also versions of the store available in Germany, France, Austria, and Switzerland.)

Getting to Know the Amazon MP3 Store

Unlike the iTunes Store, which requires installing proprietary software to access, you can get to the Amazon MP3 Store from any web browser (no proprietary software needed, as with iTunes). Just go to www.amazon.com/mp3/ and you're in.

At present, the Amazon MP3 Store has more than 18 million tracks for downloading. All its tracks are in MP3 format, with variable bitrate encoding. They aim for an

ULTIMATELY INTERESTING Some albums are accompanied by separate "digital booklets" of liner notes and such. When you see the [**+digital booklet**] notation on an item detail page, that means the item comes with a digital booklet, in PDF format.

average 256Kbps bitrate, which is near the top end of what you can expect from the MP3 format. Cover art files are included with all downloads.

You can browse for music by genre or other criteria (new releases, featured promotions, and the like), or search by title, artist, or song/album name. Purchases flow into Amazon's 1-Click payment system; the tracks you purchase are downloaded to your hard drive for immediate listening, or to Amazon's Cloud Drive for streaming to any Internet-connected device.

Since Amazon also sells physical music, in the form of CDs and vinyl LPs, many albums are also available in these other formats for purchase through the normal Amazon website. Look for the little information section under the price at the top of any album page, as shown in Figure 9.1—this will tell you what other formats are available. Click the appropriate link to view and purchase the item in CD or vinyl format.

How Do You Do
Mayer Hawthorne | Format: Audio CD
★★★★☆ ☑ (19 customer reviews) | 👍 Like (38)

Price: **$9.99** *Prime*
     Special Offers Available
In Stock.
Ships from and sold by **Amazon.com**. Gift-wrap available.

46 new from $7.92   **5 used** from $7.00

Formats	Amazon Price	New from	Used from
⊞ MP3 Download, 12 Songs, 2011	$5.00	--	--
Audio CD, 2011	$9.99 *Prime*	$7.92	$7.00
Vinyl, 2011	$17.98 *Prime*	$14.98	$14.37

FIGURE 9.1

If you want an album in another format, Amazon can accommodate you.

Amazon MP3 Store Pricing

When it comes to selling digital tracks, Amazon's pricing is similar to Apple's, with individual tracks in a three-tier pricing scheme—$0.69, $0.99, and $1.29. Amazon also offers a good number of free tracks, with the selection changing from week to week.

> **ULTIMATELY USEFUL** To view all of Amazon's free tracks, scroll down to the Top Free Albums or Top Free Songs sections of the main page and click the Browse All Free Albums or Browse All Free Songs link.

As for complete albums, pricing runs from $3.69 to $17.99 or so. Amazon also offers a number of free albums for downloading each week, although they're not likely to be recent hits.

One thing that differentiates the Amazon MP3 Music store from iTunes is that Amazon regularly puts selected items on sale. iTunes seldom if ever offers promotional pricing. So if you're looking for a bargain, Amazon is the place to go. (Look for Amazon's current promotions to be displayed prominently on the MP3 Store home page.)

> **ULTIMATELY USEFUL** If you're price-conscious, it pays to shop between the Amazon and Apple music stores. You can often save a buck or more if Amazon has a given album on sale—and Amazon's MP3 Downloader software (discussed later in this chapter) can automatically add Amazon downloads to your iTunes library.

Creating an Amazon Account

Before you can purchase music (or even download free music) from the Amazon MP3 Store, you first have to establish an Amazon account, enter payment information, and enable 1-Click ordering.

Setting Up an Account

To set up a new Amazon account, point your web browser to www.amazon.com/sign-in. Enter your email address, check the **No, I'm a New Customer** option, then click the **Sign In Using Our Secured Server** button. When the Registration page appears, enter your name, email address, birthday, and desired password, then click the **Continue** button.

That's it, you now have an Amazon account. The next time you visit the Amazon website, sign in with this email address and password.

Enabling 1-Click Ordering

Since all MP3 purchases are automatically downloaded to your computer, without you first having to go through a checkout process, you need to enable Amazon's 1-Click ordering feature and put a credit card on file for payment.

To do this, go to any page on the Amazon site and click **Your Account** in the top right corner. When the Your Account page appears, go to the Settings section and click 1-Click Settings.

When the Manage Addresses and 1-Click Settings page appears, begin by clicking the **Enter a New Address** button. When the next page appears, enter your shipping address, then click the **Save & Add Payment Method** button.

You're now prompted to add a credit or debit card to your account. Follow the onscreen instructions to do so, then click the **Use This Address** button next to the primary address items will be shipped to.

Set the address as your default by clicking the link on the address labeled **Click here to make this your 1-Click default address**. You may be prompted to associate a credit or debit card with the address, but entering one of these payment methods is not required.

When you're returned to the Manage Addresses and 1-Click Settings page, click the **Turn 1-Click On** button. You're now ready to go shopping.

Navigating the Amazon MP3 Store

What do you find when you visit the Amazon MP3 Store? Lots and lots of music for downloading, of course, organized in lots of different ways, as you can see in Figure 9.2.

FIGURE 9.2

The main page for the Amazon MP3 Store.

Navigation Controls

The top of the page is the same as what you find on any Amazon.com page. Indeed, you'll see this section of navigation controls on the top of all pages you visit in the MP3 Store.

There's a search box, which you can filter by department; if you go to the MP3 Store page directly, the MP3 Downloads filter is applied by default. This same blue bar also includes a drop-down menu to Shop All Departments, as well as buttons to access your shopping cart and overall Amazon wish list.

Beneath this blue bar is a white navigation bar. The links on this bar take you to sections within the MP3 Store, or in related Amazon stores. There are links for the following:

- **Amazon MP3 Store.** Returns you to the MP3 Store main page.
- **Music CDs.** Shifts you to the main Amazon Music store to purchase CDs and vinyl LPs.
- **New Releases.** Displays recent MP3 releases.
- **Recommendations.** Displays recommended albums and tracks based on your past purchases.
- **Advanced Search.** Opens the Advanced Search page, which you can use to search by artist, title, label, category, and other detailed criteria.
- **Browse Genres.** Displays all available MP3 genres (Alternative & Indie Rock, Blues, Classical, Country, and the like), which you can then click through to browse selections within a genre.
- **Best Sellers.** Displays Amazon's top MP3 downloads, by both paid and free albums, and tracks.
- **Amazon Cloud Player.** Opens the Amazon Cloud Player, for playing tracks you've purchased or uploaded to the Amazon Cloud Drive service. (More on this later in the chapter.)
- **Getting Started.** Displays information about how the MP3 Store and Cloud Player work.
- **Get Help.** Provides access to Amazon's online help system.

As you might suspect, this little white navigation bar is a great way to navigate the MP3 Store.

Left Column

The left column on the MP3 Store's main page is pretty much a navigational sidebar. Here you'll find links of the following types:

- **MP3 Daily Deal.** Today's featured on-sale item in the MP3 Store.
- **Featured Programs.** Links to other promotional offerings in the MP3 Store.
- **Site Features.** Links to the Amazon Cloud Player, Amazon MP3 App for Android, and to Redeem a Gift Card.
- **New Releases.** Click to view the latest releases on either CD or MP3.
- **Categories.** Click to view Bestselling Albums, Bestselling Songs, New Releases, or Free Songs & Special Deals.
- **Genres.** Click to view music by genre—Folk, Jazz, New Age, R&B, and so forth.
- **MP3 Albums by Price.** Click to view available items at selected price points—$4.99 and Under, $5.00 to $5.99, $6.00 to $6.99, and $7.00 to $7.99.
- **More in Music.** Links to Band T-Shirts, CDs, DVD & Blu-ray, and Vinyl Records.
- **More Digital Downloads.** Links to Amazon Appstore for Android, Amazon Instant Video, Game Downloads, Digital Deals, Kindle Books, and Software Downloads.
- **Connect with Us.** Click to "like" the Amazon MP3 Store on Facebook or follow it on Twitter.

And there's even more, if you keep scrolling—various promotional offers, links to give or redeem gift cards, the ability to sign up for promotional email newsletters, and a link to send Amazon your feedback.

Center Column

The center column holds a lot of interesting content—specifically, links to a lot of new and exciting music. Click the **Play** button on any album cover to preview a track, or click the album cover or title to view the product page for that item.

Here's what you'll find:

- **Recommended for You.** Tracks and albums recommended based on other items you've purchased.

9

- **MP3 Recommendations Based on Your Music**. This sounds similar to the previous section, but it's subtly different. This section makes recommendations for complete albums (not single tracks) based on items you've purchased and also on your own music you've uploaded to the Amazon Cloud Drive.

- **This Month's $5 MP3 Albums**. Albums discounted this month.

- **Amazon MP3 Exclusive Editions**. MP3 albums available only at Amazon.

- **Top Free Albums**. The most popular free albums offered for download this month.

- **New and Notable MP3 Releases**. The latest MP3 album releases.

- **More Items to Consider**. Based on the last item you viewed, albums purchased by customers who also viewed that item.

- **MP3 Recommendations**. Another section of recommendations, this time a list of individual tracks you might like. You can purchase tracks directly from this section (click the **Buy** button) or preview any track (click the **Play** button for that track). To find out why a particular track was recommended, click the **Why** link for that track.

- **Featured in the MP3 Store**. Links to various promotional offers.

- **Perennial *Genre* Favorites**. Based on your purchasing history, more recommendations in a favorite genre.

- **Top Albums $4.99 or Less**. Amazon's top-selling low-priced MP3 albums.

- **Top Free Songs**. The most downloaded free tracks from Amazon.

- ***Genre* Hot New Releases**. The top new releases in one of your favorite genres.

At the very bottom of the page are even more useful links. Scroll down far enough and you'll find **Your Recent History** (items you've recently viewed, as well as items purchased by others who viewed the same items as you) and a bunch of links to specific Amazon departments and services.

Right Column

On the right side of the home page is another narrow column, with the following contents:

- **Amazon Cloud Player**. Click this link to launch the Cloud Player, to listen to music you've purchased or uploaded.

- **Song of the Day**. Just as the title implies, a featured track that changes daily.
- **Best Sellers**. Updated hourly, Amazon's top MP3 songs and albums.
- **Movers & Shakers**. Also updated hourly, those MP3 albums that have had the biggest increase in sales.

This column also contains various promotional and informational offers.

Searching the Amazon MP3 Store

How do you find tracks to download? You can either search or browse for them. Let's look at searching first.

There are actually two ways to search the Amazon MP3 Store. You can conduct basic searches from the search box at the top of any Amazon page, or more sophisticated searches from Amazon's Advanced Search page.

Conducting Basic Searches

For most basic searches, use the search box at the top of any Amazon page. Make sure that MP3 Downloads is selected in the filter list, then enter the title of the track, album, or artist's name into the search box and click the **Go** button.

The resulting results page, like the one shown in Figure 9.3, displays a handful of matching MP3 albums along the top, as well as a list of matching songs beneath that. Click an album name to display the product page for that album; from there you can purchase the entire album or, in most cases, individual tracks from the album.

As to the track list, you can preview any individual song by clicking the **Play** button to the left of the title. View the product page for a given track or album by clicking the track or album name, or view other albums by this artist by clicking the artist name. To purchase the track, click the **Buy MP3** button.

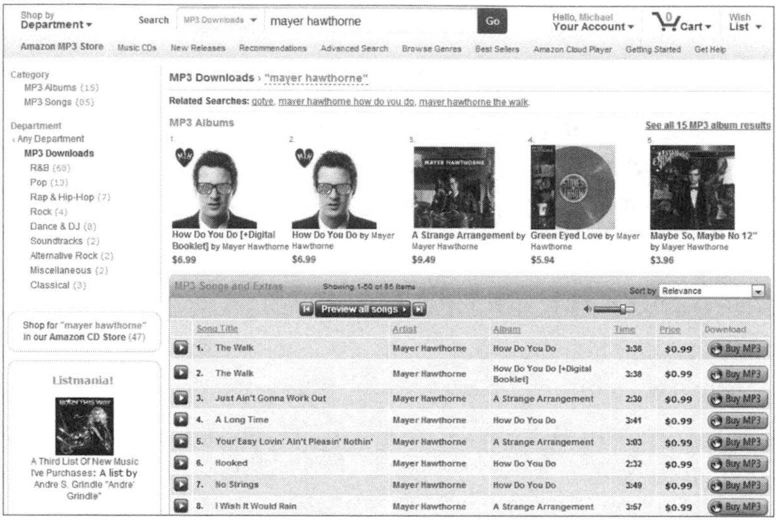

FIGURE 9.3

The results of an Amazon MP3 Store search.

Conducting an Advanced Search

If you want to fine tune your searches a bit, use Amazon's Advanced Search function. You do this by clicking the **Advanced Search** link in the top navigation bar.

The Advanced Search page, shown in Figure 9.4, lets you search by any or all of the following criteria:

- **Keywords**. Look for selected words anywhere in a track or album title or artist name
- **Artist**. Search for music by a selected performer.
- **Title**. Search only within the song or album title.
- **Label**. Limit results to music released on a specific record label.
- **Category**. Search only within a given genre—Pop, Rock, Hip Hop & Rap, and so forth.

You can also opt to sort your search results by Relevance (default), Bestselling, Song Title, Artist, Album, Time (short to long or long to short), Price, Avg. Customer Review, or Release Date. Click the search button to start the search.

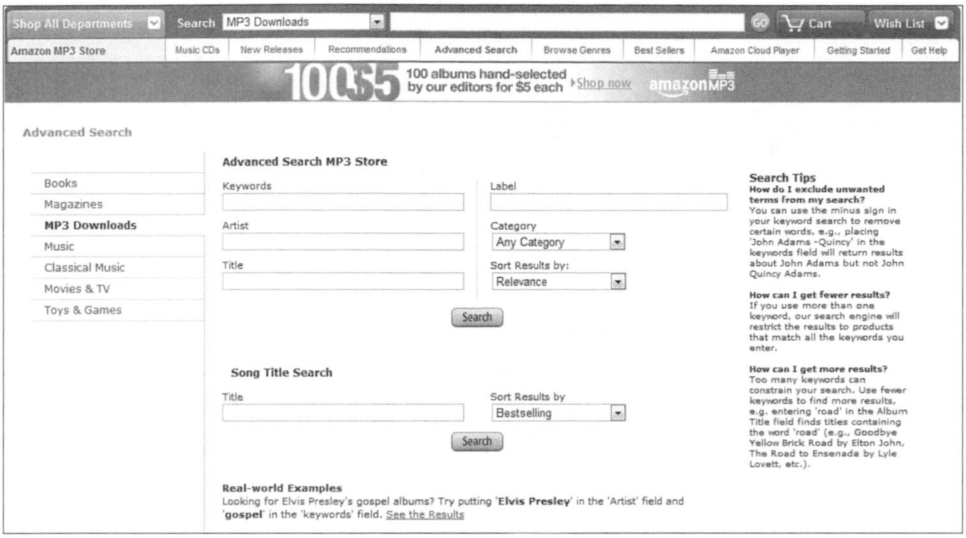

FIGURE 9.4

Conducting an advanced search.

In addition, you can perform basic song title searches. Just enter one or more words from the song's title into the Song Title Search box, select how you want the results sorted, then click the **Search** button.

Browsing the Amazon MP3 Store

If you don't have a specific track or artist in mind, you can browse the Amazon MP3 Store by genre or price.

To browse by genre, either click a genre in the left column or click **Browse Genres** in the top navigation bar, then click a genre. What you see next is a genre page, like the one shown in Figure 9.5, with selected albums displayed. You can narrow your browsing by subgenre or price; links for both are in the left column. Keep clicking until you find what you want.

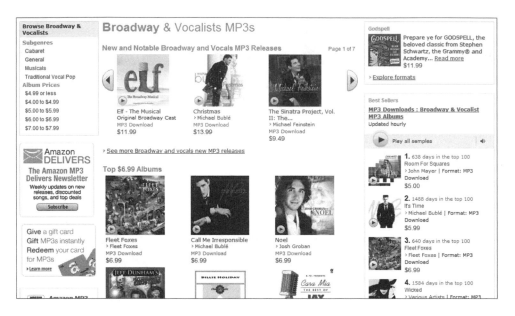

FIGURE 9.5

Browsing the Broadway & Vocalists genre.

Purchasing Items from the Amazon MP3 Store

Click far enough and you find yourself on the product page for a given item. A product page for an individual track, like the one shown in Figure 9.6, is relatively simple; you see the name of the track, the recording artist, a link to the album it came from, the price, the release date, and so forth. You can also sample the track by clicking the big **Play** button. To purchase the track, click the **Buy MP3 with 1-Click** button.

The product page for an album contains even more information. In addition to the basic stuff, you see a track listing (where you can preview or purchase individual tracks), product details, and customer reviews. In some instances, you'll even find a discussion board for this product. To purchase the album, click the **Buy MP3 Album with 1-Click** button.

> **ULTIMATELY USEFUL** You can also purchase individual tracks from any track list on the Amazon MP3 Store site. Just click the **Buy MP3** button within the list to make a purchase.

> **ULTIMATELY USEFUL** To me, the customer reviews are one of the primary reasons to purchase new music from Amazon. I can get a sense of what an album sounds like by sampling tracks, but it's also useful to hear what other music lovers have to say about a given release.

The Sinatra Project, Vol. II: The Good Life
Michael Feinstein | Format: MP3 Download
★★★★☆ ☑ (6 customer reviews) | 👍 Like (0)

Price: $9.49
Album Savings: $2.39 compared to buying all songs

Original Release Date: October 24, 2011
Format - Music: MP3
Compatible with MP3 Players (including with iPod®), iTunes, Windows Media Player
Also available in CD Format

1,000 $5 Albums
Fuel Your Kindle Fire
Shop over 1,000 albums for $5 each for a limited time.
› See more product promotions

See larger image
Share your own customer images
🔊 Listen to Samples and Buy MP3s

Buy MP3 album with 1-Click®
Give album OR song as gift
Redeem a gift card or promotion code & view balance
Requires Amazon MP3 Downloader
Add to Wish List

amazon cloud player
Launch Player

Share ✉ 📘 🐦

MP3 Songs	Play all samples				
	Song Title		Time	Price	
▶	1. Thirteen Women		3:02	$0.99	Buy MP3
▶	2. Hallelujah I Love Her So		2:47	$0.99	Buy MP3
▶	3. C'est Comme Ça		2:53	$0.99	Buy MP3
▶	4. Is You Is Or Is You Ain't My Baby?		3:17	$0.99	Buy MP3
▶	5. Sway		3:32	$0.99	Buy MP3
▶	6. Luck Be A Lady / All I Need Is The Girl		3:52	$0.99	Buy MP3
▶	7. I'll Be Around		4:23	$0.99	Buy MP3

FIGURE 9.6

Viewing a product page.

The purchasing process is fairly straightforward—after you make your first digital purchase. That's because all downloads are done through the Amazon MP3 Downloader software, which you have to install and configure before you complete any downloads. This software program not only handles all your downloads, it also automatically adds songs you've downloaded to your iTunes or Windows Media Player library, if you use one of those programs. (Both of these music players can play MP3-format files, so you're all set.)

The Amazon MP3 Downloader works with most versions of Windows (XP, Vista, and 7), Mac OS X (10.4 or higher), and Linux (Ubuntu, Debian, Fedora, and Open SUSE). To install the program, all you have to do is follow the onscreen prompts when you make your first purchase from the MP3 Store. Alternately, go to the MP3 Downloader page (www.amazon.com/gp/dmusic/help/amd.html) and click the **Install the Amazon MP3 Downloader** button. The installation program should automatically detect your computer's operating system and install the correct version of the program.

The Amazon MP3 Downloader launches automatically when you've purchased any digital music from Amazon. It downloads purchased files to the

Amazon MP3 folder within your My Music folder. (That's on a Windows PC; on a Mac, the Amazon MP3 folder is within your Music folder.)

You can also opt to have any digital music you purchase stored in the Amazon Cloud Drive secure online storage service. Any tunes stored in Cloud Drive can then be streamed to any Internet-connected computer or device via the Amazon Cloud Player, which we'll discuss next. On your first purchase from the Amazon MP3 Store you'll be asked to set your delivery preference for all store purchases; you can select **Save to This Computer** (download to your PC's hard drive) or **Save to Amazon Cloud Drive**, or both. (I recommend both.)

> ♪ ULTIMATELY **USEFUL** To configure the default download directory and other options for the Amazon MP3 Downloader program, you'll need to open the program independently. (If you're an iTunes user, you may want to change the default download directory to your iTunes music folder.) To open the program on a Windows PC, click the Start menu and select All Programs > Amazon > Amazon MP3 Downloader. To open the product on a Mac, select Amazon MP3 Downloader from your Applications folder.

Introducing Amazon Cloud Drive and the Amazon Cloud Player

Okay, so what's this Amazon Cloud Drive thing? In essence, its cloud-based online storage of all the tracks you purchase from the Amazon MP3 Store, as well as selected tracks you've previously purchased or ripped to your computer. If nothing else, Cloud Drive is a nice backup of your digital library; you can always re-download tracks stored online.

Even better, you can play the tracks stored in your Cloud Drive on any computer or portable device (including your smart phone) connected to the Internet, using the Amazon Cloud Player application. This makes Cloud Drive a streaming digital music service, which is a great way to access your music from any location, on any device.

It's a pretty neat service, comparable to Apple's iTunes Match or the Google Music service. Given that basic access to Cloud Drive is free, there's no reason not to take advantage of it—as an online backup service, if nothing else.

> ♪ ULTIMATELY **INTERESTING** Learn more about Amazon Cloud Drive and Cloud Player in Chapter 20, "Accessing Your Music in the Cloud."

AMAZON VERSUS APPLE: WHICH IS THE BEST ONLINE MUSIC STORE?

It's a battle of titans—Amazon vs. Apple in the war for your digital music dollars. Which online music store should you buy from?

There's really no clear winner here; which store you choose depends a lot on which audio file format you're wedded to, which devices you use, and which shopping experience you personally prefer. Let me explain.

Apple's iTunes Store offers tracks in Apple's AAC format. While most music player software and hardware will play AAC files, not all will. If your equipment and programs aren't compatible with the AAC format, scratch the iTunes Store off your shopping list.

Since the Amazon MP3 Store offers all its tracks in the MP3 format, you're safe playing any music purchased there on just about any program or device. That's one plus for Amazon. The minus comes from the fact that the MP3 format gives you a little lower audio quality than the AAC format, so if you're listening on a high-end home audio system, the iTunes Store might be a better choice. (That said, the best fidelity comes from ripping your own CDs in a lossless format; you can purchase those CDs from Amazon's main Music store, of course.)

If you have an iPod, iPhone, or iPad, you're going to be nudged (okay, pushed hard) to use the iTunes Store. While staying within the Apple family is certainly a good match, it's not the only way to go. You can play tracks downloaded from the Amazon MP3 Store on your Apple device; you can also play tracks downloaded from the iTunes Store on non-Apple devices. Granted, the experience is a little more holistic if you stay within the same ecosystem, but it still works.

Finally, we come down to the online store experience itself. This ultimately is a personal choice. Both Apple and Amazon do online retailing very well. I happen to prefer Amazon; I like the little extras they offer, such as detailed product info and customer reviews. I also happen to dislike having to open a separate software program to shop from the iTunes Store; why can't Apple sell products from a normal web browser, like Amazon does?

9

You can accuse me of drinking the Amazon Kool-Aid, or I can accuse others of drinking the Apple Kool-Aid, but it really is a matter of which approach one personally prefers. While I appreciate everything Apple has done in legitimizing online music downloads, at the end of the day I'm an Amazon kind of guy, I guess. Naturally, your personal tastes might differ—and that's okay.

Downloading Music from Other Online Music Stores

Apple's iTunes Store and the Amazon MP3 Store are the two biggest online music retailers—but they're not the only ones. Indeed, there are many different sites where you can find digital music to buy online, including some that specialize in ultra high-fidelity tracks.

Read on to learn about the *other* online music stores—and why you might want to frequent them.

Why Switch from Apple and Amazon?

While Apple and Amazon have a stronghold on the (legal) online music market, they're not the only players in the game. There are several big competitors to these Big Two players, and they're out to win your business.

It's a tough sell, though. Apple and Amazon do a lot of things right. Apple pretty much invented the modern online music store, after all, while Amazon defined the entire concept of online retailing. It's not in their nature to make a lot of mistakes.

That said, there are a lot of people who dislike both the iTunes Store and Amazon MP3 Store, for perfectly legitimate reasons. For example, some people dislike the one-click ordering you find in both the big stores; being able to purchase without first examining the contents of a shopping cart make it *too* easy to spend money, some think.

Some consumers don't like Apple's insistence that you install and use their software to shop their store; installing yet another software program (that must then be frequently updated) is a pain in the posterior. It's also annoying to find yourself nagged to death to install other Apple software every time the iTunes software needs updating. Why can't the iTunes Store be shopped from any web browser like Amazon can?

Pricing is an issue as well, as the iTunes Store is seldom the lowest-price alternative. Amazon is typically a little lower priced than iTunes, at least on complete albums, and some competitors can be even lower priced. That means you can often save money by shopping around—and that's important, these days.

Music lovers outside the U.S. are particularly peeved at the lack of many tracks in their own country's version of the iTunes Store. It's rare to find a European or Asian customer who hasn't encountered the message that the track she wants to buy is only available in the U.S. store, not her native store. We're talking severely limited catalogs in some countries, which is no doubt frustrating to serious music collectors.

Audio quality is an issue for many users, as you can't purchase lossless audio files from either Apple or Amazon. Instead, the Big Two limit you to files encoded with lossy compression, and it doesn't take a set of golden ears to recognize that these files just don't sound as good as files with lossless (or no) compression. If you care about fidelity, then, neither of the Big Two is an optimal choice.

But at the end of the day, choosing to purchase from some store other than Apple's or Amazon's may simply be because you don't like those guys. Some people think that big companies like Apple and Amazon are inherently evil, or just annoying and to be avoided. They prefer buying from the little guy, instead. Not everyone has to worship at the shrines of Apple and Amazon, after all; the Internet should be big enough to support multiple competitors.

10

What Can Other Stores Do That Apple and Amazon Can't?

For most consumers, however, there has to be a really good reason to switch from their current favorite online music store; it's a bit of a pain to create a new customer account, after all.

So what, then, do competitors offer that Apple and Amazon don't?

First, know that every major online retailer offers a fairly decent shopping experience. It may not be identical to what you get from the iTunes Store or Amazon MP3 Store, but the shopping and checkout process should be relatively easy to do. And once you enter your credit card the first time, it should be just as quick to check out from a new store than from your old favorite.

All these stores let you shop and order from any web browser, which makes them preferable to the iTunes Store, in the eyes of many users. Being forced to use proprietary software to spend your money is so 20th century, and Apple's competitors have moved beyond that to strictly web-based offerings; web-based stores make it easy to sign into your account from any computer, not just the one on which iTunes is installed. So if you dislike the iTunes software requirement, this may be reason alone to switch your allegiance to another retailer.

Many stores offer pricing that can, at least on occasion, save you some money compared to what you might spend with the Big Two. The iTunes Store, in particular, seldom puts music on sale—smaller online retailers do. It might only be a few pennies, but pennies add up.

You may find the selection is different at different online music stores. Not that a smaller online store is going to have more total titles available than do the Big Two, but rather that they sometimes stock different tracks from different artists—in particular, independent and emerging artists. There are some sites, such as Bandcamp and CDBaby, which specialize in offering music *not* from the big record labels that partner with Apple and Amazon. So if you're looking for music from a local or indie artist, you may be able to find it at a smaller online music store.

> **ULTIMATELY USEFUL** Even if you can find the indie music you want at Apple or Amazon's stores, the artist may get a bigger cut of the proceeds from Bandcamp or CDBaby—which is reason enough to buy there.

10

Finally, some stores offer music in different or better audio formats than what you find in the iTunes Store or Amazon MP3 Store. For example, if you really don't want to be locked into Apple's semi-proprietary AAC format, shop at a store that offers tracks in the more universal MP3 format, instead. And if you want music at higher bitrates than what Apple or Amazon offer, there are stores that specialize in that, too.

In other words, you can often find lower priced or better sounding music at smaller online music stores—as well as a more independent-oriented selection. If any of these factors are important to you, then you need to check out some of the alternatives to the Big Two retailers.

Exploring the Competition

In previous chapters you learned all about the Big Two online retailers—Apple's iTunes Store and the Amazon MP3 Store. Now let's take a look at some of the most worthy competitors, and what makes them appealing.

Google Play Music

We'll start our tour of alternative music stores by examining Google Play Music (play.google.com/store/music/), or what used to be called the Android Market. You may know Google Play in general as the place you can find apps for your Android smartphones and tablets, but it's actually a bit more than that—especially in the Music section.

As you can see in Figure 10.1, you can browse Google Play Music by genre or search for specific tracks, albums, or artists. Google offers 13 million tracks or so for download at prices from $0.49 to $1.29 per track. Downloads are high-quality MP3 files encoded at 320Kbps.

In many ways, Google Play Music functions similarly to the Amazon MP3 Store; it uses the universal MP3 format, lets you browse using your web browser, and so forth. It's certainly a decent pick if you use the Google Play Music cloud service, because it integrates well with the Google Music player. It's also a good choice if you want to download music to an Android phone or tablet. Otherwise, however, selection trails that of both Amazon and Apple, so that may be an issue.

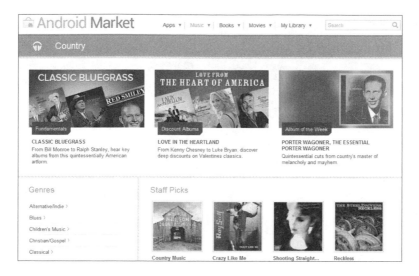

FIGURE 10.1

Google Play Music.

Bandcamp

Now we'll look at one of the more interesting smaller online music stores, Bandcamp (www.bandcamp.com). What makes Bandcamp unique is that it isn't a single monolithic store, but rather a lively marketplace where individual artists can offer their music for sale to fans.

As you can see in Figure 10.2, Bandcamp offers just over 3.2 million tracks for download from more than 200,000 artists. Some artists also choose to sell their physical CDs via Bandcamp. When you make a purchase from Bandcamp, 85% of the price goes directly to the artist; Bandcamp only takes a 15% cut (which goes down to 10% if an artist takes in more than $5,000 in sales).

Because Bandcamp is tailored to the needs of independent artists, it's the least coherent of all the major online music stores. That is, there's no single audio format used, nor pricing structure in place. Instead, individual recording artists upload their own tracks in whatever formats they prefer, and set their own pricing to whatever they thinks their music is worth.

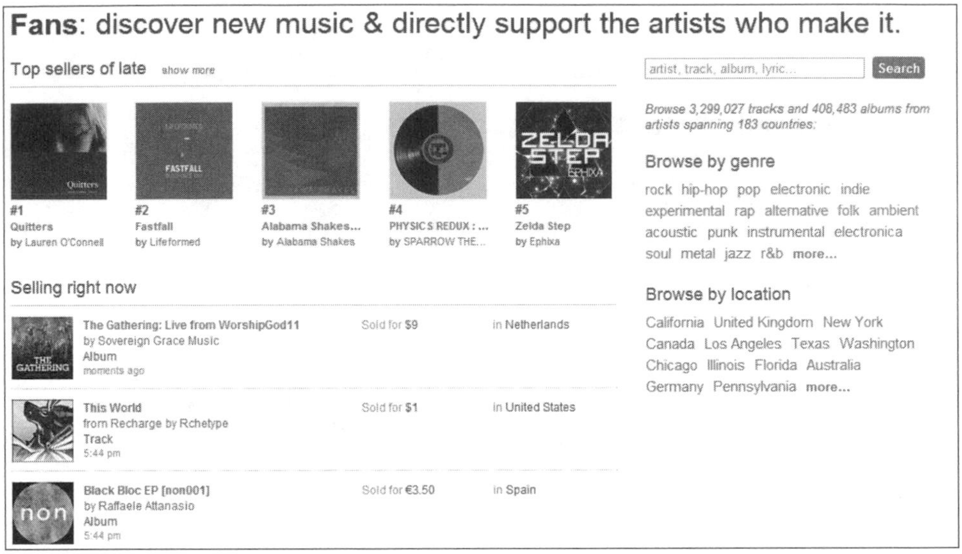

FIGURE 10.2
Bandcamp, a marketplace for independent artists.

That means you may find tracks available for download in the MP3 format, of course, but also in AAC, AAC Lossless, FLAC, or even Ogg Vorbis formats. And don't expect to see uniform 99 cents per track pricing; indeed, Bandcamp pricing is all over the board, as each artist sees fit. Some artists even use Bandcamp's name-your-own-price option, where they let fans choose how much they want to pay for an album.

Having pricing and format set by each individual artist makes shopping at Bandcamp a bit more of an adventure than what you find at competing online stores. You can browse by genre or search for specific artists. Once you land on an artist's album page, like the one in Figure 10.3, you see the various options for purchasing and downloading that artist's music. When you make a purchase, you can choose to check out immediately (payment is via all major credit cards and PayPal), or place the item in a site-wide shopping cart for later checkout.

Why use Bandcamp? In essence, you shop at Bandcamp to find music you might not find elsewhere, and to support your favorite local and independent artists. You may end up paying a little bit more for that, but it's worth it.

> **ULTIMATELY INTERESTING** Bandcamp can also be integrated into an artist's website. Most artists, however, have their own "store" within the Bandcamp site, at a URL that's typically something like *artist*.bandcamp.com.

FIGURE 10.3

Purchasing music from an individual artist's Bandcamp store.

CD Baby

CD Baby (www.cdbaby.com) is another download site that features independent artists. In fact, CD Baby has an entire infrastructure in place to help artists distribute their digital and physical music products; it also serves as a middleman for artists who want to place their music in the iTunes Store and other online music sites.

Like Bandstand, CD Baby lets artists set their own pricing on their products. Unlike the competing site, CD Baby offers all tracks in a single download format—variable bitrate MP3. As you can see in Figure 10.4, CD Baby differs from Bandstand in that it presents a more unified storefront appearance, as opposed to a collection of individual artist pages.

CD Baby currently offers more than 3 million individual tracks for download, as well as more than 250,000 albums, from more than 300,000 artists. While most of CD Baby's artists are independent, some bigger-name musicians—including Gretchen Peters, Janis Ian, Marty Balin, and Regina Spektor—also use the service.

FIGURE 10.4
The CD Baby online music store.

I find myself ordering something from CD Baby at least once a month or so, primarily because they're the designated online store for several artists I like. I like the company's vibe and the services it offers to artists who want to avoid the major label treadmill. It's worth checking it, if you're independently minded.

Classical Archives

If you're a classical music aficionado, Classical Archives (www.classicalarchives.com) is the music store for you. In fact, Classical Archives is more than just a music store for classical music lovers; it also offers a classical streaming music service.

The site's inventory is impressive—in classical music terms, anyway. Classical Archives offers more than 645,000 files for download, many of them complete albums, from more than 14,000 composers, 59,000 performing artists, and 320 record labels. Downloads are in 320Kbps MP3 format.

> **ULTIMATELY INTERESTING** Classical Archives' streaming music service costs $5.99 per month (or $59.90 per year), and also offers subscribers a 10% discount on all download purchases.

All this matters to classical music lovers because the major online music sites typically do a horrible job with classical music—just as most music stores in the real world typically give short shrift to the classical genre. Online retailers such as the iTunes Store typically chop up what classical music they offer into individual tracks for sale, with each track being a part of a longer piece of music; that's not the way classical music is listened to. What works great for organizing and selling popular music is antithetical to the way classical music works.

That's why Classical Archives focuses on selling longer pieces of music, including complete albums, instead of individual tracks. The site's classical music experts also make sure that the selection of music offered is unparalleled. As you can see in Figure 10.5, you can search or browse for music by composer, recording artist, album, or period. Download prices range from $0.49 to $3.99 per "track," depending on the length of the piece. Album prices run the gamut, as classical music often does.

FIGURE 10.5

Classical Archives—digital downloading for classical music lovers.

Classical Archives is a destination site for classical music lovers of all stripes. You'll be more comfortable—and, likely, satisfied—here than at the Apple or Amazon stores.

> **ULTIMATELY INTERESTING** Classical Archives also offers the largest collection of free classical music MIDI files on the Internet.

eMusic

Here's an interesting one. eMusic (www.emusic.com) is a typical online music store, but with a subscription option. The subscription isn't for streaming music but rather for paid downloads; subscribers get a decent discount on all purchases.

eMusic, shown in Figure 10.6, offers more than 13 million tracks for downloading in MP3 format, using DRM-free variable bitrate encoding. To purchase from eMusic, you have to subscribe to the service, which runs anywhere from $11.99 to $79.99 per month. Table 10.1 details the various subscription plans.

FIGURE 10.6

The eMusic subscription download service.

Table 10.1	eMusic subscription plans.	
Plan	Monthly price	Additional monthly bonus credit
Basic	$11.99	$0
Plus	$15.99	$1.00
Premium	$20.99	$2.00
Fan	$31.99	$4.00
Enthusiast	$41.99	$6.00
Connoisseur	$79.99	$15.00

There are also quarterly, bi-annual, and annual plans available. Obviously, the more music you intend to buy, the more you want to consider the higher-priced subscriptions.

As a subscriber, you get to take advantage of eMusic's discount pricing. You'll find individual tracks priced as low as 49 cents each, with digital album downloads running anywhere from 20% to 50% less than what you find at the iTunes Store.

> **ULTIMATELY INTERESTING** eMusic offers downloads from the four major record labels and a large number of independent labels.

Your monthly subscription fee is essentially an upfront payment for any downloads you buy that month. The way it works is that you're entitled to download as much music each month as you spend on your subscription fee—plus a small bonus credit offered by some plans. So, for example, if you subscribe to the $11.99 Basic plan, you can download up to $11.99 in music each month. Your purchases are subtracted from the subscription fee you pay, so you don't pony up additional cash for each purchase.

As noted, some subscription plans offer additional credit you can apply to your purchases. Let's say you're a heavy purchaser and sign up for the $79.99/month Connoisseur plan, which comes with an additional $15/month purchase credit. That means you can download $94.99 of music each month without spending an additional dollar.

Note that these are DRM-free downloads that you own, not DRM-protected "rentals" that you have limited access to when you stop your subscription. In the case of eMusic, the subscription fee is really just an upfront payment for the purchase you make.

eMusic says its service caters to "knowledgeable music lovers" in their 20s to 50s, who mostly purchase downloads of albums instead of individual songs.

To that end, the site offers a bevy of reviews and exclusive editorial content, such as music guides, expert columns, and editor's picks. But the main attraction is the discount pricing, abetted by the upfront subscription purchase model.

Zune Marketplace

Finally, we come to Microsoft's online music store, the Zune Marketplace (www.zune.net). The Zune Marketplace is an odd duck in that it's tightly tied into Microsoft's Xbox game console and gaming network, although anyone can purchase from it.

Like the iTunes Store, you have to download and install special Zune software, shown in Figure 10.7, to access the Zune Marketplace. (Unless, that is, you're shopping from your Xbox console, which has a direct "in" to the store.) The Zune Marketplace offers more than 14 million tracks for downloading in either the MP3 or WMA format. MP3 files are DRM-free and encoded at 256Kbps or 320Kbps; WMA files are DRM-protected, encoded at 192Kbps. (Most newer tracks are in the higher-quality MP3 format.)

FIGURE 10.7

Accessing the Zune Marketplace from the Zune software.

Somewhat confusingly, pricing in the Zune Marketplace is not in U.S. dollar, nor in any recognizable foreign currency. Instead, you pay in "Microsoft Points," Microsoft's own currency used for many Xbox network transactions. When you do the Points-to-dollars conversion, tracks end up costing anywhere from $0.99-$1.24 to purchase.

To be honest, the Zune Marketplace is just too weird and proprietary and difficult to access for most consumers—unless you're tied into the Xbox ecosystem. For Xbox users, the Zune Marketplace is a great place to download music to play on your Xbox—which can function as a multimedia player.

Discovering High Resolution Music Online

Here's one thing all the previous online music services have in common: The music they offer for downloading is highly compressed, in order to save storage space and transmittal time. Downloaded tracks sound okay on iPods and other portable music players, especially when played through stock ear buds, but lack fidelity when played on a quality home audio system.

10

If you're a music collector who also fancies himself an audiophile, downloading lossy files is not an acceptable option. Short of ripping your own CDs in lossless format, what can you do to add more high-quality tracks to your digital music library?

The answer lies in finding an online music store that offers tracks in lossless audio formats—so-called high-resolution or high-definition (HD) audio. While there aren't many of these HD music store, they do exist, and they'd like to have your business.

B&W Society of Sound

Our first HD music service is the B&W Society of Sound (www.bowers-wilkins.com/Society_of_Sound/Society_of_Sound/Music), offered by high-end speaker manufacturer Bowers & Wilkins. Figure 10.8 shows the Society of Sound website.

The Society of Sound is a subscription service. For either $39.95 for a six-month subscription or $59.95 for a twelve-month one, you get access to a rather limited library of albums (just 28, in total) in the 24-bit FLAC lossless format. Each month two new albums are added to the library, and two are removed.

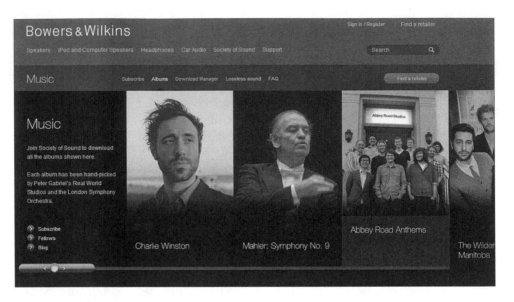

FIGURE 10.8
The B&W Society of Sound.

Now, spending sixty bucks a year to access 28 albums (plus two new ones each month) may not sound like a steal, but if you're a true believer, this is digital audio at its best. The 24-bit FLAC format is equivalent to listening to a Super Audio Compact Disc (SACD) or DVD-Audio disc—much higher fidelity than with a standard 16-bit CD.

So if you want to join the audiophile club and have access to the very best recordings available, join the B&W Society of Sound. It's a rarified experience.

> ♪ **ULTIMATELY INTERESTING** Uncompressed and lossless 24-bit audio files are not playable in all music player programs and devices. For example, you won't be able to play FLAC files on your iPod or iPhone, and you may need to install a different music player program on your system to play these files on your computer. Learn more in Chapter 24, "Playing Digital Music on Your Computer."

HDtracks

You'll find a much broader selection of HD music at HDtracks (www.hdtracks.com). This is an online music store specializing in high-resolution audiophile downloads, primarily of entire albums (although individual tracks are also available).

HDtracks, shown in Figure 10.9, offers its downloads in one of a number of DRM-free file formats. The format(s) available varies from selection to selection and include the following:

FIGURE 10.9

HDtracks high resolution downloads.

- **AIFF files**, which are CD-quality files playable in the iTunes player.
- **FLAC lossless**, which can be equal to or better than CD-quality, depending on the bitrate. 24-bit FLAC files are equal to SACD and DVD-Audio recordings in terms of fidelity.
- **MP3 files**, encoded at the top 320Kbps bitrate, which sound as good as lossy compression allows, but remains sub-CD quality.

Obviously, the AIFF and FLAC selections are going to have much higher fidelity than the occasional MP3 file you find on the site. In fact, there's a special 96Khz/24bit Store within the larger HDtracks store that offers only high bitrate 24-bit downloads; shop here for the very best audio quality. Selection, while considerably larger than at the B&W Society of Sound, is much smaller than at the iTunes Store or similar traditional online music store.

Pricing is commensurate with the sound quality. Individual tracks are typically $2.49 each, with albums priced at $17.98 and up. As with all high-resolution digital music, it will take much longer to download a track from the HDtracks store than from traditional online music stores.

> ♪ **ULTIMATELY INTERESTING**   HDtracks was founded by David and Norman Chesky of audiophile record label Chesky Records. As you might suspect, the Chesky label is well represented in the HDtracks store.

iTrax

iTrax (www.itrax.com), shown in Figure 10.10, is another service that offers high resolution digital music downloads. Tracks are available in a variety of formats, including 96Khz/24-bit PCM, WMA Lossless, WMA Pro, DTS, Dolby Digital, and MP3. Some recordings are available in both stereo and 5.1 surround.

FIGURE 10.10

The iTrax music store.

Like other HD music services, iTrax offers a limited selection—just over 700 tracks, to be specific. They also offer HD video tracks, and license their content for use in other media. Pricing is typically for an entire album, and is not inexpensive.

iTrax is the only online music store I know that offers each selection in a variety of file formats, including some surround formats not found elsewhere. It's not a big selection, of course, but it's good sounding stuff.

Linn Records

Then there's Linn Records (www.linnrecords.com), shown in Figure 10.11. This isn't an online music store, per se, but rather an audiophile music label that offers its music via high resolution online download. Linn's selections are heavy on the classical music side, as are most audiophile downloads.

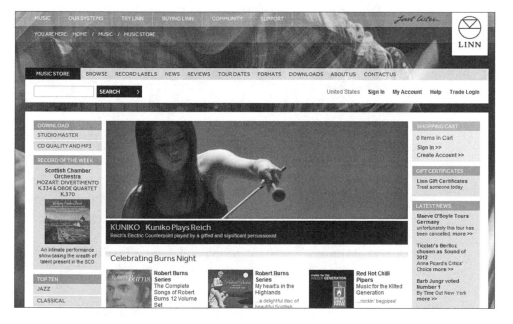

FIGURE 10.11

Audiophile downloads from Linn Records.

Linn offers its downloads in a variety of formats, including 24-bit and 16-bit FLAC lossless, 24-bit and 16-bit WMA Lossless, and 320Kbps MP3. Pricing is dependent on release and audio format; the higher-quality formats cost more, of course. Most offerings are available either by the track or in complete album format.

10

SHOULD YOU SHOP ELSEWHERE?

Okay, so there are a lot of different online music stores out there; Apple doesn't have a total monopoly in this market. (Only an effective one, it sometimes seems.) Is it worth your while to pass up the iTunes Store and do your digital shopping elsewhere?

In Apple's defense, the iTunes Store has the most comprehensive selection of music for download that you'll find online. Amazon comes close, but iTunes is typically out in front.

And pricing, while it varies somewhat from store to store, doesn't vary all that much. There are always exceptions, of course; Amazon's promotions can be appealing, and eMusic tends to be a bit lower priced across the board. But, end of the day, you get a good deal—and a good selection—if you never set virtual foot outside of the iTunes Store.

Where competing stores shine, however, is in offering music that you can't find in the iTunes Store. If you're into independent or local artists, you won't always find them on iTunes; Bandcamp and CD Baby are much better bets for this kind of thing. And, even if you can find an independent offering at the iTunes Store, chances are the artist makes more money from the same download at Bandcamp or CD Baby. That alone might make it worth your while to download from an iTunes alternative.

You may also want to skip iTunes (and Amazon) if you're interested in audiophile downloads. Let's face it, Apple and Amazon offer digital music for the digital masses; if you breathe that rarified audiophile air, shopping at iTunes is akin to partaking of Walmart's blue light specials. HDtracks and its brethren are a much more comfortable fit when fidelity matters.

Myself, I do more ripping than downloading, and tend to stick to Amazon for my downloads. When it comes to independent stuff, however, I'm a CD Baby customer. And I've been known to download a high res track or two from HDtracks, just because.

It isn't completely an Apple world, after all.

Finding Free Music to Download

In the past few chapters, we've looked at online music stores—websites where you pay to download digital music files. Not all music online has to be paid for, however; there are a number of websites that offer free MP3 files for your downloading pleasure.

Some of these sites are run by individual artists or recording labels; others are more like a community of artists, where independent musicians gather to promote their wares. Still other free sites are quasi-legal archives where others have uploaded MP3 files for sharing. And there's a whole other category of MP3 search engines, which you can use to search for free digital music files anywhere on the web.

What all these sites have in common is that the music they have for download is all free for the taking. And there's always something appealing about free...

Downloading from Official Label and Artist Sites

If you're at all cognizant of the world of music downloading, you know that most record labels and many artists really don't like the whole concept of online music—especially free online music. Understandably, the folks that do the work would like to get paid for their efforts; giving their work away for free doesn't put food on the table.

That is, unless the music they give away for free promotes other music that they can charge for. We're talking free downloads as a promotional activity, and there's a fair amount of it out there on the interwebs. That's right, you can sometimes—but not always—find free music for download from a label or artist's website.

> ♪ **ULTIMATELY USEFUL** Where can you find these official artist and label sites? Well, you'll probably need to utilize Google; a quick search should lead you to that which you seek. You can also find artist pages, complete with free downloads or streaming tracks, on MySpace and Facebook

What might you find on a label or artist site? Aside from the normal promotional messages, tour dates, and merchandise for sale, along with the latest music videos (also promotional in nature), look for previews from new albums, bonus tracks from existing albums, or sometimes streaming audio, all intended to whet your interest in the product at hand. For example, Figure 11.1 shows the bonus track offered for free download by rapper Nikki Minaj from her album *Pink Friday*.

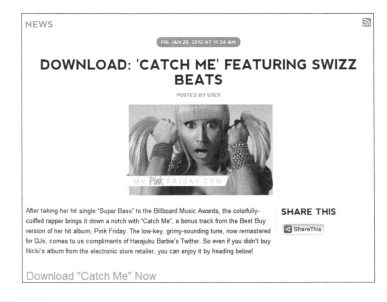

NEWS

FRI, JAN 20, 2012 AT 11:34 AM

DOWNLOAD: 'CATCH ME' FEATURING SWIZZ BEATS

POSTED BY USER

MY *Pink* FRIDAY.COM

After taking her hit single "Super Bass" to the Billboard Music Awards, the colorfully-coiffed rapper brings it down a notch with "Catch Me", a bonus track from the Best Buy version of her hit album, Pink Friday. The low-key, grimy-sounding tune, now remastered for DJs, comes to us compliments of Harajuku Barbie's Twitter. So even if you didn't buy Nicki's album from the electronic store retailer, you can enjoy it by heading below!

SHARE THIS

ShareThis

Download "Catch Me" Now

FIGURE 11.1

A free bonus track for download from Nikki Minaj's website (www.mypinkfriday.com).

Now, don't be surprised if a given site doesn't have any music for download; not all artists and labels are comfortable with the notion of giving away free samples to encourage future sales. Also, don't be surprised if any downloads that are available come equipped with some sort of DRM encoding, or if they're encoded at a fairly low bitrate. The labels and artists (labels, especially) don't really want you to build your digital music library from what are essentially free samples.

> **ULTIMATELY INTERESTING** Streaming audio is becoming more prevalent than promotional downloads, at least for major label artists. With streaming audio, there's no danger of pirating a track online, which is something the majors are constantly worrying about.

Downloading from Free Artist Communities

It's not surprising to discover that newer and independent artists are more comfortable with the concept of giving away at least some of their music online. To that end, there are several artist community websites that aggregate free downloads from a multitude of (primarily independent) artists.

Let's take a look at the major ones.

ARTISTdirect

One of the oldest of these free artist communities is ARTISTdirect (www.artistdirect.com), which was founded in 1994. Now, it's gone through a few changes (and a few different owners) since then, but it remains a great place for independent artists to showcase their music, and for music lovers to discover new music.

As you can see in Figure 11.2, ARTISTdirect offers music news, album reviews, streaming videos, photo galleries, and more from a variety of different artists. Click the **Free Downloads** link to browse through the authorized downloads, all in MP3 format.

BeSonic

BeSonic (www.besonic.com) promotes itself as "a platform for free music and procreation promotion." That's a fancy term for online artist community, which means there's a lot of free music for download here, all in the name of promoting new and independent artists. (There's also some downloads for purchase, and a fair amount of streaming music, too.)

FIGURE 11.2

Authorized free downloads at ARTISTdirect.

As you can see in Figure 11.3, BeSonic offers music from artists in a wide variety of genres, although the total selection is a little sparse. (Fewer than 15,000 tracks, in all.) The website itself is fairly easy to use, although not all of it is in English. All downloads are in MP3 format.

FIGURE 11.3

If you can figure out the language thing, BeSonic is a good site for independent music.

dmusic

The dmusic (www.dmusic.com) site is one of the oldest on the Internet for fans of independent music. In addition to lots of free MP3 downloads, you get artist news, music reviews, and a lot of interaction between fans and artists. Figure 11.4 shows the dmusic site.

FIGURE 11.4
Looking for free downloads at dmusic.

MP3.com

MP3.com (www.mp3.com) is the most established and perhaps the most popular site for authorized free music downloads. As you can see in Figure 11.5, the site features more than one million tracks for downloading, as well as a large number of tracks for streaming only. There's also a lot of support content—artist bios, photos, music videos, and the like. Not surprisingly, all of MP3.com's downloads are in the MP3 format.

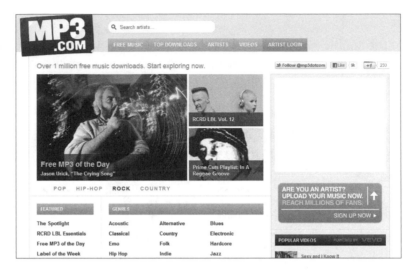

FIGURE 11.5

One of the most popular free download sites, MP3.com.

As noted, MP3.com has been around for awhile—since 1997, in fact. It's been through a succession of owners, including Vivendi Universal and CNET Networks, its current owner. The site recently went through a major revision, with the result that MP3.com is now powered by the Last.fm database, which isn't a bad thing.

PureVolume

PureVolume (www.purevolume.com) is as much a social music site as it is a free download site. As you can see in Figure 11.6, it focuses on new music and emerging artists, offering both free and paid downloads and lots of opportunities for interaction between artists and their fans.

Younger music lovers might already be familiar with PureVolume through the site's presence at top music festivals, including South by Southwest. PureVolume has also sponsored tours for various recently-emerged artists, as well as big tours such as the Taste of Chaos and Take Action tours. It's obvious that they're trying to do something more than just offer free music for download; PureVolume is a great site for anyone interested in new music.

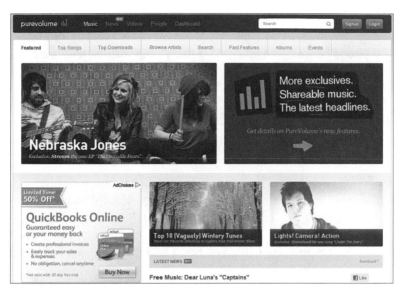

FIGURE 11.6

PureVolume, a great source for new music from emerging artists.

SoundClick

SoundClick (www.soundclick.com) is a little like PureVolume in that it bills itself as a social music site focusing on new music and emerging artists. As you can see in Figure 11.7, there's a lot of music here from indie artists as well as unsigned bands.

FIGURE 11.7

SoundClick, another community for emerging artists.

In addition to the free MP3 downloads, you get your own member profile page, streaming audio and video, music charts, custom online radio stations, message boards, and more. It's a fairly popular site, with more than 3.4 million members.

Finding Tunes with MP3 Search Sites

There's lots of free music all over the Internet, but how do you find it? The solution is to use a search engine specifically designed to find MP3 files online.

These MP3 search engines skirt on the edge of legality. Now, there's nothing inherently illegal about *searching* for free MP3 files. The legal conundrums come from where the search results lead, which is often to blatantly illegal MP3 file sharing sites. Still, you gotta find this stuff somehow, and these MP3 search sites do the job.

What can you expect from the files you find via these sites? It's a mix. Most will be in MP3 format, as expected, but bitrate is all over the place; there's some high-quality (high bitrate) stuff out there, but also a lot of poorly ripped low bitrate dreck. You get what you pay for in, any case.

> **ULTIMATELY CAUTIOUS** An MP3 search engine is likely to return a fair amount of malware masquerading as MP3 files. As such, you should download with care—and with anti-virus and anti-spyware programs fully engaged.

Here's a short list of the most popular MP3 search engines:

- **BeeMP3** (www.beemp3.com)
- **Bomb-MP3** (www.bomb-mp3.com)
- **fizy** (www.fizy.com)
- **Mp3-2000** (www.mp3-2000.net)
- **MP3 Raid** (www.mp3raid.com)
- **MP3 Search** (www.mp3searchmusic.com)
- **Search for Music** (searchformusic.eu.pn)

Downloading Music from MP3 Newsgroups

Websites aren't the only place to find MP3 files; there are also a number of Usenet newsgroups devoted to MP3 information and downloadable files.

Assuming you know what Usenet is and have a functional newsgroup reader program installed on your computer, you should check out the following hierarchies and newsgroups for MP3 files to download:

- alt.binaries.mp3.*
- alt.binaries.sounds.mp3.*
- alt.music.mp3.*

To access these newsgroups, and then download the files you find there, you need to utilize some sort of newsreader program or site. For newsreader software, I like News Rover (www.newsrover.com). To access newsgroups from within your web browser, check out the Giganews website (www.giganews.com).

MUSIC WANTS TO BE FREE

The record industry, particularly the major labels, fixates just a tad on the problem of piracy and illegal downloading, and thus tends to take a dim view of offering any music for free downloading. Giving away content is anathema to the suits at the labels, and to many artists, as well.

That said, there's a long history of providing free music for the masses; it didn't start with Al Gore's invention of Napster. Music played on AM or FM radio, after all, is free for all listeners, and nobody's complaining about that. (Or at least not that much.) And there's always been promotional giveaways, either of physical product or digital downloads. Heck, many musicians and labels provide free tunes via streaming audio on their websites. In other words, there's already a lot of free music out there—so why not provide more?

Some artists are embracing the concept of free music, either to promote their paid products or just to sell other stuff to their fans. The concept behind giving away music like this is the same as that behind the radio business. When a radio station plays a song (for free, remember), that serves as exposure and promotion for the artist and his music. Some percentage of the listening audience will like what they hear and want to buy more, thus leading to increased album sales for the artist.

11

With that in mind, why shouldn't artists give away some of their music in order to spur other sales? Maybe the artist offers a track or two from their latest album for free downloading from their website, as kind of a teaser for the full CD. Listeners who like the free tunes can then download the rest of the album, or purchase the physical CD online.

Or maybe artists should give away *all* their music. This is a radical approach, I know, but some newer artists are doing just that. They recognize that there's more money to be made in personal appearances and merchandise sales than there is in traditional music sales, so they use free downloads to hook listeners on their music and then let that drive sales of tickets, t-shirts, you name it.

The reality is that most artists, even some big names, make very little money from record sales as it is. Many artists take in much more from live performances and ancillary sales than they make from either CD sales or digital downloads; few artists get rich from selling their recordings, these days. What's the harm, then, of giving away something you don't make much money from, anyway—and then converting those free downloaders into paying customers for concert tickets and t-shirts? For today's emerging musicians, it's certainly something to consider.

Downloading Music from P2P File-Sharing Sites

In the previous chapter we addressed a number of sources for downloading free music files from the web. Well, there's another source of free music out there—and, while it's not entirely legal, it is quite popular, especially among the younger set. I'm talking about file-sharing sites, where ethically unencumbered users upload music they've ripped from CDs, and then share those illegal files with other ethically unencumbered music lovers.

Now, I'm not a big fan of these file-sharing sites. (Neither is the music industry, as you might suspect.) But I do know that this is a popular way for a lot of folks to get a lot of digital music, without spending a penny. As such, it needs to be talked about.

Understanding File Sharing

As a music lover, you're constantly on the search for specific recordings. It may be a new release from a hit artist, or a classic recording that for some reason isn't available for download from iTunes or Amazon. (That's right, even at 20 million or so tracks, iTunes doesn't have everything available.)

If you can't find the music you want at an online music store or other authorized downloading site, you're not completely out of luck. Chances are, there is another user, somewhere on the Internet, who has a copy of that particular song or album. All you have to do is find that user, and then copy the song from that computer to yours.

When users swap digital audio files like this, it's called peer-to-peer (P2P) file-sharing. That's because you're not downloading files from a big central server on a big website; it's just you and another user, swapping files.

Of course, you do have the issue of finding other users to swap files with. When you want to search other users' computers for the music you want, you have to use a P2P file-sharing service—which helps users link up to swap digital music files.

A Short History of File Sharing

Internet-based P2P file sharing started with a little service you may have heard of called Napster. That's right, Napster was the granddaddy of online file sharing, created solely to facilitate the swapping of MP3 audio files. A user connecting to the Napster network had immediate access to tens of thousands (later, millions) of other computers—and to all the MP3 files stored on those computers.

There was only one teensy-weensy problem with the original Napster concept, however—it enabled the illegal copying of copyrighted material. As such, the copyright owners had a bit of a beef with the whole thing, which resulted in Napster being taken to court by the major record labels and ultimately shut down. No good deed goes unpunished, after all.

P2P file sharing didn't end with Napster's demise, however. A number of similar file-sharing services have risen in Napster's wake, so there are still lots of different services you can use to swap digital music files with other users all around the world—copyright laws be damned.

How P2P File Sharing Works

Unlike a traditional website, where files are stored and available for downloading to your computer, a P2P file-sharing system is actually a network of personal computers connected through a central hub. You connect to the network hub and then search other users' computers for the files you want to download. When you find a match, the file is copied from that other user's computer to yours—without any interaction with the central website. This type of connection is called peer-to-peer since both computers are peers to each other; neither functions as a server, as with a traditional website.

In other words, a file-sharing network helps you find which computers have the songs you want. You then connect directly to those computers to download the files. Other computers, in turn, connect to your PC to download the files you have stored on your hard disk. Everybody shares with everyone else.

Let's say, for example, that you want to download a tune by Lil Wayne. All you have to do is launch the software for a particular P2P network, access the network's main server, and search for **lil wayne**. The P2P site then returns a list of users that have Lil Wayne tracks stored on their computers. You can then pick a computer from the list, and your computer will be connected directly to the other computer. With the click of a button, the specified file is copied from that computer to your computer's hard disk. Pretty slick.

Then There's BitTorrent...

Today's P2P file-sharing networks work pretty much the same as Napster did a dozen years ago. In fact, some of today's networks *are* yesterday's networks; gnutella (discussed later in this chapter), in particular, remains viable.

The newest and perhaps most popular file-sharing protocol, however, is BitTorrent. Where BitTorrent shines is its ultra-efficient method of distributing large amounts of data over the Internet. That makes it a popular approach for file sharing, with more than 150 million active users. In fact, BitTorrent technology is so popular that torrents now account for close to 70% of all Internet traffic. Really.

BitTorrent works different from other forms of file transfer. Instead of downloading a file from a single server, the BitTorrent protocol enables users to join a "swarm" of hosts to download and upload from each other simultaneously. As a file is being distributed, it is broken into small pieces, each sent separately across the Internet. As each peer receives a new piece of the file, that peer becomes a source for downloading the piece to other users. This allows

12

for very efficient data transfer, as well as protects against bad or interrupted transfers, since there are multiple sources for each piece of a file.

To download and share BitTorrent files, you need to install a BitTorrent client program on your computer—and connect to the Internet, of course. You can then search for files on BitTorrent master sites, and start downloading from whatever users happen to have the files you want.

> **ULTIMATELY INTERESTING** Once a computer has downloaded all the pieces and reassembled a file, it then becomes a "seed" for future downloads of that file.

> **ULTIMATELY INTERESTING** BitTorrent technology is not used exclusively for illegal downloads. Several music labels and movie studios use BitTorrent to distribute their own licensed material.

A Few Good Reasons *Not* to Use File-Sharing Sites

Before we get too much further into this discussion of file sharing, I have to tell you—I'm not a fan. In fact, I despise file sharing of this type, for a number of reasons. While I know I won't dissuade anyone inclined to download music from these P2P networks, I still have to let you know why you might not want to do so.

It's Illegal

First and foremost, you need to know that unauthorized downloads from file-sharing sites is blatantly against the law. When you download a file in this manner, you're breaking all manner of copyright laws. These are real laws with real penalties. And if you get caught, you'll have to pay—big time.

To put it bluntly, downloading music without permission is tantamount to stealing. No, that's not right; it *is* stealing. And stealing is against the law, pure and simple.

Breaking the law in this fashion can lead to prosecution on criminal charges, as well as civil lawsuits from the copyright holders. Under current law, each case of copyright violation carries a maximum penalty of five years in prison and a $250,000 fine. That's per track downloaded, by the way; download ten tracks and you could be fined $2.5 million. Ouch!

Then there's the civilian penalties, which can apply if the Recording Industry Association of America (RIAA), on behalf of the copyright owners, decides to sue you. Civil penalties for copyright infringement include a minimum fine of $750 for each work. Again, if you're a prolific downloader, this can add up.

12

How likely is it that you'll be arrested or sued for downloading music from a P2P network? Well, the odds are low, but the risk does exist. The RIAA has taken thousands of downloaders to court over the past decade, and has either settled out of court or prevailed in court in virtually all cases. It's not pretty, and you don't want it to happen to you.

Potential legal action aside, you shouldn't do something illegal just because you think you won't be caught. Breaking the law is breaking the law, whether you get caught or not. It's wrong to download illegal music, and you shouldn't do it.

You're Helping to Starve Musicians to Death

Here's another reason you shouldn't download music from P2P sites—you're taking money out of the mouths of starving musicians. Okay, Jay-Z and Rhianna aren't exactly starving, but lots of other artists with songs on P2P sites are closer to starving, and could certainly use the money they'd make if you purchased their songs from a legal downloading site.

I don't want to overstate the issue of lost revenues due to illegal downloading; it's probably not as big a deal as the major record labels contend. But it's still an issue, especially for local and emerging artists who are just getting off the ground. These kids need the money, even if Jay-Z and Rhianna don't, and you're not helping them at all by downloading their music without paying them for it. Musicians really do work hard to make a recording, and they deserve to be compensated for their work.

Quality Is Questionable

Enough about starving musicians; how does file sharing affect *you*?

Unlike an iTunes or Amazon that sells authorized copies of recordings, all supplied and vetted either by the record label or the artist himself, P2P file sharing sites are anything but authorized. The files they have for sharing don't come directly from the label or artist, but are rather uploaded by other users. And you have no idea who these users are, or where their uploads came from.

Some P2P users are quite diligent about the music they upload, and take great care to provide files encoded at a high bitrate, complete with useful metadata. Other P2P uploaders rip songs at a low bitrate and don't even bother to label the tracks accurately.

The upshot is that you never quite know what you're getting when you download a file from a P2P file-sharing network. Some tracks are high quality, others sound awful. Some files aren't even what their name implies; it's not uncommon to download a file that you think is by Bruce Springsteen but is actually something quite different from the Beastie Boys. Caveat emptor.

It's Likely Infested with Malware

When I said that files you download often aren't what you think they are, I meant it. That's because a fair number of files available on P2P networks are actually malware files—that is, they're infected with computer viruses or spyware.

Computer viruses are nasty things, rogue programs that can delete files from your hard disk or even cause your entire computer system to crash. Spyware is just as bad, capable of hijacking your system to send out spam emails, attack other computers, or just spy on your activities and send private information back to some criminal mother ship.

How big a problem is malware on P2P file-sharing sites? It's huge. One study indicates that close to 15% of BitTorrent downloads contain malware, and that BitTorrent accounts for almost half of all malware currently distributed online. That's not good odds.

I've been warning about P2P-distributed malware for some time. In fact, here's what I wrote about the problem in my 2008 book, *Is It Safe? Protecting Your Computer, Your Business, and Yourself Online:*

> On the other hand, if you or a family member (re: music-hungry teenager) are addicted to P2P music-sharing websites, you might as well resign yourself to dealing with a series of annoying and potentially harmful spyware infestations. You risk increases dramatically if you frequent these spyware-riddled sites; just expect to be infected if you do a lot of illegal downloading. It would be better if you (or your teenager) forsook the P2P sites in favor of the much safer (and completely legal) commercial download sites, such as the iTunes Store, but I know how hard it can be to shake the free download habit.

What I said then still applies today. Legalities aside, you run a significant risk of infecting your computer with some sort of malware when you download files from one of these file-sharing sites. I can't tell you how many times I had to disinfect my stepson's computer when he was in high school, because he insisted on downloading music from LimeWire and similar sites. They really are as "dirty" as some say; it's a major problem.

> **♪ ULTIMATELY INTERESTING** LimeWire is no longer a problem, as the site was forced out of business in 2010. In fact, a lot of P2P sites have gone dark over the years, as various government entities file suit to halt their illegal operations. But it seems that for every P2P site that's shut down, at least one more springs up to take its place, alas.

Yes, Virginia, There are Some Benefits to File Sharing

You've probably noticed that I'm not a big fan of P2P file-sharing sites, and it goes well beyond their illegality. Lest it be said that I'm too negative, however, I'll admit that there are some potential advantages to obtaining your music in this fashion. And it's not all about being free.

It's Free

Okay, for some users it *is* all about being free. Whether you're a music lover on a budget or just a total cheapskate, there's definite appeal in building a digital music library at zero cost. If you download a hundred tracks a month, that's $100 or more you'll save by downloading from a P2P network instead of purchasing from the iTunes Store. I'll admit, that adds up.

The free thing is probably why you see so many high school and college students using file-sharing sites. Being able to pay for your own music collection becomes more the thing when you get older; you don't have to download illegally to amass the music you love. Still, if your hunger for digital music is larger than your budget, free downloads sure are appealing.

You Can Choose Your Format

If you download tracks from the iTunes Store, you're getting okay-sounding AA3 files. If you download tracks from other online stores, such as Amazon, you're getting okay-sounding (at best) MP3 files. What you don't get from these authorized sources (short of the handful of high-def music stores, such as HDtracks) is music encoded in high bitrate or lossless format—that is, downloads for audiophiles.

Now, not every track found on a file-sharing network is in high fidelity; in fact, most uploads to these sites are piss poor when it comes to bitrate and sound quality. That said, if you do your searching you can often find higher-fidelity versions of the music you want on some of these sites. I'm talking 320Kbps MP3s and even lossless FLACs. It's all a matter of how serious the people are who upload the files to share.

It's also a matter of how seriously you search for a specific format or bitrate file. Often, you'll find the same track available from various sources, in various bitrates and even file formats. You may need to search a bit to find the highest quality file for download, but when you do, it could be a much better-sounding file than what the masses get from Apple and Amazon.

> **♪ ULTIMATELY INTERESTING** I know, the purported benefit of better-sounding files contradicts the disadvantage of worse-sounding files. The reality is the wild, wild west of file sharing consists of both extremes. You'll find a lot of crappy sounding low-bitrate tracks, as well as a smaller number of better-sounding, high-bitrate tracks. The low-bitrate stuff is more common, but the high-bitrate stuff is often there if you look hard enough.

Oh, and it goes without saying that just about every track you find at a file-sharing site is DRM-free. It wouldn't be there if it were otherwise.

You Can Find Stuff You Can't Get Anywhere Else

There's one final advantage to downloading music from a file-sharing network, and it has to do with selection. Unlike iTunes or Amazon, which can only sell those tracks that the record labels give them to sell, file-sharing networks offer just about everything that's ever been released. We're not talking about just 15 or 20 million tracks; we're talking hundreds of millions of tracks, including a lot of music that has never been officially available in digital format—or even on CD. (And, yes, there are a lot of old LPs that have yet to be reissued on CD. A lot.) We're also talking about music that's sold in other countries but not available in the U.S. because of the label's geographic restrictions. In other words, just about every song and album ever released is likely to be found on one file-sharing network or another—assuming someone, somewhere, has taken the time to rip it and upload it.

This is why file sharing networks may have some appeal to serious music collectors. I'm sure there's at least one Holy Grail album or track you've been dying to get your hands on but it just isn't available anymore, at least in the U.S. Heck, it may be an old vinyl recording that never made it to CD; a lot of uploaders do their thing by ripping LPs to digital files.

12

It may take a bit of searching, but chances are that rare recording is available on some file sharing site somewhere on the web. Even those with ethical constraints against this type of downloading may ask what's wrong with downloading something that isn't readily available for purchase. You'd buy it if you could, but since you can't, why not download it from the file-sharing universe?

So, if you have some gaping holes in your collection that you can't fill otherwise, look to the Internet's file sharing infrastructure. You can probably fill all your holes there—for free.

A Quick Look at the Most Popular File-Sharing Sites

Okay, by this time you're either interested in file sharing or you're not. If you really don't want to dip your respectable toes into these patently illegal waters, I understand; go ahead and skip the rest of this chapter and move onto topics less criminal. However, if you're willing to brave the inherent risks and don't mind too much about breaking a few laws, then the next question you're asking is where do you find all these wonderful things?

I'm not going to go into a lot of detail about the individual file-sharing networks out there (I don't want to be accused of fostering criminal activity), but I can tip you to the most popular of these havens for free music downloads.

> ♪ ULTIMATELY **INTERESTING** Given the illegality of P2P file sharing and my own distaste for the practice, I'm not going to recommend any particular client software or access sites. It's all easy enough to find by going to Google.

12

Gnutella

Gnutella may be the most popular P2P file sharing network today. Launched way back in 2000, it's is a totally decentralized network and technology, now in its second iteration (Gnutella2). That means that Gnutella doesn't have any centralized servers at all on its network; to connect, you have to log on through another PC that's currently connected to the network.

You do this by using a Gnutella client software program, most of which are open source. Once you launch the Gnutella client, you use it to connect to another computer running similar software. Once you're connected, you can search the Gnutella network for the songs you want. When you find the song, the Gnutella client handles the copying of that file from the other computer to yours.

eDonkey

The eDonkey network (also known as the eDonkey2000 network or eD2k) works much like the Gnutella network, in that it utilizes a network of decentralized servers to store and download music to connected PCs. You access the network with eDonkey client software, of course. Connecting, sharing, and downloading is virtually identical to using Gnutella.

> ♪ **ULTIMATELY INTERESTING** Some client programs can be used to access multiple file sharing networks, which makes it easier to download from multiple P2P networks.

Kad

The Kad network is similar to, and in fact tied into, the eDonkey network. Not surprisingly, many of the same eDonkey clients also work with the Kad network.

BitTorrent

BitTorrent file sharing is bigger today than traditional P2P networks, such as Gnutella and eDonkey. It works a little differently from other P2P networks, in that you can search for torrents with client software or from dedicated torrent search sites on the web. All these programs and sites work in much the same fashion; you search for a song or artist, find the track you want, and then click to download it to your PC.

> ♪ **ULTIMATELY INTERESTING** More people use BitTorrents to download movies, TV shows, and other videos than to download digital music. That means you'll find a lot of video files out there when you go searching for torrents.

Considering Legal File Sharing Networks

There are a handful of formerly outlawed file sharing networks that have since gone legit. What these sites offer is a combination of legal P2P file-sharing and subscription downloads. The file sharing is legal because the sites use sophisticated filters to remove copyrighted material; what's left, however, isn't that much or that great—which is why the sites supplement their P2P selection with DRM-protected downloads.

What you get for your subscription (typically $9.95/month) is limited access to millions of legal downloads. Since these are DRM-protected files, typically in

WMA format, they only play as long as you maintain your subscription; stop subscribing and all the files you downloaded stop playing. Any files you got from the P2P side of the service, however, are yours to keep. (Many of these sites offer P2P downloading without a subscription.)

The names here are a greatest hits list of old school P2P file sharing. It's interesting how defanged these sites now are, after their own separate legal tussles with the RIAA. Check 'em out if you like:

ULTIMATELY CAUTIOUS These legal file sharing services try to lure you in with the promise of "free music" found via their client software. This applies to those few tracks available via P2P that haven't been caught by the copyright filter. The larger library of "premium content" (15-20 million tracks, depending on the service) is only available when you subscribe to the monthly service.

- **BearShare** (www.bearshare.com)
- **iMesh** (www.imesh.com)
- **KaZaA** (www.kazaa.com)
- **Lphant** (www.lphant.com)

Protecting Yourself (and Your Computer) When File Sharing

I wrote earlier about the risk of contracting a malware infection when downloading from a P2P network. The risk is real, although there are some things you can do to mitigate that risk.

Protecting Against Viruses

First, know that real digital audio files (MP3 or other formats) cannot themselves be infected with computer viruses. It's just not technically possible. What is possible is for you to inadvertently download a file of another type that is masquerading as an MP3 file, which can contain a computer virus.

What you want to avoid are files with an EXE, PIF, BAT, or VBS extension. When you download one of these files, you're not downloading a digital music file. These files are actually program files, which—when launched—can infect your computer with a computer virus. For that reason, you only want to download files with valid digital audio file extensions, such as MP3, WMA, and WAV. If you do download a program file by mistake, just delete it from your hard disk; whatever you do, don't run the program!

The challenge comes from uploaders who surreptitiously mislabel or hide the real file type, thus making you think you have an MP3 file when in fact

12

you're downloading an executable file. For example, you might find a file labeled **yourfavoritesong-fromyourfavoriteartist-fromyourfavoriteal-bum.mp3.exe.** You might not make it to the end of the filename to discover that it's an executable file; heck, the P2P site might not be capable of displaying the entirety of an extra-long filename.

This type of subterfuge is tough to protect against. Just make sure you read the *entire* filename—no matter how long it is—before downloading.

Protecting Against Spyware

In addition to the potential for virus infection, you also have the potential for your online security to be compromised. Many file-sharing services embed so-called "adware" programs within their client software. These are spyware programs that hide in the background while you're connected for file-swapping, occasionally popping up advertisements or uploading information about your surfing habits.

You can protect against this type of spyware infection in two ways. First, don't install the client software in the first place! (Okay, I know…) Second, make sure you're running a good anti-spyware program, as we'll discuss next.

Use Anti-Malware Software

The best way to protect your system against unwanted viruses is to use an anti-virus software program. Anti-virus programs continually scan your system for any sign of infection, and also scan each file you download to make sure that it's clean. Unless you're big on risk, I think it's imperative to have your downloaded files scanned before opening them.

You should also employ a separate anti-spyware program, as spyware is technically different from a virus; anti-virus programs typically don't catch spyware. Install the anti-spyware program and keep it updated to catch any potential spyware before it's installed on your system.

Just Don't Do It

The most effective protection against virus or spyware infection, however, is to just avoid these stupid P2P sites. I have to tell you, these sites have caused me a ton of headaches over the years, as I'm tasked with "fixing" all the technical problems on my family's numerous computers. The majority of problems I encounter are malware-related, and probably 90% of the malware I encounter can be directly traced to these file-sharing sites. Avoid this type of illegal file downloading and sharing, and your risk of installing malware dramatically decreases.

THE MEGAUPLOAD SAGA

You may have heard something in the news about a big file sharing site called Megaupload that got busted in early 2012. It's an interesting story that sheds light on yet another type of file-sharing site.

Megaupload promoted itself as a file-hosting or cyberlocker service, similar to legit sites like Dropbox. Legit file-hosting sites let users both store and share large files; businesspeople use them to transfer files that are too big to send via email.

While many users did use Megaupload for its legitimate cyberstorage facilities, others used the site to upload and share pirated digital media files. In fact, Megaupload, the company, operated a number of sites devoted to specific types of media, including Megapix (digital photos), Megavideo (videos), Megabox (music), and a provocatively named site (that shall go unnamed here) for pornographic content.

At its peak, Megaupload had 180 million registered users, which would be a lot for a traditional file-hosting service. (That's big enough to make it the 13th most visited site on the entire Internet.) It's not un-reasonable to think that a goodly number of these folks were using Megaupload as way to share pirated music, movies, and photos.

That's what the authorities thought, anyway. On January 19, 2012, the United States Department of Justice shut down the Megaupload web-site and filed criminal charges against its owners. That, in itself, was a bit of an international project, as the site was based in Hong Kong but its owners, all German citizens, operated from New Zealand—and the lawsuit was filed in the U.S.

In any case, the Feds alleged that Megaupload differed from other file-storage sites in that the "vast majority" of its users didn't have any sig-nificant long-term storage capability—that is, more folks downloaded than uploaded. In addition, the site was said to have instructed users how to link to uploaded content, thus enabling file sharing at a fairly large level.

12

It was a dodge, to be sure, and one that got found out. Not that Megaupload was unique in how it operated; there are other sites, such as Mediashare and Rapidshare, which continue to operate in a similar fashion.

The moral of this story is that no matter how you couch it, wide-scale sharing of copyrighted files is illegal and will be penalized. Mega-upload joins the ranks of the original Napster, Aimster, Grokster, KaZaA, LimeWire, and similar P2P sites that have been forced out of business over the years. Illegal file sharing might be big business, while it lasts, but it seldom lasts.

Managing Your Music

Storing Your Digital Music

Where do you store all the digital music you download or rip? Should you store your music on your desktop or notebook PC? On a dedicated computer connected to your home audio or home theater system? On a media server connected to your home network? Or on multiple computers or servers, for multiple uses?

Wherever you store your digital library, it has to be someplace where you can access it from multiple computers and devices, but also convenient to manage in and of itself. You also need your library to be secure and safe from crashes and other disasters—which means effecting some sort of backup system, just in case.

When you're talking about hundreds of gigabytes, if not whole terabytes, of digital audio files, storing all those files becomes a major project. Read on to discover your options—and make the best choice(s) for you.

How Much Storage Space Do You Need?

One big factor in the type of storage you use for your digital music library is the size of the library itself. I'm talking total file size, in gigabytes (GB).

This total size is a factor of how many tracks you have in your library (each track is a separate audio file) and what kind of compression and bitrate the files are encoded at. Obviously, the larger your library, in terms of number of tracks, the more storage space you're going to need. But if those tracks are stored in lossy format (AAC, MP3, or WMA) and at a reasonable bitrate (suitable for portable playback, let's say), your space needs are somewhat mitigated.

Let's look at some quick and easy examples. A typical five-minute MP3 track ripped at 192Kbps (good for iPod/iPhone playback) will run around 9MB in size. If you have 10,000 tracks in your library (that's about 1,000 CDs), you only need 90,000MB, or 90GB, of disk space. That's not that much, these days.

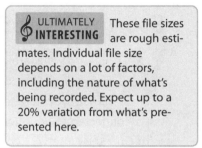

ULTIMATELY **INTERESTING** These file sizes are rough estimates. Individual file size depends on a lot of factors, including the nature of what's being recorded. Expect up to a 20% variation from what's presented here.

If you need better sound quality, however, you'll need to rip your files at a higher bit rate. So let's look at a 320Kbps MP3 file, which is as good as you can get in that format. At this bitrate, a typical five-minute track will run around 15MB in size. That equals about 150GB of total storage needed for a 10,000-track library—still not a lot, all things considered.

Move to lossless compression, however, and your storage needs increase considerably. If you encode with AAC Lossless, WMA Lossless, of FLAC, you're looking at 30MB per track or so. For a 10,000-track library, you're now up to 300GB of space.

What about storing your music in the original uncompressed WAV or AIFF format? Now we're talking about significant amounts of storage space, as you'll need about 70MB for a five-minute track. That works out to a whopping 700GB for a 10,000-track library.

Now, 10,000 tracks translates into about 1,000 CDs. If your library is larger, you'll need more space. For example, a 1,500-CD library will require 90GB of space for 128Kbps MP3, 135GB for 320Kbps MP3, 450GB for AAC/WMA Lossless, or a little over 1 terabyte (TB) for uncompressed WAV/AIFF. We're talking some serious storage needs here—which is why most users avoid these raw formats.

13

To help you determine your own storage needs, take a look at Table 13.1, which details these and other examples.

Table 13.1   Example Digital Music Storage Needs (Based on Tracks Being About 9 minutes)

	500 CDs/ 5,000 tracks	1,000 CDs/ 10,000 tracks	1,500 CDs/ 15,000 tracks	2,000 CDs /20,000 tracks	2,500 CDs/ 25,000 tracks
128Kbps MP3	30GB	60GB	90GB	120GB	150GB
192Kbps WMA/AAC	40GB	80GB	120GB	160GB	200GB
192Kbps MP3	45GB	90GB	135GB	180GB	225GB
320Kbps MP3	75GB	150GB	225GB	300GB	375GB
AAC/WMA/FLAC Lossless	150GB	300GB	450GB	600GB	750GB
Uncompressed WAV/AIFF	350GB	700GB	1TB	1.4TB	1.8TB

Storing Digital Music on Your Home PC

The first and most obvious option for storing your digital music is to use your personal computer to do the job. That may be a desktop PC or, more likely, a laptop of some sort. In fact, that's probably how most readers of this book are currently storing their digital music libraries. But is it the best way to go?

When Local Storage Makes Sense

The primary benefit of storing your entire digital music collection on your main PC is that it's easy. You already have the PC, you probably already have some music stored on it, why not make this the central repository for your entire digital music collection?

> **ULTIMATELY USEFUL** You need to plan for not just your current storage needs, but also your future needs. If you're an avid music collector, you're going to be adding several CDs a month to your collection. That might mean 50 to 100 additional CDs per year, and all the storage that signifies. You can always move to a larger hard drive, I suppose, but it's good to start with a little headroom to grow.

Local storage of this sort is certainly feasible if your library is small enough and/or your computer's hard disk is large enough. It's simple math, really; make sure the total size of your digital audio files, in gigabytes, is small enough to fit on the free space on your computer's hard disk. So if your digital

13

library takes up 200GB and you have 250GB free on a 400GB hard drive, you're ready to rock and roll. (For now, anyway; you always want to leave enough extra space to accommodate new music you'll add in the future.)

Obviously, the size of your computer's hard disk is a big factor here. If you have a newer computer with a larger hard drive, you're starting out in good shape. I'm talking about at least a 500GB hard drive, so that you have plenty of space for both your digital music collection and all your other programs and data. If you have a disk closer to 1TB in size, even better. But if you have an older PC with 200GB or smaller hard drive, it's going to be tough to amass a digital music collection of any size—at least without supplementing your storage with an external hard drive.

Also important is how much free space is left on your hard drive. Even a 1TB disk can get filled up quick if you have a lot of large programs (like photo and video editing programs) and lots of other files (videos and digital photos are big space hogs). What's ultimately important, then, is not the initial size of your hard drive (although you have to start somewhere), but how much space you can devote to digital music storage.

Finally, you need to look at the size of your digital music library. If you have fewer than 500 CDs stored in a lossy format, your space needs are different from someone with 2,000 CDs stored in a lossless format. The larger your library, the more storage space you're going to need.

Then there's the issue of growth. It's important that the computer you use on an everyday basis has enough disk space to hold not just your current library but also your library as it continues to grow in the future. You don't want to be faced with the prospect of having to delete older files to make room for newer ones; that's a not a compromise any serious music lover wants to make.

So do the math and see if you have enough disk space to comfortably store your current and future digital music library. If you do, then using your main PC to store your library is feasible—especially if you don't need to feed your music to other PCs and devices in your house. Might as well keep the music where you listen to it, on your PC.

Even if you do want to listen to your music in your living room, you can do this by connecting your main PC to your home audio system. You can even feed music to other computers and devices throughout your house, via your home network. You just have to be willing to share resources on the PC.

13

When Local Storage Isn't Enough

All that said, you may find that your everyday PC isn't suitable for hosting your digital music library. There are some stumbling blocks you may encounter.

First, your PC may not have enough free hard disk space. If you have a larger library stored in lossless format, and your PC either has a smaller hard drive or lots of other programs and files already stored on it, you simply may not have the storage capacity you need. If that's the case, consider using a dedicated computer to store and serve your music—as we'll discuss later in this chapter.

You may also find that the computer you use for other work isn't convenient for connecting to your home audio system for living room listening. Not everyone wants a computer in their living room, and you may need to keep your PC in your home office. Now, there are ways around this, such as streaming audio from your computer to another device in your living room via Wi-Fi, but give this situation careful thought.

The most common reason not to use your main PC for music storage, however, is that in order to play music anytime, anywhere, it needs to always be in place and powered up. This isn't possible if your main PC is a notebook computer that you take with you when you go to work or travel or whatever. If the PC hosting your music library isn't at home and available, you can't listen to your music.

So having your PC do double duty may not always be a viable option. Fortunately, there are other ways to go.

Storing Digital Music on a Dedicated PC

When sharing space on a heavily used PC doesn't make sense for your digital music collection, consider investing in a dedicated computer instead. I'm talking about a computer with a big hard drive that doesn't do anything else but store and serve your digital music files. (And perhaps other digital media, too, such as videos and photos.) There are plusses and minuses to this approach.

What Is a Media PC?

A computer that you dedicate to media storage is ideally placed in your living room, connected to your home audio system or home theater system. As such, this type of computer is often referred to as a Media PC, Entertainment PC, or

13

Home Theater PC (HTPC). You can call it whatever you want, as long as it does the job.

To qualify as a Media PC, you need a computer with a few key features:

- Large hard disk, at least 1TB in size, ideally.

- Wireless remote control, or wireless keyboard and mouse, for controlling it from across the living room. This is typically handled via USB add-ons.

- Appropriate outputs to connect to your audio or home theater system. For most users, an HDMI output does the job; you can run the HDMI output to an audio/video receiver to send both audio and video to your system. Other users might want to run audio separately to a receiver or preamp while sending video direct to a flat screen TV; in this instance, you can use HDMI out for video and then either left/right analog audio or optical/coaxial digital audio outputs.

> ♪ **ULTIMATELY USEFUL** For full home theater use, you may also want to include a built-in digital TV tuner (and video recording software) in your list of requirements.

- Wired or wireless network connectivity.

In addition, you want this PC to be somewhat dedicated to the task at hand. You don't want to be listening to music while you're editing videos or putting together a PowerPoint presentation; you want all system resources reserved for the media at hand.

You may also want to consider size and form factor. A notebook PC probably won't look good in your equipment rack; some folks might even object to the aesthetics of a large desktop tower. A smaller compact unit, like the Mac Mini or HP Pavilion Slimline, shown in Figure 13.1, might fit better with your other equipment.

While you can use just about any computer as a Media PC, you might want to consider a computer purpose-built for home theater use—a true home theater PC. These units meet all the previously stated requirements, have a bevy of A/V-friendly outputs, and often minimize fan noise for a quieter experience in your living room.

Most of these purpose-built HTPCs, like the one in Figure 13.2, are designed to look like traditional audio/video components. That means a horizontal design instead of the typical vertical tower, and black cases and faceplates instead of beige or white ones. Let's face it, you really don't want people to notice that you have a PC in your living room; you want your PC to fit in with your other components as much as possible.

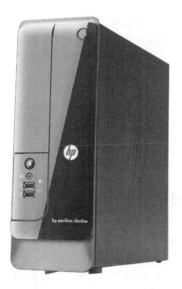

FIGURE 13.1

An HP Pavilion Slimline desktop PC—ideal for HTPC use.

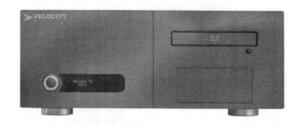

FIGURE 13.2

Velocity Micro's CineMagix HTPC.

You can also find dedicated HTPCs, for a price, from specialty manufacturers such as ASRock (www.asrock.com), Tranquil PC (www.tranquilpc.co.uk), and Velocity Micro (www.velocitymicro.com). In addition, Lenovo's Q180 is that rare HTPC from a major hardware manufacturer. If you're so inclined, you can also build your own HTPC from scratch, as many enthusiasts do.

Whether you go Windows, Mac, or even Linux depends on the file format and ecosystem you've embraced for your digital media library. If you're all Apple,

13

with AAC files, you can go with the Mac OS or even with Windows, as iTunes is pretty much cross-platform. If you've bought into the Microsoft WMA format, then go with the Windows OS. If you're all FLAC all the time, you can go either Linux or Windows. If you're an MP3 guy (or gal), you can go with any operating system; MP3 is universal.

> **♪ ULTIMATELY INTERESTING** Naturally, you'll need some sort of media player software installed on your Media PC, to play back your music files. Learn more in Chapter 24, "Playing Digital Music on Your Computer."

When Using a Dedicated PC Makes Sense

Personally, I like the concept of a computer dedicated to media storage; this is the approach I use in my own home theater system. It makes sense to centralize your media files on a single computer, and to put that computer where it's going to be doing the bulk of its work, in your living room. Naturally, the PC needs to have the right outputs to connect to the appropriate A/V equipment, but that's pretty much the norm, these days. It also helps if the PC is designed in such a way it doesn't stick out like a sore thumb, but if you have it behind closed doors in some sort of cabinet, who cares what it looks like?

The advantage here is having your music playback device alongside your other audio and video equipment. It's a short cable run from your PC to your A/V receiver and flat-screen TV; add some sort of big-screen media player program (such as Windows Media Center) and a wireless remote, and you're good to go.

As an added benefit, if your Media PC is so equipped, you can use it to play back DVDs and Blu-ray discs, any videos you've downloaded or home movies you've created, and live TV shows; you can also use it to view your digital photos and record television programs. A Media PC is a great all-in-one device for all your digital media storage and playback needs.

Naturally, you want to connect your Media PC to your home network, either via Ethernet or Wi-Fi, so that you can stream your music to other PCs and devices in your house. You'll also want to make sure the PC is handy enough to connect your iPod or iPhone, in order to sync your music collection to your portable device.

When a Dedicated PC Doesn't Do the Job

Let's face it, not everyone wants a computer in his or her living room. A PC is a big, ugly thing, not the sort of device you'd want to place next to a fancy vase or expensive couch—or sophisticated audio equipment. And how to explain away the keyboard, the mouse, or all the wires and cables and peripheral devices that tag along with the main machine? Or the *noise*?

I get it. The aesthetics of your home theater system might rule out any type of computer in your equipment rack, especially if it's not behind closed doors. Other folks might simply object to connecting a piece of complex and often questionable technology to their main TV and audio system; let's face it, computers need to be maintained and rebooted and all that, none of which is particularly living room friendly.

A personal computer also may not provide the best interface for your needs. I personally like using Windows Media Center—and I have my family properly trained—but others might find using a computer program less than user-friendly for some family members. I understand; PCs and living rooms aren't necessarily made for each other.

Storing Digital Music on a Home Server

If you like the idea of a dedicated PC for your digital music collection but don't want to place that PC in your living room, there's another option. Consider using a home server, based in your office or other out of the way location, to store your collection, and then feed your music (and other media) to other devices throughout your home. It's the increasingly preferred approach for more technical music lovers.

What Is a Home Server?

A home server, sometimes called network attached storage (NAS), is simply a computer dedicated to storing and serving files of all types. This computer typically doesn't have a monitor or a keyboard; it's a storage device, not a computer you use for computing. The server is connected to your home network, typically via Ethernet, from where it can serve its files to any other computer or device connected to the network.

What are the characteristics of a home server dedicated to storing your digital music collection? Really, a home server is just a basic computer with one or more very large hard disks; nothing more fancy than that. In terms of capacity, look for 1TB minimum and ideally more. If there are multiple hard disks, look for them to be configured in a RAID array for improved data integrity. In addition, many home servers let you swap in and out additional disks, which makes it easy to add storage space as your needs mature.

13

As you can see in Figure 13.3, most home servers are fairly small units that you can place under your desk or on a shelf or even tucked away in a corner. You configure and manage the server over your home network, using another computer, so you don't have to worry about physically accessing the machine. It's pretty much a set-up-once-and-forget-about-it kind of experience.

> **♪ ULTIMATELY INTERESTING** RAID stands for redundant array of independent disks, and describes a way of storing data across multiple hard disks. Depending on the type (level) of RAID array, identical data is written to more than one drive, essentially "mirroring" the data so that if one drive fails, the data also exists elsewhere in the array.

FIGURE 13.3
A Netgear ReadyNAS home server.

By the way, home servers are not expensive at all. You can find units for as little as $150, although you'll pay more for servers with larger storage capacity. Even the biggest, most fully featured unit won't run over $500.

While a home server sounds kind of complicated, it really isn't. In fact, just about every tech company sells these things. You can find home servers from computer manufacturers such as Acer, HP, and Lenovo, as well as from storage companies like Netgear, Seagate, and Western Digital. Your local consumer electronics store is as good as any place to buy one.

When Using a Home Server Makes Sense

The home server route is becoming the preferred way to store and serve digital media files of all sorts. It's really simple; you store all your music and media in one place, then serve them to whatever computers and other devices you have connected in your home.

The key here is that just about any type of device can access your music library stored on a home server. Yes, your computer can access the server (that's what computers do), but so can your Apple TV box, your Logitech Squeezebox or Sonos player, and any other network media player device. Many A/V receivers can connect over your network to your home server, as well, and play back your digital music without need of an additional device.

As to your portable devices, you may be able to sync your iPod or iPhone directly to your home server, or it may be easier to sync it to a computer connected to your server. Your music files don't have to be stored on your computer for iTunes or Windows Media Player to access and play the files; these programs work just fine by grabbing the files stored elsewhere on your home server.

You can download new music directly to your home server, from any computer connected to your network. Use the most convenient computer to access the iTunes Store or similar download site, then choose your home server (over the network) as the download location. You can even rip CD files to your home server, using any computer connected to your network.

In short, using a home server is an effective, efficient, and extremely convenient way to store your digital music library. Don't be scared off by the name "server;" this isn't at all like the big-ass machines the IT guys slave over at your office. A home server is truly a user-friendly device, designed specifically for use by regular guys in their homes, just like you.

When a Home Server Is Overkill

I like the approach of using a home server for digital music libraries. However, for some people it's a bit overkill.

13

For example, if you only have a single playback point in your house, why do you need to store your music separately and then serve it to that playback device? A more efficient, less costly solution is simply to connect a computer directly to your home audio system, and use that computer for both storage and playback. You don't need a separate storage device.

Same thing if you do your listening on your computer—not on your home stereo system. As you'll learn in Chapter 24, there are ways to get pretty good sound out of a computer setup; no need for a server if you go this route.

A home server may also be a bit of overkill if you're on a budget. Even at $200 or so, that may be money you don't need to spend. You can get the same benefit from dedicating an old PC to the task; you don't have to buy a fancy new home server to get server functionality. Just make sure it's a computer that's not often used for other tasks and that it has a big enough hard drive to do the job. Any computer can be a media server, after all.

Sharing Your Library Over a Home Network

What do you do when you want to play your music in multiple places in your home? There are a few options.

First, you could duplicate your music library across multiple PCs. With this approach, each PC has access to its own local copy of your music library. This isn't an approach I recommend, however; it's a lot of extra work to download or rip files to more than one computer, and you'll never be quite sure that everything is in sync.

A better approach is to share your library between multiple computers and devices, over your home network. This is, after all, how a home server works; it stores your music in one place and streams it across the network to other places in your home.

Setting up a home network is no big deal these days; most households with more than one PC have a network up and running already. What you have to get used to is the concept of storing your music on one computer and then serving it to all other computers and devices connected to your network. It's actually quite easy, nothing more than pointing your music player software to a location on your network, instead of a local library on the computer's hard disk.

In terms of what kind of home network to set up, you can go wired or wireless. A wired (Ethernet) network is faster and more reliable, but also more difficult to set up; you have to physically run that Ethernet cable from room to room in your house. A wireless (Wi-Fi) network is much easier to set up, but can be a tad slower and less reliable, especially the further you get away from the wireless router.

For listening to digital music, you can go either way. An Ethernet connection is better for streaming video, especially HD video, but not absolutely necessary for streaming music; even high bitrate audio files stream quite nicely, thank you, over Wi-Fi.

Whatever type of network you set up, configure all your computers for file sharing and make sure all your PCs can access the audio files stored on your main PC or home server. Playback should be a breeze—even when multiple PCs are playing music simultaneously.

Backing Up Your Digital Library

However you store your digital music library, you want to protect it. When you have all your music in digital format, you don't want to lose all your music if you happen to have some sort of hard drive or computer failure.

As such, it's important—no, it's *vital*—for you to back up the data in your music library on a regular basis. If, heaven forbid, your main computer or home server crashes, you can always restore your music library from the backup copy. Without a backup, all your music would be lost.

There are three ways to back up any type of computer data, including your digital music library. You can back up locally, on the same computer system on which the library resides; you can back up over your network to another computer; or you can back up over the Internet, to an online backup service. Let's look at each approach.

Backing Up Locally

The way most users today back up their data is locally. That is, you copy your data files to an external hard drive connected to your computer.

External hard drives are extremely inexpensive these days; we're talking less than $150 for a 1TB drive, which is probably big enough to hold your entire digital music library. You connect the hard drive to your computer via USB.

Most external hard drives come with some sort of backup software installed, or you can use the backup utility built into Windows or a third-party backup program. The backup process can be automated, so that it occurs once a day or once a week, and only backs up those new or changed files since your last backup.

13

Given the affordability of external hard drives and how easy most backup programs make the process, there's no excuse *not* to back up your digital music collection on a regular basis. This is the way I do it; if my house ever catches fire or floods, the first thing I'm going to grab is that backup drive!

Backing Up Over the Network

If you have multiple computers on your home network, you can back up over your network from your main computer to another PC or home server. In fact, many people purchase home servers just for the purpose of backing up data from their other computers.

The process is just as easy as backing up from a computer to an external hard drive. You schedule the backup within the backup program, then let the bits and bytes fly over your network connection at the designated time. It's even easier if you're backing up to a home server, as most of them come preinstalled with backup functionality.

> **ULTIMATELY USEFUL** How do you back up data from a home server? Well, some would say that RAID redundancy is a good enough backup, but I prefer to back up from the server to an external hard drive. Better safe than sorry in case the entire server goes up in flames.

Backing Up Online

The newest way to back up your data is to do it elsewhere, over the Internet. I'm talking about using an online backup service to copy your important files from one or more computers to the service's own servers. If your local data is lost or damaged, you can then restore the files from the online backup service's servers.

The benefit of using an online backup service is that the backup copy of your library is stored offsite, so you're protected in case of any local physical catastrophe. Most online backup services also work in the background, so they're constantly backing up new and changed files in real time.

The downside of an online backup service comes if you need to restore your files. It will take a long time to transfer lots of big

> **ULTIMATELY INTERESTING** Another form of online backup is to upload your music collection to a cloud-based music service, such as Apple's iCloud or Google Play Music. Learn more in Chapter 20, "Accessing Your Music in the Cloud."

13

files back to your computer over an Internet connection. Plus, you have to pay for the backup service—on an ongoing basis. We're talking $50 or more per year, per computer, perhaps more if you're backing up large amounts of data. It's not much, but it's not nothing.

If online backup appeals to you, check out these popular online-backup services designed for home users:

- **Carbonite** (www.carbonite.com)
- **IDrive** (www.idrive.com)
- **Mozy** (www.mozy.com)
- **Norton Online Backup** (us.norton.com/online-backup/)
- **SOS Online Backup** (www.sosonlinebackup.com)

> ♪ **ULTIMATELY USEFUL**
>
> I'm a belt and suspenders kind of guy, which means I use both local and online backup. If my entire house is destroyed by a stray meteor, that external hard drive is going to be toast, too. While it's easier to restore files from a local backup (it takes a long time to re-transfer lots of big files over an Internet connection), it's good to know that a copy of my precious music library exists safely offsite. (For that matter, I also keep all the physical CDs that I rip; if worse comes to worst, I can always re-rip them again.)

WHAT'S THE BEST STORAGE SOLUTION FOR YOU?

Okay, you know the options. Which is the best way to store your digital music library?

As with most things to do with digital music, there is no single best solution for all users. What works for me might not work for you, or might be overkill. That said, I'll make a few recommendations.

If you don't have a huge music library and only listen to music on your computer, then by all means use that computer to store your digital music library. For that matter, you can also connect that computer to your home audio system, if you're not fussy about the way things look. Even if you're using a laptop for this task, you'll probably have it at home when you need to listen to music. It's a simple if inelegant solution.

If you do most of your listening in your living room, however, I recommend connecting a dedicated PC to your home audio system. Go ahead and hide the PC in a cabinet or something if need be, and make sure you're making the best possible connections given the options

13

available. You can also stream music from this PC to other devices in your house over your home network.

For the ultimate in flexibility, especially if you have a large music library, you should go the home server route. This will take a little more time to set up and configure than the other approaches, but boy, it works like a charm once you get it going. It's also the best way to stream to multiple PCs or devices throughout your house. I prefer to connect the server to the network router via Ethernet; the router can then connect to other devices wirelessly if need be.

And remember, plan for the future and get a little more storage than you think you need. If you have 1,000 CDs in you collection today, how big will your collection be in five years? Try to build as much of a future-proof system as you can—knowing that everything's going to change sometime in the future, anyway.

Organizing Your Digital Music Collection

I f you only have a few hundred albums ripped or downloaded to your computer, keeping things organized is no big deal. But when you start to amass a *serious* collection, you have some organization issues to deal with.

For example, just how do you organize all those audio files on your computer? And how do you make sure each and every track has the right information assigned to it?

Obsessive-compulsive collectors will spend a lot of time—and I mean a *lot* of time—keeping their digital music collections neat and orderly. How you approach that affects how much time you spend at the task.

Organizing Audio Files on Your Computer

Let's start with the issue of organizing the audio files you've downloaded or ripped to your PC. As we discussed in Chapter 13, "Storing Your Digital Music," you first have to decide on what type of computer to store your collection. Whatever you decide, it needs to be one with a big hard disk, because a serious collection will take up a lot of disk space.

By default, Windows 7 stores all the audio files you download or rip in the **My Music** folder; Mac OS (and Windows Vista, as well) stores audio files in the similar **Music** folder. Within this folder are a series of subfolders.

Some of the subfolders are for specific music libraries. For example, if you download music from the Amazon MP3 Store, there will be an **Amazon MP3** folder. If you download tracks from the iTunes Store or rip tracks to iTunes, your music is stored within the **iTunes** folder in the **iTunes Media** subfolder. You may also have folders for music downloaded from other music stores.

The vast majority of subfolders in the **My Music** folder, however, are designated for individual artists. Within each artist folder are subfolders for albums from that artist. And within each album folder are the audio files for the tracks from that album.

So, for example, if you've downloaded the track "Simple Twist of Fate" from Bob Dylan's *Blood on the Tracks* album, you'd find it on your computer in this series of folders and subfolders:

C:> Users > *username* **> My Music > Bob Dylan > Blood on the Tracks > Simple Twist of Fate.mp3**

(If you're on a Mac or using Windows Vista, it's in the **Music** folder, not **My Music**.)

If, on the other hand, this was a track downloaded from or ripped via iTunes, you'd find it here:

C:> Users > *username* **> My Music > iTunes > iTunes Media > Bob Dylan > Blood on the Tracks > Simple Twist of Fate.mp3**

You get the picture.

> **♪ ULTIMATELY USEFUL** By default, these music folders are located on your computer's C: drive. If you don't have enough space on C:, or if you want to devote a dedicated drive to your music library, you can reconfigure your sites and programs to save to drive D: (or E: or whatever) instead. Same thing if you have your music files stored on a different computer or home server on your network. Just let every site and program know that you want to save to a different network location, then have at it.

Now, you don't have to do anything to accept this storage hierarchy; your operating system and whichever music program or download site you're using does this automatically. That said, you can configure your download site or ripping program to save files in a different place. I'm not sure why you'd want to, however; the default locations work just fine—unless you store your music on a different hard drive, that is.

Understanding Song Tags

By itself, an audio file is just music, nothing more, nothing less. However, audio files can be accompanied with useful information about the track—who recorded it, the song's composer, which album it came from, which musical genre it belongs to, and so forth. This information is formally called *metadata*; each individual piece of information is called a *tag*.

There's actually a formal format for tagging audio files, called ID3. The format describes a variety of different tags that can be used, and how that data is encoded. (It's in a kind of "wrapper" that encases the actual audio file.)

When you download a track from an authorized download site, basic tag information is included. When you rip a track from CD, the program you use for ripping typically goes online to find appropriate tag information, then fills in the tags accordingly.

> **ULTIMATELY INTERESTING** Technically, ID3 tags apply only to MP3-format files. AAC and WMA files have their own proprietary tagging formats, but these map fairly closely to the ID3 standard. As such, it's acceptable to refer to all audio file tags similarly.

In both instances, the metadata comes from a centralized database of music metadata. There are several of these big databases out there, including Gracenote (owned by Sony) and the Rovi Data Service (formerly known as LASSO). The major online music stores and services, as well as music player and tag editing programs, license these databases to supply metadata for the tracks they download, stream, or rip.

There are tons of possible tags detailed in the ID3 standard, but not all apply to audio recordings nor are all equally useful. To that end, Table 14.1 details the most common ID3 tags you're likely to encounter.

Table 14.1   Common ID3 Tags

Tag	Description
Album	Title of the host album.
Album Artist	Name of the artist who recorded the host album.
Author URL	Website of the record label that released the track.
Beats-Per-Minute (BPM)	Beats per minute; important in determining the tempo of dance music.
Bit rate	Bitrate at which the track was encoded.
Comments	Any additional (and optional) comments about the track.
Composer(s)	Composer of the song—not the person who recorded it.
Conductor(s)	For classical albums, the conductor of the orchestra who played on the track.
Contributing Artist(s)	Name of the artist performing this track. (Sometimes this tag is labeled just Artist.)
Copyright	Notice of copyright for the track.
Disc Number/Part of a Set	For multiple-disc releases, such as boxed sets, the disc number of the host album.
Encoded by	Name of the individual or organization that encoded (ripped) the track.
Genre	Musical genre of the track—pop, rock, dance, and so on.
Group Description	Used to group tracks into playlists.
Grouping	Used for classical works, the movement or piece of the work from which this track is taken.
Initial Key	The starting key signature of the piece; used primarily but not exclusively for classical music.
Language	The language used for the track's lyrics.
Length	Total time of the track.
Lyricist	The person or people who wrote the words for the song.
Lyrics	The words to the song.
Mood	Description of the "feel" of the track, such as "romantic" or "sad."
Official Artist Website	URL of the recording artist's website
Part of a Compilation	Checked if this track is part of a compilation album—typically an album with songs by various artists.
Publisher	Record label that released the track.
Rating	User rating for the track, from one to five stars.
Subtitle	Subtitle of the album or track.
Title/Name	Title of the song.
Track Number (#)	Track number on the album.
Year	The year the track or album was released. May be the year of original release, or the year an album or track was reissued.

Of course, not all ID3 tags are used on all tracks you download or rip, nor do they need to be. The important fields are Title, Artist (either Album or Contributing), and Genre; everything else is optional— although more serious music collectors like to fill in as much as they can, even if they have to do it manually.

The Genre tag is probably the most defined, in that a track should be assigned only a genre from the approved genre list—not one you've made up on the spot. To that end, Table 14.2 details the approved genres identified for use with the Genre tag.

> ♪ **ULTIMATELY INTERESTING**   Album Artist and Contributing Artist are not necessarily the same, especially on compilation albums. The Album Artist is the main artist for the entire album; the Contributing Artist is the artist playing on a particular track. For example, on some compilation albums, the Album Artist is "various," while each track has its own Contributing Artist.

Table 14.2   Official ID3 Genre Tags

0	Blues	43	Punk	86	Latin
1	Classic Rock	44	Space	87	Revival
2	Country	45	Meditative	88	Celtic
3	Dance	46	Instrumental Pop	89	Bluegrass
4	Disco	47	Instrumental Rock	90	Avantgarde
5	Funk	48	Ethnic	91	Gothic Rock
6	Grunge	49	Gothic	92	Progressive Rock
7	Hip-Hop	50	Darkwave	93	Psychedelic Rock
8	Jazz	51	Techno-Industrial	94	Symphonic Rock
9	Metal	52	Electronic	95	Slow Rock
10	New Age	53	Pop-Folk	96	Big Band
11	Oldies	54	Eurodance	97	Chorus
12	Other	55	Dream	98	Easy Listening
13	Pop	56	Southern Rock	99	Acoustic
14	R&B	57	Comedy	100	Humour
15	Rap	58	Cult	101	Speech
16	Reggae	59	Gangsta	102	Chanson
17	Rock	60	Top 40	103	Opera

14

Table 14.2   Continued

18	Techno	61	Christian Rap	104	Chamber Music
19	Industrial	62	Pop/Funk	105	Sonata
20	Alternative	63	Jungle	106	Symphony
21	Ska	64	Native American	107	Booty Bass
22	Death Metal	65	Cabaret	108	Primus
23	Pranks	66	New Wave	109	Porn Groove
24	Soundtrack	67	Psychedelic	110	Satire
25	Euro-Techno	68	Rave	111	Slow Jam
26	Ambient	69	Showtunes	112	Club
27	Trip-Hop	70	Trailer	113	Tango
28	Vocal	71	Lo-Fi	114	Samba
29	Jazz+Funk	72	Tribal	115	Folklore
30	Fusion	73	Acid Punk	116	Ballad
31	Trance	74	Acid Jazz	117	Power Ballad
32	Classical	75	Polka	118	Rhythmic Soul
33	Instrumental	76	Retro	119	Freestyle
34	Acid	77	Musical	120	Duet
35	House	78	Rock & Roll	121	Punk Rock
36	Game	79	Hard Rock	122	Drum Solo
37	Sound Clip	80	Folk	123	A Capella
38	Gospel	81	Folk-Rock	124	Euro-House
39	Noise	82	National Folk	125	Dance Hall
40	AlternRock	83	Swing		
41	Bass	84	Fast Fusion		
42	Soul	85	Bebop		

For most consistent organization, restrict your tagging to one of these 126 approved genres. However, it's your music collection, so feel free to create your own genres if that suits you better.

What Can Possibly Go Wrong?

Most of the time when you download a track the download site has applied the correct song information, or the right information gets added when you rip it from CD. Sometimes, however, the song information isn't right—or isn't there at all.

While you can always be surprised by a bad or missing tag or two, I've identified some very specific types of albums that are likely to generate the highest probability of error. These include:

- **Independent or self-distributed CDs.** These are not likely to be in the database at all.

- **CDs purchased from Time-Life and other special products labels.** These albums are oftentimes never listed in the database.

- **Out-of-print CDs.** You guessed it, these often get deleted from the database.

- **Re-releases.** I'm talking albums that for one reason or another have been re-released with a different track listing than the original. What often happens is that the database applies the older track listing to the newer CD—or vice versa—which really messes things up.

- **Double-album, multiple-disc, or boxed sets.** Sometimes the database only recognizes one of the discs—and applies the same track listing to all.

- **Soundtracks.** This might be an unexpected one, but I've found way too many soundtrack albums that have incorrect or irrelevant artist info for each track.

- **Classical music.** Yep, the classical music aficionado gets shafted again. Believe it or not, classical albums are perhaps the most likely to have incorrect or nonexistent track or artist info, for whatever reason.

- **Multiple-artist or compilation albums.** Whomever does these compilations often gets sloppy with their tagging; oftentimes the artist info isn't correct for all tracks.

- **Artists with commas in their names.** The master database and various tag editors seem to have trouble when there's punctuation in an artist name. For example, I've always had trouble with various editors and programs displaying the group **Blood, Sweat & Tears** as **Sweat & Tears Blood**, which just ain't right.

In addition, sometimes the info for a specific album or track is correct but not consistent with similar info on other CDs in your library. This is a particular issue for the obsessive-compulsives among us, who insist that all Broadway soundtrack albums list the specific performer's name for each track, not the character's name, or who want the Temptations listed as *The Temptations* on every single disc. If this is you, get ready to do a lot of editing!

Also be on the lookout for grossly inaccurate genre assignments—at least to your ears. Is Joni Mitchell a Folk, Pop, Rock, or Jazz artist? Is Spyro Gyra Jazz or Easy Listening? Is Bon Iver Folk, Rock, or Alternative? Chances are you have your opinion and the big music databases have theirs—and their assignments might even vary from album to album. (Which may or may not be okay with you, depending on just which way you like your consistency.) Just a warning, this sort of thing can really consume the die-hards. (Like me!)

> **ULTIMATELY USEFUL** I've found that most avid collectors would prefer that their libraries have some conformity between tracks by a single artist. That is, you want the artist names to be consistent from album to album—which, unfortunately, is not always the case in the Gracenote or Rovi databases. For example, if one track is by the "Fifth Dimension" and another by the "5th Dimension," you may want to edit one or the other track so that the artist name is the same.

Editing Tags

Fortunately, it's relatively easy to edit any of the tags associated with a digital music track. In fact, there are a number of different ways to do so.

Editing Tags Directly in a File

Since tags are nothing more than metadata amended to a digital audio file, you can edit this metadata directly in the file itself, from within your computer's operating system—if you're using Windows, that is.

All you have to do is use Windows Explorer to navigate to the file in question and then right-click the file and select Properties from the pop-up menu. This displays the Properties dialog box for the file; the information you want to edit is found on the Details tab, shown in Figure 14.1.

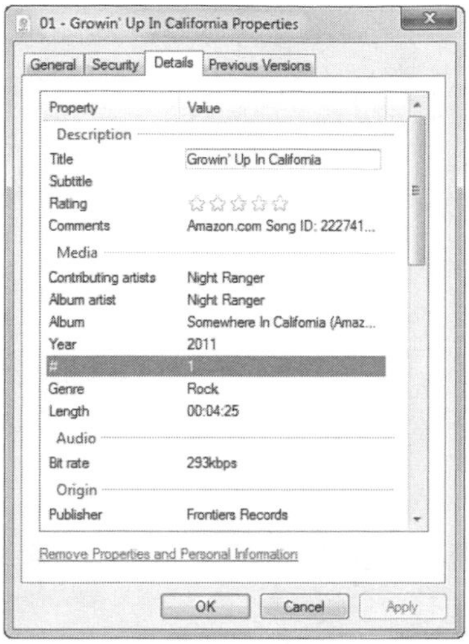

FIGURE 14.1

Editing tag data in Windows.

All the important tags are displayed on this tab. To edit a tag, just highlight that field and start typing. Make sure you click **OK** when done.

Unfortunately, you can't edit audio metadata directly on a Mac; you have to use a tag editing program, instead—which we'll address.

Editing Tags in iTunes

Before we get into third-party tag editors, you should know that you probably already have a program that can edit audio metadata. That's right, just about any music player program can also edit the tags for the tracks it plays.

Since iTunes is the most popular music player today, let's start by looking at how iTunes does the tag editing thing. You can use iTunes to edit one track at a time, or multiple tracks simultaneously.

To edit the info for any individual track, select the track in iTunes and then select **File > Get Info**. This displays the dialog box shown in Figure 14.2. Skip the Summary tab, which contains useful information but is not editable. Instead, go to the Info tab, where all you have to do is enter new information into any field. Click **OK** to save the new information.

> **ULTIMATELY USEFUL** Alternately, you can edit basic information in any iTunes track list. Just click within the appropriate field for a track, and type in the new info.

14

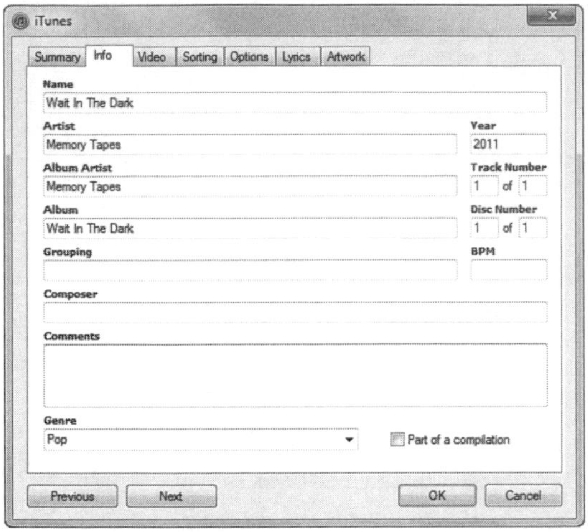

FIGURE 14.2

Editing tag data in iTunes.

Sometimes, however, you want to edit tags for multiple tracks that share the same characteristics. For example, you may want to edit the Genre tag for all the tracks on a given album. To do this, select the multiple tracks (hold down the Shift or Ctrl keys while selecting with your mouse) then select **File > Get Info**. You're asked if you're sure you want to edit multiple tracks; click **Yes** and you see the Multiple Item Information dialog box, shown in Figure 14.3. Note that you can't edit individual track titles from this dialog box, but you can edit just about anything else.

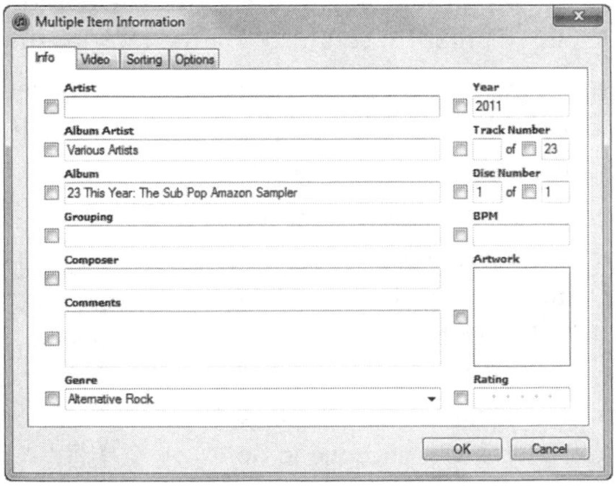

FIGURE 14.3

Editing information for multiple tracks in iTunes.

Editing Tags in Windows Media Player

You can also use Microsoft's Windows Media Player (WMP) to edit tag information for any track in your digital music library, although it's a lot more work than it used to be. WMP used to have an Advanced Tag Editor function that made tag editing a snap; beginning with WMP 12, however, the Advanced Tag Editor has been removed, and with it a certain ease of editing.

> ♪ **ULTIMATELY USEFUL** You can also use the Multiple Item Information dialog box to configure an album for gapless playback, or as a compilation album.

That means the only way to edit tags in WMP is within the track listings of the library display. The problem here is that not all the tags you may want to edit are displayed in the listing; if there's a column for that tag, you're okay, but if not, how do you edit it?

The first thing you need to do, then, is display those columns that represent the tags you want to edit. You do this by right-clicking in the column header row at the top of the listings and selecting **Choose Columns**. When the Choose Columns dialog box appears, check those columns that represent the tags you want to edit.

Now it's a simple matter of using WMP's Edit command to edit specific tags for a given track. Just right-click the column entry for the track you want to edit and select **Edit**; you can now type new information directly into the listing, as shown in Figure 14.4.

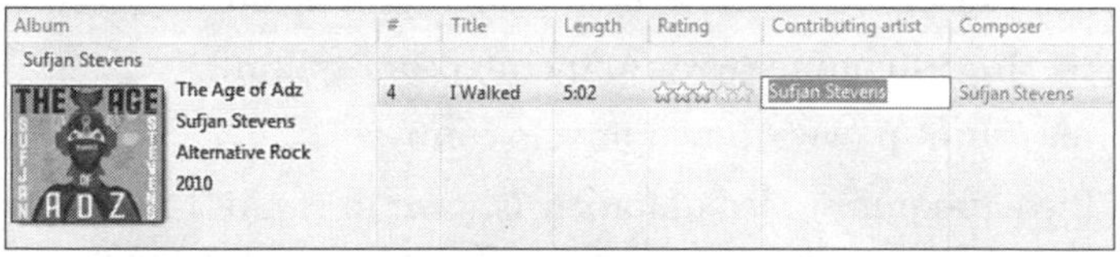

FIGURE 14.4

Editing tag information in Windows Media Player.

Editing Tags with Third-Party Software

Given the difficulty of editing tags in Windows Media Player and other music player programs, you may be better off using a third-party tag-editing program, instead. Most of these tag-editor programs work with all types of audio files—MP3, AAC, WMA, you name it.

All of these tag editors let you enter track and album data manually, and many also link up to Gracenote or other online databases to obtain more complete information. Most let you edit attributes for multiple files at one time; for example, you can change the genre or artist name for dozens of albums in a single edit.

> **ULTIMATELY INTERESTING** Many tag-editing programs also let you change the album cover art for selected, which we'll discuss further in Chapter 15, "Finding and Downloading Cover Art."

The most popular of these tag-editing programs include:

- **AudioManage Audio Library** (www.audiomanage.com)
- **Dapyx MP3 Explorer** (www.dapyx.com)
- **File Audio Processor** (www.fileaudioprocessor.com)
- **MediaMonkey** (www.mediamonkey.com)
- **mp3Tag** (www.maniactools.com/soft/mp3tag/)
- **Music Collector** (www.collectorz.com/music/)
- **MusicBrainz Picard** (www.musicbrainz.org/doc/MusicBrainz_Picard)
- **Tag Clinic** (www.kevesoft.com/TagClinic.htm)
- **Tag&Rename** (www.softpointer.com/tr.htm)
- **TuneUp** (www.tuneupmedia.com)

Of these programs, MediaMonkey (shown in Figure 14.5) is perhaps the most popular today. I like it because it will automatically flag incomplete, corrupted, or mismatched ID3 tags, so you'll know where to focus your attention. You can also edit a full battery of tags, not the limited number you can access with iTunes or WMP.

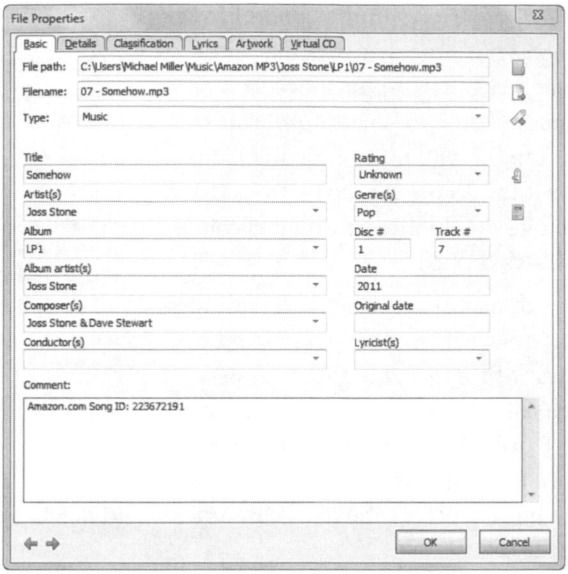

FIGURE 14.5
Editing tag information with the MediaMonkey tag editor.

Five Tricks for Better Organized Music Libraries

We all have our own ways we like to organize our music libraries. But there are a few questions and complaints that are common among a lot of serious collectors that we should probably address here.

Delete Duplicate Tracks

After you've been ripping or downloading music for a period of time, you're bound to end up with at least a few duplicate tracks—songs you've ripped or downloaded more than once, from more than one album. For example, you may have copies of the tune "Black Cow" from Steely Dan's *Aja*, *Gold*, and *Citizen Steely Dan* albums.

Now, that may not bother you, particularly if you like to play each album in its entirety. But since storage space is valuable, you may not want to keep three identical audio files on your hard disk when one will surely due.

To that end, you may want to periodically go through your library and delete those duplicate tracks, freeing up space for newer music. Some tag-editor programs, such as TuneUp, will automatically identify what it thinks are duplicate tracks, and then remove the duplicates on your command. That's a plus.

If you're not using a separate tag editing program, however, you can easily find duplicates within the ubiquitous iTunes program. All you have to do is select **File > Display Duplicates**. This lists all tracks that share the same name, in alphabetical order. Examine each of the duplicate tracks, and delete one or more instances as necessary.

> **ULTIMATELY CAUTIOUS** Not all tracks with the same name are actually the same recording. Sometimes there are more than one song with the same title; other times, it may be the same song performed by a different artist, or even performed by the same artist on a different album. (Comparing song timings is a good way to weed out false duplicates.) Make sure a track is truly a duplicate before you permanently delete it.

Combine Multi-Disc Albums into a Single Album

Here's one you may want to consider, depending on how you like your collection organized. I have a lot of two-disc (and more) sets in my collection that I don't necessarily think of as separate albums—Bob Dylan's *Blonde on Blonde*, for example. I'd rather have this as a single album in my library, not as two albums (*Blonde on Blonde Disc 1* and *Blond on Blonde Disc 2*.)

It's possible to combine a multi-disc set into a single digital album. It takes a bit of manual manipulation, however.

Here's what you need to do, in order:

1. Using whichever tag editor you prefer, rename the first disc in the set to the main album name, without the "Disc 1" in the title. For example, you'd rename *Blonde on Blonde Disc 1* to just *Blonde on Blonde*.

2. Count the number of tracks on the first disc.

3. Edit the track numbers on the second disc to start with the number following the final number on the first disc. Sticking with *Blonde on Blonde* as our example, the first disc has 8 tracks, so we renumber disc 2, track 1 ("Most Likely Go Your Way (And I'll Go Mine)") as track 9. We renumber disc 2, track 2 as track 10. And so forth.

4. After all the tracks on the second disc are renumbered, rename the second disc to the main album name, without the "Disc 2" in the title.

What your operating system, music player, and every other appropriate program now sees is a single album with all the tracks from the two discs you ripped or downloaded.

I use this little trick not only for traditional two-disc sets, but also for big boxed sets that have four or more discs. I think of these as single collections, not multiple albums, and that's how I want to hear them when I play my library.

Separate Combination Albums into Individual Albums

Sometimes you need to go the opposite route—separate individual albums that have been sold as a single CD or download. For example, the reissue label BGO sells three classic albums by the jazz/rock band Chase as a single CD. I don't want these in my library as a single album; I want to see and listen to all three original albums (*Chase, Ennea,* and *Pure Music*).

In this situation, you need to re-title and re-number all the tracks from this combination album. That means editing the tracks for each album to reflect the original album's title and track numbering. You'll also have to add the original cover art for each individual album. It's a bit of manual labor, but it creates a music library that more accurately reflects the original releases, not the way they've subsequently been rereleased.

> ♪ ULTIMATELY **USEFUL** You'll also want to enter the original release year for each album, separately, instead of using the year the albums were re-released. This goes for any album re-release, by the way, not just combo albums.

Assign Multiple Genres

Is Bob Dylan a folkie or a rocker? Is US3's *Hand on the Torch* a jazz album or a hip-hop album? Should Mel Torme be labeled a vocal or jazz artist?

Sometimes artists and albums don't fit into neatly defined categories. Instead of trying to split hairs, you can simply assign a given track or album to multiple genres. That way Dylan will show up when you're playing either folk or jazz, *Hand on the Torch* appears on both your jazz and hip-hop lists, and Mel Torme receives his due as both a talented vocalist and a jazzer.

Not all tag editors let you do this; for example, iTunes forces you to select a single genre from a list. In other tag editors (or when editing a track from within Windows Explorer) you can separate multiple genres with a semi-colon, like this: **folk; rock**, so when you display tracks by genre, the multi-labeled track will show up in both folk and rock. If your tag editor *doesn't* allow multiple-genre categorization, either switch to one that does or edit the raw files instead (if you're a Windows user).

Add Song Lyrics

Here's a final trick that adds some real value to the tracks in your music library. If you can edit the Lyrics tag (which you can do from most tag editing programs), you can add song lyrics to any track's metadata. Then, if your music player is compatible with this tag, you can read lyrics onscreen while you play your favorite tunes—which is great for karaoke, if nothing else.

One such lyric-enabled music player is our old favorite, the iTunes player. In fact, you can add lyrics information to any track from within iTunes. All you have to do is select the track, select, **File > Get Info**, and then select the **Lyrics** tab. You can then type in the lyrics, or paste the lyrics copied from another source. Click **OK** when done.

Where can you find lyrics for your favorite songs? There are several song lyrics sites on the web, including:

- **Absolute Lyrics** (www.absolutelyrics.com)
- **A-Z Lyrics Universe** (www.azlyrics.com)
- **Lyrics On Demand** (www.lyricsondemand.com)
- **Lyrics Search Engine** (www.lyrics.astraweb.com)
- **Lyrics.com** (www.lyrics.com)
- **MetroLyrics** (www.metrolyrics.com)

> **ULTIMATELY USEFUL** If you've added lyrics to a track, you can view them while playing that tune on your iPod. Just start playing the song and then press the center Select button a few times. If there are lyrics stored, they should eventually appear in the display.

THE HEADACHES OF STANDARDIZING TAG DATA

I'm a stickler for having things my way, and that's especially true when it comes to my digital music collection. With 1600+ complete albums, I have a lot of data to manage—and not all of it is as I want it from the source.

I hate inconsistency, and the online music databases are nothing if not inconsistent. Why, for the life of me, are some albums by the Boss labeled with Bruce Springsteen as the artist, while others are attributed to Bruce Springsteen and the E Street Band? (To make matters worse, sometimes it's "and" and others "&.") Then there's the problem of "The" in front of some artists names and not others. And there's always the occasional misspelling, not to mention those tracks with wholly inaccurate subsidiary information.

It gets worse when you combine data from different databases. Some companies (like Apple) get their metadata from Gracenote, others (such as Microsoft) from Rovi Data Service. Not surprisingly, there are discrepancies between the two, which means similar tracks ripped from iTunes and Windows Media Player sometimes end up with subtly different metadata.

As you might expect, this drives me nuts. I want my music data to be both accurate and consistent. Which means, of course, I spend a lot of time manually editing the tags on the tunes I rip and download. A lot of time.

Of course, I create some of this extra work for myself, because I want things my way. This means I don't always accept the generally accepted ID3 tags, especially the Genre tags. For example, I've carved out a category somewhere between Jazz and Vocals, (I call it Jazz Vocals, naturally) for singers like Ella Fitzgerald and Mel Torme. Not for Frank Sinatra and Tony Bennett, mind you, who go directly into the non-jazz Vocals category. It's just for jazz vocalists, as I define that genre in my mind.

As you can see, maintaining a detailed digital music library can be a lot of work. I suppose you can just accept the information that Gracenote or Rovi supplies when you download or rip a track, but accepting things as-is has never been my way. Thank heavens for tag editing programs.

14

Finding and Downloading Cover Art

In the previous chapter, we discussed how to edit the metadata that describes each track in your digital music library. There's one more important piece of metadata to deal with, however—the album or track cover art.

In most instances, the cover art is exactly that—a digital image of the original album cover. In some instances, special artwork is created for individual tracks sold as "singles." In all instances, however, the cover art is a digital image file that is displayed when you search for and play songs in your library. And, for many music lovers, these images are every bit as important as the music they accompany.

Understanding How Cover Art Works

The cover images that accompany digital music tracks are simple image files. In most instances, the album art is supplied automatically when you download or rip a track, the same way other metadata is supplied—from Gracenote, Rovi Data Service, and other major music databases. You can add cover images for those tracks that don't have images automatically supplied; you can change the cover image that displays for any given track.

In general, these cover images are JPG-format image files, as that format is most compatible with all file formats and music players. As to the size of the image, that's up to you. Apple's iTunes displays images at 600 x 600 pixel resolution; Windows Media Player displays at a less acceptable 240 x 240 resolution. However, you can use images of any size, from little 75 x 75 thumbnails to massive 1500 x 1500 high resolution images. In general, the bigger the screen on which you view your album covers, the higher resolution you want to go.

> **ULTIMATELY CAUTIOUS** Windows Media Player has issues with album artwork. Previous to WMP10, artwork of any size displayed at 240 x 240, but any larger files were left untouched—that is, an 800 x 800 file would remain an 800 x 800 file, but just display at 240 x 240. Starting with WMP11, however, all image files are automatically and permanently resized to 200 x 200 (but displayed at 240 x 240—go figure). So if you have an 800 x 800 image file, it becomes a 200 x 200 image. In WMP12, however, you can override the automatic file resizing by adding the following values to the Windows Registry:
>
> [HKEY_CURRENT_USER\Software\Microsoft\MediaPlayer\Preferences]
>
> "LargeAlbumArtSize"=dword:ffffffff
>
> "SmallAlbumArtSize"=dword:ffffffff
>
> WMP will still display images at the lower resolution, but will no longer resize the files themselves—which means you can still see full resolution images using another music player program.

In Windows, the album art image is by default stored in the folder for a given album, under the **folder.jpg** filename. The same **folder.jpg** image is used by all the tracks in a given folder; it also appears as the folder thumbnail when you're using Windows Explorer.

This album art can also be embedded in individual audio files. You typically have to use a tag-editing or album-art-editing program to embed image files in this fashion.

As to whether you should use the **folder.jpg** file or embed images into individual files, it all depends. Obviously, the single-file **folder.jpg** approach is easier; it's pretty much the default approach in the Windows world, and how Windows Media Player does things when it rips tracks from CD. However, the embedding approach makes sure that the artwork always travels with the audio files, even if you copy individual files from one computer to another. It also lets you use different artwork for different tracks in an album. (Some people like to do this with compilation albums.)

> **ULTIMATELY INTERESTING**   If you're using Windows Media Player to play your tracks, you'll have two additional art files in each folder—**AlbumArtSmall.jpg** and **AlbumArtLarge.jpg**. WMP automatically generates these files to display album art at various sizes within the program.

> **ULTIMATELY INTERESTING**   Most music player programs will display the embedded artwork by default when both embedded and **folder.jpg** art is available.

However, embedding artwork increases the size of the audio files themselves; the larger the images you embed, the larger the resulting audio files. Now, adding an 80Kb image file to a single 9MB MP3 file might not seem like a big deal; you're increasing the file size by a little under 1%. However, if you embed images into every track in your entire library, that starts to add up. For example, if you have a 1,000-CD library that's 90GB in size, you're going to need another 8GB to handle those embedded images for each track. It's something to consider.

What Can Go Wrong with Cover Art

If you're a devoted music lover, the cover art that accompanies each album is as important as the music itself. To that end, you want to make sure you have the right art for each album—which doesn't always happen.

Sometimes the online database that supplies the music metadata the CD you're ripping doesn't have a cover image available, so you don't get any cover art. Sometimes it recognizes the CD, but doesn't have any album art stored for that CD. Sometimes it just has the wrong artwork assigned.

15

You also can run into problems when downloading tracks. Sometimes the online music store or download site doesn't have any art for an album. Sometimes it has the wrong art. Sometimes the album art is correct, but isn't that great looking—too light, too dark, whatever. Sometimes the album art looks okay, but it's just too low-res to display well on a big-screen TV.

Whatever the reasons, there will be instances where you want to change the album art associated with a CD you've downloaded or ripped to your hard disk. There are a number of ways to do this—after you find the right cover art, that is.

Where to Find Cover Art

When it comes to finding cover art, start with what your music service or online downloads, or what your music ripping program finds. If you use a separate tag-editing or album-editing program, let that program search for artwork; it may come up with something better than what you started with.

The first place I actually look for new artwork is good old Amazon (www.amazon.com). Not surprisingly, the world's largest online retailer of CDs has the largest library of CD artwork—both its own and, in many cases, artwork uploaded by its customers. Just search Amazon for the CD in question, and the resulting product page should display the album art—but as a thumbnail. Click the thumbnail to display a larger version, then right-click the larger picture and save it to your hard disk. You can then associate this image file with the album in question, as discussed in few moments.

I'm also a big fan of Album Art Exchange (www.albumartexchange.com). As you can see in Figure 15.1, this site offers high-resolution album artwork, scanned and uploaded by other users. The artwork on this site typically starts at 600 x 600 resolution and goes up from there.

Similar is All CD Covers (www.allcdcovers.com), which lets you search a database of covers uploaded by other site users. The database on this site isn't as broad as with the previous site, but still offers a lot of high-resolution artwork.

If none of these sites have the artwork you want, nothing beats a good Google search. Use Google Image Search (images.google.com) and type in the artist and album name. You can even filter your results by file size, if that's important to you.

Then there's the albumart website (www.albumart.org), shown in Figure 15.2. This site is a search engine just for album art; it tends to return a lot of covers displayed on Amazon.com, but still.

FIGURE 15.1

Finding cover art on the Album Art Exchange website.

FIGURE 15.2

albumart, a search engine for cover art.

15

Finally, if you can't find any cover art for an album online, you can always scan in a copy of the actual CD cover—assuming you have the CD, that is. You can then use that scanned cover image, as you would any album artwork.

How to Change Cover Art

How you change album art depends on which program you're using. We'll look at a few popular options.

Changing Album Art Files Manually in Windows

This is the simple approach for those who don't mind getting their virtual fingers dirty. As you recall, Windows uses a single **folder.jpg** file in an album folder as the artwork file for all the tracks on that album. All you need to do is copy a new image file (in JPG format) into an album folder and name that file **folder.jpg**. Obviously, if the folder.jpg file already exists, either delete it first or copy over it with the new file.

ULTIMATELY CAUTIOUS The **folder.jpg** approach does not embed the artwork into the individual audio files.

Changing Album Art in iTunes

If you're an Apple devotee, you can fairly easily change your album art using the iTunes program.

To add artwork to a single track, select the track and select **File > Get Info**. When the next dialog box appears, select the **Artwork** tab, shown in Figure 15.3. Any existing artwork is already displayed in this dialog box; to delete an incorrect cover, select it with your mouse and then click the **Delete** button. To add new artwork, click the **Add** button, then browse your hard disk for the replacement art file.

To add or change artwork for all the tracks of an album, select all the tracks (hold down the Shift or Ctrl keys while selecting with your mouse) for that album in your music library, then select **File > Get Info**. Click **Yes** when asked if you want to edit information for multiple items, and you now see the Multiple Item Information dialog box. Select the **Info** tab and then double-click the large **Artwork** box; this lets you browse your hard disk for the new art file.

ULTIMATELY USEFUL iTunes and the iPod can display multiple album art files (sequentially) for any single track. You can add multiple covers from the **Get Info** dialog box, and then scroll through the covers within the dialog box.

FIGURE 15.3

Adding new album art for a single track in iTunes.

Changing Album Art in Windows Media Player

In Windows Media Player, you add new artwork using the drag-and-drop method. That is, you drag the image file from another window (Windows Explorer, for example) and drag it onto the current or placeholder art for a given album. This embeds the cover art into the file for all tracks in that album.

Changing Album Art with a Third-Party Program

There are several third-party programs that help you add album art to your digital music tracks.

Most of these programs will search your iTunes library for tracks without art, go online to find appropriate cover artwork, and then add those covers to the tracks in question. The best of these programs include:

- **Album Art Downloader** (www.sourceforge.net/projects/album-art/)
- **Album Art Fixer** (www.avsoft.nl/index.php/album-art-fixer—for Windows media only)
- **iArt** (www.ipodsoft.com—for iTunes only)
- **ID3AlbumArtFixer** (www.dalepreston.com/Blog/2009/07/id3-album-art-fixer.html)
- **TuneSleeve** (sites.google.com/site/tunesleeve/—for iTunes only)

Of these apps, Album Art Downloader, shown in Figure 15.4, is probably the most popular. It automatically searches a variety of websites (including Amazon and Google Image Search) for album covers, and often finds high-resolution images.

FIGURE 15.4
Finding cover art with the Album Art Downloader program.

In addition, many of the tag-editing programs discussed in Chapter 14, "Organizing Your Digital Music Collection," also let you edit album art. Specifically, both MediaMonkey (www.mediamonkey.com) and TuneUp (www.tuneupmedia.com) are pretty good at this task.

FINDING THE *RIGHT* ALBUM ART

As you might suspect, I'm a stickler for good album art. I want high-quality reproductions, and I want the art to be the right art—which is sometimes difficult when you're talking CD reissues of classic vinyl albums.

Take, for example, the soundtrack to the movie *Casino Royale*—the original 1960s spoof scored by Burt Bacharach, not the more recent Bond with Daniel Craig as Agent 007. Old school audiophiles will recognize the *Casino Royale* soundtrack as one of the best sounding vinyl records of that era; it remains something close to a reference CD today. It's one of my personal favorites.

15

Now, the *Casino Royale* soundtrack has been released on CD multiple times. The initial releases utilized the same artwork as the original vinyl album (which in turn used the artwork from the film's poster), as shown in Figure 15.5. I love this artwork; it's very 1960s pop artsy and conveys the spirit of the film and the soundtrack. Unfortunately, if you download the album or rip that CD today, you get the reissue artwork shown in Figure 15.6, which is notably inferior to the original.

FIGURE 15.5
The original artwork for the Casino Royale *soundtrack.*

FIGURE 15.6
The inferior re-release artwork for Casino Royale.

I'm a purist, and I want my collection to reflect the original releases. This means I can't accept the re-release *Casino Royale* artwork; instead, I have to find and download the original album artwork, and then replace the reissue artwork with the original in all my digital tracks. A bit of work, but worth it, in my mind.

You run into this a lot with reissues. For example, Columbia Jazz Masterpieces puts its own series "wrapper" around the original artwork of the albums it reissues. (Figure 15.7 shows the original artwork for Dave Brubeck's classic *Jazz Goes to College* album; Figure 15.8 shows the wrappered reissue artwork.) With each of these albums, I have to search for the original album artwork, sans reissue wrapper, and do the artwork replacement thing.

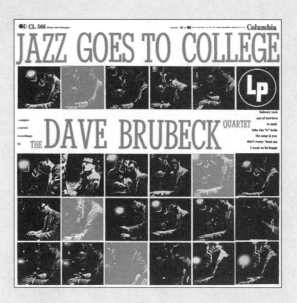

FIGURE 15.7

The original artwork for Brubeck's Jazz Goes to College—*very modernistic.*

FIGURE 15.8

The reissue artwork for Dave Brubeck's Jazz Goes to College, *complete with Columbia Jazz Masterpieces series wrapper—nothing at all like the original.*

The point is that serious music lovers need to be diligent about the cover art provided when they download or rip classic albums and reissues. Unless you're satisfied with inferior reissue art, you'll need to do your homework to discover and download the original album art—sometimes from the original vinyl LPs!

Creating the Perfect Playlist

What is the perfect playlist? Is it a bunch of inspiring tunes to accompany your run or workout? Some mellow tracks to chill out with at the end of a hectic day? A collection of up-tempo dance tunes for your next party? Some of your favorite songs from your youth? Or just a random mix of music that makes you feel good?

There's no one perfect playlist for everyone, of course. Your favorite mix is going to be much different from mine—and will probably vary on your own mood and circumstances. What all your playlists and mine have in common, however, is that they reflect one's personal taste, as represented by selected track from one's digital music library.

How do you put together the perfect playlist—or at least one that sounds interesting today? Well, as Nick Hornby wrote in his book *High Fidelity*, "there are loads of rules." Let's take a look at them.

Why Listen to Playlists?

A playlist is nothing more than a collection of songs selected for future listening. Technically, a playlist is actually a computer file that contains pointers to specific audio files stored on your computer—or, in the case of online music services, a list of selected tracks.

We create playlists for lots of different reasons. Some people use playlists as background music, to set a certain mood at a certain time or for a certain event. Others use playlists to better organize their music collection, by grouping tracks in ways other than artist or genre. Some folks create playlists for inspiration, whether they're working, exercising, or whatnot. Still others like to share their playlists with others, the better to discover new music that their friends are listening to.

For whatever reason you listen to playlists, what's ultimately important is the music contained within the playlist. Which tracks you select determine the feel and mood of the playlist; the smarter and more precise your selections, the more focused the playlist—and the more direct the listening experience.

Creating a Playlist from Your Digital Music Collection

How does one create a playlist? When it comes to creating a playlist from your own digital music library, you can easily create playlists using the same program you use to listen to your music.

> ♪ ULTIMATELY **INTERESTING** Most streaming music services also let you create playlists from the tracks they offer. The process is typically similar to that of creating a playlist in a music player program.

The process of creating a playlist differs from program to program, but typically involves clicking some sort of "new playlist" link or button, naming the playlist, and then adding tracks to the new playlist. Most music players let you add tracks in one (or both) of three ways:

- Drag a song from your master track list and drop it onto the playlist.
- Right-click a track and select the "add to playlist" option from the pop-up menu.
- Select a track and select the "add to playlist" option from the appropriate top-level menu.

For example, to create a playlist within the iTunes player, you pull down the File menu and select **New Playlist**. After naming the playlist, you add tracks by displaying your library and dragging songs onto the playlist name in the sidebar, as shown in Figure 16.1.

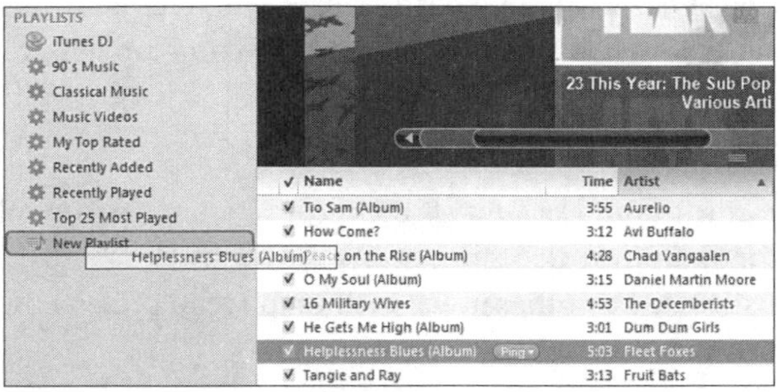

FIGURE 16.1

Adding a track to a new playlist in the iTunes player.

Many music player programs have a "smart playlist" feature. In some programs, this is as simple as you selecting a song or artist and then having the program automatically create a playlist based on that selection. Other smart playlists are even smarter; for example, iTunes lets you fine-tune selections based on one or more criteria (artist, rating, genre, time, even sample rate) and then limit the size of the playlist to a set number of tracks. (Figure 16.2 shows a smart playlist being created in the iTunes player.)

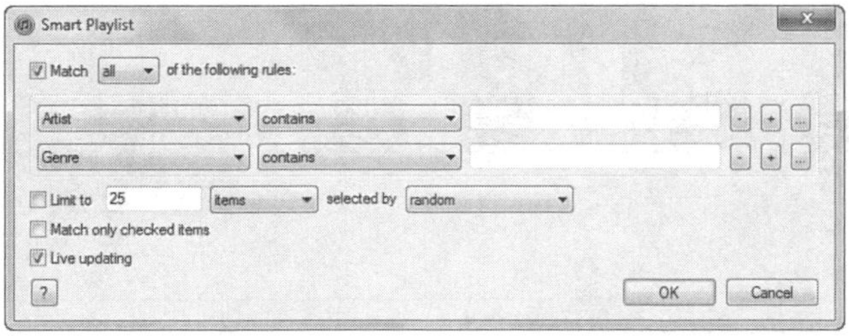

FIGURE 16.2

Creating a smart playlist with iTunes.

Listening to a playlist is as simple as selecting it in your music player and then clicking **Play**—or, in most cases, just double-clicking the playlist. You can then choose to listen to the playlist in the order that the tracks were initially added, or to shuffle the tracks in random order.

ULTIMATELY INTERESTING There are also a handful of standalone playlist builder programs, such as Advanced Playlist Builder (www.wizetech.com/apb/) and Playlist Creator (www.oddgravity.com/app-opc.php). These programs let you create playlists from tracks in your digital music library.

Creating and Sharing Playlists on the Web

Not surprisingly, there are a number of websites out there that can help you build and share custom playlists. This is where it gets interesting; some of these sites are wicked genius in what they come up with for you.

8tracks

Let's start with 8tracks (www.8tracks.com), which creates playlists in the form of personal online radio stations. As shown in Figure 16.3, you can listen to playlists created by other users, including some professional DJs, or create your own playlists online.

I like the option of searching for and refining playlists by tags or keywords—a great way to fine-tune the desired mix. Also nice is the ability to tag your own playlists and share them with others via Twitter.

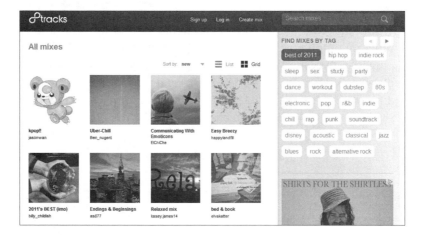

FIGURE 16.3

Finding and creating playlists with 8tracks.

FIQL

FIQL (www.fiql.com) is a straightforward playlist creation/sharing site. As you can see in Figure 16.4, you can either search for playlists or browse playlists by genre, mood/tempo (Aggressive, Brooding/Gloomy, Gentle/Warm, and so forth), or category (Dancing, Exercise, Holiday, etc.). FIQL also displays the most popular playlists each week, if that matters to you.

In terms of your own contribution, you can either upload previously created playlist files or create a new playlist onsite by typing in individual songs. FIQL also hosts a number of user-created groups, which adds a community aspect to the whole playlist thing.

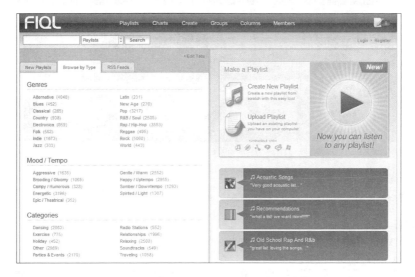

FIGURE 16.4
Browsing and creating playlists with FIQL.

Greatestplaylist

Greatestplaylist (www.greatestplaylist.com) is much like the other playlist sharing sites. As you can see in Figure 16.5, you can search for playlists by keyword, listen to random playlists, and share your own playlists with other users.

Jog.fm

If you want to find some great playlists to listen to while you're working out, check out Jog.fm (www.jog.fm). This site creates custom-selected playlists for running, cycling, or walking; just enter the time it takes you to traverse a mile and let Jog.fm suggest appropriate tracks, by matching your mile time to each track's tempo, in beats per minute (bpm). (Figure 16.6 shows how you start.) You can then add the tracks you like to a playlist and either start listening or, if you like, purchase tracks through iTunes or Amazon.

FIGURE 16.5
More playlist sharing with Greatestplaylist.

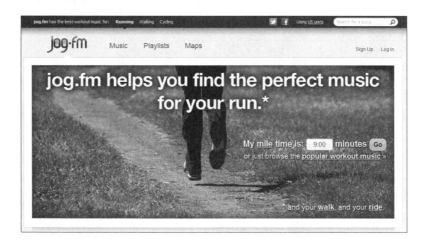

FIGURE 16.6
Creating a playlist for jogging at Jog.fm.

Mixtape.me

As you can see in Figure 16.7, Mixtape.me (www.mixtape.me) is a playlist sharing site built to resemble an old audiocassette player. You can search for playlists from other users, or build your own playlists onsite.

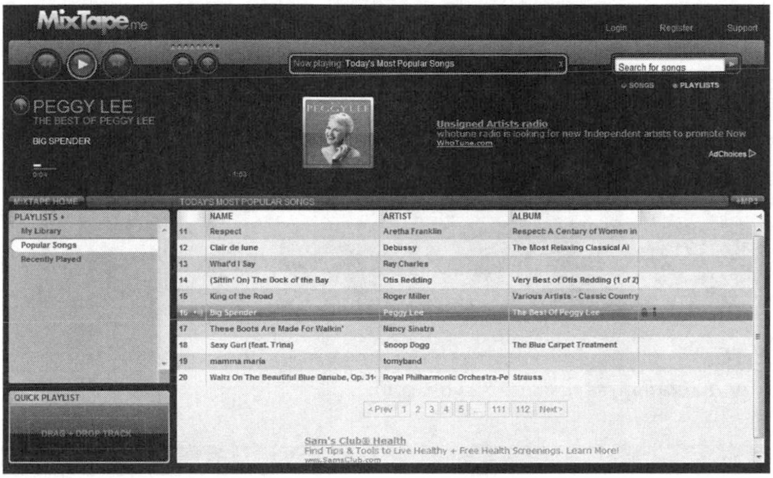

FIGURE 16.7
Listening to playlist tracks at Mixtape.me.

Playlist.com

Playlist.com (www.playlist.com), shown in Figure 16.8, is perhaps the most popular playlist sharing site on the web, with more than 48 million users. You can search for playlists by artist or song, as well as search for tracks to add to your own playlists. Once you've created a playlist, it's easy to share it with friends on Facebook, MySpace, or Twitter; you can also follow your friends' playlists on the Playlist.com site.

ShareMyPlaylists

ShareMyPlaylists (www.sharemyplaylists.com) is tied into Spotify, in that it uses the Spotify database to serve the playlists created on its own site. As you can see in Figure 16.9, you can search for and listen to other users' playlists, or create your own playlists from the Spotify database.

> **ULTIMATELY USEFUL** If you're technically inclined, you can host and serve your own playlists over the web. All you need is your own web server and Opentape, an open-source application. Learn more at www.opentape.fm.

FIGURE 16.8
Creating and sharing playlists at Playlist.com.

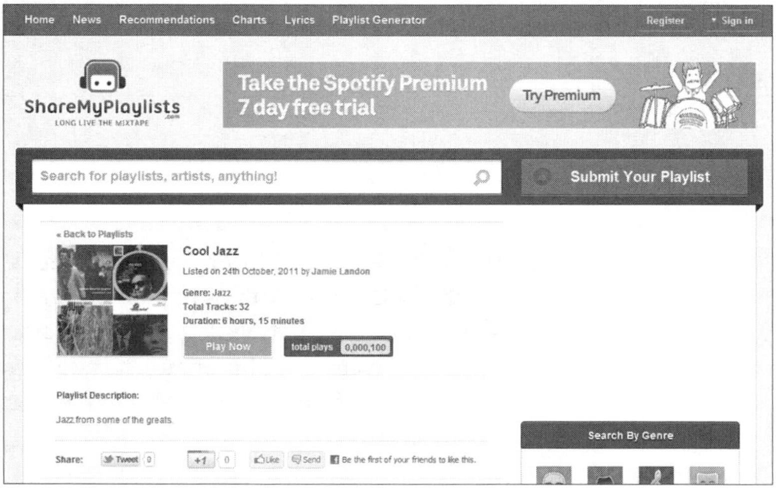

FIGURE 16.9
Listening to a playlist at ShareMyPlaylists.

Tips for Creating the Ultimate Playlist

So now you know how and where to create a playlist. We still haven't talked about what types of playlists you should create.

To that end, here are a baker's dozen tips that can help you create better playlists. (It's all about those rules, after all.)

1: Tag Tracks Before You List

The last thing you want is a rogue track in an otherwise orderly playlist. You can avoid putting the wrong tunes in the right playlists by making sure your tags are properly tagged before you start. That is, make sure each track is properly identified in terms of Title, Artist, Album, Genre, and such.

You can create even more interesting playlists if you also include some subsidiary tags for your tracks, such as Year, Composer(s), Mood, Initial Key, Beats Per Minute, and the like. Most music player and playlist builder programs will let you filter your library by any of these metadata fields.

> **ULTIMATELY INTERESTING** Since not all this metadata is added automatically when you rip or download a track, you may have to enter it manually. Learn more in Chapter 14, "Organizing Your Digital Music Collection."

2: Keep the Beat

When you're programming for a dance party, pay attention to the tempo of your selections. Assuming you want to switch seamlessly from one track to another, you'll need to select tracks with the same beats per minute (bpm). If you start mixing different bpms, you'll run the risk of interrupting the flow.

And here's an added, if somewhat obvious, tip. People like to dance to fast music, not slow. Program tracks between 120 and 140 bpm and you'll keep the feet on the floor better than if you go with slower tunes.

> **ULTIMATELY USEFUL** If a track's tempo isn't listed in the metadata, look it up at BPMdb (www.bpmdatabase.com). You can also use the MixMeister BPM Analyzer application (www.mixmeister.com/bpmanalyzer/bpmanalyzer.asp) to calculate an MP3's BPM and automatically add it to the file's ID3 metatdata.

16

16

3: Build a Mood

Professional DJs will tell you that the key to a successful set is building the appropriate mood. For example, if you want a playlist for a romantic evening with your significant other, include a lot of slow songs and forget the death metal stuff. If you're programming for a dance party, ditch the Michael Bolton and go with all up-tempo tunes.

You can get a head start on this if your tracks are properly tagged, as just discussed. Search on the Mood tag for tracks with the appropriate mood and then go from there.

4: Mix It Up

Yes, sometimes you want all the tracks in a playlist to convey a similar mood or be of the same tempo. Other times, however, you want to mix it up. Don't be afraid to include a little variety, to throw in the occasional fast song in a slow mix, or inspirational song in a blue playlist. Variety is often a good thing.

Along the same lines, you shouldn't always limit tracks in a playlist to the same genre. I'm guessing you like music across multiple genres; why not go a little JACK-FM and do some cross-genre programming? It'll break up the monotony, and you'd be surprised how tracks from different genres can often relate to one another.

5: Program by Sub Genre

The tracks in your digital library are likely tagged by major genre—folk, rock, hip hop, country, and the like. But chances are your tastes are bit more refined, so you often want to listen to a more targeted selection within the major genre.

Here's where playlist building comes in. When you'd rather listen to chamber pop or cowpunk instead of the more general pop or rock categories, you can create your own playlists containing tracks within the desired subgenre. It'll take a bit of work—you'll need to select each track individually; there's no metadata you can sort by—but you'll appreciate the results.

6: Program by Activity

This is another obvious one, but it's often useful to create playlists suitable for listening to while you're performing a specific activity. You can create playlists for studying, exercising, reading, shopping, driving, or just relaxing after dinner. Consider what things you do most often and what kind of music works best for those situations.

7: Consider the Length

When you're creating digital playlists, the temptation is to include as many similar songs as you can; there's no artificial limit on total length as there was when creating mixtapes on audiocassette. That said, you may want to consider the length of the playlist, and match it to the length of a given activity. For example, if you're hosting a party you expect to last for three hours, create a three hour-long playlist. Or if your daily run lasts 45 minutes, create a series of 45 minute-long playlists. When the playlist ends, your activity is over.

8: Put Tracks in Multiple Playlists

This should go without saying, but you don't have to put a given track in just one playlist. Any track in your library can be included in any number of playlists; playlist contents are not mutually exclusive. So "Sugar, Sugar" can go in both the Bubblegum and '60s Hits playlists, if you like.

9: Discover New Music Online

You might think you know everything there is to know about a particular genre or artist. But chances are there's a lot of music you've yet to discover, both new and catalog. Subscribe to your friends' feeds to find out what they're listening to, on both social networks and playlist sharing sites. I'm betting you'll find something new you like—or rediscover something older you'd forgotten about.

10: Share Your Playlist with Friends

Just as you can discover new music by listening to your friends' playlists, they can hear new music by listening to the playlists you create. To that end, take advantage of the playlist sharing sites discussed earlier in this chapter, as well as the ability to share via Facebook, Google+, Twitter, and other social networks. We live in a social world now, and music is a part of that sharing.

11: Experience Serendipity

I'm a big believer in serendipity, so here's a tip I particularly like. When you're searching for tunes to add to a playlist, just type in the beginning of a title

16

and let your software do the auto-complete thing. You might be pleasantly surprised with the suggestions your software makes—and find some interesting tracks you weren't otherwise thinking of.

12: Don't Stop Editing

A playlist isn't set in stone until you say it is. You can always add new tracks to an older playlist when you buy or download a new CD; you can also delete tracks from an existing playlist if you decide they really don't work that well. There's nothing that says you can't keep editing a playlist forever, if that's your want.

13: Get Creative

Yes, playlists are often used to convey or set a mood, but sometimes they can just be fun. Consider different ways that different tracks relate to one another, and build some interesting playlists in this fashion. For example, how about a playlist with songs that have the day of the week in the title? Or songs that begin with the letter "p?" Or songs about the weather? Or songs that all run under two and a half minutes long? You get the idea—and have some fun with it!

AN ODE TO THE HUMBLE MIXTAPE

I love the book (and the equally charming movie) *High Fidelity*, by Nick Hornby. In the characters of Rob Fleming and his oddball record store pals, Hornby captured the essence of the obsessive music lover—and extolled the joys of creating the perfect mixtape:

"To me, making a tape is like writing a letter—there's a lot of erasing and rethinking and starting again. A good compilation tape, like breaking up, is hard to do. You've got to kick off with a corker, to hold the attention (I started with 'Got to Get You Off My Mind,' but then realized that she might not get any further than track one, side one if I delivered what she wanted straightaway, so I buried it in the middle of side two), and then you've got to up it a notch, or cool it a notch, and you can't have white music and black music together, unless the white music sounds like black music, and you can't have two tracks by the same artist side by side, unless you've done the whole thing in pairs and...oh, there are loads of rules."

The mixtape is the analog predecessor of today's digital playlist. You recorded a mixtape on audiocassette, of course, by playing one song after another from one album after another. You had to plan it out in advance, and try to get the timing to come out just right, so you didn't cut off the last song mid-chorus or end up with too much blank space at the end of a side. And, as record store owner Rob Fleming opined, "there are lots of rules" in terms of which tracks you select and how you program them.

In comparison, it's almost too easy to put together a playlist today. A few drag and drops of your mouse and it's done, you don't have to worry about overall timing or bother with actually listening to each song as you record it to the mix. The result is a plethora of uninspired mixes, most overly long and overly inclusive, the stuff of background music, not of inspiration.

Contrast today's insipid playlists with the personal genius of mixtapes in their day. A great mixtape created a mood, had a personality, expressed a point of view. It showed off the musical knowledge and experience of its maker, in the way that certain tracks were chosen and contrasted with each other. The best mixtapes took you on a journey, complete with emotional peaks and release, much the way the best albums of the time delivered a complete musical experience from start to finish. There was a degree of skill involved, to be sure.

Today's playlists, while purportedly serving much the same function, deliver a much different experience. It isn't just the ease of which they're created, it's the method in which we listen to them, typically with the songs shuffled randomly. This sort of arbitrary listening order belies any attempt to define a listening experience; at best, you get to experience some degree of serendipity from the indiscriminate play-back order of the tracks selected, but more often than not it just becomes a random assortment of songs.

To recreate the old school mixtape experience, you'd have to limit the number of tracks in a playlist and dictate non-shuffle playback. But who does that, these days? Indeed, who sits and actually listens to music anymore, without multi-tasking with a book, iPad, or television show? Who takes music seriously today?

16

16

Well, I do. And I miss the blood, the sweat, and yes, the tears that went into creating a heartfelt mixtape. Remembering those good old days almost makes me want to create a top five list of my favorite mix-tapes—which is something I imagine Rob from *High Fidelity* could do with ease.

PART

IV

Streaming Music

Understanding Streaming Music

For music collectors, it's about building a library of the music you love—which means downloading or ripping your favorite tunes and albums. But there's another way to listen to a lot of music, if you don't mind not adding it to your permanent collection.

I'm talking about listening to streaming music over the Internet, which is the online equivalent of listening to AM and FM radio stations. In some instances, you choose the music you want to listen to; in other cases, you just sit back and listen to whatever's served up—just like old school radio.

What's different about streaming music is that you don't download or rip any files to your computer; it all comes at you in real time via any device connected to the Internet. (Not just your computer…) Streaming music is becoming more popular every day, and you need to consider it as part of your online music mix.

Understanding Streaming Audio

There are two basic ways to listen to digital music. The first requires the creation, either via download or CD ripping, of an audio file, which is then loaded into a media player program and played from start to finish. The second, called *streaming audio,* serves up tunes in real time over the Internet, much the same way music is broadcast over the radio airwaves.

Streaming audio uses many of the same technologies found in traditional audio files, but streams those digital bits and bytes over an Internet connection to your computer, smartphone, or other device. You don't have to wait for a file to download before you can start listening, nor do you have to allocate disc space to store all the music you listen to. For many listeners, it's the perfect way to hear a wide variety of music—at a relatively low cost.

How Streaming Audio Works

Streaming audio is the Internet equivalent of broadcasting music from one central point to multiple listeners. It works by sending multiple packets of data from the broadcasting server. Playback starts as soon as the first packet is received; other packets follow in a continuous stream. The process is much faster than waiting for a traditional audio file to download.

A good way to think of streaming audio versus normal file downloads is to envision a glass placed under a faucet. Normally, you'd turn on the faucet, fill the glass with water, and then take your drink. This is the way normal file downloads work; you can't access the file (drink the glass of water) until the file is completely downloaded (the glass is completely full).

With streaming audio, however, you can access the stream immediately. This is the equivalent of placing your head under the faucet and drinking directly from the tap; there's no glass to fill up first.

Streaming media can be either live or on demand. The former is used to broadcast concerts and other live performances; the latter is used by most streaming music services and Internet radio stations. In most instances, all you have to do is sign into the service from your computer or other device and select what you want to listen to; streaming commences within a few seconds.

Compromises and Requirements

As we've talked throughout this book, you often have to make compromises in audio quality to reduce the size of the audio files you download or rip. This is also true of streaming audio, where the audio is often of lower quality than what you'd expect from other formats.

Streaming fidelity is dependent on the format (AAC, WMA, etc.) and bitrate of the stream. In general, streaming music services want a smaller packet size so that the streaming music can play back as smoothly as possible. You end up sacrificing some degree of quality to ensure a faster streaming playback— although different services often make different choices in this regard.

As you might suspect, the faster your Internet connection, the smoother the streaming playback. If you try to listen to streaming audio on anything less than a broadband connection, you'll likely experience herky-jerky playback and frequent pauses and freezes. It's definitely not for dial-up.

Streaming audio also isn't for those with inconsistent Internet connections, however. If your connection goes down (or if you don't have Internet access), you can't listen to any streaming music. Sigh.

Fortunately, you don't need any special hardware on your PC, beyond a standard sound card and speakers, to listen to or watch streaming media. Most streaming music services play back in your web browser; others have their own software you have to install first to access the services.

In addition, streaming music is becoming increasingly popular on portable devices, which have limited storage space for large music collections. It's relatively easy to "dial into" a streaming music service or Internet radio station on your iPhone or similar device, and listen to your favorite music wherever you happen to be at the moment.

That said, there's a definite downside of listening to streaming music on a portable device, in the form of excess data usage charges. All those tunes you stream eat up what bytes you have in your mobile provider's data plan—at least when you're not connected via Wi-Fi. Overdo the 3G listening and you'll end up paying by the minute for the excess. (It's interesting that all the mobile services try to get you to buy smartphones and sign up for data plans, but then get all upset when you actually use that data.)

> **♪ ULTIMATELY USEFUL** One of the drawbacks of streaming audio, at least to serious collectors, is that the music is transitory; there's nothing to download or store. What do you do, then, when you hear something on a streaming music service or Internet radio station that you'd like to save? Check out Tubemaster++ (www.tubemaster.net), an application that lets you grab audio (or video) from any Flash-based web page. You can use it to record most streaming audio that plays from within your web browser (but not from standalone applications, such as Spotify's). In addition, if you're interested in saving Internet radio broadcasts for posterity, use Screamer Radio (www.screamer-radio.com) to both listen and record Internet radio.

17

Exploring Streaming Music Online

There are two primary types of delivery services for streaming audio over the Internet. You can listen to music from a streaming music service, or from an Internet radio station. (And, yes, there is some overlap between the two.)

Streaming Music Services

A streaming music service is typically a paid service that lets you listen to an unlimited amount of music, via streaming audio, for a flat monthly subscription fee. (Some call these "all you can eat" plans.) Most services let you browse or search for specific tracks or albums, or music by a given artist or in a given genre. Some services let you create playlists of your favorite tracks; some even create custom "radio stations" based on your listening habits. A few services are social in nature, in that they let you share your favorite music with friends on Facebook and other social networks.

Table 17.1 compares the most popular streaming music services today.

Table 17.1   Streaming Music Services

Service	URL	Price	Selection (number of tracks available)	Bitrate
Grooveshark	www.grooveshark.com	$6.00-$9.00/month, plus free plan	15 million	128Kbps-320Kbps
Last.fm	www.last.fm	Free	12 million	192Kbps
MOG	www.mog.com	$4.99-$9.99/month, plus free plan	14 million	320Kbps
Pandora Radio	www.pandora.com	Free	900,000	192Kbps
Raditaz	www.raditaz.com	Free	14 million	N/A
Rara.com	www.rara.com	$4.99-$9.99/month	10 million	72Kbps
Rdio	www.rdio.com	$4.99-$9.99/month, plus free plan	12 million	"Up to 320Kbps"
Rhapsody	www.rhapsody.com	$9.99-$14.99/month	14 million	128Kbps
Slacker Radio	www.slacker.com	$3.99-$9.99/month, plus free plan	8 million	128Kbps
Spotify	www.spotify.com	$4.99-$9.99/month, plus free plan	15 million	160Kbps/320Kbps (Premium plan)
Turntable.fm	www.turntable.fm	Free	11 million	128Kbps
Zune Music Pass	www.zune.net	$9.99/month	11 million	192Kbps

Internet Radio

There's a fuzzy line between streaming music services and Internet radio stations. The way I like to think of it, streaming music services let you pick your own music to listen to, whereas Internet radio stations determine which songs they broadcast. That is, streaming music services are all about you making the choice, where Internet radio stations make the choice for you.

ULTIMATELY **INTERESTING** Learn more about Spotify in Chapter 18, "Listening to Music with Spotify." Learn more about Last.fm and Pandora in Chapter 33, "Discovering New Music with Last.fm and Pandora Radio." And learn more about the other streaming music services in Chapter 19, "Listening to Music with Other Streaming Music Services."

Just as there are all different formats of terrestrial radio stations, there are also all manner of Internet radio stations. You can find stations that specialize in just about every musical genre, and then some. Some stations broadcast audio books, others news and opinion. There are even a lot of terrestrial radio stations that simulcast over the Internet, which is a great way to listen to stations that you can't pick up on your local AM or FM radio.

Tuning into an Internet radio station is as easy as clicking a link in your web browser. One benefit of Internet radio over traditional radio is that many Internet radio stations display the title and artist of the currently playing song right on your computer screen. In addition, many Internet radio sites let you create your own custom "stations," based on your own listening preferences.

ULTIMATELY **INTERESTING** Learn more about Internet radio in Chapter 21, "Listening to Internet Radio."

Cloud-Based Music Services

Then we have the newest type of streaming audio service, those based in the cloud. Cloud-based music services stream your own music back to you over the Internet, on any device wherever you might happen to be.

To do this you first have to create a cloud-based library, or upload your ripped and downloaded tracks to the service; your music is stored on a collection of Internet-based servers dubbed the "cloud." When you want to listen, the music is streamed from the cloud servers to your Internet-connected computer or device.

17

There are a number of big players competing in the cloud music market—Amazon, Apple, and Google among them. The ability to listen to your own library when you're away from home is appealing; the fact that it's accomplished via a combination of cloud storage and streaming audio technology makes it interesting.

> ♪ ULTIMATELY **INTERESTING** Learn more about cloud-based streaming audio in Chapter 20, "Accessing Your Music in the Cloud."

STREAMING AUDIO FOR THE SERIOUS MUSIC LOVER

Where does streaming audio fit into the pantheon of digital music options? It's probably different if you're a casual listener than if you're a true enthusiast.

For casual listeners, streaming music services are godsends. For a low monthly fee (or free, in some instances), you get to listen to music whenever you want, wherever you happen to be. Whether you want background music while you're studying or something funkier for an upcoming party, listening to streaming music is as easy as tuning the dial on an FM radio. In fact, that's the comparison; streaming audio is just like listening to AM or FM radio, but with more channels available and the ability (in some instances) to customize your own channels. It's all the music you can listen to, served to you in real time.

The true music lover, however, will be less enthusiastic, for a number of reasons.

First, streaming music is not audiophile quality. Far from it, as a matter of fact. For example, most Internet radio stations stream between 64Kbps and 128Kbps, which is well below CD quality. Now, the paid music services are a little better, streaming between 128Kbps and 320Kbps, but the sound quality is still notably compressed compared to any lossless files you've ripped from CD—definitely not music to an audiophile's golden ears.

Then there's the issue of not actually owning the music you listen to. I know, you don't own the music you listen to on FM radio, either, but we're talking about the appeal to collectors here. With streaming music, there's nothing to collect. It's all rather transitory.

That said, I think that streaming music services have some appeal to music lovers—including collectors. For a relatively low monthly fee (or free, in some instances), you get exposure to a large variety of music, including a ton of new music. Personally, I use streaming audio not to listen to my favorite tunes (I already have them in my own collection) but rather to discover new music. Maybe that's a new artist I've been hearing some buzz about, perhaps it's a new album from an artist I'm familiar with but on the fence about. In any case, I can listen for free (more or less) and then determine whether I want to buy the album and add it to my collection.

In addition, many streaming services are great for social sharing online. Want to spread the news about a great new album? Listen to it on Spotify or another service and then share it via Facebook to the world at large. In return, your friends will share their latest discoveries—which, again, you can decide to buy and add to your library. It's music sharing, pure and simple.

Will streaming music services replace music downloads? Not for the true audiophile or collector, that's for sure—although it may be a different story for the casual listener. But even golden-eared collectors can find something to like with these streaming services; it's another option for music lovers everywhere.

17

Listening to Music with Spotify

S potify is arguably the fastest-growing streaming music service today. It lets you stream music to any computer or mobile device, so you can listen to all the music you like anyplace you happen to be.

Spotify offers a combination of a large music library, relatively high bitrate streaming, and easy social sharing. That makes the service attractive to digital music lovers everywhere—and worth a further examination.

Getting to Know Spotify

Spotify is a relatively new music service, at least in the U.S. It launched on our shores in July of 2011, but has been around in Europe for a lot longer; it went live in Sweden way back in October of 2008, and has more than 10 million European users. That makes Spotify one of the world's largest online music services, right up there with iTunes and Pandora.

Of course, Spotify isn't at all like iTunes; instead of offering tracks for sale and download, it streams all the music in its library to any computer or device connected to the Internet, for a low monthly fee. Currently, Spotify offers more than 15 million individual tracks for streaming, from all four major music labels and a large number of independent labels. You can find everything from the latest pop and hip-hop hits to classic rock tunes, country and blue-grass, and even jazz and classical music.

One of the unique features of Spotify is that it can consolidate its online music database with music you've previously downloaded or ripped to your PC. When you first install the Spotify software, it scans your hard disk for existing tracks and creates a Local Files library. You can then create playlists that combine tunes on your PC with tunes you stream from Spotify.

Spotify also does a good job on the social sharing front. It integrates tightly with Facebook and can automatically post everything you listen to to your Facebook account. You can also easily share your favorite tracks and albums with friends via Facebook, Twitter, and email.

Subscribing and Getting Started

To use the Spotify music service, you first have to sign up as a subscriber. Spotify offers three levels of subscription access, ranging in price from free to $9.99 per month. The more you pay, the more music you get to listen to.

The three plans are as follows:

- **Free**. No doubt the most popular plan, because you don't have to pay anything to use it. This plan displays occasional ads in the application and comes with some limitations—there's no mobile version, you can't use it in offline mode, and you're limited to 10 hours of listening each month. (Although you get unlimited streaming for the first six months of your subscription.)

- **Unlimited**. This plan costs $4.99 per month, and eliminates both the ads from the interface and the listening time limit. With this plan you can listen to your music as long and as often as you like. However, there is still no mobile component to this plan.

- **Premium**. This is Spotify's ultimate plan, at $9.99 per month. This plan gives you everything you get with the Unlimited plan and adds access via your mobile devices, as well as the ability to listen to your own music while offline. You also get enhanced sound quality (up to 320Kbps), which makes all your music sound better, and the ability to play Spotify through whole house media players, such as those offered by Sonos, Squeezebox, and Boxee.

To use Spotify, you have to first download the Spotify application for your computer. You do so by going to www.spotify.com and clicking the **Download Spotify** button. Follow the instructions from there to get up and running. (You also need to have a Facebook account, which you use to log into the new service.)

> 🎵 ULTIMATELY **INTERESTING**   At present, the Spotify software is available for computers running the Windows XP/Vista/7 and Mac OS X 10.5.0 or higher operating systems.

Getting Around Spotify

When you launch Spotify, the application opens and connects via the Internet to the Spotify service. You need to be connected to use Spotify; all the music you listen to is streamed live over the Internet.

As you can see in Figure 18.1, the Spotify application consists of several panes and sections, as follows:

FIGURE 18.1

The Spotify program.

■ **Menu bar**, with five pull-down menus for access to specific functionality.

■ **Navigation bar**, with right and left arrows for moving back and forward through the site, as well as a Search box to search for music to listen to.

■ **Navigation pane**, on the left side of the window, which provides access to a variety of features and functions; click an item in this pane to display specific content in the center content pane. The three primary section of the navigation pane are Main (What's New, People, Inbox, Play Queue, and Devices), Apps (access to Spotify's add-on apps), and Collection (access to your personal library and playlists). At the bottom of the navigation pane is the now playing section—the album cover for the track you're currently listening to.

■ **Main content pane**, in the center of the window, which displays whatever content is selected in the navigation pane.

■ **People list**, on the right side of the window. The top half of this pane displays your favorite friends—those Spotify and Facebook friends you've opted to share music with. The bottom half of the pane displays tracks recently listened to by these friends.

■ **Playback controls**, at the very bottom of the window. Use these controls to play and pause playback.

Importing Local Files into Spotify

One of the unique aspects of Spotify is that it blends a typical streaming music service with the playback of music you have stored on your own PC. This way you can supplement Spotify's 15 million-track library with other tracks that you own and aren't available from Spotify.

Importing Files

Spotify lets you import tracks you've either downloaded to your PC from other websites or ripped from CDs you've purchased. In fact, when you first install the Spotify software, it automatically scans your hard disk for existing tracks and creates a Local Files library. You can then create playlists that combine tunes on your PC with tunes you stream from Spotify.

> ♪ ULTIMATELY
> **INTERESTING** Spotify lets you import music files in the universal .mp3 format, as well as Apple's .m4a (AAC) format—which means you can consolidate your entire iTunes library into Spotify. Unfortunately, Spotify is not compatible with Windows' .wma audio file format, nor can it import files in FLAC and other lossless formats.

You can also configure Spotify to manually import tunes stored anywhere on your PC. Just select **Edit** > **Preferences** to display the Preferences page, then scroll to the Local files section and check those locations that contain music you want to import. Spotify will then automatically scan that location for compatible files and import them into the library.

> ♪ ULTIMATELY **INTERESTING**   When Spotify "imports" a file into its library, it doesn't actually upload that file onto Spotify's servers. Instead, it links its library to that file on your computer's hard drive. For this reason, you can play local files only on the computer on which they reside, not on other computers connected to the Spotify service.

Viewing and Playing Imported Music

All of the files you import from your computer are stored in Spotify's Local Files library. To view the files you've imported, select **Local Files** in the Collection section of Spotify's navigation pane. All imported files are flagged by an icon of a musical note.

To play a local file, you have to be logged onto Spotify from the computer that hosts that file. You can then initiate playback in the normal fashion (discussed shortly).

Listening to Local Files on Your Mobile Device

You can also use your compatible mobile device to listen to local files stored on your computer—if both your PC and mobile device are connected to the same Wi-Fi network.

To listen to local files on your mobile device, you first have to create a playlist on your computer that contains the local music you want to listen to on your mobile device. Then connect your mobile device to the same Wi-Fi network that your computer is connected to and launch the Spotify app on your device. Mark the newly created playlist as an Offline Playlist, and that playlist will now be available for playback on your mobile device.

Viewing and Playing Music

The first link in the Collection section of Spotify's navigation pane is for the Library. This is not Spotify's library, but rather *your* library. This is where Spotify lists your personal music, including playlists you've created or listened to, favorite tracks you've "starred," and local tracks you've imported into Spotify.

In short, the Library is the master collection of your favorite and personal music. It does not contain all 15 million tracks in Spotify's database—just those tracks and playlists you like best.

To view the Library, click **Library** in the Collections section of Spotify's navigation pane. As you can see in Figure 18.2, each track listed displays a variety of information, including the track name, recording artist, time, and album name.

FIGURE 18.2
The Spotify Library.

Playing an Individual Track

Wherever you find music in Spotify, playing an individual song is relatively easy. In fact, there are three ways to start playback of a given track:

- Double-click the track name.
- Right-click the track name and select **Play** from the pop-up menu.
- Select (single-click) the track name and then click the **Play** button in the transport controls.

The track you're currently playing is highlighted in the now playing area at the bottom of the navigation pane. You can control playback by using the transport controls at the bottom of the Spotify window.

Playing an Album

Playing an entire album is just as easy as playing individual tracks. To play all the tracks from an album, simply navigate to the album, right-click the **album's name** or **cover**, and select **Play**.

Alternatively, you can double-click the album name or cover to open the album page, like the one shown in Figure 18.3. From here you initiate playback by right-clicking the **album cover** and selecting **Play**. (If you double-click a single track within an album list, only that track will play back.)

> **ULTIMATELY USEFUL** To play an album's tracks in their original order, make sure you deactivate Spotify's shuffle mode by clicking "off" the **Shuffle** button at the lower right corner of the application win-

> **ULTIMATELY INTERESTING** Many classic albums feature an in-depth review of the recording. Most newer albums do not.

FIGURE 18.3
Viewing an album page.

Playing Music in a Queue

You can play back one track at a time, or select multiple tracks to add to a temporary playback *queue*. All tracks you add to a queue are played back in order of when they were added—unless you're in shuffle mode, of course, then tracks are played back in random order.

To add one or more tracks to a queue, select those tracks then right-click and select **Queue** from the pop-up menu. To view your current queue, select **Play Queue** in the Main section of the navigation pane.

All the tracks you've queued up are listed on the Play Queue page. Queued tracks will play immediately following the currently playing track; after all tracks in the queue are done playing, playback of the currently selected album or track will resume.

Viewing Artist Information

Recording artists are all over Spotify. Every track you play, every album you open, has at least one artist associated with it.

For example, all the tracks in your Library have an associated Artist column. Every track in a playlist has a similar Artist column. Even the Tracks and Albums lists on the Top Lists page have artists associated with each track or album.

You can also search Spotify for specific artists. Just enter the artist's name into the search box at the top of the Spotify window, then select the artist from the resulting drop-down list.

To view more information about a given artist, all you have to do is click the artist's name, wherever it appears on Spotify. This displays the artist page, like the one shown in Figure 18.4. From here you can read a brief overview or a detailed biography of the artist, as well as view related artists—which is a good way to discover new music.

18

FIGURE 18.4
Viewing an artist page.

Listening to Spotify Radio

Spotify Radio is a special app built into the Spotify service. It lets you create virtual radio stations based on a single track or artist. These radio stations include music similar to the track or artist you selected—including other music by the original artist. The station's music streams to your computer over the Internet, and you can easily skip from track to track as you listen.

Spotify creates radio stations based on its intelligent recommendation engine. It uses what it knows about a given track and artist to identify other similar music, and adds those tracks to the station. You'll probably hear a lot of artists you've never listened to before—which makes Spotify Radio a great way to discover new music.

Creating a New Radio Station

There are a number of different ways to create a new Spotify Radio station. Here are a few:

- Drag a track from any Spotify listing, such as your Library, onto the Radio item in the Apps section of Spotify's navigation pane.

- Go to any track listing, right-click a given track, then select **Start Radio**.
- Go to any artist page and click the **Start Artist Radio** link at the top of the page.
- Click **Radio** in the Apps section of Spotify's navigation pane. When the Radio page appears, click the **Create a New Station** button. When the search pane appears, enter the name or an artist or song, then select the matching track or artist from the pull-down list.

Playing a Spotify Radio Station

When you create a new radio station, playback starts automatically. To view the current station, click **Radio** from the Apps section of the navigation pane. As you can see in Figure 18.5, the currently playing track is displayed at the top of this page. You can pause playback by hovering over the album artwork and clicking the **Pause** button; hover and click the **Play** button to resume playback.

FIGURE 18.5

Listening to a Spotify Radio station.

Artist and track information is displayed beneath the now playing artwork. To skip to the next track, click the **Fast Forward** button to the right of the album artwork.

At the bottom of the radio page is a list of the recent radio stations you've listened to. Click any given station thumbnail to begin listening to that station; click the right arrow at the top right of the stations list to view more stations you've created.

Working with Playlists

A Spotify playlist can include up to 10,000 individual tracks. Playlists can include tracks from multiple artists and albums, or can be constructed from tracks from a single artist.

Once you create a playlist, it is listed in the Collection section of Spotify's navigation pane. You can easily play back an entire playlist, either in the track order listed or in random order, by shuffling the tracks.

Creating a New Playlist

To create a new playlist, go to the Collection section of Spotify's navigation pane and click the **New Playlist** item. This creates a new unnamed playlist at the top of the playlist list. Enter a name for the playlist into the "New Playlist" text box then press Enter.

Adding Tracks to a Playlist

There are two ways to add new tracks to a playlist:

- Navigate to a track you wish to add, then use your mouse to drag and drop that track onto the name of the playlist in the navigation pane.

- Navigate to and right-click a track you wish to add. When the pop-up menu appears, select **Add To** and the name of the playlist.

Using either method, you can add multiple tracks at once by selecting more than one track first. To select consecutive tracks, hold down the Shift key while clicking; to select nonconsecutive tracks, hold down the Ctrl key while clicking. You can then right-click or drag the selected tracks to create a new playlist or to add tracks to an existing playlist.

Playing a Playlist

There are two ways to play a playlist. You can

- Right-click the playlist name in the navigation pane and click **Play** from the pop-up menu.

- Double-click the playlist name in the navigation pane.

18

With either approach, the playlist opens in the main content pane and begins playback. The currently playing track is indicated with a green speaker icon to the left of the track name. The number of tracks and total elapsed time of playback is displayed at the top of the pane, next to the playlist name.

> 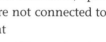 **ULTIMATELY USEFUL** While playing back a playlist, you can play the tracks in the original order added, or you can shuffle the playback—that is, play the tracks of the playlist in random order. To shuffle the playback, click the **Shuffle** button at the lower right corner of the Spotify window. (The button turns green when activated.)

Listening to Spotify Offline

Spotify is a streaming music service, which means that it feeds music over the Internet, in real time, to your computer or portable device. But what do you do if you don't have an Internet connection and still want to listen to music?

Good news—if you're a Premium or Ultimate subscriber, Spotify offers a special Offline mode, which works when you're not connected to the Internet. You decide in advance which playlists you want to listen to while you're offline, then those tracks are downloaded to your computer in advance. The next time your Internet connection is disconnected, Offline mode lets you play those playlists from within Spotify.

> **ULTIMATELY CAUTIOUS** Offline mode is not available for Free subscriptions.

As you can imagine, this is especially helpful when you know you're going to be without an Internet connection for some time. For example, Offline mode lets you listen to your favorite playlists when you're on an airplane or traveling in your car.

Spotify's Offline mode works with playlists only, not individual tracks. You can sync your Offline playlists for up to three devices at once—for example, your notebook computer, iPad, and iPhone. Spotify lets you sync a maximum of 3,333 individual tracks for Offline listening.

Making a Playlist Available for Offline Listening

You need to activate Offline mode for each playlist you want to listen to while offline. Start by clicking the playlist name in the navigation pane to open the playlist. At the top of the playlist page, click the **Available Offline** switch to the right, so that the green "available" icon is displayed.

Listening Offline

To listen to your selected playlists offline, you don't have to do a thing—other than sever your Internet connection, that is. When your computer isn't connected to the Internet and you open Spotify, it launches in Offline mode. This is indicated by an icon in the lower right corner of the window.

Playlists activated for Offline playback are indicated with a green down arrow icon. You can play the tracks in these playlists as you would normally. All other music is greyed out, and cannot be played until you re-establish an Internet connection.

Spotify will return to normal mode when you re-establish your Internet connection.

Sharing Your Music with Spotify Social

As the company goes to great lengths to point out, Spotify is more than just a music streaming service, it's a *social* music streaming service. That means you easily share the music you listen to with your friends—and they can share their music with you.

You can share music with other Spotify members, and with anyone on your Facebook friends list. (You actually sign into Spotify with your Facebook ID and password; this links your Spotify and Facebook accounts.) You can also share to your Twitter followers or to friends via email.

The key to social sharing is the concept of *friends*. You already know about Facebook's friends list; to share your favorite music, you need to assemble a similar list of your Spotify friends—what Spotify calls a *People list*. Your Spotify People list can include any other Spotify member, as well as anyone on your existing Facebook friends list.

Spotify displays your People list in the top half of the left-hand people pane. Sharing to a Spotify friend then becomes as easy as dragging a track to a name in the People list.

Adding Facebook Friends

Let's start by examining how you can add your Facebook friends to your Spotify People list. Assuming that you've signed into Spotify with your Facebook ID, and thus linked your Spotify and Facebook accounts, it's a relatively easy process.

18

Go to the Main section of the navigation pane and click **People**. This displays your entire Facebook friends list in the center content pane. To display only those friends who are already subscribing to Spotify, click **On Spotify** at the top of the pane.

Hover over the person you want to add and click the **Add Favorites** button; the selected friend is now added to your People list. To remove a person from your People list, right-click that person's name and select **Remove from Favorites** from the pop-up menu.

Adding Other Spotify Users

You can also add any other Spotify user to your People list. To do so, however, you need to know the person's Spotify user ID or otherwise locate them on the Spotify site; at present, there is no way to search Spotify's master user list.

To add a user to your People list, click through to this person's profile page, then click the **Add to Favorites** button at the top of the profile page. That's it.

Sharing Tracks

Sharing an individual track with a friend is quite easy. Just navigate to the track you want to share, right-click the track, and select **Share To** from the pop-up menu. When the sharing pop-up appears, as shown in Figure 18.6, select the tab for the service you want to share with. Enter a message to accompany the shared track, then click the **Share To** button.

FIGURE 18.6

Sharing music with your friends.

Sharing Albums

Sharing an entire album is similar to sharing a track. Navigate to and right-click the album you want to share, then select **Share To** from the pop-up menu. When the sharing pop-up appears, select the tab for the service you want to share with. Enter your message and then click the **Share To** button.

Sharing Playlists

To share a complete playlist, right-click the playlist in the navigation pane and select **Share To**. When the sharing pop-up appears, select the tab for how you want to share, enter an accompanying message, then click the **Share To** button.

Sharing Artists

To share your favorite artists, navigate to a track or album and click the artist name. When the artist page appears, click **Share** at the top of the page. When the sharing pop-up appears, select the tab for the service you want to share with, enter an accompanying message, and click the **Share To** button.

Sharing Everything You Listen To

Once you link your Spotify and Facebook accounts, everything you listen to on Spotify is sent to Facebook automatically. These tracks are displayed in your Facebook ticker, that piece of real-time real estate displayed in the top right corner of the Facebook News Feed page. The tracks you listen to also contribute to the Spotify gadget displayed on your Facebook profile or timeline page.

You don't have to do anything to have the music you listen to sent to Facebook in this fashion; it's automatic. You can, however, disable this feature if you feel that it's sharing a little too much. To disable this automatic sharing, select **Edit > Preferences**; when the Preferences page appears, go to the Activity Sharing section and uncheck the **Show What I Listen To on Facebook** option.

Collaborating on a Playlist

A *collaborative playlist* is one that you not only share with others, but that others can also edit. You and your friends all see the same playlist in the Collection section of your Spotify navigation panes; when one person makes a change to the playlist, that change appears in everyone's version of the playlist, in real time.

Collaborative playlists let multiple music lovers team up to share their musical likes and dislikes. It turns music curation into a team sport, and helps you build better playlists with the musical knowledge of others.

You can turn any playlist into a collaborative playlist. In the Collection section of the navigation pane, right-click the playlist you want to collaborate on and select **Collaborative Playlist** from the pop-up menu.

Now, return to the navigation pane, right-click the playlist, and select **Share To**. When the sharing pop-up appears, select the Spotify tab. Enter the person's name you want to share with into the To box, then enter an optional message into the Optional Message box. Click the **Send Playlist** button when done. (Obviously, your potential collaborator has to be a Spotify member to join in the fun.)

Your friend now receives a message in their Spotify inbox. When they open the message they see the playlist page. To collaborate on the playlist, they need to click **Subscribe** at the top of the playlist page.

Once they've subscribed to the collaborative playlist, your friends can add tracks to and delete tracks from the playlist. Their changes appear on your playlist page as they make them, as your changes appear on their versions of the playlist.

Extending Spotify with Apps

An app is a small application designed for a specific purpose. Spotify has opened its underlying technology platform so that other companies can develop apps for use by Spotify members. You can add apps to your version of the Spotify software that provide enhanced value when you're using Spotify.

There are more than a dozen apps currently available for Spotify, including the following:

- Billboard Top Charts
- Fuse
- Last.fm
- Moodagent
- Pitchfork
- Rolling Stone Recommends
- ShareMyPlaylists
- Songkick Concerts
- Soundrop
- Spotify Radio
- Spotify Top Lists
- The Guardian
- Top10
- TuneWiki
- We Are Hunted

Of these apps, I particularly like Last.fm (for discovering new music), Moodagent (for creating new playlists), Songkick Concerts (for finding out when my favorite artists are performing nearby), and TuneWiki (for displaying song lyrics onscreen).

To install a Spotify app, go to the Apps section of the navigation pane and click **App Finder**. This displays the App Finder page in the content pane, as shown in Figure 18.7. Navigate to any app you find interesting.

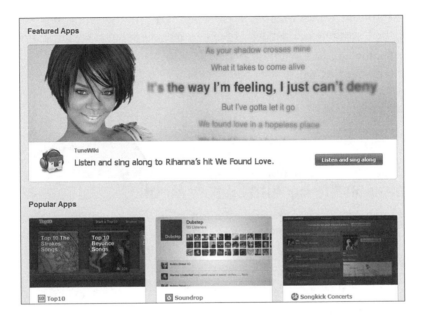

FIGURE 18.7

Discovering Spotify apps with the App Finder.

To learn more about a given app, click its title. This displays a dedicated page for that app, provided by the app's developer. To install an app, click the blue **Add** button in the top right. A link to that app is now added to the Apps section of the navigation sidebar.

Scrobbling to Last.fm

Spotify tightly integrates with Last.fm, to help you discover new music. Last.fm analyzes the music you listen to on Spotify and uses that information to recommend similar music you might like.

For this to work, you have to have a Last.fm account and then activate Last.fm scrobbling within Spotify. To do this, select **Edit** > **Preferences** to display the Preferences page. Go to the Activity Sharing section and check the **Scrobble to Last.fm** option. Enter your Last.fm username and password into the Username and Password boxes, and you're done.

Spotify will now send information about each track you play to Last.fm. You can then visit the Last.fm site to view your personalized recommendations—or use the Last.fm app within Spotify to the same effect.

> **ULTIMATELY INTERESTING** Learn more about Last.fm in Chapter 33, "Discovering New Music with Last.fm and Pandora Radio."

Listening on the Go with Spotify Mobile

If you subscribe to Spotify's Premium plan ($9.99/month), you can stream music from Spotify on your iPhone or other mobile device. You do this by installing the Spotify Mobile app for your device. Spotify has apps for the following smartphones and devices:

- iPhone and iPod Touch, shown in Figure 18.8
- Android
- Windows Phone
- Palm OS
- Blackberry
- Symbian

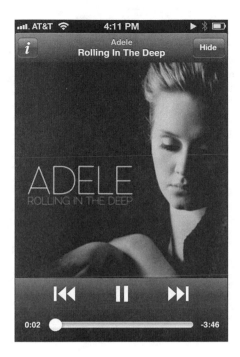

FIGURE 18.8
Listening to Spotify Mobile on an iPhone.

You can find the Spotify Mobile app in your phone's app store, or learn more online at www.spotify.com/mobile/.

WHY EVERYBODY LIKES SPOTIFY

Spotify is getting lots of attention and lots of new users. It's growing faster than any competing streaming music service. Why is this?

I could go on about Spotify having a larger library than its competitors (about a million tracks more, which really isn't that much), having better sound quality (not really true; you have to subscribe to the Premium plan to get the top 320Kbps streaming, and even then, not everything streams at that rate), and being so easy to use (not that much easier than its competitors—and a lot less easy than Raditaz or Rdio).

So what's really different about Spotify? It's the Facebook connection, pure and simple. To subscribe to Spotify, you have to have a Facebook account, and sign in with your Facebook ID and password. From there on out, Spotify is tightly connected to Facebook, posting each track played to Facebook's news feed and timeline.

This is how many new users hear about Spotify—by seeing Spotify-related (actually, Spotify-created) posts by their friends. Obviously, Spotify makes it easy for Facebookers to join up and start listening, and once they're hooked, they're hooked. I doubt Spotify would be this popular without the close integration with the world's largest social network.

Spotify's free plan also plays a part. Free is always good, and even better when you get unlimited streaming for the first six months. After that, you're throttled back to just 10 hours of listening per month, which will either turn off a lot of users or get them to pony up $4.99/month to continue the unlimited streaming. In any case, signing up from Facebook for free is what's appealing; the fact that Spotify does everything else reasonably well is probably enough to make everybody happy—at least until something better comes along.

18

Listening to Music with Other Streaming Music Services

I n the previous chapter we discussed Spotify, one of the most popular streaming music services. But they're not the only streaming music service out there; you actually have a lot more choices available, at a variety of monthly price points. (Including free!)

Let's look, then, at the remaining big music streaming services. Who knows—you might find something you like better.

Grooveshark

With more than 35 million users, Grooveshark (www.grooveshark.com) is one of the largest and most established music services out there. It offers an ad-supported free plan, which has appeal. You can also pay $6/month to get rid of the ads, or $9/month if you want access on your mobile device.

Grooveshark, shown in Figure 19.1, has a 15 million-track library, which is among the largest of these streaming services. The sound quality varies wildly, however, depending on what bitrate a track was uploaded at; some tracks sound great at 320Kbps, others not so much, at 128Kbps or less.

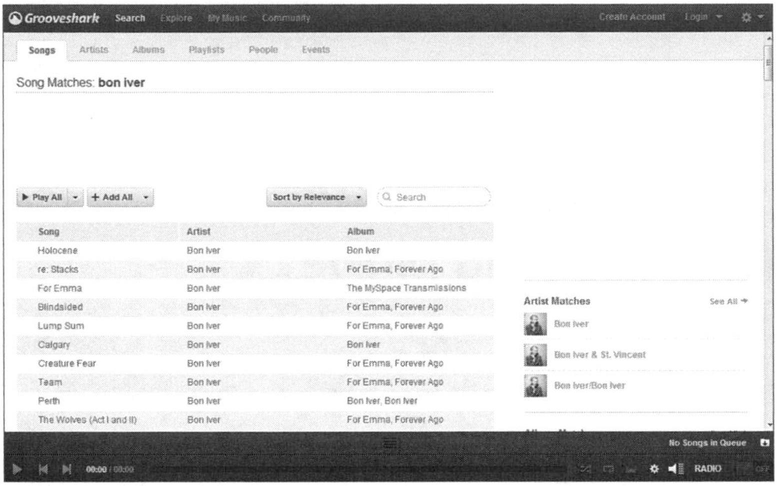

FIGURE 19.1

Searching for music on Grooveshark.

The variance in bitrate is because not all tracks come from the labels themselves. Users can upload their own MP3 rips to the site, as long as Grooveshark has authorization to offer those songs to its members. It's kind of a mish mash, if you ask me, but does allow for some music you can't find on other sites.

For mobile listeners paying that $9/month subscription, you can access Grooveshark from iOS, Android, Blackberry, Windows Phone 7, and Palm devices. Any user can create and share playlists with others; the site also offers genre- and artist-based radio stations.

ULTIMATELY INTERESTING Grooveshark operates in a legal grey area, as witnessed by the plethora of user uploads coexisting with licensed product from various record labels. That said, the company is currently being sued by EMI Music Publishing, Sony Music Entertainment, Universal Music, and Warner Music Group—all the major labels, in other words. Charges vary from label to label, ranging from general copyright infringement to not paying royalties due. We'll see how it all plays out.

Last.fm

Last.fm (www.last.fm) has a decent sized library (around 12 million tracks), charges no subscription fees, and has a large and loyal customer base, with more than 30 million active users. But Last.fm does more than just stream music; it also serves as a first-class music recommendation service. In fact, Last.fm was designed to introduce listeners to new music, based on their current musical tastes, and it does a fine job of it.

Last.fm is a free service, at least in the U.S., the U.K., and Germany. (You have to pay 3 Euros a month outside these countries.) Music is streamed at an acceptable 192Kbps rate. Last.fm offers apps for the iPhone/iPad, Android, Windows Phone 7, and Blackberry devices.

> **♪ ULTIMATELY INTERESTING** We'll discuss Last.fm in detail in Chapter 33, "Discovering New Music with Last.fm and Pandora Radio." Turn there to learn more.

MOG

MOG (www.mog.com) receives a lot of critical plaudits, and for good reason. It offers high quality playback (320Kbps), a good selection of music (14 million tracks and growing), and a reasonable subscription price ($4.99/month for listening on your PC; $9.99/month if you add mobile devices). There are MOG apps for iOS and Android.

As you can see in Figure 19.2, MOG is an easy service to use, and does a good job of recommending new music based on your past listening habits. MOG even creates automatic playlists based on any artist you select.

19

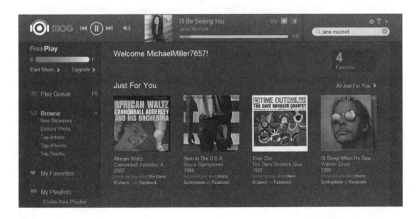

FIGURE 19.2

Listening to high-quality music on MOG.

All that said, MOG's claim to fame is its audio quality. As noted, MOG uses 320Kbps streaming, which is as good as you can get today. You can also tell that MOG encodes its music with care; when it's good, it's very, very good, and when it's bad, it's good enough. Suffice to say, if you're an audiophile, MOG is likely to be your service of choice.

Pandora Radio

Pandora Radio (www.pandora.com) is an old hand at the streaming music biz. Like Last.fm, Pandora is as much a music recommendation service as it is a traditional streaming music service, creating "stations" based on artists or songs you select. You help fine-tune the recommendations by giving each suggested track a thumbs up or thumbs down rating.

Pandora's library is relatively small compared to the competition, at just under a million tracks. The service is free, however, and you get your music streamed at 192Kbps. Pandora has mobile apps for iOS, Android, BlackBerry, and Palm devices—but not Windows Phone 7.

> ♪ **ULTIMATELY INTERESTING**   We'll discuss Pandora in detail in Chapter 33, "Discovering New Music with Last.fm and Pandora Radio." Turn there to learn more.

Raditaz

Raditaz (www.raditaz.com) is the newest kid on the streaming music block. Launched in January of 2012, Raditaz takes direct aim at Pandora with a completely free service.

At launch, Raditaz had a 14 million-track library, which is pretty good. It works by creating on-the-fly "stations" for a specific artist, genre, year, or the like. You can easily share the stations you create via Facebook, Twitter, or email.

As you can see in Figure 19.3, Raditaz offers a fairly simple (some might say too simple) interface, with big buttons and cover art. It offers apps for iOS and Android phones.

As I write this, Raditaz is actually a little too new to get a firm grip on its pros and cons. (For example, I have no idea what bitrate they're using; the company hasn't published this spec yet.) It does promise no advertisements, which sounds good but makes you wonder how they plan to make money.

19

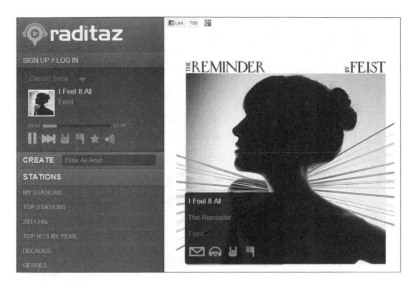

FIGURE 19.3

The newest streaming music service, Raditaz.

Rara.com

Rara.com (www.rara.com) is another new service, launched in December of 2011. On the surface, Rara.com (www.rara.com) looks a lot like other streaming music services. After a low-priced (99 cents/month) initial three month trial period, you pay $4.99/month for web access or $9.99 ($1.99/month for first three months) for web plus mobile access. (Rara offers iOS and Android apps.) The U.K.-based service launched with 10 million or so songs in its library, which is a little behind the curve these days. Rara.com is aimed at less technical users, which explains the image-heavy interface, shown in Figure 19.4. It relies heavily on curated playlists, which it dubs "stations," thus taking some of the serendipity out of the process—which might be fine for the target audience. The emphasis is certainly on ease of use.

As to audio quality, here's where it gets a little interesting. Technically, Rara streams its web music at 72Kbps, which would appear to offer substandard quality compared to the 192Kbps and better you find with several other services. However, Rara uses Dolby Pulse encoding, which delivers higher fidelity than other formats at the same bitrate. Still, you're looking at sound quality comparable to 128Kbps-192Kbps streaming from other services—not quite as good as the 320Kbps you get from MOG and Spotify Premium.

19

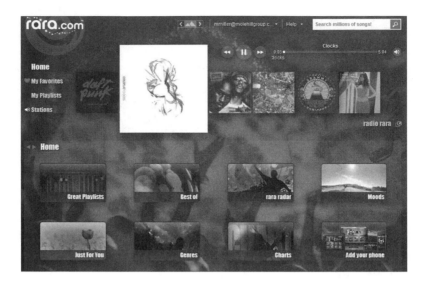

FIGURE 19.4

Rara.com, another new streaming service.

Rdio

Rdio (ww.rdio.com) has a nice pedigree, launched in 2010 by the founders of Skype and KaZaA. (It's actually owned by Skype.) It's a decent service, with the typical $4.99/month subscription plan ($9.99/month for mobile access) and over 12 million songs in its database. Oh, there's also a free plan, which serves a limited number of songs per month. (They don't tell you how many, unfortunately.)

Anyway, Rdio is a bit of a social service, in that it encourages you to follow other users. You can follow "influencers," suggested users, top listeners, and your own friends, listening to their playlists and the tracks they like. You can also easily connect Rdio to your Facebook, Twitter, and Last.fm accounts. Figure 19.5 shows what Rdio looks like.

ULTIMATELY INTERESTING Dolby Pulse, released in 2009, is a relatively new audio codec designed specifically for mobile devices. Compared to other encoding schemes, Dolby Pulse delivers high-quality audio at relatively low bitrates, which means better sound without hogging the datastream.

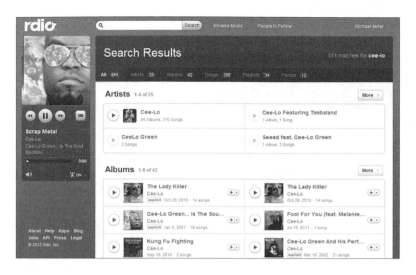

FIGURE 19.5

Searching and listening for music on the Rdio.

On the mobile front, Rdio offers apps for iOS, Android, Windows Phone 7, and BlackBerry devices, which is a pretty good spread. As to sound quality, Rdio refuses to divulge its streaming bitrate, other than saying it streams "up to 320Kbps." There's no way of knowing how many tracks are at this high bitrate and how many aren't. To my ears, it sounds comparable to Spotify.

Rhapsody

Now we come to Rhapsody (www.rhapsody.com), which is one of the largest and most established streaming music services on the web. You get a good selection of music (14 million tracks) served up at a decent-if-not-spectacular bitrate (128Kbps) for an acceptable monthly subscription fee ($9.99/month for both web and mobile). Ho hum.

> ♪ **ULTIMATELY INTERESTING** Rhapsody recently folded in its sibling Napster service.

I hate to be too hard on Rhapsody, because it certainly has its proponents, but I just don't see anything distinctive here. Yes, they do what they do as well as anybody else, but what makes them different? Couple the stale functionality and interface (shown in Figure 19.6) with an old-school 128Kbps bitrate, and you get nothing special with substandard fidelity. Seems to me that there are more attractive options out there.

19

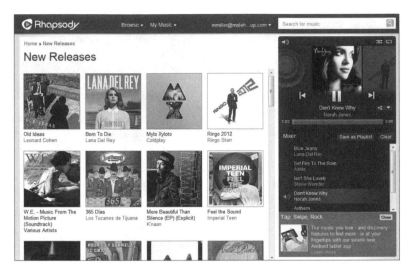

FIGURE 19.6

Viewing Rhapsody's new releases.

As to mobile access, the $9.99 Premier subscription lets you listen on one mobile device (plus your PC, of course). The $14.99 Premier Plus lets you listen on up to three mobile devices. Apps are available for iOS, Android, Windows Phone 7, and BlackBerry.

Slacker Radio

Slacker Radio (www.slacker.com) is a mix between a streaming music service and an Internet radio provider. Slacker started (in 2004) as an Internet radio service, and still provides access to a variety of online radio stations programmed by in-house DJs. Since then, however, Slacker has added features that are more akin to streaming music. How you view it (or listen to it) depends to a degree on which subscription plan you sign up for.

The Basic service (free) offers access to thousands of programmed Internet radio stations, but with ads. The Radio Plus plan ($3.99/month) offers similar Internet radio access, but is ad free. The Premium Radio plan ($9.99/month) is more like a traditional streaming music service, in that you can listen to songs and albums on demand, and create your own playlists.

The result is kind of a mish-mash. The interface, shown in Figure 19.7, is probably better suited to Internet radio than it is to searching and playing individual tracks. Add to that Slacker's somewhat anemic 8 million-track selection and sonically anemic 128Kbps streaming, and you get a service that doesn't have a lot of appeal—unless you add in those proprietary Internet radio stations, that is.

FIGURE 19.7
Listening to tracks on Slacker Radio.

Turntable.fm

Turntable.fm (www.turntable.fm) is a mix of streaming music and playlist sharing service. It has a lot of music sharing functionality, and integrates closely with Facebook and Twitter.

This service works a bit differently than others we've discussed. You start by creating or entering a room, typically devoted to an artist or style. You then share turns picking music to play—in Turntable's terms, you become a DJ. As you can see in Figure 19.8, you can even chat with the other DJs in your room. It's a fun way to discover new music, or just pass the time listening with others who like the same stuff.

Turntable.fm is a free service. It has 11 million tracks or so in its library, that it streams at 128Kbps. There's an iPhone app available, but that's it in terms of mobile access.

19

FIGURE 19.8

Sharing DJ duties in the I Love the 80's room on Turntable.fm.

Zune Music Pass

Finally, we have Zune Music Pass (www.zune.net), Microsoft's attempt at a music streaming service. It's not much of an attempt—unless you're wedded to the Microsoft ecosystem, that is.

Zune Music Pass shines if you're an Xbox user and you want to listen to music in between playing games. It's also quite functional on a Windows Phone 7 smartphone, where it's tightly wedded to the phone interface.

On other devices—including your computer—it's not so great. Oh, there's the expected $9.99/month subscription fee (includes mobile access) and the 11 million track library, and streaming is at a better-than-average 192Kbps. But it's a weird bird. The interface, shown in Figure 19.9, looks more like a typical online music store than a streaming music service, and you're constantly bombarded with prompts to buy tracks and albums. (It's also a tad slow, in my personal experience.)

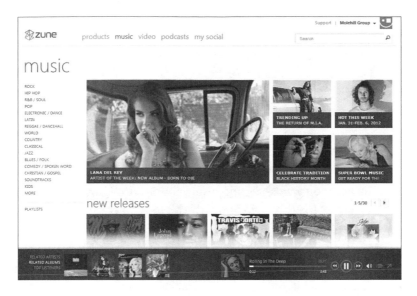

FIGURE 19.9
The store-like interface of the Zune Music Pass.

In any case, if you have a phone running Windows Phone 7 or play an Xbox, take a look at Zune Music Pass. It won't play on any other smartphone or tablet, however, and your experience browsing from the web may be somewhat disappointing.

COMPARING THE SERVICES

So, which of these streaming music services (as well as Pandora and Spotify, which we discuss in other chapters) is the best for you? I think there are some clear recommendations to be made.

In terms of audio quality, you can't beat MOG. You get consistent 320Kbps streaming, which you don't get with any other service. (Spotify's Premium plan promises 320Kbps streaming, but in my experience it only occasionally hits that level.) MOG also has a quite-acceptable 14 million-track library, and a good design for its mobile apps.

If you absolutely positively want the largest selection of music, then Spotify and Grooveshark are the way to go. With 15 million tracks, they're a hair beyond the rest of the competition.

19

Spotify is also good if you're into sharing your music on social networks—particularly on Facebook. While other services offer some degree of social sharing, no other service integrates as well with Facebook.

If you're interested in discovering new music, it's hard to beat either Last.fm or Pandora Radio (discussed in Chapter 33. Most streaming music services also recommend new music via playlists and personalized stations, but these two do it the best.

Finally, if you want eye candy, Rdio and Raditaz have the prettiest interfaces. That may not mean much if you have to click too far to find what you want, but still.

It really depends, then, on what matters to you. If it's selection or social sharing, go Spotify or Grooveshark. (Although MOG isn't bad, either.) If it's audio quality, go MOG. If it's a fancy interface, go Rdio or Raditaz. And if it's price—well, any of the free services (Last.fm, Pandora Radio, Raditaz, or Turntable.fm) are good bets. Heck, even the paid services tend to have free previews; you might as well sign up for a test drive if you're at all interested.

19

Accessing Your Music in the Cloud

The latest development in streaming audio is something called cloud streaming. In essence, this technology stores your personal music collection in the "cloud"—an ephemeral collection of Internet-based servers. You can then stream your music to any computer, smartphone, or other device connected to the Internet. Cloud streaming lets you carry your music collection with you pretty much anywhere there's an Internet connection.

Cloud streaming looks to be a big deal, and has attracted some pretty big players—chief among them Amazon, Apple, and Google. Some say that cloud streaming will supplant traditional music streaming services, at least for users with big music collections. Is this an accurate prognostication? Read on to form your own opinion—and find out how cloud streaming can work for you.

IN THIS CHAPTER

- How Cloud-Based Music Services Work
- Pros and Cons of Streaming Music from the Cloud
- Comparing Cloud Music Services
- Streaming Music from Your Own PC

How Cloud-Based Music Services Work

To understand cloud-based music services, you first have to understand the cloud. I'm not talking the cumulonimbus variety, but rather that congregation of anonymous computers that store and serve data over the Internet. It all has to do with something called *cloud computing*, which signals a major change in how computer applications are run and information is stored.

With traditional desktop computing, your computer applications and data are stored on each individual computer you use. While data can be accessed from other computers over a network (or over the Internet), they can't truly be shared—that is, they can't be used on by multiple devices in real time. The whole scene is very device-centric.

With cloud computing, the software programs and data you use aren't stored on your personal computer, but are rather stored on servers accessed via the Internet. If your computer crashes, the data isn't lost; it's still out there in the cloud, available for you to access from some other device. Unlike traditional computing, this cloud computing model isn't device-centric, it's data-centric; which device you use to access your data simply isn't important.

When we're talking about cloud music services, sometimes called *music clouds*, we're actually talking about how the music is stored. When you download or rip music to your computer, that's where your files are stored—locally, on your computer. When you listen to music from a streaming music service, you're not actually listening to your files; instead, you're listening to the music service's files, stored on their computers.

But with cloud music services, it's your music that's stored out there in the Internet cloud. In most cases, the music files on your computer are uploaded to the cloud servers; you can then listen to these files, via streaming technology, over the Internet on any connected device. In other instances, the cloud service discovers which tracks you have on your computer, and rather than uploading all of them, simply grants you access to the same tracks already stored on the service's servers; any tracks the service doesn't have in its library are then uploaded from your computer to fill in the gaps in the cloud.

As you can imagine, it can take a bit of time to upload all the tracks in a large music collection—literally days of uploading for collections of 10,000+ tracks. Once your music is in the cloud, however, it's a simple matter of streaming any individual track to any computer, smartphone, or music player device that has a connection to the Internet.

20

Note that most cloud music services charge for this privilege—actually, for the data storage itself. It's typically not too expensive, just a few bucks a month or even a few bucks a year, depending on how much storage space you need.

Oh, and most of these services put limits on how many tracks you can upload, or how much storage space you can use. This may be a problem if you have very large music collections, or tracks stored in lossless format (which creates much larger files). Check out the limitations before you sign up for any given service.

Finally, know that streaming your own music back to you might deteriorate the audio quality. When you listen to music on your own computer, you're listening at the original bitrate encoded—which can be quite high, if you go the lossless route. However, the music you stream back down from the cloud may not be at the original bitrate, but rather a lower bitrate determined by the cloud music service. (The download bitrate varies from service to service; some claim to stream at the original bitrate.) So your great-sounding lossless music might come back to you with poor-sounding lossy compression.

Pros and Cons of Streaming Music from the Cloud

So, is a cloud streaming service a good deal or not? Like all things in the digital music world, it depends on what you want to get out of it.

Advantages of Cloud Streaming Services

What's good about cloud streaming music? There's a lot, including the following:

- You can access your personal music library anywhere, anytime, from any Internet-connected device. This means you can listen to your music collection from a notebook computer when you're at the office or on the road, or from your smartphone when you're on the bus or taking a walk. It's the only way to access your own music collection over the Internet.

- You can use cloud streaming to serve music throughout your house. Just dial in each connected device to your cloud account, and you're good to go.

- You can listen to your entire music collection, not the limited number of tracks available from a typical streaming music service. (Given the limitations of the cloud service, that is; some won't upload certain types of files.)

20

- It's relatively low priced, compared to the monthly prices from some streaming music services.

- It serves as a backup of sorts for your music collection, essentially duplicating your library in the cloud. This would let you repopulate your library if your computer happens to get lost or damaged. (Note, however, that this duplication may be at a lower bitrate than the originals in your library.)

To me, the big advantages of cloud music is that you can access your library, not someone else's, from any computer, smartphone, or other device. That's big.

Disadvantages of Cloud Streaming Services

Not that all is pears and honey with cloud music streaming. There are some drawbacks, including the following:

- If you don't have an Internet connection, you don't have any music. That makes listening to your music problematic when you're on a cross-country plane flight or if you're on vacation out in the sticks.

- If you don't have a fast Internet connection, you'll probably have play-back problems. You need a broadband connection, no question about it, or you'll experience unwanted pauses and jerky playback. That also means connecting at anything less than 3G cellular service will proba-bly be unacceptable.

- Not all cloud services support all file types. You're good to go if your entire collection is in MP3 format, but if you have WMA-format files, you won't be able to upload your collection to Amazon's cloud service, for just one example. And few cloud services will accept lossless-format files, which stinks if you're into high-fidelity sound.

- The cloud service may not allow enough storage for your entire collec-tion. If you have a very large digital music collection (tens of thou-sands of tracks) or have your music in lossless format (which takes up lots of disk space), you may not be able to upload your entire library to a given cloud service. Do you really want to pick and choose which music you can access with your other devices?

- Downstream audio quality will probably be less than that in your orig-inal files. Most cloud services convert the music you upload to lower-quality files for storage, and then stream it back to you at this lower

20

rate. (Amazon is actually an exception here, as is MP3tunes.) That means that the music you listen via the cloud service will sound worse than your original files—which is an issue if you're using cloud streaming inside your house.

- If you stream cloud music to your smartphone, it'll eat up a lot of data, which can cost you big if you don't have an unlimited data plan. (And who does, nowadays?) Now, this is an issue with any streaming music service on your phone, but definitely the case if you're streaming higher-quality files from your cloud collection. Looking at the numbers, streaming an hour of music to your phone at a 128Kbps rate, which ain't that great, uses about 56MB of bandwidth an hour. Listen to 20 hours of music on your phone at this rate and you've used 1GB of data; increase the bitrate to 320Kbps and you double your data usage. (Fortunately, most cloud player apps let you select lower bitrate streaming to your phone, but still…)

To me, the biggest issues are finding a service that accepts the file format(s) you use and finding a service that has enough capacity to accept your entire music collection. As well, you need to be sure you can live with the downstream quality of your chosen service; if you're an audiophile, it probably won't be as high as what you'd like.

Comparing Cloud Music Services

Currently, there are a half-dozen major cloud music services—all of them relatively new. The big three (all launched in 2011) are from Amazon, Apple, and Google, with three smaller services (MP3tunes, mSpot, and MyMusicCloud) also worth considering.

These services are not identical. While all can accept MP3 files and non-DRM, lossy AAC files, not all are compatible with WMA file or lossless files of any format. Storage limits differ wildly from service to service, with some offering unlimited storage and others capping your uploads to a few gigabytes or 20,000 or so tracks. Downstream bitrates also vary, from an abysmal 96Kbps to streaming at the same quality as the original file. Pricing varies wildly, as well.

For your edification, Table 20.1 offers details about each of these services.

20

Table 20.1   Cloud Music Services Compared

Service	URL	Price	Storage Capacity	Audio Files Supported	Downstream Bitrate	Mobile Apps Available
Amazon Cloud Player	www.amazon.com/cloudplayer/	Free (up to 5GB storage); $20/year (unlimited)	Unlimited	.mp3, .m4a (AAC); individual files must be 100MB or smaller; does not support lossless formats	Original bitrate	Android
Google Play Music	play.google.com/music/	Free	20,000 tracks	.mp3, .m4a (AAC), .wma, .flac, .ogg; FLAC, OGG, and AAC files are transcoded to 320Kbps MP3	320Kbps max	Android
iTunes Match	www.apple.com/itunes	$24.99/year	25,000 tracks	.mp3, .m4a (AAC and Apple Lossless), .wav, .aiff	256Kbps	iOS
MP3tunes	www.mp3tunes.com	Free (up to 2GB), $4.95/month for 50GB, $7.95/month for 100GB, $12.95/month for 200GB	200GB	.mp3, .mp4, .m4a (AAC), .aac, .wma, .ogg; does not support lossless formats or DRM-encoded files	Original bitrate	Android, iOS
mSpot	www.mspot.com	Free (up to 5GB), $3.99/month for 40GB	5GB free, up to 40GB paid	.mp3, .mp4, .m4a (AAC), .aac, .wma; does not support DRM-encoded files	96Kbps	Android, iOS
MyMusicCloud	www.mymusiccloud.com	Free (up to 2GB), $10/year for additional 5GB	2GB free, up to 7GB paid	N/A	N/A	Android, iOS, BlackBerry

20

Which of these services offer the best deal? It depends.

- If you're concerned about sound quality, avoid mSpot and look instead at Amazon and MP3tunes, both of which stream at the original file quality—although neither Amazon or MP3tunes accept lossless files, which could be an issue. Google Play Music might be a good compromise, in that it's compatible with lossless files and streams them back at 320Kbps.

- If you have a huge library, consider Amazon's unlimited storage capacity. (Google Play Music and iTunes Match, while not unlimited, have pretty big limits, too.)

- If you're an Apple junkie, go with iTunes Match; it ties directly into the iTunes software and iPhone/iPad hardware.

- If your library is in WMA format, avoid Amazon and iTunes and look instead at Google Play Music and MP3tunes.

- If cost is an issue, Google Play Music is free—although Amazon's $20/year plan for unlimited storage ain't bad, either.

> **ULTIMATELY INTERESTING** Since some services limit use to X number of tracks and others to X amount of storage (in gigabytes), there's no easy way to compare one with the other—especially since a given track can be encoded at a variety of bitrates, resulting in much different file sizes. That said, if you're looking at an average track being 5 minutes long and encoded at 192Kbps, then Google Play Music's 20,000 track limit equates to about 180GB, and iTunes Match's 25,000 track limit equates to about 225GB—both considerably larger than the other services' single-digit gigabyte limits.

All in all, I'd gravitate towards the Amazon Cloud Player, as long as your music is in MP3 or AAC format. If you're a WMA fan, then you have to skip Amazon (which doesn't support WMA) and consider MP3tunes or Google Play Music, instead.

Let's take a few moments, then, and look at each of these services separately.

Amazon Cloud Player

Amazon is making a big play in the world of cloud computing, and part of that play is the Amazon Cloud Player (www.amazon.com/cloudplayer). Launched in March of 2011, it's essentially a cloud storage service for music files, that you play back via any web browser on any computer or connected device.

20

First things first. Amazon will automatically store in the cloud any music tracks you purchase from the Amazon MP3 Store. It's a matter of clicking the **Save to Your Amazon Cloud Drive** button when you purchase a track; Amazon does the rest.

> ♪ ULTIMATELY **INTERESTING** MP3 files you purchase from Amazon are not counted towards any storage limits for Amazon Cloud Player.

You can then upload files from your own personal music library to the cloud service. Amazon lets you upload MP3 and AAC files, but doesn't let you upload any lossless files, WMA files, or DRM-protected files. That may or may not be a deal breaker for you. On the plus side, your files are streamed back to you at their original bitrate.

Amazon offers two plans for its cloud music service. You can store up to 5GB of music for free, or pay $20 a year to get unlimited storage. If you have a large collection, the latter option is appealing.

> ♪ ULTIMATELY **INTERESTING** The Amazon Cloud Player is actually built into the Amazon Fire tablet.

Once you sign up, you have to download Amazon's upload application. Run this app and tell Amazon where your music files are stored on your computer, and it does the rest, uploading all compatible files to the Amazon cloud. As with any of these services, the uploading can take a while, especially if you have a large library or a slow Internet connection.

Playback is through your web browser on any computer or smartphone, no additional software necessary. Figure 20.1 shows how it looks; you can view your library by songs, albums, artists, or genres.

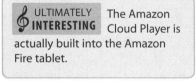

FIGURE 20.1

Listening to music with the Amazon Cloud Player.

20

Not surprisingly, Amazon offers a Cloud Player app for Android phones and tablets, but not for iPhones or Windows phones. You can still access Cloud Player from non-Android phones, you just have to do so using your phone's web browser.

I happen to like Amazon Cloud Player. I particularly like the unlimited storage and the playback at the original bitrate. I don't like the fact that it won't work with WMA files, but if you're in the Apple or MP3 camps, that won't be a concern. The player itself is easy enough to work with, not a standout performer but nothing wrong with it, either. All in all, Amazon's cloud offering is definitely worth your consideration.

Google Play Music

Google is another big player in the cloud computing market, and Google Play Music (play.google.com/music) is the company's cloud music service. It's a nice service, with only a few limitations—and it's free.

Google Play Music is compatible with all popular audio file formats, including MP3, AAC, WMA, and FLAC. FLAC, OGG, and AAC files are automatically transcoded to 320Kbps MP3 files for storage, however. Playback quality tops out at 320Kbps, lower if that's what your tunes were encoded at.

> **ULTIMATELY INTERESTING** Google Play Music (formerly known as just Google Music) is also an online music store, having officially opened in the Google Play store (formerly known as the Android Market) in November 2011. As we discussed in Chapter 10, "Downloading Music from Other Online Music Stores," it works like any other online music store, with similar selection and pricing.

Now to the free part. Like most of Google's online services, Google Play Music is totally free to use. All you need is a Google Account (also free) and you're good to go. For that low, low price you get to store up to 20,000 tracks, which will be enough for all but the largest digital music libraries.

As with the Amazon service, to use Google Play Music you have to first download and install Google's upload app. You use this app to identify the files you want to upload and then upload them. Again, this uploading can take a while, especially if you have a lot of files.

Playback is through any web browser. As you can see in Figure 20.2, you can display your music by song, artist, album, or genre. Google also offers discrete prompts throughout to purchase related music through its online store.

20

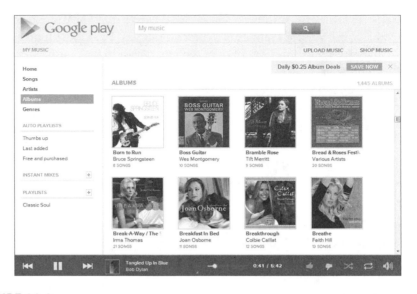

FIGURE 20.2

Listening to music with Google Music cloud app.

There is a Google Play Music app for Android devices, but not for other smartphones or tablets. (It's unlikely you'll ever see a Google Play Music app for iPhones...) You can always access Google Play Music through your phone's web browser, of course.

I like Google Play Music because it lets me upload and listen to all my WMA-format files, of which I have a lot. Unfortunately, I also have a lot of files, period, and have bumped into (crashed into, actually), Google's 20,000-track limit. I certainly like the price (free), but would gladly pay a little extra to be able to upload my entire library.

> **ULTIMATELY INTERESTING** Tracks purchased from the Google Play Music store do not count against the 20,000-track limit.

iTunes Match

Apple is the big dog in digital music, and it didn't take long for this dog to get into the cloud music show. (November 2011, to be precise.) Apple does it via the iTunes Match service, which is closely integrated with its existing iTunes software.

iTunes Match works a little different from the other cloud music services, however, in that it doesn't upload every single audio track in your library. It does upload information about each track, however, and matches that to all the tracks available in the iTunes Store. When there's a match—which there is, more often than not—you can then stream that track from Apple's database direct to any connected device. If you have a track on your computer that is not in Apple's database, then iTunes uploads it to the cloud for you to stream to your other devices.

What you end up with is a cloud-based library that looks like the library on your computer, but in actuality includes mix of Apple's files and your files. In day-to-day usage, you don't know the difference between one or the other.

Since iTunes Match is part of Apple's infrastructure, it has all the requirements and limitations that you're used to with all things iTunes-related.

You activate iTunes Match within the iTunes software; all you have to do is select Store > Turn On iTunes Match and follow the onscreen instructions from there. iTunes will "match" the music in your library with songs in the iTunes Store, then upload any track it doesn't have access to.

To listen to your cloud music on other computers, follow these same instructions. As you can see in Figure 20.3, tracks from the cloud are noted with a cute little cloud icon; playback is the same as it always is in iTunes.

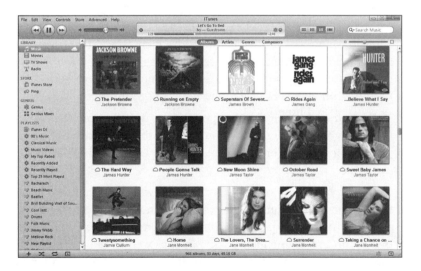

FIGURE 20.3

Listening to music from the cloud with iTunes Match.

You pay $24.99 a year to use iTunes Match, although any track you purchased from the iTunes Store is served for free and doesn't count towards your storage limit of 25,000 tracks. iTunes Match is compatible with MP3 and AAC files, including AAC Lossless. Playback is at 256Kbps, not quite as good as with Amazon or Google.

Naturally, iTunes Match is built into the Music app in iPhones and iPads. There is no corresponding app for other phones or devices; it's solely an Apple thing.

MP3tunes

Amazon, Google, and Apple are the Big Three in cloud music services—but they're not the only ones. MP3tunes is a smaller competitor (although it's been around longer than the big boys) that works in much the same fashion as the larger services. You upload files from your music library, they're stored on MP3tunes' cloud servers, and then streamed to your computer, smartphone, and other devices.

MP3tunes (www.mp3tunes.com) has a lot going for it, especially for serious music lovers. First, it's compatible with most popular audio file formats—MP3, AAC, WMA, and OGG. (It doesn't support lossless formats, however, nor DRM-encoded files.) Playback is at the original bitrate, which audiophiles will like.

You can upload up to 200GB of music, which should be plenty, depending on the plan you purchase. MP3tunes' basic free plan gives you 2GB of storage; for $4.95/month you get 50GB; for $7.95/month you get 100GB; and if you need the full 200GB of space, you pay $12.95/month.

Uploading is via an uploading program or directly from the service's web page. Playback is via any web browser, as shown in Figure 20.4; you can view your music by artist or album, but not by genre. Android and iOS apps are available.

On paper, MP3tunes certainly looks good, with its large storage capability, near-universal file compatibility, and original bitrate playback. However, the service's interface is quite a bit different from the norm, with its hierarchical tree list and recommended tracks pane, as well as the slideshow of artist pictures instead of standard album art. It's certainly clunkier in terms of navigation, as you have to select an artist here and album there and then click a track to play. You're either going to like the interface or you're not; there's nothing standard about it.

20

FIGURE 20.4

Listening to music with MP3tunes.

So if you're an independent-minded sort, MP3tunes might be worth checking out. If you like your music services a little more polished and familiar, however, stick with the big boys.

mSpot

Another smaller competitor in the cloud music space is mSpot (www.mspot.com), shown in Figure 20.5. This one is difficult to recommend; it has limited storage capacity and extremely low bitrate playback, along with a very bare bones interface.

The good news first. mSpot lets you upload MP3, AAC, and WMA files. It also offers a free plan, with 5GB of file storage. If you need more, there's a 40GB plan that costs $3.99 a month. That's kind of limiting, however, if you have a larger music library.

> **ULTIMATELY INTERESTING** MP3tunes is technically a *music locker* service, in that it stores users' original files in an online "locker" (and then streams them back, of course). The company was sued by EMI for copyright infringement, because users uploaded copyrighted files to the site. A federal court found in EMI's favor, primarily because MP3tunes did not remove offending files when EMI notified the company about them. That said, the Digital Millennium Copyright Act (DMCA) generally provides safe harbor for music lockers, as long as the companies take down offending material when notified.

FIGURE 20.5

Listening to cloud music with mSpot.

On the playback front, mSpot offers the lowest fidelity of all the cloud services. We're talking playback at a whopping 96Kbps, which pretty much sucks, even on a portable device. (Speaking of which, mSpot apps are available for Android and iOS devices.)

I'm not sure why you'd want to bother with this one, but it is an option— especially if you're looking for a cross-platform (iOS and Android) solution. And they do claim a million users, so somebody likes 'em.

MyMusicCloud

The final cloud music service we'll discuss is called MyMusicCloud. It's another small player, in all senses of the term.

First, it's small in terms of how much music you can store. The basic free services lets you store a measly 2GB of songs. Even if you upgrade to their top plan ($10/year), you only get an additional 5GB of storage, for 7GB in total. That's not much at all, even if you have a small library encoded at low bitrates.

MyMusicCloud doesn't say which file formats it works with, nor does it disclose its streaming bitrate, neither of which says anything good about the service. The playback interface, shown in Figure 20.6, tries to be flashy but just ends up being difficult to use.

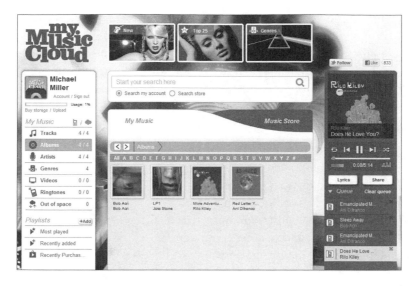

FIGURE 20.6

Listening to cloud music with MyMusicCloud.

On the plus side, MyMusicCloud is the only cloud music service with an app for BlackBerry phones. It also has iOS and Android apps.

Streaming Music from Your Own PC

As you've seen, a cloud music service uploads your music (or copies of it) to the cloud, and then streams it back from the cloud to any Internet-connected computer or device. That's fine, but do you really need that middleman storing your music for you? Wouldn't it be more efficient to stream your own music from your own computer to your remote devices?

That's the concept behind the following two services, Audiogalaxy and Subsonic. Both services turn your home computer into a cloud music server, so that you can listen to your own music, stored on your own PC, anywhere you may happen to be, via any Internet–connected device. You don't have to upload anything to anywhere; your music stays where it is, but then streams across the Internet as you need it.

> **♪ ULTIMATELY INTERESTING** Cloud server services are sometimes called *placeshifting services*.

This process requires a bit of technical expertise, as you have to turn your computer into a streaming server, with all the necessary configuration that requires. You also need an always-on broadband Internet connection, of course, and need to have the server software constantly running in the background. But once you get it set up, it's pretty sweet.

Audiogalaxy

The first streaming server service we'll look at is Audiogalaxy (www.audiogalaxy.com). The new Audiogalaxy is a combination of software application and cloud music player that lets you stream music from your computer to any other computer or mobile device that's connected to the Internet.

> ♪ **ULTIMATELY INTERESTING** The new Audiogalaxy cloud server shares the same name as the previous Audiogalaxy subscription service (2002-2010)—and, prior to that, the Audiogalaxy P2P file-sharing service (1998-2002). This new service was launched in mid-2010.

At the heart of the system is the Audiogalaxy Helper software that you install on the PC that hosts your digital music library. Once this software is installed and configured (it's actually quite easy), your computer is turned into a web server. (The server software works on systems running Windows XP/Vista/7 and Mac OS X 10.5 and above.)

You then use the cloud player on Audiogalaxy's website to access and play your music from remote computers, as shown in Figure 20.7. You can also use the Audiogalaxy app (available for iOS and Android devices) to play your music on your smartphone. Audiogalaxy supports all popular file formats—MP3, AAC, WMA, FLAC, and OGG.

While the concept of turning your home PC into a cloud server is obviously new and has some kinks to work out, there's a lot to like about it. You can start serving music immediately without having to bother with uploading a ton of files, and your entire music collection is compatible. (There's a limit of 200,000 tracks you can serve, but that's a pretty big nut to crack.) Better yet, both the Audiogalaxy server software and cloud player are free. It's worth checking out.

20

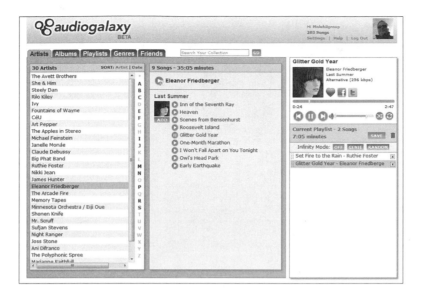

FIGURE 20.7

Streaming music from your own PC via Audiogalaxy.

Subsonic

Another approach to creating home-based cloud server exists in the form of Subsonic (www.subsonic.org.) Subsonic is an open-source web-based music streamer application that you install on the same computer where you have your digital music library stored. Once configured (and configuration is more involved than with the simpler Audiogalaxy service), Subsonic turns your computer into a web-based music server.

With Subsonic streaming your music over the Internet, you can listen to your library from any Internet-connected computer or device. (Figure 20.8 shows Subsonic's web-based music player.) There are apps available for iOS, Android, and Windows Phone 7 devices.

The Subsonic software works on Windows, Mac, Linux, and UNIX computers. It can serve all manner of audio files, including MP3, AAC, WMA, FLAC, and OGG. You can configure the software to stream at any desired bitrate; Subsonic resamples your music to serve it at the selected quality level.

Like Audiogalaxy, Subsonic is free to use—although the developers request a 20 Euro (approximately $26) donation if you're streaming to mobile devices.

20

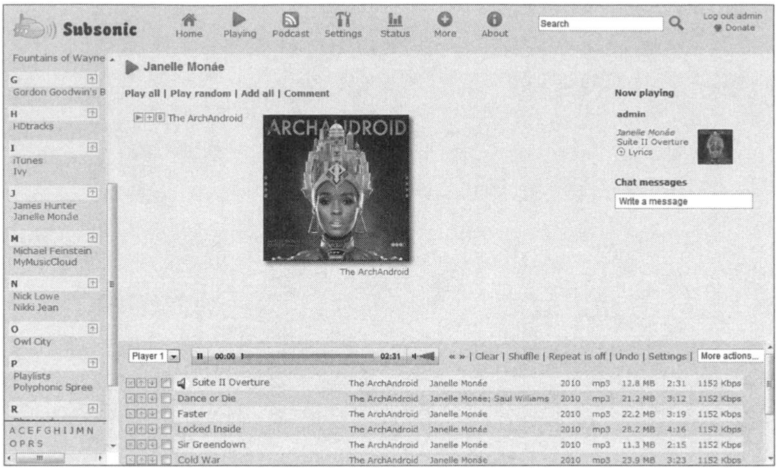

FIGURE 20.8
Streaming music from your own PC via Subsonic.

IS CLOUD STREAMING FOR YOU?

I happen to believe that cloud streaming could be the future of online music delivery, especially for serious music collectors. I don't think it's there yet, but it's getting close.

The big advantage that cloud streaming offers over traditional subscription download or streaming services is that you own the music you listen to, and listen to the music you own. It opens up your personal collection for listening anywhere, anytime, on any device. You don't have to rely on a third party's database of tracks when you're listening in the car or on the run; it's literally just like taking your music library with you, wherever you go.

That said, I think today's cloud streaming services have a lot of faults. (They're the upload-based services from Apple, Amazon, and Google are not universal in terms of what files they'll accept, and most stream back to you at substandard bitrates. Good enough for phone use, but not for use in the home.) In addition, most put limits on the number of files or gigabytes of data they'll store, and such limits rule out using them with today's largest digital libraries.

All these issues are understandable, given how young these services are (most less than a year old), and easily addressed. For example, Amazon already has unlimited storage, and plays back tracks at their original bitrates. If Amazon would add WMA and FLAC compatibility, as well as accept lossless files, you'd have a near-perfect service.

Of course, any of these services could make a few tweaks and add these desired features. I don't expect Apple to add cross-format compatibility, but Google certainly could. Open it up all the way and let's see how it works then.

Then there's the home music server option, which might be the best way to go for folks with very large music collections. There's nothing to upload, you serve your music directly from the same PC where it's currently stored. Bandwidth may be an issue, but we're always getting more of that. Why deal with a cloud service that (a) gets in the way, by enforcing its own technical limitations and (b) costs money, when you can do it all yourself?

Cloud computing is certainly making things interesting in the online music space. Stay tuned to see how it all shakes out.

20

Listening to Internet Radio

There's one more type of streaming music we need to discuss. Internet radio is the online equivalent of terrestrial AM/FM radio, full of all sorts of radio stations that operate over the web, using streaming audio technology.

Some Internet radio stations exist solely online. Others simulcast existing AM/FM stations. And some let you create own personal stations, just for you, in real time. It's an interesting way to hear old favorites and new music alike, town to town and up and down the dial.

Understanding Internet Radio

Internet radio is a form of streaming audio that broadcasts specific programming over the Internet. The key here is the word "programming;" unlike other forms of streaming music, the songs you hear on Internet radio stations are (typically) programmed in some fashion. That is, someone (or some thing, in the form of a automated application) puts together the songs that are broadcast on a specific channel. This programming flows from or defines the channel's nature.

You access most Internet radio stations via your web browser. All you need is a reliable Internet connection, desirably a broadband one, and the aforementioned web browser. Once you tune in, you hear whatever it is that the radio station is broadcasting at the moment.

In this fashion, Internet radio is a lot like terrestrial or satellite radio, in that you have little choice in what is broadcast. Your choice comes in picking a particular station to listen to; once you've made that choice, you pretty much have to listen to whatever the station has programmed.

Not that that's really an issue. Many people listen to Internet radio while they're working at their computers or lounging around at home. Just dial into a station broadcasting the kind of music you like, then press play and leave the Internet radio site up and running in the background while you work or relax. It's just like listening to a traditional radio, except it's on your computer desktop rather than on your physical desktop.

Of course, you can also listen to Internet radio on your smartphone or tablet. It's streaming audio, so as long as you have an Internet connection, you're good to go.

When comparing Internet radio to traditional radio, you'll see that most Internet radio stations display the title and artist of the currently playing song, right on your computer screen. You don't get that with all AM or FM stations; if you've ever wondered what it was you were listening to when you heard a song on the radio, you'll like this feature. In addition, many Internet radio sites let you create your own custom "stations," based on your own listening preferences.

In terms of audio quality, Internet radio is typically at the low end of the fidelity spectrum. That is, you're likely to experience much lower bitrates with Internet radio than you are with other forms of streaming music. That might be fine when you're listening to an all-talk station, but if you're in it for the music, be prepared for an aural disappointment.

> **ULTIMATELY CAUTIOUS** The speed of your Internet connection also affects sound quality. A slower connection (dial up is the worst) is prone to audio dropouts, unexpected pauses, stuttering playback, and other issues.

What's Out There

If you can imagine it, there's probably an Internet radio station devoted to it. There's that much variety in terms of programming; there's a station for every taste.

21

It isn't just Internet-only programming, either. Internet radio is a great way to listen to terrestrial AM and FM stations. Whether you want to listen to your hometown radio station or some foreign-language station in another part of the world, you can probably find it on the web—and play it back through your own PC or smartphone.

What else can you find on Internet radio? Here's a list of some of what you can expect to find online:

- Simulcasts of local radio stations (from around the world)
- Web-only broadcasts of format-specific music
- Live or taped broadcasts of talk radio programs
- Rebroadcasts of classic "old time" radio programs
- Live news, sports, and weather reports
- Audio books
- Live interactive celebrity chat sessions

Listening to Web-Only Radio

There are a large number of sites that create their own original radio programming and beam it over the Internet. This programming is typically genre-specific music; many of these sites offer dozens (or hundreds) of channels, each devoted to a specific type of music. So whether you're interested in '70s pop hits or classic polka tunes, one of these sites probably has a channel just for you!

Here's a short list of some of the most popular Internet-only radio sites:

- **AccuRadio** (www.accuradio.com). Listen to programmed stations (typically by genre) or create your own custom stations. Figure 21.1 shows some of what's available.
- **AOL Radio** (music.aol.com/radioguide/). A large number of genre-specific radio stations, created specifically for online listening.
- **Goom Radio** (www.goomradio.us). A variety of genre-specific Internet radio stations, as well as user-created stations.
- **Groovera** (www.groovera.com). A number of online stations specializing in down-tempo "chill" techno music.
- **iHeartRadio** (www.iheart.com). Presents more than 850 terrestrial and web-only stations, plus user-created custom stations.

21

- **Jango** (www.jango.com). A mix of genre-based stations and user-personalized programming.

- **Live365** (www.live365.com). One of the largest Internet radio sites, with more than 5,000 stations in more than 260 different genres. As you can see in Figure 21.2, if you can't find it on Live365, you probably can't find it anywhere.

- **Radio.com** (www.radio.com). From the CBS Interactive Music Group, a handful of big-media channels and the ability to create your own custom channels.

- **Radioio** (www.radioio.com). Dozens of genre-focused web-only channels.

- **RadioMOI** (www.radiomoi.com). Features a mix of programmed channels (browsable by genre) and on demand content.

- **SHOUTcast** (www.shoutcast.com). Part of the AOL empire and one of the oldest and most reliable Internet radio sites. Amalgamates more than 50,000 free Internet radio stations in a single site. You can browse by genre or search by station, artist, or genre.

- **SomaFM** (www.somafm.com). More than 20 channels of listener-supported, commercial-free, underground and alternative stations.

- **VirtualDJ Radio** (radio.virtualdj.com). Dance music, with live mixes selected by real-life DJs.

FIGURE 21.1

Listening to genre-specific stations at AccuRadio.

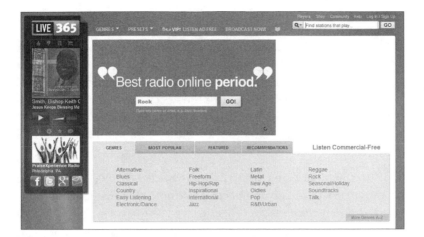

FIGURE 21.2

Live365, one of the largest collections of Internet radio stations on the web.

> **♪ ULTIMATELY USEFUL** You can also listen to Internet radio via a dedicated radio player program, such as Screamer Radio (www.screamer-radio.com). This particular program lets you listen to more than 4,000 different web-based and terrestrial stations—and record what you're listening to!

In addition, there's free Internet radio available via iTunes. As you can see in Figure 21.3, select Radio in the Library section of the navigation sidebar, then click a category to view all the stations available. Double-click a station to begin playback.

FIGURE 21.3

Using iTunes to listen to Internet radio stations.

21

Searching for Internet Radio Stations

I purposely excluded individual radio stations from the prior list, focusing instead on sites that aggregate multiple channels. Because there are a lot of individual stations on the web, you need a way to find that one station you want. To that end, you might want to check out a directory or search engine for Internet radio programming. Most of these sites let you search for both web-only stations and sites that simulcast traditional radio stations online.

Here's a list:

- **Classical Live Online Radio** (www.classicalwebcast.com). Links to more than 160 online classical radio stations from more than two dozen countries.
- **InternetRadio** (www.internet-radio.com). Links to numerous web-based and terrestrial stations. Browse by genre or search for specific stations.
- **radio-locator** (www.radio-locator.com). My favorite Internet radio search engine, with links to more than 10,000 AM and FM stations, as well as 2,500 web-only stations. As you can see in Figure 21.4, you can search this site by city or ZIP code, country, or call letters.
- **RadioTuna** (www.radiotuna.com). Lists thousands of online and terrestrial stations, searchable by genre, artist, or station.
- **Web-Radio** (www.web-radio.com). Lists both terrestrial and web-only radio stations by call letter, location, and format.

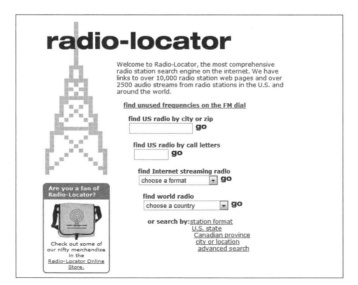

FIGURE 21.4
Searching for Internet radio stations at the radio-locator site.

Listening to Terrestrial and Satellite Radio Online

Finally, we come to the topic of terrestrial radio on the Internet. That is, being able to listen to traditional AM and FM stations over the Internet.

Personally, I like listening to terrestrial radio online. Sometimes you just want local news and views, or to listen to your local DJs; there's no reason you should be deprived of this just because you're listening online. Of course, you're not limited to listening to just *your* local stations; via the magic of the Internet, you can listen to local stations from anywhere in the world, in real time.

> **ULTIMATELY INTERESTING** You're not limited to just AM and FM radio online. If you have a subscription to Sirius/XM satellite radio for your car, you can also listen to it over the web.

- **Live Radio on the Internet** (www.live-radio.net). A great guide to AM/FM simulcasts from all around the globe.

- **Online Radio Stations** (www.webradios.com). Includes listings of local radio stations online, by location or genre.

- **radio-locator** (www.radio-locator.com). We discussed this one previously; this is a search engine with links to more than 10,000 AM and FM stations, searchable by city or ZIP code, country, or call letters.

- **Sirius/XM Radio** (www.siriousxm.com/player/). Satellite radio online, with more than 130 channels of music, news, and talk—including several web-only channels that aren't available via normal satellite radio.

- **TuneIn Radio**. Shown in Figure 21.5, this is my favorite site for listening to terrestrial radio stations. You can browse local stations in any city or state, as well as listen to local police and fire bands. Each station shows what's currently playing, which is great when you're browsing for something interesting to listen to.

> **ULTIMATELY USEFUL** If you're searching for a particular radio station online, try entering the station's call letters between the **www.** and **.com** of a URL. For example, San Francisco's KFOG can be found at www.kfog.com. (This doesn't always work, but it's a good first guess.)

21

FIGURE 21.5
Browsing local AM and FM stations with TuneIn Radio.

SEARCHING FOR LOCAL RADIO

I mentioned previously my love of TuneIn Radio, a great site for listening to local radio stations on your computer (or, via the appropriate app, on your smartphone). But given the mass customization possible with today's streaming music and download services, why in the world would you want to regress to local radio's force-fed programming?

I'll be honest. I don't listen to much AM or FM radio these days. Back in the Top 40 era, yes; radio stations back then played an amazingly wide variety of music, exposed listeners to all sorts of new artists, and actually helped to create a community of listeners with a shared listening experience. Today's radio stations, in general, are tragedies of corporatism, with your local Emmis or Clear Channel station playing a disturbingly short playlist culled from an increasingly narrow genre classification. You hear the same playlists (and sometimes the same DJ banter) on multiple stations across the country; there's no regionalism, no personalization, no personality period. Corporate radio today sucks, and I don't want to listen to it, either over the air or over the Internet.

21

That said, some cities do have truly local stations that distinguish themselves from the corporate competition. I'm fortunate enough to live in the Twin Cities market, and we have several local channels that are actually worth listening to. I particularly like 89.3 FM (KCMP), The Current, which is a public radio station that plays a great selection of new indie and alternative rock, the kind of stuff that none of the corporate stations play. I also like 88.5 FM (KBEM), a pretty good local jazz station; I'm always a sucker for a good jazz station. We also have a true local news and talk station (even though it happens to be owned by CBS) in the form of 830 AM (WCCO), which features a minimum of syndicated national talk and a powerful portfolio of smart local talkers.

As I said, I'm fortunate to live in a city with such rich local media. Previously I lived in Indianapolis, which is the home of very little local anything anymore. Contrast Minneapolis' WCCO with Indy's WIBC, which has a similar storied history but a much different current presence. WIBC used to be the premier local news and talk station, home of talents such as morning man extraordinaire Gary Todd and local news legend Fred Heckman; it was *the* station you listened to for breaking news and local events. Imagine my surprise when last I visited my home town and discovered that not only had WIBC been moved from its historical home of 1070 on the AM band to the 93.1 FM space occupied in my youth by FM rock legend WNAP, but that the programming day was comprised almost exclusively by the same ubiquitous syndicated right-wing windbags you hear on every other talk radio station across the country. I don't fault corporate owner Emmis Communication for trying to make a little money on their local flagship station (Emmis is an Indianapolis-based company, and I have a good friend who works for them), but eviscerating a once-great local landmark is not only sacrilegious, in my view, but also makes for boring, plain-vanilla, location-generic radio. Yuck.

You know, it would be great to listen into Indy's WIBC from my home in Minneapolis, if indeed it was worth listening to. As is, I can use TuneIn Radio to listen to other local stations across the country, from San Francisco's legendary rocker KFOG (which, admittedly, is owned by corporate powerhouse Cumulus Media—but has a strong local orientation) to Atlanta's eclectic low-power WMLB. If you can sift through the corporate crap on the airwaves today, there are still some real gems out there—and you can listen to them, wherever you are, over the Internet.

21

PART

V

Playing Your Music—At Home

Understanding Home Digital Music Playback

There are lots of places you can listen to digital music. You can listen in your office, via your work PC. You can listen on the go, via your iPhone, iPod, or similar portable device. And, lest we forget, you can listen to digital music in your home.

In fact, there are a lot of different ways you can listen to digital music in your home. You can listen on your computer, of course, or on your iPhone or iPod while exercising or just lounging around. You can connect your computer or other device to your main audio system and listen to digital music in your living room. You can even stream your digital music across your home network to listen in any room of your house.

Depending on how fancy you want to go, listening to digital music at home can be as simple as tapping the **Play** button on your iPhone or as complex as setting up a whole-house audio system in multiple rooms throughout your abode. In this chapter I present an overview of the topic, and talk about why—and how—you might want to listen to digital music at home.

Music Is for the Home

If you're a true music lover, you listen to music both for enjoyment and edification. That is, you really *listen* to music, not just use it for background noise. (Although there's probably some of that, too, if you're honest with yourself.) Of course you want to listen to music in your home—in fact, you probably want to listen to music in multiple rooms, depending on what activity in which you're engaging at the moment.

So let's think about it. Where in your home do you want to listen to music?

If you're like me, your listening locations include some or all of the following:

- Living room
- Bedrooms (yes, your kids might want to tap into your music collection, too—or at least some of it)
- Home office or den
- Kitchen (nothing like a little background music when you're cooking dinner)
- Bathroom (while taking a shower or bath—or performing other duties…)
- Outdoor deck or porch

Now, you probably have one room set up as your main listening room. This could be your living room but it may also be your den, library, or maybe your basement. Chances are this room is also wired for video, in that you have a home theater system installed, complete with 5.1- or 7.1-channel sound; if this is the case, you have to decide whether to listen to music through all your surround sound speakers, or be a bit more pure and listen to front-channel stereo speakers only.

The challenge, then, is setting up a system that delivers your digital music collection to all these rooms in your house. You have to figure out how to store your digital music and how to serve it. This typically means hooking up devices in each room to your home network, although you can duplicate your collection on multiple devices throughout your home. The former method is more efficient, of course; the latter route is most often accomplished by using an iPod for storage and moving it from room to room.

Different Ways to Listen to Digital Music in Your Home

Streaming music from room to room is one challenge. What you stream is something else to consider.

I'm not talking about choosing music genres here, although that's probably worthy of a private conversation, especially if you have a lot of 80s hair band stuff in your collection. No, I'm talking about your playback source—what media you use to store and play the music you like.

When I wrote *The Complete Idiot's Guide to Home Theater Systems* back in the ancient days of the year 2000, there was really only one viable source for music playback—a CD player. Napster had launched a year before, but didn't yet have a big audience, at least outside of the hacker community. Apple's iPod was a year away from introduction, and the MP3 player market was in its infancy. No, given the practical death of the LP a decade or so before, the music scene at the turn of the century was a compact disc world.

Now, CDs are still around today, even if the market has contracted a tad. It's possible to build a whole-house audio system today based around a CD player (actually, it's probably a multi-purpose Blu-ray, DVD, and CD player), but that's definitely an old-school solution. It also isn't near as versatile as other options, especially when it comes to streaming different tunes to different rooms.

> **ULTIMATELY INTERESTING**   If you're into audiophile music, you may want to keep an SACD player in your equipment rack. SACD (stands for Super Audio Compact Disc) delivers audio four times the quality of the standard CD format. Even though it hasn't been a success in the mass market, it's seen acceptance in the audiophile community.

Today, you want to base your home audio system around digital storage and playback. (That's what we've been discussing in this book, in case you haven't noticed.) That means using a personal computer or server to store a collection of digital audio files, and to serve those files over your home network to devices in various rooms of your house.

> **ULTIMATELY INTERESTING**   We discussed storage options back in Chapter 13, "Storing Your Digital Music." Re-read that chapter if you've forgotten any details; there might be a test later.

There are a number of ways to do this, of course. Let's look at the most popular approaches.

Digital Music via PC

The first option is to use some sort of computer to play back the digital audio files you've previously ripped or downloaded. There are actually a number of options within this option, as follows.

22

First, you can simply listen to music on the same computer where your audio files are stored. You'll need to have some sort of music player program (such as iTunes or Windows Media Player) installed, but it's a fairly simple thing to play back audio files. Unfortunately, the sound quality of PC playback typically leaves much to be desired, but there are ways to improve PC sound, including upgrading to better speakers, using quality headphones (not ear buds, sorry), and utilizing a digital-to-analog converter (DAC) box to ensure higher-fidelity playback. All in all, this is the simplest approach to home music playback.

If you want better quality sound, all you have to do is connect your PC to your existing home audio system. You still have to choose a music player program, but in this instance you probably want one with some sort of "ten foot interface," as you'll be controlling playback from your couch across the room. You still might want to employ a DAC box to improve playback quality, and consider the best type of connection to make from your PC to your receiver or preamp.

Another approach is to use a computer for storage, but not place it in the same room as your main audio system. Instead, you stream audio from the computer over your home network to a playback device connected to your home audio system. This can be another, smaller computer, a Media Center Extender, or some sort of network music player—which we'll discuss next.

> 🎵 ULTIMATELY **INTERESTING** Learn more about computer-based playback in Chapter 24, "Playing Digital Music on Your Computer."

Digital Music via Network Music Player

If you don't want a computer in your living room, consider using another type of playback device instead. Non-PC playback devices are typically called *network music players* or *network media players*, and can include any of the following:

- Standalone media players, such as those sold by Apple (Apple TV), Boxee, Logitech (Squeezebox), Netgear, Sonos, Sony, and Western Digital.

- Media Center Extenders, a specific type of network media player designed to work with a computer running Windows Media Center. There aren't a lot of these still being sold today (they fizzled in the marketplace), although an Xbox game console can serve this function quite well.

22

- A/V receivers, Blu-ray players, and even widescreen TVs with DNLA functionality, which lets them grab and play media files from other PCs on your network.

- High-end whole-house audio system, such as designed for professional home theater installations. (This is the uber-expensive stuff, by the way.)

In this scenario, you store your audio files on your office computer or home server, and then stream music from that device to the network music player connected to your home audio system or home theater system. This type of approach is both less functional (you lose all the computer-specific functionality) and more reliable (you lose all the computer-specific quirkiness) than connecting a true PC to your system. You do, however, gain the benefit of being able to stream different music to different devices in different rooms, at the same time; you're not limited to listening to the same song throughout your entire house.

> ♩ ULTIMATELY **INTERESTING** Learn more about network media players in Chapter 25, "Playing Digital Music on a Home Media Player."

Digital Music via iPod

There's yet another option for storing your digital music library, one that doesn't involve a computer or a network media player. If you have all your tunes ripped or downloaded to an iPod, or similar portable music player, you can use it to stream music to your main audio system and even throughout your house.

There are several ways to do this:

- Connect your iPod to an iPod speaker system—a self-contained set of speakers with a dock for an iPod.

- Connect your iPod to a dock that connects to your home audio system or home theater system for playback.

- Connect your iPod to your home network wirelessly using Apple's Airport Express or some other streaming technology, and then stream from your network to your home audio system.

While all these options are great for utilizing your iPod as both a storage and playback device, it's not always a perfect solution; in particular, you're limited to the lossy sound quality of the files on your iPod. While the audio quality might not be quite to an audiophile's liking, it's probably good enough for less discerning listeners or background music. It's also a relatively convenient and low-priced option; there are lots of iPod docks, speakers, and streamers out there that are pretty much plug-and-play solutions.

> **ULTIMATELY INTERESTING**   Learn more about play-back via iPod in Chapter 29, "Playing Your Portable Music in the Living Room."

Other Items to Consider

Whichever approach you embrace, you probably want to feed your digital music throughout your house, so you can enjoy your library wherever you may happen to be at the moment. That means installing some sort of playback device in each room where you'd like to listen to music. (You may want to choose different playback options for different rooms; in most instances, you're not limited to a single solution throughout your house.)

> **ULTIMATELY INTERESTING**   Learn more about whole house streaming in Chapter 26, "Building a Whole House Digital Audio System."

Once you have all your devices in place, it's a relatively simple matter to get everything connected to everything else over your home network, get all the devices recognizing and reading from your main music library, and start listening. In theory, anyway.

In practice, setting up digital music playback in the home can be a confusing and frustrating experience. There are a ton of decisions you have to make, and each one locks you into a defined set of options. It's not uncommon to get half way through the process and discover you've ripped most of your music in a format that your playback device can't read, or find that a given device just doesn't want to talk to your main PC or server. Oy!

And, as I've oft repeated throughout this book, there is no one single solution that fits every home. So don't expect me to lay out the perfect system that you can implement by following a series of simple steps. Every situation is different, and the steps aren't always simple. Most music lovers will do a lot of experimenting before making any final decisions.

So that's what you need to do, in a nutshell. There are lots of choices to make, along with a bit of testing and trial and error. But once you get it set up, you're going to like the results.

MUSIC IN MY HOME

I've been listening to music at home since I was old enough to remember doing so. Some of my earliest memories consist of listening to the day's hits on a transistor radio; for some reason, Barry Mann's "Who Put the Bomp (in the Bomp, Bomp, Bomp)" and "I'm Henry the Eighth, I Am" by Herman's Hermits stand out five decades later. (My tastes have always been eclectic.) Moving into the late 1960s and early 1970s, I listened to Top 40 hits on Indianapolis' WIFE-AM (home of the "Good Guys") and collected a small mountain of 45 singles that I played on my portable phonograph player. Later, I gravitated to album rock on WNAP-FM and started buying albums instead of singles—which I still played on that toy-like phonograph. And somewhere in there I got a cassette recorder and made my fair share of bootleg tapes from friends' LPs and by recording off the radio. (Good old WNAP, again.)

Fortunately, I abandoned the cheap record player and moved into more audiophile equipment once I got into high school. The father of the girl I was dating (she became my wife about thirty years later, but that's another story) was into high-end audio gear, plus I had a friend who worked at a local Lafayette Radio store, so I got exposed to and hooked on the good stuff early on. By the time I left for college I had a continuing subscription to *Stereo Review* magazine, along with a Sansui quadraphonic receiver, Technics direct drive turntable, Sansui cassette deck, a good pair of Koss headphones, and four fairly massive Lafayette-brand speakers. Maybe not true audiophile quality, but pretty good for a high school kid in the mid-1970s.

I upgraded my equipment frequently over the years, exchanging vinyl and tape for CDs, and in the late 1990s migrated into an audio/video home theater system. (Yes, I had a Laserdisc player, long before DVDs hit town.) Today I have two home theaters in my house (living room and basement), with digital music streamed to both theaters and several other rooms, besides. My 1,600+ CDs are stored in boxes in my basement, along with several hundred DVDs and Blu-rays.

As to my current equipment, I'm actually a tad behind the state-of-the-art systems I write about in this book. On the plus side, all my music is stored in WMA Lossless format, the vast majority ripped from CDs, with just a handful of tracks being downloaded from Amazon and iTunes.

22

On the minus side, I'm storing and controlling everything from a dedicated Niveus Denali media center PC that cost me four grand several years ago. (Niveus no longer makes them, in case you're wondering.) I run audio and video through a B&K Reference 70 preamp and Reference 200.7 200 watts/channel dedicated amplifier. (B&K went belly up a few years ago, too, although ATI recently purchased the company's assets and is in the process of resurrecting the brand.) My speakers come from another defunct firm, Onix, and are true audiophile quality. I watch it all on a Panasonic 58" plasma TV and control it with a Logitech Harmony One remote. (Both Panasonic and Logitech are still in business, last time I looked.)

My main music interface is Windows Media Center (although my PC is running Windows Vista, not the somewhat-improved Windows 7). I stream music to multiple rooms using Media Center Extenders from Linksys, which are less than reliable (and also discontinued). So you can see, I have a system that works (mostly) but could be upgraded.

Taking my own advice from this book, my intent is to sometime soon switch from the dedicated media center PC to a home server. I can then stream music from that server to either smallish PCs (running Windows Media Center) or other devices connected to the various TVs and audio systems throughout the house. Since my CD collection is ripped in lossless format, I'm in good shape there. I did choose WMA Lossless, which locks me into the Windows ecosystem to some degree, but I could always convert those files to FLAC or Apple Lossless if I really needed to. (And, worse comes to worst, I still have those 1,600+ CDs in my basement, in case I ever need to start from scratch.)

In any case, having had a whole-house digital music system for several years now has totally sold me on the concept. Whenever I want to listen to music, whether that's a favorite album or a mood-reflective playlist, it's a matter of calling it up on the Media Center menu and pressing the **Play** button. I can display a slideshow of family pictures while the music's playing, and it works great for both background music and intensive listening. It's a hell of a lot more convenient (and conducive for serious listening) than physically picking through the shelves of a CD collection in search of that one CD you want. Access to tens of thousands of songs at the push of a button—what's not to like about that?

Ripping Your Physical Music Collection

I f you're older than a certain age, you have probably amassed a substantial music collection in physical format. Depending on that certain age, we could be talking about CDs, vinyl records, audiocassettes, or maybe even 8-track or reel-to-reel tapes. You don't want to toss this treasure trove of classic music; there must be a way to convert it from physical to digital format.

Well, there is a way—actually, lots of ways, depending on the nature of your collection. It's actually quite easy to rip CDs to digital audio files, and not that much harder (once you get the right equipment) to do the same with your discs and tapes. You do, however, have to make some choices ahead of time, such as file format and bitrate, but then the actual conversion process is as easy as clicking a button or two.

Ripping CDs to Digital

Let's start with the easiest and most common type of conversion, from compact discs to digital audio files. This is relatively easy because CDs are already in digital format, so it's really just a matter of converting one format of digital file (on the CD) to another (on your computer). It's so easy that most music player programs (including iTunes and Windows Media Player) do it.

> ♪ ULTIMATELY **INTERESTING** The process of converting music on a CD to digital audio files is called *ripping*, as in "I'm ripping my old Bob Seger discs to digital." That's not to be confused with the process of transferring digital audio files to a CD, which is called *burning*, as in "I'm burning all my Bob Seger tracks to CD."

Understanding the Process

The process is simple. In general, here's what happens:

1. You insert the CD you want to copy into your computer's CD/DVD drive.
2. You launch your music player or music ripping program.
3. You configure your program to rip files in a specific file format and bitrate.
4. You click the "rip" button in your program.
5. The program reads the music files from the CD, converts them to digital audio files in the chosen format and bitrate, then writes those files to a designated location on your computer's hard drive.
6. The program goes online and retrieves metadata (album title, recording artist, song titles, and so forth) for the newly created digital audio files.
7. The newly ripped files are added to your digital music library.

As I said, pretty simple. The only really complicated thing is choosing the file format and bitrate for your ripped files, which you only have to do a single time; once you configure your program, it will rip all future CDs using those same settings.

Choosing the Best Digital File Format and Bitrate

But which settings should you choose? I won't go over all the different variations again here, but will offer the following suggestions:

- If you listen to your collection through a decent home audio system or good headphones, go with one of the three lossless formats— Apple/AAC Lossless (if you're into the Apple ecosystem), WMA Lossless (if you're in the Windows ecosystem), or FLAC (if you're somewhat of an iconoclast).

> **ULTIMATELY INTERESTING** Learn more about file formats and bitrates in Chapter 4, "Understanding Digital Audio File Formats."

- If you listen through an unmodified PC (stock speakers, etc.), an iPod or other player with good headphones (not the stock earbuds), or in a good car audio system, go with a high-bitrate lossy format, like 256-320Kbps AAC (Apple), WMA (Windows), or MP3 (universal).

- If you listen primarily via an iPod or other portable music player using earbuds, go with a mid-bitrate lossy format, like 192Kbps AAC, MP3, or WMA.

> **ULTIMATELY INTERESTING** If you want to be relatively futureproof—that is, you want the option of ripping to a different format sometime in the future—go with one of the lossless formats. You can always re-rip (or, more technically, re-transcode) an AAC/WMA/FLAC Lossless file to a lower-bitrate lossy file, if need be.

In other words, let the quality of your playback system dictate your file format and bitrate. For best sound, go with a lossless format. Otherwise, let your ears be the judge and choose a lower-bitrate lossy format.

Choosing the Best Ripping Application

When it comes to ripping CDs, just about any music player application can do the job. There are also dedicated ripping apps that we'll also examine.

First, a short list of music players that double as CD rippers:

- **iTunes Player** (www.apple.com/itunes/download/, free). Supports AAC and MP3—but not WMA or FLAC.
- **MediaMonkey** (www.mediamonkey.com, free). Supports MP3, AAC, WMA, FLAC, and OGG.
- **WinAmp** (www.winamp.com, free). Supports MP3, AAC, WMA, and FLAC.
- **Windows Media Player** (included with Microsoft Windows, free). Supports WMA and MP3—but not AAC or FLAC.

- **VLC Media Player** (www.videolan.org, free). Supports MP3, AAC, WMA, and FLAC.

These programs all work pretty much the same way. After you've configured them for your file format/bitrate of choice, you insert a CD and click the **Rip** button. Nothing much to it, really.

There is, however, a class of CD ripper programs that provide a bit more functionality, chiefly in the realm of bit checking and therefore theoretically cleaner rips (that is, with fewer dropouts and other errors). These standalone programs will typically check the ripped file to the original for any discrepancies, and then re-rip as necessary. They also will rip to more formats than most music player programs, and may (or may not) do a better job at grabbing metadata from multiple music databases. Some of these apps also function as audio conversion programs—that is, they'll convert existing digital files from one format to another.

> **♪ ULTIMATELY INTERESTING** A ripping error typically manifests itself as a short dropout—that is, blank space or a missing section, typically of less than a second. These errors are relatively rare, even when ripping with general music player apps. I've only experienced glitches in a handful of the 25,000+ tracks I've personally ripped, which leads me to think you probably don't need to use a standalone ripper program if you don't want to.

The most popular of these single-function CD ripping programs include the following:

- **Audiograbber** (www.audiograbber.org, free). Bypasses your PC's sound card during ripping for more accurate conversion. Can also capture audio from your computer's microphone input, or rip multiple tracks to a single file. Rips to WAV files (initially), then to MP3 and WMA files (with external codecs).

- **dBpoweramp** (www.dbpoweramp.com, $38). A suite of apps, including the popular CD Ripper program (converts to MP3, AAC, WMA, FLAC, and OGG), Batch Ripper (for automated ripping from multi-disc CD players, up to 120 CDs per hour), and Music Converter (for converting existing audio files from one format to another).

- **Exact Audio Copy** (www.exactaudiocopy.de, free). A popular Windows-based ripping program, big on reliability and error correction. Rips to most popular formats, including MP3, WMA, FLAC, and OGG—but not AAC. Can also rip specific time ranges in addition to complete tracks.

■ **FreeRIP Basic** (www.freerip.com, free). Rips to most popular formats, including MP3, WMA, FLAC, and OGG—but not AAC.

All of these ripping programs will do a good job, and may produce more reliable results than ripping with a general music player program.

Ripping a CD with iTunes

How do you rip a CD? The details differ from program to program, so we'll look at a few of the most popular apps—starting with the iTunes player.

Start by configuring iTunes for your chosen file type and bitrate. Select **Edit > Preferences** to open the General Preferences dialog box, then select the **General** tab. Go to the When You Insert a CD section and click the **Import Settings** button.

When the Import Settings dialog box appears, as shown in Figure 23.1, pull down the Import Using list and select the desired file type—AAC Encoder (for standard AAC lossy files), AIFF Encoder, Apple Lossless Encoder (for AAC Lossless files), MP3 Encoder, or WAV Encoder. Next, pull down the Setting list and select the desired rip quality, which differs depending on the file type you selected. For example, if you selected the AAC Encoder, you have the option of High Quality (128Kbps), iTunes Plus (256Kbps), Spoken Podcast (64Kbps), or Custom anything from 64Kbps to 320Kbps). Click **OK** when done.

FIGURE 23.1

Configuring iTunes for ripping.

Once everything is properly configured, all you have to do to rip a CD is insert that CD into your computer's CD/DVD drive. As you can see in Figure

23.2, all the tracks from the CD are now listed in the iTunes window. Check those tracks you want to copy, then click the **Import CD** button at the bottom of the iTunes window.

FIGURE 23.2
Getting ready to rip a CD with iTunes.

iTunes now extracts the selected tracks from the CD and converts them from their original CD Audio format to the file format you selected, sampled at the bitrate you selected. The converted files are written to your PC's hard disk and automatically added to the iTunes library.

ULTIMATELY INTERESTING Make sure you're connected to the Internet before you start ripping, so that your program can download album and track details. If you don't connect, you won't encode track names or CD cover art—and will have to do so manually, later.

Ripping a CD with Windows Media Player

Note, however, that the iTunes player doesn't rip to WMA format. So if you're invested in the Windows ecosystem, you'll need to use a different ripper—such as Microsoft's own Windows Media Player (WMP).

Of course, you'll first need to configure WMP for your file format and bitrate of choice. Assuming you're using WMP 11, you should right-click anywhere at the top of the window and select **Tools > Options** from the pop-up menu. When the Options dialog box appears, select the **Rip Music** tab and go to the Rip Settings section, shown in Figure 23.3.

FIGURE 23.3

Configuring Windows Media Player for Ripping.

Pull down the Format list and select your file format—Windows Media Audio (WMA lossy), Windows Media Audio Pro, Windows Media Audio Variable Bit Rate, Windows Media Audio Lossless (WMA Lossless), MP3, or WAV (lossless). Then adjust the Audio Quality slider to select the desired bitrate; the available options vary by the type of file you selected. Click OK to apply your settings.

Now it's time to start ripping. All you have to do is insert the CD you want to copy into your PC's CD/DVD drive and, when the Now Playing window appears, click Rip CD.

Alternatively, you can rip a CD from the main WMP window, shown in Figure 23.4. Check all the tracks you want to copy, and then click the **Rip CD** button.

Whichever method you use, Windows Media Player now extracts the selected tracks from the CD and converts them to the file format you selected, sampled at the bit rate you selected. The converted files are written to your PC's hard disk and added to the Windows Media Player Library.

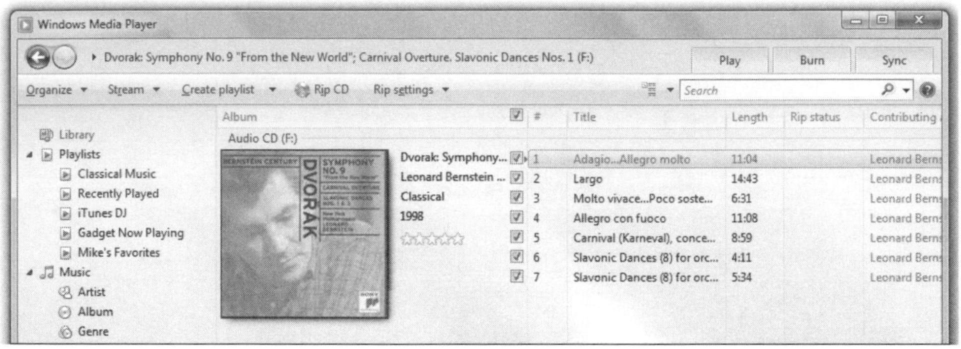

FIGURE 23.4

Getting ready to rip a CD with Windows Media Player.

Ripping Lots of CDs

When you rip your CDs to hard disk, one of the biggest issues is time—especially if you're trying to rip your entire CD collection.

You see, it takes about 3-4 minutes to rip an entire CD. But that doesn't take into account the time it takes to locate the CD, remove the disc from the jewel case, and insert the disc into your computer's CD drive—and then afterwards remove the CD from the computer, reinsert the disc into the jewel case, and return the CD to storage. Let's say the whole process takes 5 minutes per disc.

So, if you're ripping 100 CDs, that's 500 minutes, or almost 8 1/2 hours. If you have 500 CDs, we're talking close to 42 hours; if you have 1,000 discs, that's 85 hours or so. With this in mind, we can assume you won't do your ripping in one marathon session. (For what it's worth, when I originally ripped my then-1,000 CD collection, I did it in bits and pieces over a period of six weeks.)

Fortunately, there are options.

First, you can buy yourself a multiple-CD changer and use dBpoweramp Batch Ripper to rip multiple CDs at a time. That's if you can find a multiple-CD changer, of course—there are only a few manufacturers sill making them these days.

> **♪ ULTIMATELY INTERESTING** As of mid-2012, five- and six-CD players are still available from Denon, Onkyo, Teac, and Yamaha—although you might have to special order them. In my experience, however, the best unit for big batch ripping was a 400-CD megachanger that Sony used to make, which you could load up and let it do its thing overnight. That machine is long out of production, unfortunately, but you can still find used units on eBay and in the Amazon marketplace.

You also have the option of having somebody else do your CD ripping for you. Short of hiring migrant labor for the job, there are several companies that offer more professional solutions. The way it works is you box up your entire CD collection and ship it to the company; a week or so later you get your CDs back, ripped either to an external hard drive or a batch of DVDs (which can then be copied to your PC's hard disk). In most instances you choose the file format and bitrate for the ripped files.

You'll pay about a buck a disc for this service, offered by the following companies:

- **dmp3music** (www.dmp3digital.com)
- **MusicShifter** (www.musicshifter.com)
- **ReadyToPlay** (www.readytoplay.com)
- **Rip2iPod** (www.rip2ipod.com)
- **RipDigital** (www.ripdigital.com)

Know, however, that this type of service is only for those who won't get nervous shipping their entire music collection cross-country. If you're skittish about this, do it yourself instead.

Filling in the Metadata

In most instances, your music player or CD ripper program, after ripping a CD, will go out via the Internet to one of the big online music databases to retrieve all pertinent metadata about the ripped tracks. (Assuming, of course, that your computer was connected to the Internet while you were ripping.)

> **ULTIMATELY INTERESTING** Learn more about metadata and the big music databases in Chapter 14, "Organizing Your Digital Music Collection."

On the off chance that no metadata is retrieved, or that the wrong tags are applied for a given disc, you'll need to either use another (better) program to retrieve tag data or enter it yourself. I discussed all that back in Chapter 14, "Organizing Your Digital Music Collection," so turn back there if you need help doing this.

Ripping Vinyl Discs and Analog Tapes to Digital

If you have a collection of old vinyl records and audio cassettes (or even 8-track or reel-to-real tapes!), you're not out of luck. It's possible to transfer any collection of physical media to digital format and burn them onto CDs; all you need is the right equipment and software. Converting your vinyl and tape to digital will help your collection last longer than it would have otherwise, and make all your old music accessible to any state-of-the-art digital music system.

Understanding the Process

When you think about it, it's a bit of a challenge to digitize physical media. Not only are you going from a physical disc or tape to a computer file, you're also converting analog music to digital format. Fortunately, the technology behind both conversions is relatively simple.

Ripping a CD to digital format is no more complex than reading one type of digital file and converting it to another file type. (CD tracks are nothing more than digital audio files in an industry-specific format.) In the case of vinyl records and tapes, you have to intercept the output signal from the playback device, convert it from analog to digital, and then save the new digital file.

Here's how it works, in general:

1. You connect a turntable or tape deck to the appropriate inputs on your audio receiver (or amp/preamp combo), and then connect the left and right analog outputs from your receiver to the mic input on your computer. (You may need a converter cable to go from RCA outputs to mini-jack input.)

   OR

   You connect your turntable or tape deck to a special USB capture device, which then connects to your computer via USB.

   OR

   You use a special USB turntable or tape deck, which connects directly to your computer via USB.

2. You launch a special digital recording program on your computer.

3. You begin playback of a given disc or tape on your original equipment.

4. The recording program records the signal coming from your turntable or tape deck as a digital audio file on your computer.

You can typically choose the file format and bitrate for the recorded file. Some programs record an entire album side as a single file; others will automatically create separate files for each track on the album. You can then listen to your newly ripped digital tracks, or burn the digital files to a CD for posterity.

So what equipment do you need? Here's the list:

- Traditional turntable or cassette deck, audio amplifier/preamp or receiver, along with appropriate R/L stereo cables (and some sort of R/L RCA to single mini-jack converter)

  OR

- Traditional turntable or cassette deck and USB capture device (R/L audio in to USB out)

  OR

- USB turntable or cassette deck
- Digital recording software
- Personal computer

> **ULTIMATELY INTERESTING** When your old records and tapes are in digital format, you can copy them to audio CD just as you would any digital audio file, and have yourself a brand-spanking new (sort-of) CD of your favorite old album. Learn more in Chapter 30, "Burning Your Music to a CD or USB Drive."

Choosing the Right Equipment

If you go the traditional route—that is, you connect your turntable/tape deck to your receiver and then to your PC's mic input—you don't need any additional equipment other than what you already have. (Save for a Y-connector from your receiver to your computer's mic input.)

That said, there are several ready-made solutions for converting discs and tapes to digital format. You may find these easier to deal with.

First, you can insert a simple USB audio capture device into the chain between your turntable/tape deck and PC. These devices convert the analog audio signal to digital format and output it via USB. Just connect the R/L RCA outputs from your turntable or tape deck to the RCA inputs on the capture device, then connect the capture device to your PC via USB.

As you can imagine, using this sort of conversion gadget is a tad easier than doing the old R/L RCA connections to your PC's mic input. Figure 23.5 shows one such device; you can find them at Radio Shack or Fry's, or online at Amazon. Price is typically under $20.

> **ULTIMATELY INTERESTING** Many of these USB capture devices are actually audio/video in nature, in that they also include inputs for composite video and S-Video. This makes them also useful for converting VHS tapes to digital format.

FIGURE 23.5

A typical USB audio capture device—analog inputs and USB output.

Then there's the all-in-one solution, as typified by ION Audio's TTUSB USB turntable—or what the company calls a "high-performance LP conversion system." As you can see in Figure 23.6, what you get is a decent quality turntable with its own analog-to-digital converter built in, and USB output. Connect the turntable directly to your computer via USB, use the included EZ Vinyl Converter software, and you're ready to rock and roll. The whole shebang sells for around $100; find more information at www.ionaudio.com/products/details/ttusb.

Sony also makes a similar USB turntable, model LX300USB. It's a belt-drive unit, sells for under $150, and comes with Sony's Audio Studio software for recording your vinyl records. Figure 23.7 shows what this one looks like; you can find it online at Amazon, Crutchfield, and similar dealers.

> **ULTIMATELY INTERESTING** ION's TTUSB can also be used as a traditional turntable with traditional R/L RCA outputs. It also has line inputs to which you can connect a tape deck to convert your audiocassettes, 8-track, and reel-to-reel tapes. By the way, the ION unit is also sold under the Numark professional brand, same model number, same price.

23

FIGURE 23.6
The ION TTUSB analog-to-digital turntable.

FIGURE 23.7
Sony's LX300USB turntable.

On the tape side of things, ION makes a similar Tape 2 PC USB audiocassette deck, shown in Figure 23.8. It has the requisite built-in analog-to-digital converter, along with USB output. It comes with the EZ Tape Converter program for recording your old cassettes. This unit sells for around $120; more info available here: www.ionaudio.com/products/details/tape-2-pc.

> **ULTIMATELY USEFUL** If you have a good quality turntable, you'll probably get better results using it for playback, connected to a USB audio capture device (or directly to your PC's mic input). These USB turntables are fine for casual listeners, but aren't quite the quality of a good audiophile unit.

FIGURE 23.8
ION's Tape 2 PC USB audiocassette deck.

Choosing the Right Software

When it comes to recording tracks from your discs and tapes, you need to install some sort of recording software on your computer. You can go one of two routes.

The first route is to use a general digital recording program, which records the signals you input as WAV files. You can then convert the WAV files to MP3, AAC, WMA, or whatever file formats you like, as well as manually add your own track splits and metadata. Good programs for this include:

- **Audacity** (audacity.sourceforge.net, free)
- **GarageBand** (www.apple.com/ilife/garageband/, $14.99, Mac OS only)
- **GoldWave** (www.goldwave.com, lifetime license $49, one-year license $19)

■ **Sonar X1 Essential** (www.cakewalk.com/Products/SONAR/ X1-Essential/, $100)

■ **Sony Sound Forge Audio Studio** (www.sonycreativesoftware.com/soundforgesoftware, $65)

For that matter, you can also use the Sound Recorder app built into Windows, or the SimpleSound app built into the Mac OS—both free, but somewhat limited in terms of features.

The second route is to use a program specifically designed for recording music from vinyl and tape. The most popular of these conversion programs is **Golden Records Vinyl Converter** (www.nch.com.au/golden/), which works for both vinyl and tape conversion. It includes various audio restoration tools, to remove clicks and hiss, and also does a good job determining track breaks and creating files for individual tracks. It encodes the final files in either WAV or MP3 format, and sells for $60.

Also popular is a program called **Spin It Again** (www.acoustica.com/spinitagain/). This one offers advanced track detection technology, along with very effective track cleaning. It also looks up and applies metadata for each recorded track. The software sells for $34.95, and records to WAV, MP3, WMA, and OGG format files.

> **ULTIMATELY CAUTIOUS** You may have noticed that I previously mentioned two additional programs, EZ Vinyl Converter and EZ Tape Converter. These programs, however, are not available for individual purchase; they're only packaged with the ION and Numark USB turntables and tape decks. So unless you buy one of those products, you'll have to use another software program.

Splitting a Side

When you're recording audio from an analog medium, you have the choice of recording all the songs as separate files, or recording the entire side of an LP or tape as one large file. While making one large file might be more convenient, recording separate files provides more flexibility when it comes to listening to the songs from your digital music library.

The challenge comes when the recording software doesn't do a good job of determining where one track ends and another begins—or simply doesn't offer a separate-track recording option. In this instance, you'll need to use your recording program to cut one large track down into several smaller ones. It's a manual process, but you can do it.

For that matter, your recording program might leave some unnecessary blank space at the beginning and end of the recorded file. You can use your recording program to trim the blank space from the beginning and end of the file; read your manual for instructions. (And if your recording program doesn't offer audio trimming, change programs.)

> **ULTIMATELY CAUTIOUS** The one downside of recording from vinyl or tape is that you don't get any metadata with your files. (Heck, many of the LPs and tapes you'll be recording have never been reissued in CD or digital format!) That means you'll have to manually edit the tags for each track; see Chapter 14 for instructions.

PONDERING THE VINYL TO DIGITAL THING

If you're a long-time vinyl collector, you don't want to abandon your record collection just because you're going digital. You probably have lots of LPs (and maybe a few 45s) that have never been released on compact disc or digitally, so there's value in moving them into your digital library.

If you're not into old-school vinyl, you might find it hard to imagine that there are albums that have yet to see digital release, but it's true. Even with the efforts of Rhino, Hip-O, Wounded Bird, and other reissue labels, there are a lot of lesser-known LPs of the 60s and 70s that remain buried in the vaults. If you have those albums on vinyl, you're a step ahead.

A quick word on my favorite reissue label, Wounded Bird Records. Wounded Bird has reissued quite a few of hidden gems and guilty pleasures of my youth, albums without big followings but that occupy a warm place in my musical heart. I'm talking little-known albums such as *New City* by Blood, Sweat & Tears; Dave Brubeck and sons' *Two Generations of Brubeck*; Harry Chapin's *Heads & Tales*; Don Ellis' *Tears of Joy*; Ellen Foley's *Night Out*; most every LP Gordon Lightfoot ever cut; the whole basketful of 1970s M.F. Horn LPs from Maynard Ferguson and his big band; and assorted albums from the likes of Bay City Rollers, Laura Branigan, Brownsville Station, Samantha Fox, Grand Funk Railroad, Howard Jones, Nicolette Larson, Melissa Manchester, Passport, Redbone, Sister Sledge, Wendy and Lisa, and Edgar Winter. If you're into any of this stuff, check 'em out at www.woundedbird.com.

Rhino used to be my favorite reissue label, but they seem to have gone straight in recent years. Still, there's no denying the sheer genius of their collections of the past, including *Super Hits of the 70s: Have a Nice Day*, *One Kiss Can Lead to Another: Girl Group Sounds, Lost & Found* , and the legendary *Nuggets: Original Artyfacts from the First Psychedelic Era* boxed set. All a step above your typical box or collection, with some surprising tracks and great liner notes.

But I digress. The point is that if you're a vinyl collector, you probably have some titles in your collection that are not available today, and therefore worth your while to rip and add to your digital music library. It's not so much that digital is a replacement for vinyl in this regard, but rather it lets you listen to your hidden gems along with the rest of your modern music tracks.

There is the additional question, of course, of whether there's value in digitizing vinyl albums that are also available on CD or available for digital download. If you're a die-hard vinyl devotee, you might think that the supposed warmth and fidelity of the vinyl release would trump the CD release, and thus justify ripping your vinyl to digital. But that's a fool's argument; if a commercial CD can't reproduce the warmth of the original vinyl, then neither can a homemade rip. I suppose there might be some argument made for ripping ultra-high fidelity discs, such as those from Mobile Fidelity Sound Lab in their heyday, but that still misses the point. If it's the audio quality of analog you crave, digitizing a vinyl record won't give you that analog sound. You might as well buy the CD version, and not record all those pops and cracks from the LP.

In any case, ripping your LPs to digital is relatively easy to do (if you follow my advice in this chapter), if a bit time consuming. I'd do it for those LPs unavailable in commercial digital format, but probably not for albums that have been reissued (often in higher fidelity) on CD. But that's just me; serious vinyl collectors might think otherwise.

23

Playing Digital Music on Your Computer

For many music lovers, home base for music storage and playback is the humble home computer. Whether it be Windows or Mac (or even Linux), notebook or desktop, networked or not, using your computer as the hub for all your digital music activity makes a lot of sense.

It's also quite versatile. Not only can you listen to your music library on your computer (via speakers or headphones), you can connect your computer to your home audio system for even better sounding playback. You can also connect your computer to your home network to play music on other computers and devices throughout your house, which is always fun.

IN THIS CHAPTER

- Choosing and Using a Music Player Application

- Improving Your Computer's Sound

- Connecting Your Computer to Your Home Audio System

The challenge, though, is maximizing the sound quality of your digital music playback while minimizing the effort of connecting everything together and making it all work. As with all things related to digital music, there are choices to be made.

Choosing and Using a Music Player Application

When it comes to playing digital music on a personal computer, it all revolves around the music player application you use. You use your music player not only to play your digital tracks, but also to organize your library, create playlists, rip and burn CDs, and a lot more.

What a Music Player Does

Most music player programs share a similar feature set. Whether you're using Windows Media Player (built into the Windows operating system), the iTunes player (installed when you first connected your iPhone, iPod, or iPad), or another quality program, what you can do is pretty similar. The big differences are in some of the ancillary functionality, as well as file format compatibility.

In terms of what you see onscreen, most music player apps have a big open area in the middle of the display. What's displayed here depends on what function you're using. You may see artwork for the currently playing track, a collection of album covers, a list of available tracks, or even some sort of groovy graphic "visualization" that moves in time to the music. (If your player also functions as a digital video player, which most do, this area of the screen will also display the picture when you're playing back videos.)

Of course, all digital music players include an area of playback controls, typically located at the very top or bottom of the window. These are the normal transport buttons you'd find on any physical CD player or music player, including Play/Pause, Stop, Rewind, and Fast Forward. Most players also include Next and Previous track buttons, along with a volume control and mute button.

Most digital music players also include a playlist section, where you can view and edit the contents of any playlist you've created. Most players let you create your own playlists to better organize the music you most like to listen to. (You may also use the playlist function to set up a group of songs for burning onto CD or USB drive.)

Whichever digital music player you use, you follow the same general steps to play a digital audio file. You start by launching the program, then you select the item to play, typically by browsing to the desired genre, album, or playlist. Start the playback by double-clicking the track, album, or playlist, or by clicking Play in the transport controls. You click Pause to pause playback, and start up in the same place by clicking Play again. You can stop playback altogether by clicking Stop.

Evaluating Music Player Programs

There are many different music player programs available. You probably have at least one of them already installed on your computer; others are readily available for download over the Internet. All of these programs do exactly what you'd think—they play back digital audio files. Not all programs play back all types of files, however, which is an issue. On the plus side, some of these programs include additional functionality. You need to look at the whole package before you make a decision.

> ♪ ULTIMATELY **USEFUL**   Most of these programs are Windows only. If you're a Mac user, your choices are more narrow—the iTunes player, obviously, but also RealPlayer, Songbird, VLC Media Player. (WinAmp also offers a Mac version, although it's currently in beta.)

All that said, Table 24.1 details some of the most popular music player programs, along with some brief details about each.

Okay, that's a fair number of choices. How do you choose one player over another?

The first criteria for choosing a music player program is which file formats it supports. If you're tied in the Apple ecosystem, for example, you need a player that supports AAC-format files—which all do *except* MusicBee. If you're in the Windows ecosystem, you need a player that supports WMA-format files—which all do *except* the iTunes player. If you want to go the FLAC route, you can go with any player *except* the iTunes player, RealPlayer, and Windows Media Player. Obviously, if you're in the MP3 world, just about everything will work.

Next, look at the player's functionality. Obviously, all will play back digital files and all will rip files from CD, but not all will burn files to CD. If that's important to you, avoid MusicBee, Songbird, Spider Player, and VLC Media Player.

Table 24.1   Music Player Applications

	Audio Playback	CD Ripping	CD Burning	Playlist Creation	Video Playback	Other Features	Supported Audio Formats	Operating Systems Supported	More Information	Price
iTunes Player	Yes	Yes	Yes	Yes	Yes	Tight integration with other Apple products, connects to iMatch cloud-based music service, necessary to connect to iTunes Store	AA, AAC, AIFF, MP3, WAV	Mac, Windows	www.apple.com/itunes/download/	Free
MediaMonkey	Yes	Yes	Yes	Yes	Yes	Tag editor, file format conversion, iPod sync	AAC, FLAC, MP3, OGG, WMA	Windows	www.mediamonkey.com	Free
MusicBee	Yes	Yes	No	Yes	No	Personalize with skins and plug-ins, tag editor, Internet radio playback	AIFF, FLAC, MP3, OGG, WAV, WMA	Windows	www.getmusicbee.com	Free
RealPlayer	Yes	Yes	Yes	Yes	Yes	iPod sync, evolving into more of a video player than audio player	AAC, MP3, RA, WAV, WMA	Mac, Windows	www.real.com/realplayer/	Free
Songbird	Yes	Yes	No	Yes	Yes	Displays extra info from web for each track	AAC, FLAC, MP3, OGG, WMA	Mac, Windows	www.getsongbird.com	Free
Spider Player	Yes	Yes	No	Yes	No	32-bit audio processing, Internet radio playback and recording, file format conversion, tag editor	AAC, AC3, FLAC, MP3, OGG, WAV, WMA	Windows	www.spider-player.com	Free
VLC Media Player	Yes	Yes	No	Yes	Yes	File format conversion, Internet radio playback	AAC, FLAC, MP3, WMA	Linux, Mac, Unix, Windows	www.videolan.org	Free
WinAmp	Yes	Yes	Yes	Yes	Yes	Personalize with skins and visualizations, Internet radio playback	AAC, AIFF, FLAC, MP3, WMA	Windows, Mac (BETA)	www.winamp.com	Free
Windows Media Player	Yes	Yes	Yes	Yes	Yes	Built into Windows OS (not available for separate download), tight integration with Windows OS	AAC, MP3, WMA	Windows	windows.microsoft.com/en-US/windows/products/windows-media	Free

24

What are my recommendations? Given how similar most of these programs are, once you get past compatibility issues, any of them will probably do the job. Obviously, if you're invested in the Apple ecosystem (have an iPod or iPhone, have all your files in AAC format, or download from the iTunes Store), you're best off with Apple's very own iTunes player. And if you're invested in the Windows ecosystem, your best bet is Windows Media Player. Otherwise, the better all-round music player is probably MediaMonkey. (WinAmp looks good on paper, but is rapidly aging—and there's no telling how much longer AOL will support it.)

> ♪ ULTIMATELY **USEFUL**   One important feature to look for in a music player is *gapless playback*—the ability to play one track after another without long silences in between. This may not seem like a big deal until you listen to an album where one track flows directly into one another, such as the last half of *Sgt. Pepper's Lonely Hearts Club Band* or, for something more obscure, Spirit's *Twelve Dreams of Dr. Sardonicus*. It's particularly important when listening to classical music, where a single movement may be broken up into multiple tracks; you don't want the music to stop just because the tracks changed. Most (but not all) music players offer some sort of gapless playback or cross-fading between tracks; in fact, gapless playback is enabled by default in the three major music players (iTunes, Windows Media Player, and MediaMonkey).

With that in mind, we'll take a closer look at all three recommended players—iTunes, Windows Media Player, and MediaMonkey.

Using the iTunes Player

Like it or not, but the most popular music player program today is Apple's iTunes player. It's a simple function of how many iPods, iPads, and iPhones that Apple has sold; to use your i-device, you need to install the (free) iTunes software. Hence for many users, iTunes has become their default music player app.

That's not necessarily a bad thing; iTunes is a decent enough program. It's a little too cluttered for my personal liking, and while innovative at the time, it's starting to show its age a little. Still, it'll do everything you need it to do. (Except play WMA-format files, of course; you should never expect Apple to play nice with the competition.)

You can download the iTunes player (for free) from www.apple.com/itunes/download/. As noted elsewhere in this book, you have to use iTunes if you want to download items from Apple's iTunes Store.

As you can see in Figure 24.1, the iTunes window is divided into two or three panes. (The third pane is optional.) The left pane (dubbed the Source pane) is for navigation, and includes the following sections:

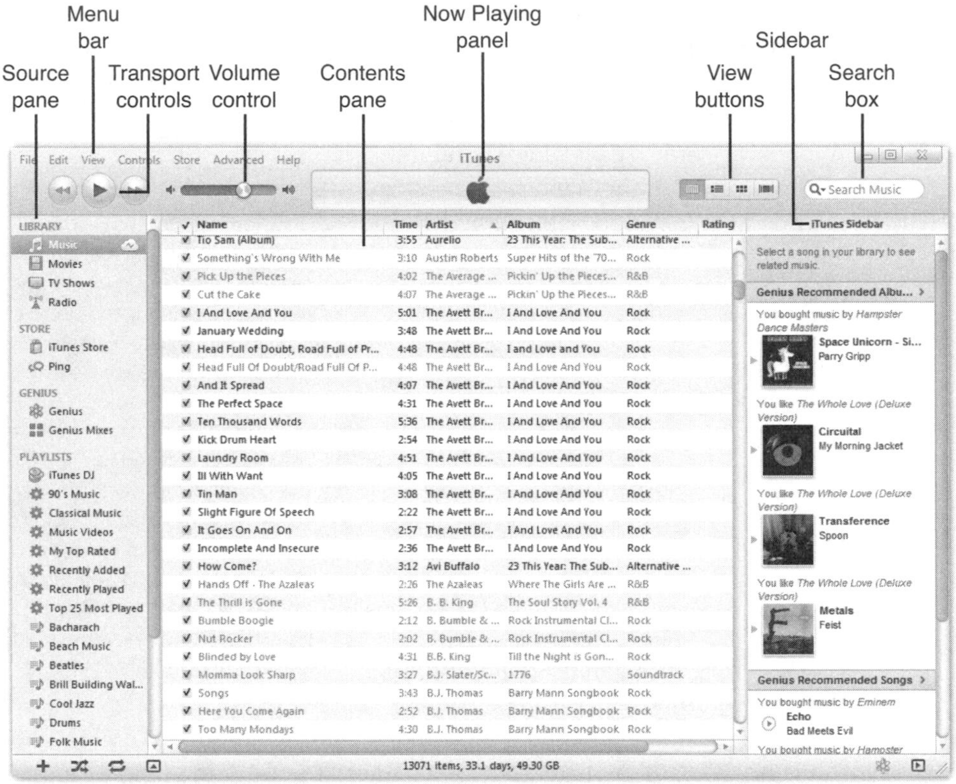

FIGURE 24.1

The iTunes player, with contents in song list view.

■ **Library**. Displays either your Music, Movies, TV Shows, Radio, or Apps libraries—that is, all those items stored on your computer.

■ **Store**. Connects to and displays the iTunes Store or, optionally, iTunes Ping.

ULTIMATELY INTERESTING Ping is the social networking arm of iTunes; it displays recent activity from your favorite artists.

■ **Genius.** Genius is iTune's recommendation engine; it recommends artists and tracks related to other music you're listening to. Click Genius to create and play Genius playlists (automatic playlists based on a selection), or click Genius Mixes to play pre-selected mixes based on your library's contents.

> ♪ **ULTIMATELY INTERESTING** When you connect your iPod, iPhone, or iPad, there's an additional section for your connected device. Click this item to sync your two devices, and to manage your portable device.

■ **Playlist.** This section displays all the playlists you've created, or that iTunes has created for you automatically. Click a playlist to view, edit, and play it.

The center pane displays the contents of whatever you've selected in the Source pane. For example, if you select Music in the Library section, the center pane displays all the music in your library. If you select iTunes Store from the Store section, it connects to and display's Apple's iTunes Store.

You can, by the way, change how the contents in the center pane are displayed. Just click one of the four buttons at the top right of the window. You can choose any one of the following four views:

■ **Song list.** Displays all tracks in a long list. You can sort the song list by track name, track time, artist, album title, genre, rating, and number of plays.

■ **Album list.** Displays all tracks sorted by album. That is, the list is sorted by album, with the tracks for each album listed within each album's section.

■ **Grid.** Displays album, artist, genre, or composer thumbnails, as shown in Figure 24.2. Click each thumbnail to see the tracks within.

■ **Cover flow.** Somewhat unique to iTunes, a "flow" of album covers, as shown in Figure 24.3.. Flip left and right through the covers using your mouse or the left and right arrow buttons on your computer keyboard. Contents for the selected album are displayed in a list beneath the covers.

FIGURE 24.2

iTunes in grid view, displaying artist thumbnails.

FIGURE 24.3

iTunes in cover flow view.

At the very top of the iTunes window is a menu bar, with pull-down menus for common functions. Beneath that are iTune's transport controls (Rewind, Play/Pause, Fast Forward), the volume control slider, the now playing pane, buttons for changing the display of the contents pane, and a search box. At the very bottom of the window are buttons for Create a Playlist, Shuffle, Repeat, and Show/Hide Artwork; stats for your library; and more buttons to Show Genius and Show/Hide Sidebar. (That's the right sidebar.)

That right sidebar is imaginatively named the iTunes Sidebar. It displays information related to the current selection, Genius results (if you have that feature enabled), and Ping results about your favorite artists.

Playing songs with iTunes is relatively simple. Make sure you have **Music** selected in the Library section of the Source pane, and then iTunes displays all the music you have stored on your computer. Depending on the view you've selected, you may see individual tracks, albums, or artists.

If you're displaying an album or artist, click the thumbnail for that album or artist to view all related songs. To play a track, either double-click it or select it and then click the **Play** button in the transport controls.

Using Windows Media Player

If you're a Windows user, you have another free media player program already installed. This one is Microsoft's own Windows Media Player (WMP), and it's every bit as versatile as the iTunes player. It even plays Apple's AAC-format audio tracks.

By the way, if you somehow don't have Windows Media Player on your PC, you're out of luck; the only way to get it is with Microsoft Windows. That also means you can't upgrade from one version of WMP to another, without also upgrading the entire Windows operating system.

Like the iTunes player, WMP features three panes, as shown in Figure 24.4. The left pane is the Navigation pane, and includes sections for any libraries you've created or can access.

> **ULTIMATELY INTERESTING** The latest version of Windows Media Player (WMP 12, included with both Windows 7 and Windows 8 and discussed here) supports Apple's AAC format. Previous versions did not, so if you're still using WMP11 or older (on Windows Vista or older), it may be worth upgrading.

(Typically, each computer you have access to over a network shows up as a separate library.) Within each library are sections for Playlists, Music (filterable by Artist, Album, and Genre), Videos, Pictures, Recorded TV, and Other Media.

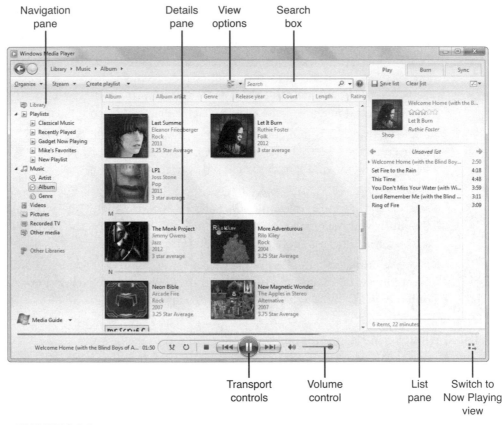

FIGURE 24.4

Microsoft's Windows Media Player.

Whatever you select in the Navigation pane is displayed, in detail, in the center pane, which Microsoft calls the Details pane. Click the **View Options** button, directly above this pane, to change the way these details are displayed—Icon (thumbnails for artist, album, or genre), Tile (kind of like a thumbnail but with summary information beneath), or Details (a basic list).

The contents of the right-hand, or List, pane, depend on the tab you select above the pane. The **Play** tab displays details about what you're currently playing; for example, if you're playing a playlist, the List pane displays information about the currently playing track at the top, along with all the tracks in the playlist at the bottom. The **Burn** tab is used for burning CDs; drag items to this pane to create a burn list. And the **Sync** tab is used for synchronizing content to a portable audio player.

One interesting aspect of WMP 12 is the Now Playing view. Instead of keeping the entire big WMP window open while you're playing music, you can switch to a much smaller window by clicking the **Now Playing** button at the lower right corner. This window, shown in Figure 24.5, displays the current tracks' album cover, along with playback and volume controls; as you can see, it takes up a lot less space. Return to the big WMP window by clicking the **Library** button at the top right of the little window.

Switch to Library view

Volume control

Transport controls

FIGURE 24.5

WMP's Now Playing window.

To play a single track in WMP 12, all you have to do is use the Navigation pane to navigate to the song you want to play, and then either double-click the **song title** or select the **song** and click the **Play** button.

To play an entire album, select **Album** in the Navigation pane, navigate to the album, and then click the **Play** button. Same thing with playing back all the songs by a particular artist or in a particular genre: Select either **Artist** or **Genre** in the Navigation pane, navigate to the artist or genre you want, and then click the **Play** button.

Using MediaMonkey

MediaMonkey is a good option if for some reason you don't like or don't want to use iTunes or WMP. It plays back all major audio formats, including Apple's AAC and Microsoft's WMA, as well as MP3, OGG, and FLAC. It's very effective at managing large digital music collections, offers an excellent tag editor, can convert existing audio files from one format to another, and even syncs with your iPod/iPad/iPhone. Given that it's every bit as free as the Apple and Microsoft offerings, what's not to like?

You can download MediaMonkey (for free, remember) from www.mediamonkey.com. They also offer an upgraded version, dubbed MediaMonkey Gold, for $24.95; this version offers more sophisticated library management, AutoPlaylists, and advanced error detection when burning CDs.

Like the other popular media players, MediaMonkey utilizes a navigation pane on the left, a contents pane in the middle, and a Now Playing pane on the right. (Figure 24.6 shows the MediaMonkey player.) There's a menu bar and search box at the top of the window, and transport controls and various other buttons at the bottom.

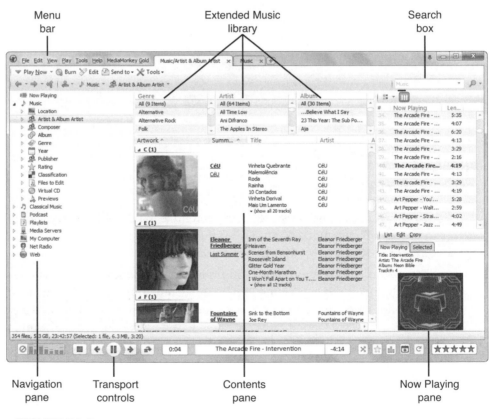

FIGURE 24.6

The MediaMonkey music player.

Whatever you select in the navigation pane is displayed in the contents pane. For most items, the contents pane is divided into four sections—three at the top and a big one below. The top three sections help you drill down through your selection, with sections for Genre (Composer if you've selected Classical Music), Artist, and Album. Filter your collection by any or all of these criteria, and matching tracks appear at the bottom of the contents pane.

You can also filter your collection by expanding any item in the navigation pane. Expand the Music item to display items by Location, Artist & Album Artist, Composer, Album, Genre, Year, and so forth. It's a lot more versatile than competing players.

To change the view in the contents pane, pull down the View menu and select from the options there. You can also use the **Show** buttons at the top of the now playing pane.

Playing a single track is as easy as navigating to that track in the contents pane and then either double-clicking it or selecting it and then clicking the **Play** button. Same thing with playing an album or a playlist or all tracks for a given artist; double-click the album/playlist/artist to start playback.

> **ULTIMATELY USEFUL** One thing that power users tend to like about MediaMonkey is that it's very easy to customize. For example, you can rearrange any of the items in the contents pane by simply dragging and dropping the item's header to another position in the pane. You can also change the look and feel of the player by adding different *skins*, which you can find online at www.mediamonkey.com/addons/browse/appearance/skins/.

Improving Your Computer's Sound

Ripping your music library and installing a music player app gets you started with digital music on your PC. For many users, that's enough; you can now play back all your favorite music, digitally, on your computer.

The problem, though, is that most personal computers have lousy sound systems. The sound cards are functional at best, and the speakers small and tinny. The sound is somewhat short of high fidelity—to be honest, it pretty much sucks.

So what can you do to improve the sound quality of music playback on your computer? Fortunately, quite a bit.

24

Using an External Digital to Analog Converter

Let's start with how the sound is generated inside your PC. Your computer has either a sound chip on its motherboard or a separate sound card inside the case. These sound chips/cards are fine for reproducing system sounds, videogame soundtracks, and what audio you typically get over the Internet. But they fall short when reproducing high fidelity music; they're just not built for that.

This is primarily due to the quality of the digital-to-analog converter (DAC) found on most soundboards. The DAC is a little piece of technology that converts digital audio into audio signals that can then be amplified and sent to your computer's speakers or headphones, or to an external audio system. You can find DACs in just about any device that plays digital audio; there's a DAC in your iPod or iPhone, in your Apple TV or Squeezebox device, in your notebook or desktop computer, and in your audio/video receiver.

A computer-based DAC works by taking the digital audio signals generated from a music player program, web-based streaming audio, or even CD playback and converting those digital signals into analog. The analog signals are then fed to your computer's speaker outputs.

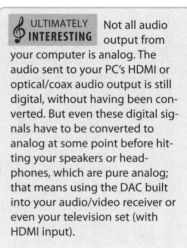

ULTIMATELY INTERESTING Not all audio output from your computer is analog. The audio sent to your PC's HDMI or optical/coax audio output is still digital, without having been converted. But even these digital signals have to be converted to analog at some point before hitting your speakers or headphones, which are pure analog; that means using the DAC built into your audio/video receiver or even your television set (with HDMI input).

The better quality the DAC, the better the resulting sound. Unfortunately, many devices (including most personal computers) use somewhat mediocre DACs, which means you get fairly noisy sound with limited dynamic range; most PC DACs sound somewhat muddled, lacking the clarity you're used to on a quality audio system.

Fortunately, you don't have to use the DAC that's built into your computer. It's easy enough, and not that expensive, to replace the built-in DAC with an external one of higher quality. It's really one of the easiest and lowest-cost ways to dramatically improve the audio quality of your computer for music playback.

ULTIMATELY USEFUL Some higher-end DACs will also upsample your audio to 24-bit/192KHz format, which approaches the quality of the SACD format. This upsampling is necessary to achieve the full effect of the so-called HD audio from HDtracks and similar high-end online download stores. (Learn more about HD audio in Chapter 10, "Downloading Music from Other Online Music Stores.")

An outboard DAC connects to your computer via either USB or optical/coaxial digital cable, and thus taps into your PC's sound system before the internal DAC. The outboard unit coverts your computer's digital audio to analog, and then feeds it to the unit's right and left analog RCA-jack outputs.

You can find several classes of outboard DACs designed for personal computer use. *Ultra-compact* units are small enough to carry with a notebook PC and offer basic digital-to-analog conversion; *desktop* DACs work fine with desktop PCs, and some offer 24/192 upsampling; and *component-style* DACs look right at home alongside your home audio equipment and offer many advanced features, including upsampling and filtering. All will improve the sound you get from the digital music on your computer.

Here's a short list of some of the more popular external DACs for computer use, lowest priced first:

■ **NuForce uDAC-2** (www.nuforce.com, $129). This ultra-compact DAC, shown in Figure 24.7, also functions as a headphone amplifier and includes both R/L RCA and minijack headphone outputs, as well as optical digital output. Features USB input only—and, in fact, is powered by that USB input.

24

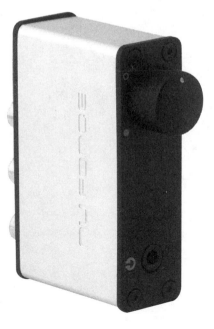

FIGURE 24.7

NuForce's compact uDAC-2 DAC/headphone amp.

- **Audioengine D1** (www.audioengineusa.com, $169). A compact 24-bit DAC, with both USB and optical digital inputs. Includes both R/L RCA outputs and headphone output.

- **Musical Fidelity V-Link II** (www.musicalfidelity.com, $189). This compact unit offers three types of inputs (USB, Toslink optical, and coaxial digital) and 24/192 upsampling.

- **Calyx Coffee** (www.calyxaudio.com, $199). An ultra-compact unit, about the size of a smartphone, with USB input.

- **NuForce Icon** (www.nuforce.com, $249). This desktop unit also includes a 12 watt/channel stereo amplifier, so you can use it to feed non-powered speakers. Input is via USB, output is via speaker connectors or stereo minijack, for headphone listening.

- **Music Hall dac15.2** (www.musichallaudio.com, $299). A palm-sized unit, shown in Figure 24.8, designed specifically for use with PCs and streaming media boxes. Offers 24/192 upsampling, along with USB, optical, and coaxial digital inputs.

FIGURE 24.8

The compact Music Hall dac15.2.

- **NAD DAC 1** (www.nadelectronics.com, $299). A desktop unit with Wi-Fi connectivity. Includes 24/192 upsampling, USB input, and both R/L analog and coaxial digital outputs.

- **Musical Fidelity V-DAC II** (www.musicalfidelity.com, $349). A higher-quality version of the V-Link unit, this one offers similar inputs/outputs with improved frequency response, signal-to-noise ratio, and total harmonic distortion.

- **Peachtree Audio DAC*iT** (www.peachtreeaudio.com, $449). A compact desktop unit, shown in Figure 24.9, with triple inputs (USB, optical, coaxial) and 32-bit processing.

FIGURE 24.9

The back panel of the Peachtree Audio DAC*iT.

- **Arcam rDAC** (www.arcam.co.uk, $479). A desktop unit with USB, optical, and coaxial digital inputs, along with 24-bit/192KHz upsampling. Also available in a $599 Wi-Fi version.

- **Cambridge Audio DacMagic Plus** (www.cambridgeaudio.com, $599). A component-type unit, shown in Figure 24.10, with a variety of inputs (USB, Toslink optical, and coaxial digital). Also features 24/192 upsampling and offers a selection of digital filters for customized sound.

- **Musical Fidelity M1DAC A** (www.musicalfidelity.com, $749). A component-style DAC that looks like a high-end audio component. Includes upsampling and oversampling, accepts four types of inputs (USB, coaxial and optical digital, and XLR), and features both RCA and XLR outputs for higher-end audio equipment.

FIGURE 24.10

The Cambridge Audio DacMagic digital to analog converter.

As you can see, there's a lot of variation in terms of price and functionality. If you want the most bang for a little buck, go with a compact unit like the Audioengine D1 or Calyx Coffee. For better performance and upsampling for HD audio tracks, try a desktop unit like the Musical Fidelity V-DAC II or NuForce Icon. If you want a unit to insert between your PC and a good home audio system, go with a fully featured component-style unit, such as the Cambridge Audio DacMagic Plus or Musical Fidelity M1DAC A.

Whichever unit you choose, connect it to your computer via USB, then feed the output to a pair of powered computer speakers or the R/L inputs of your audio or audio/video receiver. I guarantee you'll notice the improved sound quality—it's a good investment.

Choosing Better Speakers

The other major factor in improving your computer sound is the speaker system you use. Most speakers that come with desktop PCs are small and tinny; the speakers built into notebook PCs are even worse. If you're going to spend much time at your PC listening to music, you need to upgrade your speakers—now.

Browse through your local Best Buy or Fry's and you'll see a wide variety of replacement PC speaker systems. These range from slightly-larger stereo speakers to complicated 5.1- or 7.1-speaker systems designed for surround sound movies and PC games. Since we're interested in music, we'll focus on *stereo* speaker systems instead of surround sound ones—although there are a lot of good PC surround sound speaker systems on the market, if that's your want.

It's important to note that most computer speakers are *powered* speakers—that is, one or both of the speakers in a stereo pair contains a power amplifier, and thus needs to be connected to AC power. You don't drive these speakers from an audio receiver or preamp/power amp combo; it's all built into the speakers themselves.

Some stereo speaker systems are actually three-piece systems. The third piece is a subwoofer, which is useful for supplementing the inherently weak bass of small desktop or bookshelf speakers. If you go this route, make sure you make space for the sub on the floor near your PC.

Most PC speaker systems are designed for computer use. That is, they connect to either your PC's stereo mini-jack output or to an optical or coaxial digital output. They're powered, of course, and also shielded, so that the speaker magnets won't affect a traditional CRT computer monitor.

Here are some of the more popular PC hi-fi stereo speaker systems on the market today, lowest-priced first:

> ♪ **ULTIMATELY INTERESTING** Speaker shielding is only necessary if you're using an older CRT monitor, which can be really screwed up by a strong magnetic field—like that found in a speaker. Newer LCD monitors are not affected by magnetic fields, so the shielding and placement of your speakers is less important.

24

■ **Altec Lansing Expressionist Ultra** (www.alteclansing.com, $125). As shown in Figure 24.11, a neat-looking, decent-sounding 2.1 system. (That is, right and left speakers with a separate—and rather large—subwoofer.) Probably more known for its looks than its sound, it still delivers much better sound than typical computer speakers—and will look great on your desktop.

FIGURE 24.11

Altec Lansing's futuristic-looking Expressionist Ultra speaker system.

■ **Klipsch ProMedia 2.1** (www.klipsch.com, $149). A somewhat traditional but decent-sounding 2.1-speaker system, shown in Figure 24.12. One of the better values for the price. Also available with wireless R/L speakers for $50 more.

FIGURE 24.12
Klipsch's ProMedia 2.1 speaker system.

■ **Audioengine 2** (www.audioengineusa, $199). These are affordable two-way (woofer and tweeter) ported speakers in a handsome but somewhat plain cabinet, as shown in Figure 24.13. Features both mini-jack and RCA inputs.

■ **Audioengine 5+** (www.audioengineusa.com, $399). Larger powered speakers, in beautiful wood cabinets, as shown in Figure 24.14. These look more like traditional two-way (woofer and tweeter) bookshelf speakers, with no separate subwoofer, and are among the best-sounding of the speakers listed here.

FIGURE 24.13

The (somewhat) affordable Audioengine 2 speakers.

FIGURE 24.14

The high-end, all wood Audioengine 5+ speaker system.

■ **Bose Companion 5**
(www.bose.com, $399). Compact
but powerful 2.1 desktop speaker
system. Includes R/L speakers on
short stands, as shown in Figure
24.15, and a larger subwoofer for
positioning on the floor.

> ♪ **ULTIMATELY INTERESTING** I tend to think that Bose products are a tad overpriced, but others really like them, so that's why I include them here. They are quality products, no matter what you think of the price/value equation.

FIGURE 24.15
Bose's top-of-the-line Companion 5 speaker system.

■ **Focal XS Book** (www.focal.com, $399). Compact and stylish desktop
speakers, as shown in Figure 24.16, that deliver a big bang for their
size.

■ **Bowers & Wilkins MM-1** (www.bowers-wilkins.com, $499). Now we're
talking high-end. This is arguably the best-sounding (and certainly the
most expensive) of these desktop computer speakers. As you can see in
Figure 24.17, this two-way, two-speaker (no subwoofer) system features
innovative design and all the high-end hi-fi this and that for which
B&W is known among audiophiles.

FIGURE 24.16

The compact Focal XS Book speakers.

FIGURE 24.17

B&W's audiophile-quality MM-1 computer speakers.

You're not limited to traditional computer speakers, however. Believe it or not, but the near-field monitor speakers found in recording studios are perfect for audiophile computer music playback. Near-filed monitors are small, self-powered, deliver reference-quality sound, and are designed to be placed about three to six feet from the listener's ears—perfect for desktop computer use. Most studio monitors include decent woofers, so they don't even need subwoofers. And, surprisingly, prices—at least on the lower-end units—are right in line with higher-end PC speakers.

> **ULTIMATELY USEFUL** Personally, I use M-Audio AV 40 near-field monitors with my desktop PC. They sound better than any traditional computer monitors I've evaluated, at lower cost. That's a hard-to-beat combination. (I also have a set of Samson Resolv monitors connected to the system I use for home recording; although more expensive, they are perfect for home studio use.)

Here are some of the more popular near-field monitors best suited for use with a home PC, also ordered from lowest- to highest-price:

- **Behrenger MS40** (www.behrenger.com, $169/pair). As shown in Figure 24.18, these ported speakers feature 4.75" woofers and 2.5" tweeters with a 20 watt/channel amplifier. Includes both analog and digital inputs; use the digital inputs to utilize the built-in 24-bit/192KHz digital-to-analog converter.

FIGURE 24.18
Behrenger MS40 studio monitors.

- **Alesis M1Active 520USB** (www.alesis.com, $199/pair). This good-sounding system connects to your computer via either 1/4-inch analog inputs or USB. As shown in Figure 24.19, these are two-way speakers with 5" woofers and 1" dome tweeters, driven by a 30 watt/channel amp.

FIGURE 24.19

Alexis M1Active 520USB studio monitors.

- **M-Audio AV 40** (www.m-audio.com, $229/pair). Excellent fidelity at a surprisingly affordable price. As you can see in Figure 24.20, these speakers fit fine on an office desktop and are shielded to reduce interference. Each speaker sports a 4" woofer, 1" tweeter, and a rear port, and are driven by a 20 watt/channel amp. Connections are optimized for computer systems, complete with a

> **ULTIMATELY INTERESTING** M-Audio makes a full line of studio monitors that can be adapted for personal computer use. The line starts with the compact AV 30 ($149), includes the new BX5 D2 and BX8 D2 bi-amplified systems ($399 and $599, respectively), and tops out with the 180-watt Studiophile DSM3 ($949 a pair). There's something for everyone, at a variety of price points.

1/8-inch stereo mini-cable that connects to your PC's mini-jack connector and to the speakers' 1/4-inch RCA connectors.

FIGURE 24.20

M-Audio AV 40 studio monitors.

■ **KRK Rokit 5 G2** (www.krksys.com, $298/pair). A compact two-way monitor with 5" woofer, 1" dome tweeter, and front-firing port, driven by 30 watt/channel low frequency and 15 watt/channel high frequency amps. Includes RCA, XLR, and mini-jack inputs. Colorful design with a bright yellow woofer, as shown in Figure 24.21.

FIGURE 24.21

KRK Rokit 5 G2 studio monitors.

■ **Samson Resolv A6** (www.samsontech.com, $299/pair). As shown in Figure 24.22, a great sounding set of studio monitors in beautiful piano black lacquer finish. Features a 6.5" woofer and 1.25" dome tweeter, driven by powerful 75 watt/channel low frequency and 25 watt/channel high frequency amps. Also available in 5" and 8" woofer models.

FIGURE 24.22

Samson Resolve A6 studio monitors.

■ **Mackie MR8 Mk2** (www.mackie.com, $500/pair). As shown in Figure 24.23, this higher-end studio speaker pair features a big 8" woofer, 1" tweeter, and rear port, driven by 100 watt/channel low frequency and 50 watt/channel high frequency amps. Includes RCA, TRS, and XLR inputs.

FIGURE 24.23
Mackie MR8 Mk2 studio monitors.

Note that none of these studio monitors come with a subwoofer; they don't need it. Their fidelity is pure and flat without need of an extra bass boost. Lesser-trained ears, however, might perceive the studio monitor sound as *too* flat compared to what they're used to. If this bothers you, either add a sub (Samson's $229 Resolv 120a subwoofer is a nice match to any of these pairs) or go with one of the traditional computer speaker systems that we examined previously.

ULTIMATELY **USEFUL** The only issue you may run into with some studio monitors is making the right connection. Models with USB or digital inputs are nice, in that they easily connect to your PC. Models with mini-jack inputs also connect easily to your computer's mini-jack speaker output. Models with RCA connectors, however, will require a converter cable to go from a single mini-jack to two RCA connectors.

Using Headphones

Another option when it comes to listening to music from your computer is to use headphones—*good* headphones. I'm not talking iPod-quality earbuds, folks, but rather the kind of covered-ear cans that audiophiles are more than familiar with.

We won't go into the various types of headphones available here, but know that a good pair of stereo headphones will probably sound better than a comparably priced speaker system; that's just the nature of the beast. There's some real enjoyment to be had with a good set of headphones. (Plus, they're quiet—that is, you can crank up the sound without disturbing everyone else in the house.)

> ♪ ULTIMATELY **INTERESTING** Learn more about quality headphones in Chapter 27, "Playing Music on a Portable Music Player or Smartphone."

Connecting Your Computer to Your Home Audio System

There's another way to improve the sound quality when playing digital music on your computer. Instead of upgrading your speakers, connect your computer to your existing home audio system. This lets you take advantage of the more powerful amplifier and better speakers you use to listen to the rest of your music.

Making the Connection

We talked previously about which types of computers you can connect to your home audio system; basically, any PC will do, but a smaller desktop model (or a dedicated media PC or home theater PC) might fit better, both physically and aesthetically. Whatever type of computer you use, you want to place it relatively close to your receiver, to minimize the cord run. (That's true of all audio/video components, of course.)

Depending on your particular computer, you may have several types of jacks available for connecting your PC to your audio or audio/video receiver—stereo mini-jack, R/L RCA, optical digital, coaxial digital, or HDMI. Table 24.2 details each type of connection.

> ♪ ULTIMATELY **INTERESTING** Learn more about selecting a computer for living room use in Chapter 13, "Storing Your Digital Music."

Table 24.2 Audio Connection Options

Computer Jack	Cable Plug	Name	Analog or Digital?	Details
Green		Stereo mini-jack	Analog	Most receivers do not have mini-plug inputs
White — L, Red — R		RCA	Analog	Most PCs do not have RCA audio outputs
(Toslink)		Optical (Toslink)	Digital	Typically the lowest-cost digital cable
Orange		Coaxial	Digital	Uses RCA connector with shielded coaxial cable; better for longer runs
		HDMI	Digital	Transmits both audio and video; may be the only digital connection offered on lower-priced receivers and most flat-panel TVs

As to which type of cable you use, it depends on what connections you have on your computer and receiver, and what your ultimate goals are. Here are some examples:

■ If your computer doesn't offer any digital audio outputs, and if you don't have an outboard DAC connected to your PC (shame on you!), then you'll have to use your computer's stereo mini-jack output. The problem with this type of connection is that your receiver probably doesn't have a mini-jack input, so you'll need to connect a mini-jack to RCA cable or adapter (like the one shown in Figure 24.24) between the two.

FIGURE 24.24

A mini-jack-to-RCA adapter cable.

- If you have a good DAC connected to your computer, you want to make an analog connection to your receiver. (Most outboard DACs have R/L RCA audio outputs.)

- If your computer has an optical or coaxial digital output (some but not all do), then use the appropriate optical or coaxial cable to connect from your computer to the similar input on your receiver. (This relies on your receiver having a decent digital-to-analog converter, which most decent receivers do.)

- If you also want to view video from your computer on your home theater system, connect an HDMI cable from your computer to your audio/video receiver. (Most newer PCs have an HDMI output.) This transmits digital audio as well as video signals.

> **ULTIMATELY USEFUL** When you're listening to music, there's nothing magical about a digital connection. It depends on where the best DAC is in your system. If it's an outboard unit connected to your PC, then go digital to the DAC and analog to your receiver.

As I said, the connection you choose is partially if not primarily dependent on the connections your equipment offers. Use the best-quality connection available.

There's one more alternative to consider, especially if you don't want to place your PC right next to your audio/video equipment rack. Several networking manufacturers offer wireless devices that beam the audio/video output from your PC to a device that connects to your A/V receiver or flat-screen TV. You plug a USB transmitter into your computer then connect the receiving device to your audio/video system, typically via HDMI; the audio and video signals from your computer are then beamed from your computer to the receiving device, via WiFi. While these devices are more expensive than a simple set of cables (they run anywhere from $50 to $100), they do simplify the whole connection process. You can find such devices from Belkin (ScreenCast), Netgear (Push2TV), and others.

> **ULTIMATELY USEFUL** While we're focusing on audio connections here, you'll probably also want to make a video connection from your PC to your A/V receiver or flat screen TV. HDMI connects both audio and video simultaneously, which is why most folks like it. But if you prefer one of the audio-only connections discussed here, you'll still want to connect the video output from your computer to your home theater system. While most PCs are somewhat limited in video output connections (HDMI might be your only choice), you may have the option of connecting via S-Video, VGA, DVI, or, in rare instances, three-connector component video. For best picture, use the highest resolution of the available connections.

Choosing a Ten Foot Interface

Okay, so you have your computer connected to your audio system. How do you control the darned thing?

This is where connecting via HDMI is a good idea. When you use an HDMI connection, you feed not only audio but also video from your computer to your receiver. Of course, you'll need to have an audio/video (A/V) receiver, not an audio-only one, but most of us do, these days.

> **ULTIMATELY USEFUL** You can also connect HDMI from your computer directly to a flat panel television, and listen to music through your TV's speakers—although, given the poor quality of most TV's built-in speakers, I'm not sure why you'd want to.

When you're connected this way, your system's flat-panel TV functions as a computer monitor. This is all well and good, but do you really want to view your computer programs in your living room, on your television screen?

The challenge is that operating a computer in your living room is a much different experience than operating a computer in your office. In your office, you're sitting 10 inches away from the computer screen; everything you see is small and compact yet still visible from the 10-inch level. In your living room, you're sitting 10 *feet* away from the television screen; all the onscreen icons and buttons need to be big enough to be seen from the extended distance. It's the difference between a 10-inch interface and what is formally known as a *10-foot interface.*

What you need to do, then, is use some sort of graphical user interface (text won't do) that runs on top of your normal Windows or Mac desktop and enlarges the onscreen elements for better ease of reading from your comfy couch. There aren't a lot of options here, but there is one solid recommendation.

If you're using a Windows computer, you have a 10-foot interface built into the operating system. It's called Windows Media Center (*not* Windows Media Player—that's a separate app), and you can find it right there on your Windows Start menu. Windows Media Center (WMC, for short) is actually a very good interface, one that works quite well for listening to digital music in your living room. (It's also great for watching movies, viewing digital photos, recording TV shows, and the like, but we'll stick to music for the purposes of this discussion.)

Windows Media Center lets you perform most common home entertainment operations, using a Media Center remote control. (More on that in a moment.) It's not designed for desktop applications; there's no built-in web browser, or word processor, or email client. If you want to do office work, shut down Media Center and revert to plain old Windows. But if you want to listen to music (or watch DVDs or record television programs or whatever), Media Center is the perfect interface. It's simple, it's intuitive, it's easy to read from across the room; it's a computer interface that

ULTIMATELY INTERESTING Windows Media Center is built into all versions of Windows prior to Windows 8. In Windows 8, Media Center is no longer part of the basic consumer edition of the operating system, but only available as an add-on pack to Windows 8 Pro edition. (The Windows 8 version of Media Center is functionally identical to the Windows 7 version.)

ULTIMATELY USEFUL Windows Media Center is an interface that runs on top of the Windows operating system; it's not an operating system itself. That said, you can configure WMC to launch automatically when you turn on your computer, and to automatically display full screen (not in a smaller window). To launch WMC automatically, go to the main screen, select Tasks > Settings > General > Startup and Window Behavior, then select Start Windows Media Center When Windows Start and click Save. To keep it displayed full-screen (what Microsoft calls "media mode,") select Tasks > Media Only.

doesn't look like a computer interface. And you don't need to take a training course to learn how to use it. It's easy enough to use that your spouse and children can probably figure it out without much help.

The first page you see when Media Center launches (or when you press the **Green** button on the Media Center remote control) is the Start page, shown in Figure 24.25. This is a lot different from the main desktop in Windows; it's much more streamlined, with only a handful of important options. It's also designed to be seen from clear across the living room, which makes it the perfect 10-foot interface.

FIGURE 24.25

The Windows Media Center Start screen.

Since WMC sits on top of Windows, it utilizes all the settings you've already configured in Windows and in Windows Media Player. So if you've used WMP to rip and manage your music collection, WMC picks up on all you've done and displays your library and playlists spot-on. After a brief initial configuration on first launching WMC, everything should be ready to go.

> ♪ **ULTIMATELY USEFUL** You can further configure your WMC libraries by selecting **Tasks > Settings > Media Libraries**, but you probably won't need to.

To play music in WMC, all you have to do is click **Music** > **Music Library** from the Start menu. This tosses you into your digital music collection, shown in Figure 24.26, which you can sort by Albums, Artists (AKA contributing artists), Genres, Songs, Playlists, Composers, Years, Album Artists, and Shared (music you've shared with other computers on your network). You use your remote to scroll left or right through the selections, and click an item to see more.

FIGURE 24.26

Accessing your music library in WMC.

When you select an album, you see the album pane shown in Figure 24.27. You can scroll down to and click an individual track to play it, or click **Play Album** to play the entire album. Same thing if you select a playlist; click **Play Playlist** in the playlist pane and get grooving.

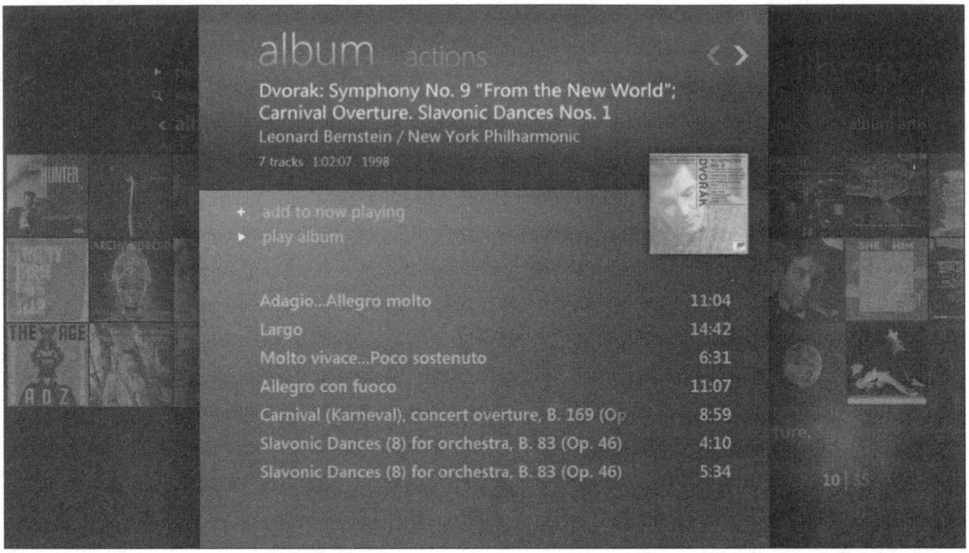

FIGURE 24.27

Getting ready to play an album in WMC.

During playback, you can view the default playback screen, shown in Figure 24.28, which displays all your album artwork as a kind of scrolling background, with album or track details on top. You can tap the **left** button on your remote to display a subsidiary menu and then choose to display one of those funky visualizations or a picture slideshow. (You can also use this menu to turn on or off the shuffle mode.)

Of course, Windows Media Center is just one of several 10-foot interfaces available for living room use. I highlight it because it's so widely available (and free if you're running Windows 7 or prior). But there are other options, including the following:

> ■ **JRiver Media Center** (www.jriver.com, $49.98). A standalone media player app that features several different skins, including the Theater View 10-foot interface, shown in Figure 24.29. This one's a Windows-only GUI, and the most expensive of the bunch. Before buying it, you can try it out for free for 30 days to see what you think.

> **ULTIMATELY USEFUL** WMC's default picture slideshow displays all the photos in your My Pictures folder. To display pictures from a subfolder or another location, just back out to the Start menu (with the music playing, of course) and select **Pictures + Videos > Picture Library**, navigate to the folder you want, then select Play Slide Show.

FIGURE 24.28
Playing digital music in Windows Media Center.

FIGURE 24.29
JRiver Media Center's Theater View.

■ **MediaPortal** (www.team-mediaportal.com, free). Originally part of the XBMC project, MediaPortal has developed into its own unique operating environment. Like XBMC, it's an open source project, but runs only on Windows. The main menu looks a lot like Windows Media Center, while the music section (shown in Figure 24.30) uses an iTunes-like cover flow approach.

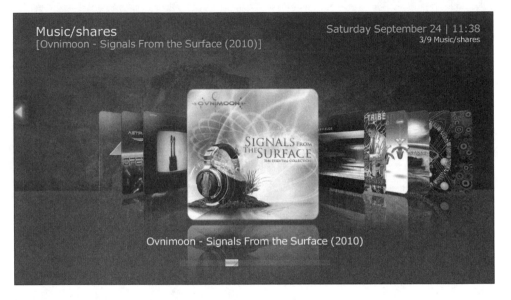

FIGURE 24.30

Browsing through MediaPortal's music library.

■ **NextPVR** (www.nextpvr.com, free). Developed primarily as a personal video recorder (PVR) app, NextPVR also features robust digital music playback and management. This is a Windows-only interface, similar to that of WMC's, as shown in Figure 24.31.

■ **XBMC** (www.xbmc.org, free). This is a freeware interface designed for home theater PC (HTPC) use, probably the most popular competitor to Windows Media Center, and runs on Windows, Mac OS, and Linux. As an open source project, there are a lot of user-developed skins you can choose from, like the one in Figure 24.32, which makes it a highly customizable option.

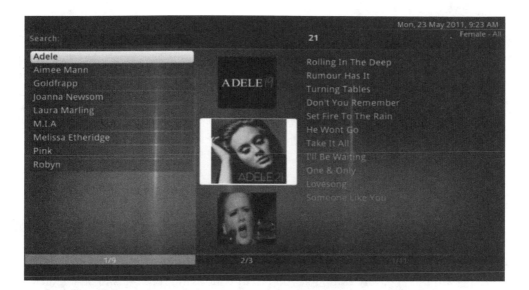

FIGURE 24.31
Playing music with NextPVR.

FIGURE 24.32
Playing an album with XBMC.

All of these interfaces work pretty much like Windows Media Center. They all have a central home or start menu, from which you select various playback options—music, photos, TV, movies, and so forth. They're all designed for use from across the living room, and all work with one or another types of remote controls, including most universal remotes. (In addition, many are designed to work with Microsoft's Media Center remote.) It's hard to go wrong with any of them.

Controlling Your System

The other big difference between having a PC in your office and in your living room is how you operate it. You're accustomed to using a keyboard and mouse in your office, but both of those peripherals seem out of place in a typical living room environment. In your living room, you're used to using a remote control unit—just point it at the screen and click.

To this end, any computer you put in your living room has to be remote control operable. The 10-foot interface you choose has to include big buttons and controls that you can operate with a click of the remote control. No fiddling about with the diminutive buttons and sliders found in a traditional music player app; in the living room, big is beautiful—and necessary. And forget about typing; anything you select on screen has to be done with a simple remote control, not a keyboard or mouse.

What you need then, is some sort of remote control unit that can control the 10-foot interface on your computer. The de facto standard in this regard is Microsoft's Media Center remote, shown in Figure 24.33. Not only will the Media Center remote control Windows Media Center, it will also control most of the alternative 10-foot interfaces we previously discussed. All you have to do is connect the remote receiver to your PC (typically via USB), then you can operate the whole shebang via infrared remote.

Naturally, you can also program just about any universal remote to control the media center interface on your computer. (You will have to first connect an infrared receiver to your computer, typically via USB.) I happen to like Logitech's Harmony One remote, shown in Figure 24.34; you can set it up over the web just by adding a "Media Center PC" device to the remote's device list.

> ♪ ULTIMATELY **INTERESTING** You can find Media Center remotes, from various manufacturers, online at Amazon, Fry's, and similar retailers; expect to pay $15-$35 or so. You'll pay more for a full-featured universal remote such as Logitech's Harmony One, which sells for $199 at www.logitech.com.

FIGURE 24.33

Use a Media Center remote control to control your living room computer.

FIGURE 24.34

Program a universal remote, such as the Logitech Harmony One, to control your living room PC.

Finally, there are apps available that can turn your iPhone or iPad into a media center remote for your PC. Your phone or tablet communicates to your computer via your Wi-Fi network, and performs all the functions that the app provides. Some of the more popular of these apps include the following:

- **HippoRemote** (www.hipporemote.com, $4.99). Not a media center remote per se, but rather an app that lets you control all your computer functions from your iPhone or iPad. It's easy enough to configure the app to provide media center-specific controls via customized "PlayPad" screens, like the one in Figure 24.35.

FIGURE 24.35

Configure the HippoRemote app to control media center playback from your iPhone.

- **My River** (www.4bay.dk/MyRiver.htm, $2.99/iPhone, $4.99/iPad). An iPhone app specifically for the JRiver Media Center. Available in both iPhone and iPad versions; the iPad version, shown in Figure 24.36, is particularly useful, and even lets you stream music directly to your iPad.

FIGURE 24.36

Control the JRiver Media Center program with your iPad, using the My River app.

- **Remote Kitten** (www.kared.net/rk/, $2.99). Designed specifically for Windows Media Center. As you can see in Figure 24.37, this app lets you control most Media Center functions via push button operation.

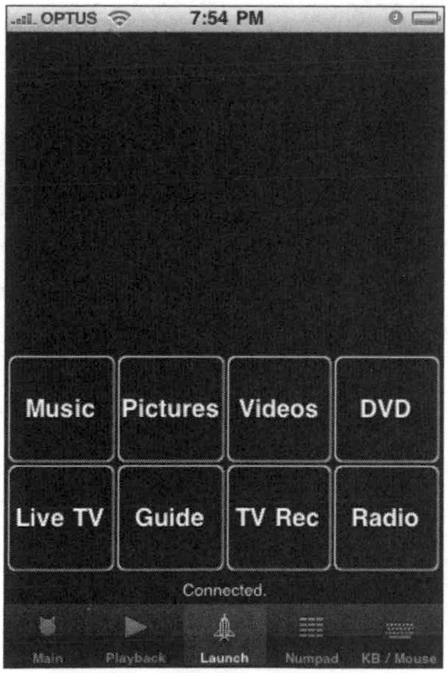

FIGURE 24.37

Control Windows Media Center with the Remote Kitten iPhone app.

■ **vmcMote** (vmcmote.blogspot.com, $7.99). One of the more fully functional Media Center control apps. As you can see in Figure 24.38, this app does a decent job adapting the WMC interface and functionality for the smaller smartphone and tablet screens. Available in both iPhone and iPad (vmcMote HD) versions.

FIGURE 24.38
vmcMote for both iPads and iPhones.

■ **WiFi-Remote Control for Media Center** (www.halcomputing.com, $3.99). A Windows Media Center-specific app, similar to Remote Kitten. As you can see in Figure 24.39, this app puts all the necessary controls on the iPhone screen.

♪ **ULTIMATELY INTERESTING** You can find all these apps in Apple's App Store, or link to the download from their individual websites. Naturally, similar apps are available for Android and Windows phones, so look in the appropriate app store if you use a non-Apple phone.

FIGURE 24.39

Control basic WMC functions with WiFi-Remote Control for Media Center.

Without question, the most powerful of all these apps is vmcMote (and its iPad companion, vmcMote HD). Before you use the app on your portable device, you have to download and install on your Media Center PC a free server program from the company's website. The server program is what gives your iPhone access to Media Center on your computer. What's cool about this app is that it's more than just a simple one-way controller; it offers two-way access that lets you view and search your entire music library from your phone, and then control playback however you want. It's actually much more functional than traditional Media Center remote, and well worth the $7.99 price.

THE JOYS (AND HEARTBREAKS) OF WINDOWS MEDIA CENTER

I've been using Windows Media Center since the Windows XP days. I even wrote a book about Media Center. (That's *Creating a Digital Home Entertainment System with Windows Media Center*, published by Que back in 2006 and still in print.) So I know Media Center pretty well.

On a good day, I really like Media Center. It does exactly what I need it to do, especially with my focus on playing selections from my large music library. It's easy to dial up a particular artist, album, or playlist, and listen in whichever room I happen to be in. (I have Media Center Extenders in various rooms in my house; we'll discuss those in Chapter 26, "Building a Whole House Digital Audio System.") I also use Media Center to view our similarly huge library of digital photographs and all the home movies I've shot since getting married (and inheriting stepchildren and grandchildren) four years ago. It's an elegant solution.

That's on a good day. On a bad day, I curse Media Center with all the fury of a Midwestern thunderstorm in August. Because it's Windows-based and runs on a personal computer, it exhibits all the expected Windows and PC foibles. It's not Media Center's fault, but PCs being PCs, my system does freeze from time to time, and rebooting (thanks to my huge media library) takes a good 10 minutes or so. Then there are the obligatory Windows system updates, which can't be managed from within Media Center and thus require the use of a wireless keyboard and mouse (I use the Logitech diNovo Edge combo keyboard/trackpad, which costs $179 but gets the job done) and being able to read that extremely small print from across my extremely large living room. In addition, the Media Center Extenders, which work fine when they're working, tend to freeze and disconnect with a disturbing regularity. Cursing abounds.

Then there's the constant fear that Microsoft is going to abandon Media Center. Oh, they haven't yet, but it's becoming more and more of an afterthought from the folks out in Redmond. There was a rumor that Media Center wouldn't be included in the new Windows 8 release, but Microsoft instead decided to extract it from the core operating system and offer it as an optional (paid) add-on to the Pro edition of the operating system. (That's less than ideal but better than dropping it altogether; at least interested users can pony up for the add-on pack.)

It's certainly true that Media Center hasn't caught on the way Microsoft hoped it would back in the waning days of the last century. That's despite some very significant upgrades to Media Center's features and functionality (it's a lot better now than in the Windows XP days), as well as a shift in focus that positioned Media Center as a fancy movie player and computer-based DVR.

We Media Center aficionados have also had to deal with the drying up of third party support. Nobody makes Media Center Extenders anymore (if you want an Extender, you have to use an Xbox game console for that function), and Microsoft gobbled up, absorbed, and pretty much evaporated The Green Button website, which used to be a vital hangout for all Media Center users. It's not surprising that a lot of custom home theater installers, who used to push Media Center as part of their custom installs, have turned their backs on Microsoft and use more proprietary solutions. It's tough dealing with a product that its parent neglects.

All that said and done, I haven't really found a better computer-based solution for playing music in my living room. (Remember, I'm not an Apple zombie, so I'm focusing on Windows-based solutions.) Despite all the FUD and flaws, Media Center continues to do what I need it to do. And here's the real selling point—my wife and stepkids and even my five year-old grandson have all figured out how to use Media Center. If you've ever tried to share your digital music jones with your family, you know that's not a small thing. Anybody in my house can pick up the Logitech Harmony One remote, press the Listen to Music function, and start picking and playing all the music, photos, and videos they want. Until, that is, the damn computer freezes on them again and I hear someone calling "Mike, the music isn't playing," and I have to go into home tech support mode yet again. Damn you, Microsoft—and thank you for giving us Windows Media Center to loathe and love.

24

Playing Digital Music on a Home Media Player

After reading the previous chapter, you may not be totally convinced that you really want a personal computer in your living room. I understand; it's a level of technological complexity one step beyond what less tech-savvy folks (like the rest of your family) are comfortable with. Really, there ought to be a less-complex way to listen to your digital music on your home audio or audio/video system.

Well, there is. Or rather, there are. That is, there are lots of other devices that can connect to the computer or home server where you store your digital music library, and play those tunes (as well as videos and photos) on your home theater system in your living room. Since these devices are more mission-specific (that is, they don't do all the ancillary tasks that a PC does), they also tend to be simpler to operate and more trouble free. In other words, a winning combination—especially for us music lovers with spouses and children.

What Exactly Is a Home Media Player?

There are a lot of "black boxes" that connect to your home theater system and play music stored elsewhere on your home network. These devices have lots of different names—home media player, network media player, streaming media player, and so forth. Whatever the name, these devices all let you listen to your digital music library in your living room (or other room in your house), without having to connect the host PC directly to your A/V receiver.

The concept is simple. The home media player (or whatever you want to call it) sits in your living room, next to your existing audio and video equipment. It connects to your A/V receiver or flat-screen TV, typically via HDMI (so you can also view videos and photos, as well as see onscreen menus and graphics). It also connects to your home network, either wirelessly (via WiFi) or via Ethernet cable. Using your home network, the home media player grabs music (and videos and photos and more) from your host PC or media server, which can be then be placed anywhere in your house—as long as it's also connected to your network, of course.

Most of these home media players are smallish boxes, smaller than a similar PC or piece of audio equipment. They're small because they can be; there's not a lot inside, no hard disk or (in most instances) CD/DVD drive or the like. You have the expected connections on the back and maybe a USB connector (to play media on USB memory drives), but that's it. All the functions are accessed via remote control, which is typically included in the price of the unit. You sit across the room in your comfy chair or couch and press the appropriate buttons to browse through and play music from your library.

The advantage of one of these boxes over a full-featured PC is simplicity. These devices are designed to play back music and other digital media, and nothing else. As such, they're relatively simple to set up and use, less prone to crashing and freezing, and less expensive. In other words, they're much more user friendly, as opposed to personal computers, which unfortunately require a moderate level of technical expertise to set up and keep running.

As to price, these home media players are fairly affordable—in most instances, considerably lower priced than a media center PC. Many units hover around the $100 range, although those units designed for audiophiles, with better digital-to-analog converters and such, can be priced closer to $1,000 (and up). But don't think you have to spend a grand to get something decent; the $100 boxes perform just fine, thank you.

Note that most of these units aren't just for playing music. Most of them also let you view digital photographs, watch movies and home videos, and even stream TV programs and other media from the web. For music lovers, all that other media playback is just icing on the cupcake, although it's obvious that a large part of the audience is buying these devices primarily for their video playback capabilities.

Choosing a Home Media Player

At the start of this chapter, I noted that there are lots of these home media players on the market today. I wasn't kidding; we're looking at more than a dozen different units from a similar number of manufacturers. There's a lot of variety to choose from.

That said, most of these devices do pretty much the same thing—play media stored on a networked computer or streamed from the Internet. Yes, you'll find units with different sets of connections, different graphical displays, different remote controls, and (of course) different prices. Some units come from consumer electronics manufacturers, some from computer manufacturers, some from networking companies. You'll also find that some units play some file formats and not others; format compatibility remains a largish bugaboo. And, to be honest, some of these units are simply better at what they do than others.

When all is said and done however, choosing a home media player is as simple as comparing the specs and the functionality and the prices, finding the one that does what you need it to do the way you want it to. Which specs should you pay attention to? Here's what I think you should consider:

- **Compatibility**. You want a home media player to be able to play your particular media. That means if you have an Apple-focused library, you need a media player that plays back AAC files. If you have a Windows-focused library, you need a media player that plays back WMA files. Not all media players can play all formats, so peruse the specs to find out for sure.

- **Connections**. Most media player boxes have an HDMI output, which may be all you need; just connect an HDMI cable between your media player's output and the input on your A/V receiver or flat-screen television. However, if you need additional types of outputs, do your homework to determine which media players meet your criteria.

- **Graphical interface.** Just about every digital media player has a user interface of some sort, but there are significant differences in what and how things are displayed. If you have the opportunity, play around with the interface a bit to see if you like it. If you're shopping online, search for screenshot images from the media players you're considering. You have to deal with the interface every day, so make sure you get one that does what you need it to do in a way you're comfortable with.

- **WiFi.** Your media player has to connect to your home network. Some do this wirelessly, via WiFi; others connect in a wired fashion using Ethernet. Naturally, WiFi is easier to connect, since you don't have to run any wires. But not all media players have built-in WiFi; you may have to purchase some sort of WiFi adapter to go that route. Most media players have an Ethernet connection, however, and Ethernet is not only faster but more reliable than WiFi. Of course, you may not be able to run an Ethernet cable from your network server to your digital media player, in which case WiFi makes more sense. Figure out how you want or need to connect, then make sure your media player accommodates your wishes.

- **Features and performance.** Make sure the media player you use lets you do what you want to do; in particular, look for playlist creation (easier with some than with others) and customizable photo slideshows while you're playing music. If you're using the media play box as a digital-to-analog converter, make sure the included DAC has acceptable specs. This becomes less critical if you're going digital out from the media player box; in this instance, make sure your A/V receiver has a suitably high performance DAC built in.

- **Price.** Finally, there's the money. Can you make do with a unit in the $100 range, or are you committed to a higher priced (and, presumably, higher performance) device? If you have to stay within a budget, make every dollar of that budget count.

These features (and more) are compared in Table 25.1; I've arranged the units in order of price. Out of all the available units, there should be at least one that meets your personal requirements.

> **ULTIMATELY INTERESTING** Roku (www.roku.com) makes a line of affordable streaming media players, but they don't play music (or other media) stored locally. That is, you can only use your Roku box to stream music and movies from the Internet, not from your PC—which is why I don't list those units here.

Table 25.1   Home Media Player Features

Unit	Website	List Price	Video Playback	Photo Viewing	Audio Formats Supported	Outputs	Network Connection
Sony SMP-N200	store.sony.com	$79	Yes	Yes	AAC, MP3, WAV, WMA	HDMI, component video, composite video, optical digital audio, RCA R/L analog audio	WiFi, Ethernet
Apple TV	www.apple.com/appletv	$99	Yes	Yes	AAC, AIFF, MP3, WAV	HDMI, optical digital audio	WiFi, Ethernet
Western Digital WD TV Live	www.wdc.com	$99	Yes	Yes	AAC, AIFF, FLAC, MP3, OGG, WAV, WMA,	HDMI, composite video, optical digital audio, RCA R/L analog audio	WiFi, Ethernet
Seagate FreeAgent GoFlex TV HD	www.seagate.com	$129	Yes	Yes	AAC, FLAC, MP3, OGG, WAV, WMA	HDMI, component video, composite video, optical digital audio, RCA R/L analog audio	Ethernet
Microsoft Xbox 360	www.xbox.com	$199+	Yes	Yes	AAC, MP3, WMA	HDMI, composite video, optical digital audio, RCA R/L analog audio	WiFi, Ethernet
Netgear NTV550	www.netgear.com	$199	Yes	Yes	AAC, FLAC, MP3, WMA	HDMI, component video, composite video, optical digital audio, RCA R/L analog audio	Ethernet
D-Link Boxee Box	www.dlink.com/boxee/	$229	Yes	Yes	AAC, AIFF, FLAC, MP3, OGG, WAV, WMA	HDMI, optical digital audio, RCA R/L analog audio	WiFi, Ethernet
Logitech Squeezebox Touch	www.logitech.com	$299	No	No	AAC, AIFF, APE, FLAC, MP3, OGG, WAV, WMA	Optical digital audio, coaxial digital audio. RCA R/L analog audio	WiFi, Ethernet
Sonos Connect (ZonePlayer)	www.sonos.com	$349	No	No	AAC, AIFF, FLAC, MP3, OGG, WAV, WMA	Optical digital audio, coaxial digital audio, RCA R/L analog audio	Ethernet (connects wireless via separate $49 Sonos Bridge device)
Denon NDP-720AE	usa.denon.com	$499	No	No	AAC, FLAC, MP3, WAV, WMA	Optical digital audio, RCA R/L analog audio	WiFi, Ethernet
Pioneer N-30	www.pioneerelectronics.com	$499	No	No	AAC, FLAC, MP3, OGG, WAV, WMA	Optical digital audio, coaxial digital audio, RCA R/L analog audio	Ethernet
Marantz NA7004	us.marantz.com	$799	No	No	AAC, FLAC, MP3, WAV, WMA	Optical digital audio, coaxial digital audio, RCA R/L analog audio	Ethernet
NAD C446	www.nadelectronics.com	$799	No	No	AAC, FLAC, MP3, WAV, WMA	Optical digital audio, coaxial digital audio, RCA R/L analog audio	Ethernet
Logitech Transporter SE	www.logitech.com	$1,299	No	No	AIFF, FLAC, MP3, WAV, WMA	Optical digital audio, coaxial digital audio	WiFi, Ethernet
Musical Fidelity M1 CLiC	www.musicalfidelity.com	$1,999	No	No	AAC, FLAC, MP3, OGG, WAV, WMA	RCA R/L analog audio	WiFi, Ethernet

25

Evaluating Home Media Players

Preliminaries out of the way, let's look at some of the most popular digital media players available today. We'll look at units in price point order—that is, the lowest-priced units are first and the higher-priced ones last.

♪ ULTIMATELY
ULTIMATELY
INTERESTING   I'm limiting this discussion to models from major consumer electronics and computer companies. It's not that lesser-name brands are less suitable, but rather that you're more likely to find these more popular units where you generally shop.

Sony SMP-N200

The lowest-price offering in the home media player market is Sony's SMP-N200 Streaming Media Player, at $79. As you can see in Figure 25.1, it's a compact little box, although it has a surprising number of output connections—not just HDMI and stereo audio, but also component video, composite video, and optical digital audio. It handles all the popular audio formats, including AAC, MP3, and WMA, but not FLAC or OGG. It includes built-in WiFi and an Ethernet connection.

FIGURE 25.1
Sony's affordable SMP-N200 Streaming Media Player.

All that is good and fine, but users complain about its difficult-to-navigate interface and some underlying connection problems. It's certainly attractive enough at the price, but make sure you check out the interface first—and buy from a dealer with a decent returns policy, just in case.

Apple TV

For many, if not most, music lovers, Apple TV may be the best home music player. It's certainly affordable, at just $99, has a great user interface, and works exceedingly well with other Apple products, such as the iPhone and Mac computers. It also works well with Windows PCs, as long as you music is in Apple's AAC or the universal MP3 format; it doesn't play Microsoft's WMA files, of course.

(Figure 25.2 shows the Apple TV unit; it's very small.)

FIGURE 25.2

The Apple TV unit and the interface's home screen.

Connection is typically via HDMI, although you also have a single optical digital audio output, if you prefer that. It includes built-in WiFi, as well as an Ethernet connection.

Not only can you use Apple TV to stream music from your networked computer, you can also stream music over the web via iTunes Match and iCloud. Of course, you also have access to a variety of streaming media services, including Netflix and Vimeo. If you like, you can also stream music and other media from your iPhone or other iOS device using Apple's AirPlay technology.

You can control the Apple TV unit with the included seven-button remote, or you can install Apple's Remote app on your iPhone, iPad, iPod touch and control things from there.

Bottom line, Apple TV (despite its video-centric moniker) does an exceedingly good job playing music and other media—if you're a supporter of the Apple ecosystem. If you don't need it to play WMA or FLAC files, it may be the media player for you.

Western Digital WD TV Live

Now we come to the first of two home media players from computer hard drive manufacturers. The Western Digital WD TV Live offers quite a lot for its $99 price, rivaling Apple TV for features and functionality. As you can see in Figure 25.3, it's a little box with an accompanying remote that can play back music, movies, and photos from any computer connected to your home network. It also lets you play streaming media from Netflix, Hulu Plus, Pandora, Spotify, and other web sources. Also, like Apple TV, you can opt to control the WD TV Live from your iPhone, via the free WD Remote app.

> **ULTIMATELY INTERESTING** My son-in-law has an Apple TV unit, and he's a somewhat technical Mac devotee. He has been known to exclaim that it's "magic" how the Apple TV device automatically picks up any new photos or videos he's shot on his iPhone, as well as new music he's added to his MacBook Pro. (The former is Apple's AirPlay technology at work; the latter is simple media streaming.) He, his wife, and their kids also do a lot of media streaming on their Apple TV, primarily from Netflix and Pandora. They like it very much.

FIGURE 25.3

The affordable and extremely versatile WD TV Live.

In fact, given this unit's ability to play almost all audio file formats (including AAC *and* WMA, plus MP3, FLAC, and OGG) and the plethora of audio and video outputs on the back (Apple TV is pretty much an HDMI-only device),

WD TV Live might be a better option for most music lovers. You're not tied exclusively to the Apple ecosystem, which is probably a good thing, and you have a lot more options in terms of what it can do—all for the same price. It certainly makes the WD TV Live worth consideration.

> ♪ **ULTIMATELY INTERESTING** Western Digital also offers the WD TV Live Hub ($199), which includes a 1TB hard drive and lets you stream your media to other units on your home network.

Seagate FreeAgent GoFlex TV HD Media Player

Seagate is another hard drive manufacturer in the home media player market. The company's FreeAgent GoFlex TV HD Media Player (their marketing folks need to learn how to be a bit more concise) is a $129 unit that does pretty much everything the lower-priced Western Digital unit does.

Like the WD unit, the FreeAgent GoFlex etc. etc. is a compact box that comes with its own remote, or can be controlled via an iPhone app. It plays all major audio formats, including AAC, WMA, MP3, FLAC, and OGG, and also offers photo viewing, video playback, and all sorts of streaming media. (Figure 25.4 shows the device and its remote control.) The higher price tag doesn't buy you much if anything extra; in fact, the two units are very, very similar—which makes the Seagate player also worth looking at.

FIGURE 25.4

Seagate's FreeAgent GoFlex TV HD Media Player.

Microsoft Xbox 360

Yes, I know Microsoft's Xbox 360 is a videogame console. But the Xbox, shown in Figure 25.5, also includes a Windows Media Center interface, so it can function as a Media Center Extender.

25

FIGURE 25.5

Microsoft's Xbox 360 game console also functions as a Media Center Extender.

This means that if you have an Xbox console connected to your home theater system, you can scroll through the main menu, select Media Center, and then use your Xbox to play music (and watch movies and photos) on your main system. The Xbox connects to your main Windows PC (as an Extender) and accesses the digital music library stored there. The experience is just like using a PC with Windows Media Center, except you're doing it through your game console.

Since the Xbox in this configuration essentially turns into a Media Center extender, you can do everything with the Xbox that you can with a computer running Windows Media Center. That means playing back audio files in AAC, MP3, and WMA format, as well as viewing pictures and videos and all sorts of other stuff. With the proper cables, you can connect your Xbox to your system via HDMI or digital or analog audio. The latest Xboxes include both WiFi and Ethernet connectivity.

Microsoft sells a number of different consoles in different configurations. For music playback, the most basic 4GB console is all you need, and it sells for $199. That's about the same price as a lot of the other home media players, with the added benefit that the Xbox is also a fully-featured videogame console!

> **ULTIMATELY INTERESTING** Learn more about Windows Media Center in Chapter 24, "Playing Digital Music on Your Computer." Learn more about using an Xbox 360 as a Media Center Extender in Chapter 26, "Building a Whole House Digital Audio System."

Netgear NTV550 HD Media Player

Netgear's NTV550 HD Media Player is the networking manufacturer's entrée into the home media player game. It's a decent enough entry, but somewhat overpriced at $199. The Netgear unit, shown in Figure 25.6, plays all major audio file formats (including AAC, FLAC, MP3, and WMA) and comes with a good assortment of connection options, from HDMI on down. Unfortunately, it's an Ethernet-only device, so there's no wireless connection available.

FIGURE 25.6

Netgear's NTV550 HD Media Player and remote.

D-Link Boxee Box

Then there's D-Link's Boxee Box. As you can see in Figure 25.7, this puppy has a distinctive form factor—it literally looks like a box, albeit one sat on its corner and pushed into a tabletop.

FIGURE 25.7

The unique looking Boxee Box.

25

Looks are nice, but in this instance you pay for them; the Boxee Box sells for $229. Fortunately, it plays all major file formats (including AAC, WMA, MP3, FLAC, and OGG) and offers both Wi-Fi and Ethernet connectivity. I also like the unit's remote control, which does double duty as a standard remote and, when you turn it sideways and flip it over, a mini keyboard.

> **ULTIMATELY INTERESTING** Boxee started out as cross-platform HTPC ten-foot interface software. The company changed its focus, however, and now markets its software exclusively on its own Boxee hardware. The original software has essentially been abandoned.

Logitech Squeezebox Touch

Now we come to the first audio-only home music player. All the previous units we've discussed also play photos and videos; the Logitech Squeezebox Touch, shown in Figure 25.8, only plays digital music.

True to its digital music roots, the Squeezebox Touch plays all popular audio file formats, including, AAC, WMA, MP3, FLAC, OGG, even APE. It comes with all three types of audio connections—optical digital, coaxial digital, and stereo analog. The unit connects to your home network via either WiFi or Ethernet.

FIGURE 25.8

The Logitech Squeezebox Touch digital music-only player, complete with touchscreen display.

At $299, the Squeezebox Touch might appear a tad on the expensive side, especially when you consider it only plays music, not photos or videos. Some of that cost is explained by the fact that it comes with a 4.3" touch screen, which serves both as its graphic display (there's no HDMI or video connector on the back) and as a controller for the unit. (There's a traditional wireless remote included, as well.)

The Squeezebox Touch's higher price is also explained by its superior 24-bit digital-to-analog converter. This is better than the DACs included in the lower-priced multimedia offerings we've been discussing.

In short, the Squeezebox Touch is a dedicated home music player that offers better

> **ULTIMATELY INTERESTING** Logitech also offered, for a time, a home media player dubbed the Logitech Revue. It was the first (and so far only) device running the Google TV technology. In many ways the Revue mirrored Apple TV in features, but was plagued by all sorts of issues that led one to believe that Logitech released the product before Google was finished with the underlying technology. In any case, you still might be able to find a Revue unit on the cheap; it's worth looking at, but probably best left alone.

25

sound quality and more audio flexibility than you get with lower-priced combo players. For music lovers, that's a lot to like.

Sonos Connect

Sonos offers a family of digital music players designed primarily for whole house audio use. That said, the Sonos Connect product, shown in Figure 24.9, can be used by itself as a digital music player for a home audio system. It's a little pricey at $349 (especially when you consider it doesn't include built-in WiFi connectivity), but it has a lot of fans.

FIGURE 25.9
The Sonos Connect digital music-only player.

Like the Logitech Squeezebox Touch, this is an audio-only device, so you won't be able to play videos or view photos. It handles all major audio formats, including AAC, WMA, MP3, FLAC and OGG, and offers the hat trick of audio connections (optical digital, coaxial digital, and stereo analog). You can also use the Sonos Connect to

 ULTIMATELY INTERESTING The Sonos Connect was formerly known as the ZonePlayer. We discuss Sonos' whole house audio systems in more detail in Chapter 26.

play streaming audio over the 'net from Pandora, Rhapsody, SiriusXM, Last.fm, MOG< and other web-based services.

It's an Ethernet-only device; if you need a wireless connection, you have to add the $49 Sonos Bridge device elsewhere in your system.

Since there's no onscreen display (or display on the unit, as with the Squeezebox Touch) you need to purchase the optional $349 Sonos Control remote control, or opt to control the unit with an app on your iPhone, iPad, Kindle Fire, or Android phone or tablet.

A lot of folks like Sonos when they're putting together a whole house system. If that's your ultimate goal, great. However, comparing the Sonos Connect as a standalone digital music player, it seems to be somewhat overpriced for what it delivers. Not that there's anything wrong with the unit itself, because there isn't, it's just a price/value thing.

Denon DNP-720AE

With Denon's DNP-720AE, we move up into a whole different level of performance—and price. At $499 you get a music-only player that connects to your computer via either WiFi or Ethernet. It plays back all major audio formats (including AAC, WMA, MP3, and FLAC) and includes both optical digital and stereo analog outputs.

Now, all that's to be expected. What you really get for the price is audiophile sound quality, thanks to the 192KHz/24-bit DAC. This makes for a noticeable improvement in fidelity, especially when playing lossless-format audio. (The Denon supports AAC Lossless, WMA Lossless, and FLAC formats.)

By the way, the Denon unit also includes Apple AirPlay technology, which lets you stream music directly from your iPhone, iPod touch, or iPad. (You can also use your Apple device as a remote control for the Denon unit, which is nice). The Denon also streams music from Internet radio stations and audio streaming services such as Pandora and Rhapsody.

Not surprisingly, given its roots, the Denon looks more like an audio component than do the lower-priced players discussed previously; it even has a front panel text display. (You can see what I mean in Figure 25.9.) If you're a serious audiophile, this is a digital music player worth serious consideration.

25

FIGURE 25.10

Denon's NDP-720AE digital music player.

Pioneer N-30 Audiophile Networked Audio Player

New to the home media player market is Pioneer's N-30 Audiophile Networked Audio Player, priced at $499. As you can see in Figure 25.11, it shares similar look and feel to the Denon unit; it'll fit right in with your other audio components.

FIGURE 25.11

Pioneer's N-30 Audiophile Networked Audio Player.

Spec-wise, you're looking at compatibility with all major audio formats (AAC, WMA, MP3, FLAC, and OGG), with optical and coaxial digital outputs, along with stereo analog connections. It features a 192KHz/24-bit upsampling DAC for audiophile-quality playback, and works

> ♪ ULTIMATELY
> **INTERESTING**
>
> Pioneer also sells the $699 N-50 digital audio player, which adds gold connectors, an "armored chassis," and Advanced Sound Retriever technology to enhance playback quality of compressed files.

with both DLNA and AirPlay devices. It's an Ethernet-only device, although you can connect an optional (and extra $129) WiFi adapter for wireless connectivity.

Marantz NA7004 Network Audio Player

Next up for audiophile music lovers is the Marantz NA7004 Network Audio Player, shown in Figure 25.12. It's a lot like the Denon and Pioneer units in terms of performance, but with slightly different functionality. It's also priced considerably higher, at $799.

FIGURE 25.12

The Marantz NA7004 Network Audio Player.

25

The Marantz unit is Ethernet only, with no wireless connectivity. It offers optical digital, coaxial digital, and stereo analog outputs, and plays back AAC, WMA, MP3, and FLAC files. It also includes Apple AirPlay playback, as well as streaming audio capability.

On the fidelity front, the unit boasts a Cirrus CS4398 192KHz/24-bit DAT for audiophile playback. It also includes Marantz's Dynamic Audio eXpander circuitry that purports to improve the sound quality of compressed audio sources.

In short, this is another worthy competitor for audiophiles looking for a player for their digital music libraries.

NAD C446 Digital Music Tuner

The NAD C446 Digital Music Tuner is similar to both the Denon and Marantz units. It's an Ethernet-only device that handles all major audio file formats (AAC, WMA, MP3, and FLAC) and connects via optical digital, coaxial digital, or stereo analog. It also boasts a 192KHz/24-bit DAC for audiophile-quality sound. As you can see in Figure 25.13, it looks right at home in any audio component rack.

FIGURE 25.13

NAD's C446 Digital Music Tuner.

Logitech Transporter SE Network Music Player

I wouldn't necessarily think of Logitech when considering high fidelity audio components, but then there's this puppy, the Logitech Transporter SE. At $1,299 it's certainly not a cheap little media player. What it is, is a true audiophile-quality player, complete with 96KHz/24-bit DAC. (That's right; the Transporter's DAC isn't quite as good as that of the lower-priced units from Denon, Pioneer, Marantz, and NAD. Go figure.)

The Transporter offers a sleek backlit remote control and dual fluorescent displays on the unit itself, as you can see in Figure 25.14. It handles all the major audio file formats, with the notable exception of Apple's AAC format, and includes optical digital, coaxial digital, and stereo analog outputs. It also has both WiFi and Ethernet connectivity.

FIGURE 25.14

The Logitech Transporter SE Network Music Player.

The Transporter has a lot of fans, although I'm wary both of the price and the inability to play AAC-format files. Still, if you're in the market for an audiophile-quality digital music player, the Transporter should be on your short list.

> **ULTIMATELY INTERESTING** The Logitech Transporter uses Squeezebox software, installed on your PC, to drive its system. That's the same software used by the Squeezebox Touch and other Squeezebox devices.

Musical Fidelity M1 CLiC

Finally, we come to the highest-priced unit in our list, the M1 CLiC from Musical Fidelity, shown in Figure 25.15. At a cool two grand ($1,999, actually), you'd expect a high-performance device, and the M1 CLiC delivers.

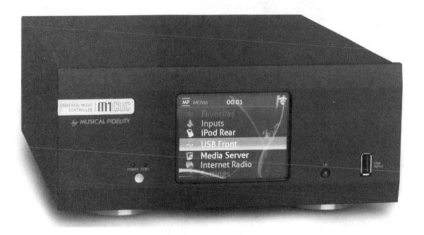

FIGURE 25.15

The highest of the high end—Musical Fidelity's M1 CLiC.

First, you get all the standard stuff—playback of all major file types (including AAC, WMA, MP3, FLAC, and OGG), WiFi and Ethernet connectivity, streaming Internet audio, and the like. You only get stereo analog outputs, because the CLiC has a 192KHz/24-bit upsampling DAC. It also features jitter reduction circuitry to re-clock the digital audio signal and eliminate timing errors in the data stream that can cause distortion, as well as a high-resolution processor that produces a more-than-acceptable 119dB signal-to-noise ratio.

You can also use the CLiC as a DAC for all your other digital equipment. It has multiple USB, coaxial digital, and optical digital inputs, so you can connect just about any other digital playback device, from a CD player to your iPod or iPhone, and let the CLiC do the decoding. In this fashion, the device lives up to its billing as a "universal music controller."

In short, the CLiC impressive audiophile-quality performance and versatility, but at a price. When nothing but the best will do, this is the unit to buy.

Connecting via DLNA

With all this discussion of connecting a home media player device to your home audio or home theater system, know that this isn't the only way to play music stored elsewhere on a networked computer. Believe it or not, many standard audio and video components—A/V receivers, Blu-ray players, even flat-panel TVs—are capable of accessing and playing your digital music, photo, and video files over your home network.

It's all due to a technology called Digital Living Network Alliance (DLNA). Any device that's DLNA certified can discover, access, and play media stored on any computer or network storage device (such as an external hard disk drive) connected to the same home network. And there are a lot of DLNA—certified devices on the market today.

> **ULTIMATELY INTERESTING** The DLNA 1.5 spec supports MP3, WAV, and WMA audio files, as well as JPEG and PNG digital photos and a variety of MPEG-format video files.

For example, the mid-priced ($649) Denon AVR2112CI audio/video receiver, shown in Figure 25.16, features DLNA capability. It connects to your home network via Ethernet, and then plays back MP3, WAV, and WMA-format audio files—as well as displays your JPG digital photos. (It can also stream AAC-format music from your iPod or iPhone via Apple's AirPlay technology, as well as decode FLAC files via non-DLNA technology.) With this or a similar DLNA receiver in your equipment rack, you don't need to buy a separate home media player; this puppy serves that function.

FIGURE 25.16

Listen to your digital music library via the Denon AVR2112CI audio/video receiver.

There are a slew of DLNA-capable A/V receivers available, as well as DLNA Blu-ray players and LCD and plasma TVs. It isn't just high-end models, either; Samsung's $99 BD-D5100 Blu-ray player is fully DLNA compatible, as is the same company's $599 LN40D550 40-inch LCD television. If you want to minimize the number of components in your audio/video rack, this is the way to go.

Just search out DLNA-compatibility when you're comparing equipment specs, and then you can access your music library after a little initial setup. I'm not sure that listening to music through a TV's speakers make sense, but I'm definitely a fan of DLNA functionality on a decent A/V receiver or Blu-ray player.

MUSIC OR MOVIES?

If you've been shopping for one of these home media players, especially those in the sub-$500 range, you've probably noticed that they don't prominently play up the music playback feature. In fact, you'd be hard pressed to find any promotional information about music playback for some of these devices, and there are even a few that barely mention this functionality in their user manuals. (Now *that's* really helpful.)

Instead, you hear all about how these units can stream movies and TV shows from Netflix and Hulu Plus and the like. It's all about streaming video, with digital music playback an afterthought, at best.

This speaks, I suppose, to a trend away from serious music listening and towards passive video watching. More folks would rather catch up on *Mad Men* via streaming video than listen to music in their living rooms. This makes me sad, but there's no bucking the trend. If you want to sell a home media player device, you have to give the public what it wants—which is a kind of cable TV box replacement.

Fortunately, the same technology that lets these devices stream and play back digital video also lets them stream and play back digital music. One digital file is the same as the next, at least where the hardware and software is concerned. You just have to make sure that the music interface is as functional and easy to use as you need; you don't want music to take a back seat to video when actual day-to-day use is concerned.

Still, I do get annoyed at how some of these manufacturers—including Apple—back burner their music playback capabilities. I mean, just start with the name; it doesn't say "Apple Music" or "Apple Media" or "Living Room iPod," it flat out says "Apple TV." The heading on the Apple TV web page says "With the best HD content and AirPlay, there's always something good on TV." Not "always something good to listen to," but "always something good on TV." Matter of fact, Apple only mentions music *once* on the entire page, buried in a sentence that reads "Wirelessly play video, show off photos, and enjoy music and more…" That's it. Apple, which made its bones selling iPods and downloads from the iTunes Store relegates music to the last media position on its living room playback device. We music lovers thank you for your continued support, Apple. Let us know what we can do for you sometime.

It's not just Apple, and it's not just standalone digital media players. Look at how Microsoft pushes Windows Media Center, the perfect ten-foot interface for digital music playback in the living room. Microsoft bills WMC as "The best way to experience TV," not "The best way to listen to music." Bah, humbug.

This may just be sour grapes on my part. After all, there are a good number of music-only digital players—all priced at $500 and up, of course. We may be ignored, but at least we're not totally forgotten—at least, not yet.

I'd like to see music hold its rightful place in the pantheon of digital media, of course. But if the average consumer is more interested in watching streamed TV shows than listening to Adele or the Beatles, then you might as well give 'em what they want—as long as us music lovers have a few scraps left to fight over at the end of the day.

25

Building a Whole House Digital Audio System

If listening to your digital music collection in your living room is great, then why not extend your listening to other rooms in your house? I like to listen to music in the bedroom and basement, out on the deck, and even in the bathroom while I'm showering and shaving. (Too much information, I know.)

The good news is that it's not that difficult or expensive to pipe your digital music, stored in a central location, to any other location on your property. All you need is the proper devices and a home network—and just a little bit of technical expertise, to get it all running correctly.

How Whole House Audio Works

The concept of a whole house audio system is not a new one. Even before the advent of easily streamed digital audio files, audiophiles were wiring their homes to feed their favorite music to multiple rooms in the house.

Back in the pre-digital days, however, setting up such a multi-room system was quite a task. In fact, most of these installations were custom, and extremely pricey. Before wireless networks and digital media servers, you had to install a fancy audio switching device off your main audio receiver or pre-amp, plug in an extra audio amplifier or two, run CAT-5 cable to all the rooms in your house, install in-wall speakers in each room, and then program a custom remote control system to operate it all. Lots of work and lots of money, and for your expenditures you got to listen to the same music in your bedroom that was playing in your living room. That's right, old school multi-room audio systems essentially played a single source in multiple rooms; you couldn't listen to one thing upstairs and another down.

Today's whole house audio systems are more versatile, much easier to set up, and much less expensive than those systems of old. When you've digitized your entire music collection, it's easy to store those files in one central location and then access them from multiple devices in multiple locations; this lets you play different tunes at the same time in different parts of the house. Set up is a lot easier than before, because you can do it all wirelessly via your home network; no cables to run. And the cost—well, today's $100-$200 home media servers are a lot less expensive than the custom equipment you used to need. All in all, it's a big improvement.

The question, then, becomes one of what type of equipment you need. You actually have several options, and can choose different options for different rooms in your house. You can opt to use any or all of the following:

- **Personal computers**. Yes, you probably have your digital audio files stored on one computer (or media server), but you can access and play those files from other computers in other rooms, over your home network.

- **Networked media players**. These mission-specific devices are both lower cost and easier to use than more fully featured personal computers, which makes them ideal for playing music elsewhere in your house.

- **Freestanding music players**. If you don't have an audio system in a given room, connect a freestanding music player to your network to play your digital music library on its self-contained speakers.

Which type of device you choose depends a lot on what you want to do and what other equipment you have in a given room. As I said, you can use a PC for playback in one room, a networked media player in another, and a freestanding music player in a third. They all connect to your home network to access the digital music library you have stored on a central PC or server.

How much money should you budget for a whole house audio system? It depends on how many rooms you're talking about and what type of equipment you need. If it's a simple matter of putting a few networked media players into rooms where you already have audio systems and speakers, your additional cost can be as low as a few hundred dollars. (Assuming your home network is already up and running, of course; if not, throw in another hundred bucks for a wireless router.) If you need to put freestanding music players in a handful of rooms, double or triple that budget. And if you need to buy receivers and speakers for any of those rooms—well, you can see how it all starts adding up fairly fast.

> **♪ ULTIMATELY USEFUL** If all you want is to run audio to a second room, without having to deal with a lot of network and equipment issue, you may be able to do this directly from your audio receiver. Many receivers include both "A" and "B" speaker outputs; it's easy enough to use the "B" outputs to drive a second set of speakers in another room. Even better, many mid- and high-end receivers feature multi-room/multi-source outputs, which send line-level signals to an optional second amplifier. The benefit of this second output is that it can be switched to a different source than your receiver's main selection; push a button on your remote and send the sound from your CD player to a second room, while you watch cable TV in your main home theater room.

In any case, do your homework (meaning, read the rest of this chapter) and determine just how you want to set up your system and what specific equipment you'll need. I think you'll be pleasantly surprised at how affordable this sort of system can be!

Using Personal Computers

If you have a personal computer connected in your living room, why not connect other PCs in other rooms of your house? That's certainly an option, and one that isn't that wacky when you consider how inexpensive computers have gotten these days. Granted, a network media player will probably cost less, but you get more functionality with a full-featured PC.

The thing here is to not duplicate your music library on each PC. Instead, connect each computer to your home network and access your master music library on whatever PC or media server on which it resides. It's easy enough to connect one computer to another over a network, whether you're using WiFi or Ethernet, and to point your music player (or Windows Media Center) to the computer where your library is stored.

The disadvantage to this approach, of course, is cost. Instead of spending $100-$200 on a network media player, you spend $400 or more on each computer in your system—maybe more, since you need to add a remote receiver to each PC to operate it via remote control. And if you're really fussy about sound, you'll add an outboard DAC to each PC. You see where we're going here.

Still, if you already have an audio/video system installed in a given room (and it needs to be an A/V system, as you'll need a TV screen to navigate the PC), adding a smallish, low-cost PC is as good an approach as any. Consider it if you're technically proficient and like the added benefits you get from having a full-featured computer handy.

> ♪ **ULTIMATELY INTERESTING** Learn more about using a computer for music playback in Chapter 24, "Playing Digital Music on Your Computer."

Using Networked Media Players

For most users, however, using a networked music player in a second room makes more sense than using PC for that same purpose. Not only are most media players lower priced than most PCs, you also have a simplicity of installation and operation that isn't possible on the PC side.

You can install any number of network media players on your home network, and connect them all to your digital music library stored on a central computer or media server. Each music player can play different selections; that is, you can listen to the Like in the living room, Dylan in the den, Kraftwerk in the kitchen, and Bach in the bedroom, all at the same time.

Connecting a networked media player is simplicity itself—assuming you have an audio system or home theater system already in the room. For most lower-priced players, you'll need to make both audio and video connections (you need a screen to control playback), which means you need an A/V receiver and flat-screen TV. Connect the media player to the receiver, typically via HDMI, and you're good to go.

For example, if you're in the Apple eco-system, installing Apple TV boxes (like the one in Figure 26.1) in each room in your house isn't a bad way to go. You pay $99 per box, and they hook up to any A/V receiver or, if you only have a TV in a given room, directly to a flat-screen TV via HDMI. These little boxes work great, the interface is easy to use, and each box

> **ULTIMATELY USEFUL** If you're not an Apple devotee, Western Digital's WD TV Live box does everything the Apple TV does, but adds compatibility with WMA, FLAC, and OGG files, all at the same $99 price.

accesses your main iTunes library independently for music, photos, movies, whatever. I have to admit, this is an attractive option for many folks.

FIGURE 26.1

Install Apple TV boxes throughout your home to build a whole house audio/video system.

If you want to go audio only, most of the higher-priced media players ($500 and up) have front-of-unit displays and full-featured remote controls, so you don't need a TV to see what you're doing. This type of player has much better audio fidelity, so this is always a good choice if you want the best possible sound in a given room.

> **ULTIMATELY INTERESTING** Learn more about networked music players (AKA home media players) in Chapter 25, "Playing Digital Music on a Home Media Player."

26

Using Media Center Extenders

Then there's the subject of Media Center Extenders. This is a specific option if your main PC is running Windows Media Center and you want to replicate that experience in other rooms. Instead of installing additional PCs running WMC in those rooms, you instead install low-priced ($100-$200) Media Center Extenders, which are small media player-like boxes that connect to your main PC and provide the Media Center experience and interface, remotely. (Figure 26.2 shows a Linksys Media Center Extender, with both WiFi and Ethernet connections.)

The challenge in setting up a whole house system using Media Center Extenders is that nobody makes them anymore. That's right, as promising as the concept was, it ended up being a failed experiment—to a point, anyway. While you can still find used Media Center Extenders from D-Link and Linksys on eBay (and believe me, some enthusiasts are hording extra boxes), there are no new units to be had, which means this really isn't a viable option.

FIGURE 26.2

A Media Center Extender from Linksys—no longer available.

Except that it is. That's because there is still one type of Media Center Extender available today, and that's Microsoft's Xbox 360 game console. Yes,

26

the Xbox plays videogames (and quite well, thank you), but it also functions as a Media Center Extender. Just select the Media Center option off the main menu and get the full Media Center experience, right through your game box.

Given that most households have at least one Xbox set up and ready to go (and if you don't, you can buy one for just $199), this is a very attractive option for many music lovers. Granted, Xboxes can be a little noisy (although the noise level, due to the internal fan, is much reduced on newer units) and they don't really have an audio equipment design aesthetic, but it may be the easiest way to set up digital audio in a second or third room in your house.

> ♪ **ULTIMATELY INTERESTING**   Interestingly, freestanding Media Center Extenders didn't quite replicate the entire Media Center experience; for example, they didn't include transition effects when playing photo slideshows. The Xbox 360, on the other hand, functions just like Windows Media Center on a PC, transition effects and all.

Using Freestanding Media Players

What do you do if you want to listen to your digital music library in another room that doesn't have an audio system or home theater system installed? You need to purchase a freestanding music player that connects to your home network and then plays tunes through its own internal speakers.

There are a number of these freestanding music players available. Most offer both WiFi and Ethernet connections; going wireless is probably the best choice in a large home. Many of these boxes also let you listen to streaming audio over the Internet, so Pandora and Last.fm and the like can be easily accessed.

Controlling one of these units is typically via a full function remote control; many feature color screens so you can view cover art and the like. Many units also have a decent front panel display, so you can see what you're listening to from across the room.

The most versatile of these units not only include their own amps and speakers, but also have outputs you can run to an external audio system. This way you can keep using the unit (for access and control) if you decide to move it to a room with a better audio system.

What kinds of freestanding music players are we talking about? Here's a list of some of the most popular:

- **Grace Innovator X** (www.gracedigitalaudio.com, $149). Connects via WiFi only, offers both network audio playback and Internet streaming radio. As you can see in Figure 26.3, this tabletop unit features a single speaker and a four-line LCD text display.

26

FIGURE 26.3
Grace's Innovator X Wireless Radio and Media Streamer.

■ **Grace Bravado-X** (www.gracedigitalaudio.com, $179). This unit features two up-firing speakers with rear ports for improved sound. Like the Innovator X, this unit is Wi-Fi only with a four-line LCD text display. It looks more like a traditional audio component, as shown in Figure 26.4.

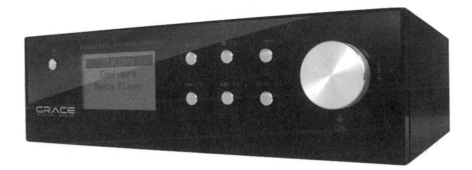

FIGURE 26.4
Grace's Bravado-X Wi-Fi Radio.

■ **Logitech Squeezebox Radio** (www.logitech.com, $179). Connects via WiFi or Ethernet, and also plays music from your iPod/iPhone or other portable music player. Sound is from a two-way mono speaker system. Features a nice color LCD screen on the front, as shown in Figure 26.5.

FIGURE 26.5

Logitech's Squeezebox Radio, available in white, black, or red.

■ **Sonos Play:3.** (www.sonos.com, $299). Connects via Ethernet, or wireless with an optional $49 Bridge unit. As shown in Figure 26.6, this is a three-way mono speaker system. You can purchase an optional Sonos Controller remote control, or use your iPod, iPad, or Android device to control playback.

■ **Sonos Play:5** (www.sonos.com, $399). The Play:3's big brother, shown in Figure 26.7. Features the same connections and control, but with five-speaker stereo sound. (That's two tweeters, two midrange, and a single woofer.)

> ♪ **ULTIMATELY INTERESTING** The Sonos units (previously dubbed "ZonePlayers") are part of the more inclusive Sonos Wireless HiFi System. The Sonos system has a lot of fans, as many music lovers like the simplicity of going with a whole house system from a single manufacturer—and the Sonos system is easy to set up and works quite well. The complete system includes the Connect networked media player, Connect-Amp media player with built-in amp (but not speakers), Play:3 and Play:5 freestanding music players, and Bridge wireless connector. (You need one Bridge per system to connect other devices wirelessly.)

26

FIGURE 26.6

The Sonos Play:3.

FIGURE 26.7

The Sonos Play:5.

Sound varies, of course; the higher-end units are going to sound a lot better than the lower-end ones. Still, for background music in a room without a formal audio system, these are good options for listening to your digital music library.

GOING WHOLE HOG FOR WHOLE HOUSE AUDIO

I like the digital music revolution, especially when it comes to whole house audio. It's really easy to pop a $99 network media player onto a living room or bookshelf audio system and have access to your entire music library, whatever room you're talking about. And the freestanding units, like the Logitech Squeezebox Radio, put that same music in rooms without existing audio systems. It's easy enough that a technophobe can do it, and surprisingly affordable.

That's a far cry from the way whole house audio used to be—and the way it's still presented in the custom installation trade. Believe it or not, there are still manufacturers out there pimping their $10,000+ proprietary solutions, which you see a lot in new construction and custom remodels. I'm talking about systems from companies like Niles, NuVo, Russound, Vidabox, and ZON. Pricey systems, all of them.

What these custom systems have in common is the use of multi-zone audio servers, connected via CAT-5 cabling to custom audio or audio/video systems in each major room of the house. But here's the thing; there's nothing these expensive systems do music-wise that you can't also accomplish with $99 Apple TV or WD TV Live units connected via a WiFi network to a desktop PC or home server. Oh, some of these custom systems let you add home automation controls and the like (which you can also do from a PC, by the way), but when it comes to music playback, the consumer-oriented products we discuss in this book are just as good as the pricey custom stuff.

And that's a good thing, at least in my opinion. (Custom installers might disagree; they like the technical support they get from the high-end companies, as well as the way proprietary equipment locks customers into future purchases from them.) Digital audio brings both quality playback (at least in theory; don't get me going on lossy compression) and versatility to the average consumer. You don't need to break the bank or consult a pricey professional to add digital music in any room you like; the power is now in the hands of the consumer. Good for us!

26

PART

VI

Playing Your Music—On the Go

Playing Music on a Portable Music Player or Smartphone

For millions of music lovers, their listening device of choice is either a portable music player or smartphone. It's certainly convenient to take your music with you wherever you go and be able to listen to tunes while you commute, exercise, study, or whatever.

There's not much complicated about playing music on a portable music player or smartphone. You have to somehow get the music to the portable device, of course, and then navigate through the menus to find the track, album, artist, genre, or playlist you want to listen to. From there, it's a simple matter of plugging those little earbuds into your ears and getting your groove on.

Choosing a Portable Music Player

When it comes to choosing a portable music player, we can pretend that it's otherwise but it's truly an Apple world. Apple pretty much defined the market for portable music players, and a decade later it's still Apple's game.

Apple's iPods

If you're in the market for a new portable music player, your quest starts and probably ends with a member of the iPod family. And even though the company's emphasis is not-so-subtly shifting to the iPhone (which also functions as a portable music player), Apple still sells a boatload of its market-leading music player devices.

While there have been rumors about Apple paring its iPod offerings, as of Spring 2012 that hasn't happened. There are still four primary types of iPods to choose from, including the following:

▪ **iPod shuffle.** The shuffle is Apple's smallest, lightest, and least expensive iPod. There's no screen; playback literally shuffles through the tunes you've loaded onto the device. It's great for joggers and exercisers of all types; as you can see in Figure 27.1, the unit is small enough to clip onto your shirt or belt or whatever. The iPod shuffle's capacity is 2GB, it comes in a variety of pretty colors, and it sells for just $49.

FIGURE 27.1

Apple's teeny-tiny iPod shuffle.

■ **iPod nano.** Next up is the iPod nano, which in its current iteration (there have been several variations of the nano over the years) is just a smidge larger than the iPod shuffle, but with a small color LCD screen to control all playback operations. (Figure 27.2 shows the nano and its various screens.) The nano is also a favorite with athletic types and comes in 8GB ($129) and 16GB ($149) versions, in a variety of colors.

FIGURE 27.2

An assortment of iPod nanos.

■ **iPod classic.** Apple's biggest iPod, in terms of both size and storage, is the iPod classic, shown in Figure 27.3. This unit is the most like the original iPod, and plays both music and videos. You get a whopping 160GB of storage, enough for a fairly large music library, for $249. This is the iPod for serious music collectors.

■ **iPod touch.** The iPod touch can best be described as an iPhone without the phone. Instead of physical controls, the entire front of the device is a touch-screen display, as you can see in Figure 27.4. Like the iPhone, you can install all sorts of apps for games and other functionality. The touch also has built-in WiFi connectivity, so you can go online (to surf the web, grab email, send messages, and such) whenever you're near a wireless hotspot. There are three versions of the iPod touch available, in 8GB ($199), 32GB ($299), and 64GB ($399) versions. This is the iPod for people who want to do more than just play music.

27

FIGURE 27.3

The classic look of the iPod classic.

FIGURE 27.4

Apple's iPod touch.

All of these units, save for the classic, use solid state flash memory for storage. The classic uses a small, high capacity hard drive instead, which is why it has so much more capacity than the others.

> **ULTIMATELY INTERESTING** All of Apple's portable devices (iPods, iPhones, and iPads) are compatible with AAC- and MP3-format audio files. They are *not* compatible with WMA, FLAC, or OGG files.

Which iPod is best for you? If you want something small and inexpensive, the shuffle does the job. If you like small but want more functionality and storage, go with the nano. If you have a huge music library you want to take with you, choose the classic. And if you want to do more than just listen to music, like play games, then the touch is the unit you want.

> ♪ **ULTIMATELY INTERESTING** You can find more information about Apple's iPods online at www.apple.com/ipod/.

Other Portable Music Players

What do you do if you're in the market for a portable music player but don't want to give your money to Apple? The choices are few and far between, but they do exist—although you might have to seek them out. Here's a sampling of what's available:

- **Creative ZEN Style** (www.creative.com, $49/$69/$89). Creative's been a steady competitor to Apple since the early days of the iPod, and continues with the ZEN Style, a lower-priced alternative to the iPod nano. It's a touchscreen operated device, as you can see in Figure 27.5, and comes in 4GB ($49), 8GB ($69), and 16GB ($89) versions. Unlike it's Apple competition, the ZEN Style has a built-in FM radio.

FIGURE 27.5

Creative's ZEN Style MP3 player with touchscreen display.

- **SanDisk Sansa Clip Zip** (www.sandisk.com, $49). As you can see in Figure 27.6, the Sansa Clip Zip unit is a cross between Apple's shuffle and nano, with 4GB of storage, a variety of colors to choose from, and a small color touchscreen display.

27

FIGURE 27.6

SanDisk's Sansa Clip Zip nano-like music player.

■ **SanDisk Sansa Fuze+** (www.sandisk.com, $59/$89/$119). As shown in Figure 27.7, the Sansa Fuze+ is a bigger version of the Clip Zip, with a larger screen and either 4GB ($59), 8GB ($89), or 16GB ($119) of storage.

FIGURE 27.7

SanDisk's Sansa Fuze+.

■ **Sony Walkman** (store.sony.com, $79/$89/$109). Yes, Sony is still making something they call the Walkman, although it's a far cry from the portable audiocassette players of old. As you can see in Figure 27.8, this 21st-century Walkman sports either 4GB ($79), 8GB ($89), or 16GB ($109) of solid state storage and a 2-inch color LCD display.

FIGURE 27.8

Sony's new-generation Walkman.

■ **Creative ZEN X-Fi3** (www.creative.com, $99/$139/$169). This ZEN model is a tad larger than the ZEN Style, with improved audio playback, support for FLAC files, and Bluetooth connectivity to similarly equipped car audio systems. Available in 8GB ($99), 16GB ($139), and 32GB ($169) versions, as shown in Figure 27.9. Includes a built-in FM radio.

■ **Samsung Galaxy Player** (www.samsung.com, $199). As you can see in Figure 27.10, this unit looks a lot like one of Samsung's Galaxy smartphones, but without the phone part. You get a big full-face touchscreen display and 8GB of storage.

27

FIGURE 27.9

The Creative ZEN X-Fi3 MP3 player.

FIGURE 27.10

Samsung's Galaxy Player.

All of these units use solid state flash memory for storage. All play MP3-format files; some also play WMA files, but few if any can play Apple's AAC files. They're all decent-enough alternatives to an iPod, but really don't do anything that an iPod doesn't. (Except, in some cases, play WMA-format files—and, in the case of the Creative players, offer a built-in FM radio.)

Playing Music on a Smartphone

Many people today have abandoned their dedicated portable music players to instead listen to music on their smartphones. For most folks, this is a simple step sideways from an iPod to an iPhone; the music player functionality is nearly identical between the two.

After all, why not carry one multi-function device (smartphone) in place of two single-function devices (mobile phone and portable music player)? Even though a smartphone might not have as much storage capacity for your music library (especially when you start adding games and other apps to the phone), it's considerably more convenient than juggling two separate devices in your purse or pocket.

Apple's iPhone

The dominant smartphone today is, no surprise, Apple's iPhone. The iPhone's music storage and playback functionality is identical to that of an iPod touch, and similar to that of non-fullscreen iPods. With the latest 4S iteration, shown in Figure 27.11, you can find models with either 16GB ($199), 32GB ($299), or 64GB ($399) of storage. (All prices are subsidized by your purchase of a corresponding service plan with your wireless carrier.)

FIGURE 27.11

Use Apple's iPhone for music playback.

27

Using an iPhone for music playback is appropriately intuitive. Tap the Music icon to launch the playback function. You can then browse through your playlists, artists, songs, or albums. As you can see in Figure 27.12, the iPhone displays the album cover fullscreen during playback, along with the necessary transport controls—while the device is held vertically. Flip the phone on its side and you get Apple's cover view mode, shown in Figure 27.13, where you can flip back and forth through the albums on your device.

FIGURE 27.12

Playing music on an iPhone, in vertical mode.

Naturally, your iPhone connects to the iTunes software on your computer to manage your music library and synch tracks between the two devices. It's also a cinch to purchase and download tracks directly from the iTunes Store to your phone. The Apple ecosystem is tight. (Just don't expect to play WMA-format files on your iPhone; that's not allowed.)

ULTIMATELY **INTERESTING** Learn more about Apple's iPhones at www.apple.com/iphone/.

FIGURE 27.13

Hold the iPhone sideways to view your music in cover view mode.

Android Phones

If you have an Android phone, such as a Samsung Galaxy, you can also play music while you're on the go. While many phones come with proprietary music player apps preinstalled, there are lots of other music player apps available from the Google Play app store. The most popular of these Android music player apps include the following:

- AudioGalaxy
- Cubed, shown in Figure 27.14
- Meridian Music Player
- MixZing Media Player
- PlayerPro, shown in Figure 27.15
- PowerAmp
- TuneWiki
- WinAmp

FIGURE 27.14
The Cubed music player for Android devices.

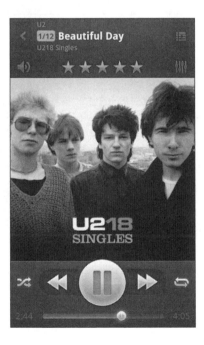

FIGURE 27.15
The PlayPro Android music player.

Most of these apps are free or certainly affordable, with the most expensive ones topping out at $4.99. Most of these apps play all file formats, including MP3, AAC, and WMA; some even play FLAC and OGG files. Check out the specs and reviews before you down load from the Google Play app store.

Windows 7 Phones

Windows Phone is a distant number-three player in the smartphone market. That's a shame; I kind of like the interface. If you do too, Microsoft includes a Music+Videos hub in Windows Phone 7. The music function is dubbed Zune, and it does everything you'd expect a music player to do.

As you can see in Figure 27.16, music playback is simplicity itself, with transport controls above the current track's artwork. There's also a Smart DJ feature that automatically creates playlists based on tracks you select, which is nice.

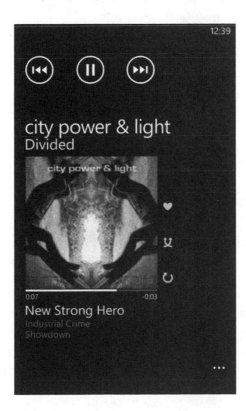

FIGURE 27.16

Playing music on a Windows 7 Phone.

The one advantage to playing music on a Windows Phone is that you get to tap your library of WMA-format tunes, if that's what you have. Naturally, there's also MP3 playback, as well as Apple's AAC-format files. That makes a Windows Phone a good fairly universal music playback device.

Playing Music on a Tablet

Not surprisingly, there are also music player apps available for all the major tablet computers, including the Apple iPad. Most of these apps work similarly to the phone-based music players for the same operating system.

> 𝄞 **ULTIMATELY** Microsoft says
> **INTERESTING** that the
> music/video playback function in Windows Phone 7 is kind of like having a Zune player on your phone. (The Zune was Microsoft's ill-fated attempt to compete with Apple's iPod players.) Since Microsoft has long since discontinued its actual Zune portable music player, I'm not sure how that's smart marketing. To sync media between your computer and phone, you do have to install Zune software on your PC, so there's that.

Apple's iPad

If you have an Apple iPad, you have the iPad version of music player found on the iPod; it's kind of like playing music on an iPod, only bigger. There are also numerous third-party music player apps available, if that's your want. (I'm guessing most users are just fine with Apple's built-in music player, however.) Search Apple's App Store and see what comes up.

Amazon's Kindle Fire

The number-two bestselling tablet out there (okay, a distant number two, but still) is Amazon's Kindle Fire. The Fire has its own built-in music player which functions as a music player should. When you hold your tablet horizontally, which seems to be the preferred orientation for the fire, the screen looks like the one in Figure 27.17. You get album cover art on the left, transport controls and track info on the right. As you might suspect, the Fire's music player is tightly tied into the Amazon.com website, in particular the Amazon MP3 Store.

The music you play on your Fire isn't stored locally, however. Instead, the Fire takes advantage of Amazon's Cloud Drive service, which streams your library (including Amazon MP3 Store purchases) to you over the Internet. It certainly helps, then, if you have a consistent WiFi connection, but that's true about anything you do with the Fire. So if you have one of Amazon's tablets, you're pretty much good to go out of the box.

> 𝄞 **ULTIMATELY** Learn more
> **INTERESTING** about Ama-
> zon's cloud music services in Chapter 20, "Accessing Your Music in the Cloud."

FIGURE 27.17

Playing music on an Amazon Kindle Fire tablet.

Other Android Tablets

If you have another brand of Android tablet (yes, the Kindle Fire runs a variation of the Android OS), you can find a variety of music player apps to use. In fact, most of the music player apps for Android phones, discussed previously, are also available for Android tablets. Search the Google Play apps store to see what's available.

Managing Music on Your Portable Device

Whichever type of portable device you use to listen to music on the go, you have to somehow get your music onto the device, and then manage it. While each and every device will do this a little differently, the basic concepts are the same.

In general, you manage your music library on your computer, not on your portable device. That is, you download tracks you purchase to your computer, you rip CDs to your computer, and you assign genres and create playlists on your computer.

What you do next is connect your portable device to your computer, and synchronize ("sync") selected music files between the two devices. In essence, you copy the tracks and playlists you want from your computer to your portable device.

You can use just about any music player program to do this synchronization, but assuming you have an iPod, iPhone, or iPad, you're probably going to be using the iTunes software for this task. And, to be fair, this synching is done pretty much automatically.

27

Syncing Your iPod or iPhone

You connect your i-device to your computer via the supplied cable which connect on one end to the dock connector on your portable device and on the other end to a USB port on your computer. (If you have an iPod shuffle, there's no dock connector; instead, there's a mini-jack connector that you use.)

When your iPod is connected to your PC, the portable device automatically enters a special sync/charge mode. Your PC should automatically recognize your device and launch the iTunes software. Within iTunes, a new Devices section appears in the Source pane, with your iPod or iPhone listed. In addition, the main window changes to display information about your iPod in a series of tabs, as shown in Figure 27.18.

FIGURE 27.18
Viewing information about a connected iPhone in iTunes.

The Summary tab displays the name, capacity, version information, serial number, and such for your i-device. In addition, the Version section lets you update your iPod's firmware or restore the iPod to its factory condition (useful if you have corrupted data or some sort of operational problem).

> **ULTIMATELY CAUTIOUS** Do not disconnect your iPod from your computer until synchronization is complete, otherwise you might corrupt the files on your iPod.

At the bottom of the Summary tab is a visual representation of what's currently stored on your iPod. You'll see how much total space is available, how much space is devoted to each type of media (audio, video, photos, apps, books, and other), and how much free space is left to use.

> 🎼 ULTIMATELY **INTERESTING** Connecting your iPod or iPhone to your PC also recharges the iPod's battery. Even if you don't need to sync your iPod, you still need to connect it to your PC to recharge it—or use the power adapter to recharge it directly from a wall outlet.

Configuring Sync Options

Scroll down to the Options section of the Summary tab to determine how your i-device syncs to your computer. The following options are available:

- **Open iTunes when this iPod/iPhone is connected**, the default operational mode.

- **Sync with this iPod/iPhone over Wi-Fi**, available for devices with WiFi connectivity, lets you perform the sync operation over your wireless network, no cables needed.

- **Sync only checked songs and videos**, which is useful when you're syncing a device that has less storage capacity than you have songs stored on your PC. When this option is selected, only those tracks you've checked in your iTunes library are copied to your portable device. When this option is not selected, all the songs in your library are automatically transferred to your iPod or iPhone—which works well if you have a larger-capacity device (or a smaller music library).

- **Prefer standard definition videos**, which keeps you from filling up your portable device with large HD video files.

- **Convert higher bit rate songs to XXX AAC**, which is an easy way to load lower bitrate versions of files stored on your computer at a higher bitrate—and save storage space on your i-device.

- **Manually manage music and videos**, which you can use to sync only selected tracks to your portable device.

If you have a large-capacity iPod classic and you want to transfer all the songs on your PC to the iPod, uncheck all but the first option. If you have a smaller-capacity iPod nano or iPod shuffle, or want to transfer only selected songs to your iPod, check the first and second options. If you want to manage the music already stored on your iPod, check the first and third options.

27

Syncing Your Music

To configure what music files are synced, you need to access the Music tab, shown in Figure 27.19. From here, you can choose to sync everything in your music library or just selected playlists, artists, albums, or genres—that is, those items checked in your iTunes library. You can also choose to include music videos in your sync, if you wish.

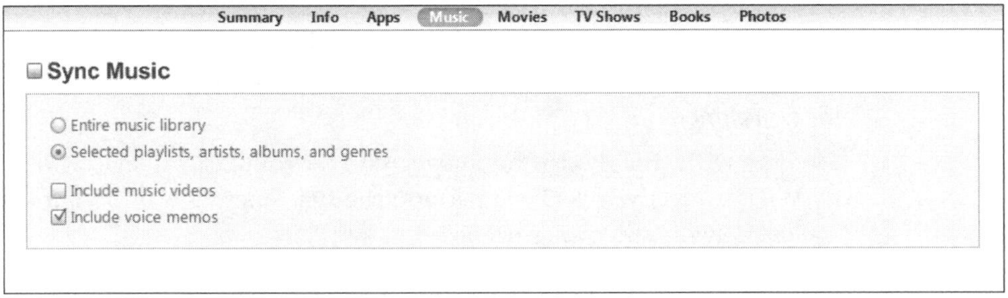

> ♪ **ULTIMATELY USEFUL** After you make a change on the Music, Movies, or similar tabs, click the **Apply** button to register the change and make the new sync.

FIGURE 27.19

Selecting music sync options in iTunes.

Improving Your Device's Sound Quality

When you play music on your portable music player or smartphone, you're playing back audio files encoded with lossy compression, typically at a midgrade bitrate. That means the music isn't that great to start with, but probably good enough for listening on the go.

That said, there are ways to make your iPod, iPhone, or whatever device it is you're using sound better when you're listening to your favorite tunes. I'm not talking about encoding at a higher bitrate or using lossless compression, both of which will increase file size and let you store less music on your device. Instead, I'm talking about improving playback by changing what you use to listen to your portable player.

Upgrading Your Earbuds (or Headphones)

Let's start with the obvious. Whatever type of portable device you're using, even one of Apple's, the little earbuds that come from the factory are fairly low grade. Oh, they're fine for most folks who just want background music, but they don't have the fidelity that audiophiles and other serious music lovers are accustomed to.

To that end, the quickest and easiest way to improve the sound quality of your iPod, iPhone, or whatever is to upgrade from the stock earbuds. You can choose a better pair of earbuds or replace the buds with a set of good headphones. The difference in fidelity will be impressive.

How easy is it to switch from the stock earbuds? Very easy, since all earbuds and most headphones sold today either come with a mini-jack plug or with a mini-jack adapter for the traditional 1/4-inch plug. This makes it easy to connect just about any buds or phones to your portable device.

What kind of earbuds can you choose from? Here's a short list of some of the more popular models—excluding low-end replacement items:

- **Kicker EB101** (www.kicker.com, $39)
- **Klipsch Image S4** (www.klipsch.com, $79)
- **Bose IE2** (www.bose.com, $99), shown in Figure 27.20
- **Beats by Dr. Dre iBeats** (beatsbydre.com, $119)
- **Beats by Dr. Dre Tour** (beatsbydre.com, $149)
- **Bowers & Wilkins C5** (www.bowers-wilkins.com, $179)

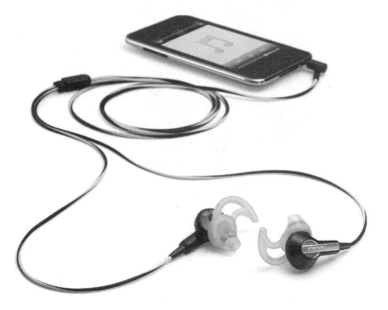

FIGURE 27.20

Bose's IE2 "in-ear headphones."

27

And here are some of the more popular headphones for portable use:

- **Koss Porta Pro KTC** (www.koss.com, $79), shown in Figure 27.21
- **Sennheiser HD 558** (www.sennheiserusa.com, $179)
- **Beats by Dr. Dre Solo HD** (www.beatsbydre.com, $199)
- **Bose QuietComfort 15** (www.bose.com, $299), shown in Figure 27.22
- **Bowers & Wilkins** (www.bowers-wilkins.com, $299)
- **Beats by Dr. Dre Studio** (www.beatsbydre.com, $299), shown in Figure 27.23.

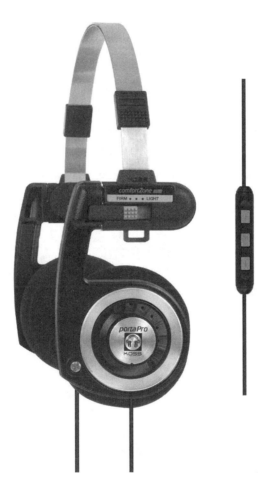

FIGURE 27.21

Koss's affordable Porta Pro KTC headphones, complete with microphone and controls for iPhone use.

FIGURE 27.22

Bose's QuietComfort 15 noise-canceling headphones.

FIGURE 27.23

Beats by Dr. Dre Studio headphones.

27

Of these units, the hottest on the market today are the various Beats by Dr. Dre. Listeners love the enhanced fidelity (and slightly pumped bass) you get from all Beats models; the higher-end Studio model is true audiophile quality. (My book editor got some Beats for his birthday and says he's in nirvana—and not the grunge type.) They're definitely worth a listen.

Adding an Outboard DAC

The other way to improve music playback on your portable device is to use an outboard digital-to-analog converter (DAC). That's because most portable devices, especially smartphones, have fairly mediocre internal DACs. Bypassing the internal DAC with an external one provides much better conversion to analog, which will improve playback over either earbuds or headphones.

The challenge is finding an outboard DAC that is compatible with the iPod's digital audio output, via the dock connector. There are only a handful, including the following:

- **Pure i-20 Digital Dock** (www.pure.com, $99)
- **High Resolution Technologies iStreamer** (www.highresolutiontechnologies, $199)
- **NuForce Icon iDo** (www.nuforce.com, $249)
- **Fostex HP-P1** (www.fostexinternational.com, $649), shown in Figure 27.24
- **Peachtree iDac** (www.peachtreeaudio.com, $999)

ULTIMATELY USEFUL If you listen to your iPod or iPhone while cutting the grass, traveling on a plane, or in other situations where there's a lot of loud background noise, consider investing in a set of noise-canceling earbuds or headphones. These units, such as those Bose's QuietComfort line, use active noise-canceling technology to cancel out background noise and deliver a much cleaner listening experience. I've found they definitely reduce in-flight headaches when flying cross-country.

ULTIMATELY INTERESTING Learn more about DACs in Chapter 24, "Playing Digital Music on Your Computer."

ULTIMATELY CAUTIOUS Don't assume that just any outboard DAC can connect via USB to your iPod or iPhone. Even though you can run a cable from the iPod's dock connector to your DAC's USB input, very few DACs can decode the encoded digital signal coming out of the iPod. That's right, Apple encodes its digital signal and has only given the "keys" to a handful of DAC manufacturers.

27

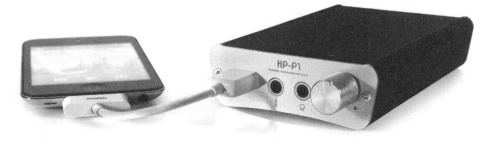

FIGURE 27.24
The Fostext HP-P1, designed especially for iPod/iPhone use.

The question is, is it really worth it to add an outboard DAC to your iPod or iPhone? It certainly does up your total expense. To be honest, you'll get more immediately noticeable results by spending that same money (or less!) on a good set of headphones. But past that, if you really want the best sound possible, an outboard DAC does deliver—albeit subtly. Frankly, if you can notice the difference from an outboard DAC, you probably should be encoding your audio files at a higher bitrate, which also improves the sound quality.

It's all a matter, I suppose, of how much effort and expense you want to go to maximize the sound quality of your portable playback. For some music lovers, no effort should be spared. For others, upgrading from the stock earbuds is effort enough. As with all things musical and digital, let your own ears be your guide.

WHO CREATED THE iPOD?

In Apple's post-Steve Jobs era, it's fashionable to give the late Mr. Jobs sole credit for all of his company's successes. (And to conveniently forget his failures, such as the Apple Lisa and, some would say, Apple TV.) Yes, Jobs had a great feel for his customer base and an unerring sense of design, but he didn't run the company by himself. Case in point is Apple's signature digital music product, the iPod.

The story of the iPod begins in the year 2000, when Apple was staging a comeback after a somewhat-disappointing period in the late 1990s. The low-priced iMac was a newfound consumer hit, and Jobs was thirsting for additional opportunities to tap into the mass market. As part of this effort, Jobs' staff began looking at all manner of digital devices that could connect to a computer and drive sales of the company's line of Macintosh products.

27

One of the opportunities that Apple recognized was that of digital music; people were downloading songs (for free) from Napster, using their PCs to listen to this music, and ripping and burning their own mix CDs. Since Apple didn't have its own music player app, the company licensed the SoundJam MP music player program from third-party developer Casady & Greene. Apple also hired the software's head programmer, Jeff Robbin, and directed him to turn SoundJam into a music player that Apple could distribute with all its Macintosh computers. That music player would be called iTunes and was introduced to the public at Macworld Expo on January 9, 2001.

Simultaneous with the launch of the iTunes software, another group within Apple was looking at opportunities revolving around digital devices for the mass market. As part of this effort, the group focused on the market for MP3 players. The MP3 players of that era were either big and bulky or small and fairly useless, lacking in both performance and sexiness. Most of the smaller MP3 players used fairly low-capacity flash memory chips that could only hold a few dozen songs. The larger MP3 players incorporated a 2.5" Fujitsu hard disk drive and could hold thousands of songs, but were bigger and heavier than that era's portable CD players, making them singularly unappealing. Neither type of player was taking the market by storm.

This, then, was the opportunity that Apple was looking for.

Apple's engineers began to strategize how they could improve on the current crop of portable music players. Users wanted to carry an entire library of songs with them, not just a CD's worth of music, so higher capacity was the way to go. This meant focusing on hard drive players. But a smaller size was also desirable, which argued for some sort of compromise between size and capacity—or the use of newer technology.

With this in mind, Apple engineer Jon Rubinstein traveled to Tokyo to talk to Apple's current supplier of hard drives, Toshiba. Executives there showed him a new 1.8" drive that could hold 5GB of data—enough storage for about a thousand songs. Rubenstein realized that this new drive could be used to construct a smaller and lighter music player than the competition, which was still using the larger 2.5" Fujitsu drive.

Rubinstein also decided to take advantage of other technology advances to improve upon the performance of competing music players. Better displays and longer-lasting batteries were appropriated from the cell phone industry, and a FireWire connection was utilized to provide faster song transfer than was available with the current USB 1.1 standard.

The basic components in place, Apple hired an outside consultant, Tony Fadell, to put all the pieces together and design the player itself. One of the first things Fadell did was to contract with Silicon Valley startup PortalPlayer, which was already working on reference designs for several different types of digital music players. Fadell picked a design already in progress, then had his team work closely with PortalPlayer to get the player on the market as quickly as possible.

The software for the new music player was acquired from Pixio, a privately-held software company that developed operating systems for cell phones. Apple's interface design group, led by Tim Wasko, then built the iPod interface on top of the Pixio OS. Apple's head of marketing, Phil Schiller, came up with the idea for the iPod's innovative scroll wheel, and also suggested that menus scroll faster the longer the wheel is turned.

Prototype after prototype were turned out by Apple's design group, headed by Jonathan Ive. This group worked closely with PortalPlayer and Apple's engineers, constantly tweaking and refining the design. The development of the final player wasn't the result of a sudden flash of genius, but rather the step-by-step design process itself.

As the project developed, Apple leader Steve Jobs became more and more personally involved. By the time the first prototypes were built, Jobs was giving his input on a daily basis. He was focused on ease of use—how many button pushes it took to play a song, how fast the menus displayed, and so on.

As the product neared its final stage, Apple's marketing department had to come up with a name for the thing. Vinnie Chieco, a freelance copywriter who was part of a team of marketing consultants hired by Apple, came up with the iPod moniker, thinking of the device as one of several "pods" that connect to the central Macintosh hub.

27

It all came to a head on October 23, 2001, when the iPod was introduced to the public at a special event at Apple's Cupertino headquarters. The rest, as they say, is history, with more than 300 million units sold in the ensuing decade or so.

So that's how the iPod was developed. Yes, Jobs was involved (and truly instigated the entire project), but he must share the credit with other individuals such as Jon Rubinstein, Jeff Robbin, Tony Fadell, Tim Wasko, Phil Schiller, Jonathan Ive, and Vinnie Chieco, as well as companies like PortalPlayer, Pixio, Casady & Greene, and Toshiba. The iPod wasn't a one man show, but rather a group effort—and the results speak to the power of the group.

Listening to Streaming Music on a Portable Music Player or Smartphone

For some reason, consumers haven't bought into large-capacity portable music players with enough space to hold really big digital music collections. Yes, Apple still sells the 16GB iPod classic, but doesn't sell very many of them. (In fact, many tech pundits have been predicting the imminent demise of Apple's biggest iPod—although that hasn't happened yet.)

The reality is, whatever portable music player or smartphone you're using, it probably doesn't have enough storage space to hold your entire digital music library. If you want to listen to more tunes than your device can hold, you have to get the music another way—streamed to your device, over the Internet.

Evaluating Streaming Audio on Portable Devices

More and more people are using multi-purpose smartphones instead of single-purpose iPods to listen to music, but a smartphone has less storage capacity than a dedicated music player. That makes it increasingly difficult to take a large library of music on the go, which limits your listening options.

You have the same problem if you use a tablet, like the iPad or Kindle Fire. Tablets have notoriously little storage space; in the case of the Kindle Fire, the storage space is almost totally absent.

What's the solution when you don't have enough capacity to store your entire digital music collection? Streaming audio.

As we've discussed, streaming audio is music that isn't stored locally, but rather is piped in real time over the Internet to a playback device. That device can be a computer or network music player in the home, or a WiFi-equipped smartphone, tablet, or portable music player (like the iPod touch) on the go.

> ♪ ULTIMATELY **INTERESTING** Learn more about streaming audio in Chapter 17, "Understanding Streaming Music."

To listen to streaming audio on a portable device, all you need is an Internet connection of some sort (which rules out Apple's iPod shuffle, iPod nano, and iPod classic) and an app for your streaming music service of choice. That Internet connection can be WiFi, which is fine if you're near a WiFi hotspot or wireless network, or it can be a 3G or 4G data service from your mobile phone carrier. (Assuming, that is, that your music player or tablet has 3G/4G functionality.)

Listening to streaming music via WiFi is actually fairly seamless—that is, if you have a decent WiFi connection. If your wireless network is a bit dodgy, expect all sorts of stuttering and pauses in your music playback. And, if you're in a place without a WiFi network (like driving in your car!) you don't get any streaming music at all. Still and all, WiFi is probably the best way to listen to streaming music on a portable device.

Listening to streaming music via a 3G/4G network is more problematic. First off, if your cellular service is like mine (thank you, AT&T!), you don't always have a good connection. And if you don't have a good connection, your streaming music won't stream. It's no good to be listening to your favorite Spotify playlist while driving through the wilds of central Iowa, lose your cellular signal, and lose your playlist.

Second, you probably pay a set amount each month for a fixed amount of download data; if you exceed that amount, you pay through the nose. Well, get ready to pay through the nose, because streaming audio takes up a lot of data bandwidth. If you listen to a lot of music over a data network you're going to bust right through your data plan's ceiling, and fairly quickly. The mobile service providers want you to use their fancy 3G data networks, but not too much—which means you don't want to rely on 3G networks for the majority of your music streaming.

Still, if you have a device (like the Kindle Fire tablet) that has little to no inboard storage, streaming music is the only way to go. Even if you have a larger-capacity iPhone, streaming music may be the best way to listen to a wide variety of music. It's all a matter of picking the streaming service that best suits your needs—and making sure you're always around some sort of WiFi network.

Listening to Streaming Music Services on the Go

One of the benefits of a streaming music service is that it lets you listen to a wide variety of music on your iPhone, Android phone, tablet, or similar portable device. You connect your portable device to the streaming service of choice and listen to your favorite tunes, streamed over the Internet direct to your phone or tablet.

Most of the major streaming music services have apps for most major types of smartphones and tablets; certainly, you see iOS (iPhone/iPad) and Android apps aplenty. (Table 28.1 shows the available apps for the major streaming music services.) Note, however, that you often have to pony up for a pricier subscription plan to access a service on your mobile device.

Table 28.1   Streaming Music Mobile Apps

Service	iOS (iPhone/iPad)	Android	Windows Phone 7	BlackBerry	Palm
Grooveshark	Yes	Yes	No	Yes	Yes
Last.fm	Yes	Yes	No	No	No
MOG	Yes	Yes	No	No	No
Pandora Radio	Yes	Yes	No	Yes	Yes
Raditaz	Yes	Yes	No	No	No
Rara.com	No	Yes	No	No	No
Rdio	Yes	Yes	Yes	Yes	No
Rhapsody	Yes	Yes	Yes	Yes	No
Slacker Radio	Yes	Yes	Yes	Yes	Yes
Spotify	Yes	Yes	Yes	Yes	Yes
Turntable.fm	Yes	No	No	No	No
Zune Music Pass	No	No	Yes	No	No

28

Listening is as easy as you'd expect. Depending on the service, you can browse albums and artists, search for specific songs, and listen to any playlists you've created previously on your computer. It all streams in real time, in the palm of your hand.

>
> **ULTIMATELY USEFUL** If a web-based music service doesn't have an app for your phone or tablet, you can still listen in by using your device's web browser to go to the service's website. (This doesn't work for those services that employ their own software, such as Spotify and Zune.)

For example, Figure 28.1 shows the Spotify app for the iPhone. This app has five tabs, accessible from the bottom of any screen—Playlists, Search, What's New, Friends, and Settings. When you want to listen to your favorite music, the **Playlists** tab is a good place to start, as it lists all the playlists you've created in Spotify. To view a playlist, simply tap its **name** to display the playlist screen. To start playback in Shuffle mode, tap the **Shuffle Play** icon. To view the currently playing track, tap the **Now Playing** button.

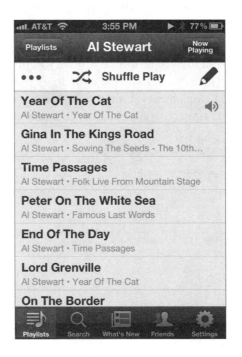

FIGURE 28.1

Playing a playlist from Spotify's iPhone app.

Pandora's iPhone app works in a similar fashion. Pandora lets you create artist-specific "stations," which you can then play from the app's Stations tab. As you can see in Figure 28.2, song playback is like that of any music player app, with the addition of thumbs up and thumbs down voting buttons.

FIGURE 28.2

Listening to a streaming station on Pandora's iPhone app.

Listening to Internet Radio on the Go

Beyond traditional streaming music services, there are a number of apps that let you listen to Internet radio on your smartphone or tablet. The most popular include AOL Radio, the aptly named Internet Radio, and Internet Radio Box. Look for them in your phone's app store.

Personally, I like listening to terrestrial radio when I'm on the go. This makes the TuneIn Radio app, shown in Figure 28.3, a must-have. I can browse through all my local AM and FM stations (even the HD substations), or look for out-of-town stations that fit my fancy. If I'm in the right mood, I can even use TuneIn to listen in on the police and fire bands. It's way cool.

28

FIGURE 28.3

Browsing local radio stations on the iPhone via the TuneIn Radio app.

Listening to Streaming Music from the Cloud

The final way to listen to streaming music on your portable device is to use a cloud music service. These services let you listen to your own music library, stored in the ephemeral cloud that is the Internet, then streamed over the Internet to your smartphone or tablet.

> **ULTIMATELY INTERESTING** Learn more about streaming music from the cloud in Chapter 20, "Accessing Your Music in the Cloud."

Naturally, to stream tunes from a cloud music service, you first have to subscribe to said service and upload all your music to the cloud. You can then install the app for that service on your phone or tablet and play your own music anywhere you go. You're not relying on a service being able to duplicate your library; you're literally listening to your own home-based music library on your phone or tablet, from wherever your current location happens to be.

28

The major cloud music services include Amazon Cloud Player (www.amazon.com/cloudplayer/), Google Play Music (play.google.com/music/), and iTunes Match (www.apple.com/itunes/). There are also two services (Audiogalaxy, www.audiogalaxy.com, and Subsonic, www.subsonic.org) that let you turn your home PC into a cloud server, without needing to upload your music to another server. (Figure 28.4 shows the Google Play Music app for Android devices; Figure 28.5 shows the Amazon MP3 Android app; you play iTunes Match music through your regular iPhone/iPad Music app.)

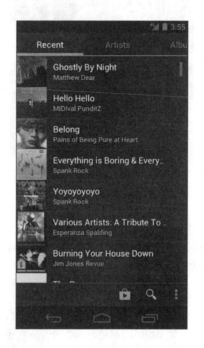

FIGURE 28.4

The Google Play Music Android app.

FIGURE 28.5

The Amazon MP3 (with Amazon Cloud Player) Android app.

Whichever cloud service you choose, they work in much the same fashion. After you've uploaded your library to the service, you install the service's app on your phone or tablet. (Or, if the service doesn't have an app for your device, go to the service's website on your device's web browser.) Log into your account and you see your entire music library displayed onscreen. Pick the music you want to listen to and it's streamed in real time to your device.

Personally, I like the concept of streaming cloud music to my iPhone. It's the only solution that lets me, in effect, take my entire music library with me, wherever I go.

> **ULTIMATELY CAUTIOUS** I must repeat, if you listen to a lot of music streamed over a mobile data network, even if it's stored in the cloud, you're likely to bump up against the upper limits of your mobile data plan— and incur high overage charges.

28

WHY YOUR iPOD ISN'T AN AM/FM RADIO

When I was a kid, everybody listened to Top 40 music on AM transistor radios. FM came a little later, and the radios were a little larger. But it's ingrained in my mind that portable music means, in addition to everything else, listening to AM and FM radio.

It's perplexing to me, then, that Apple didn't initially include an AM/FM radio in its iPod music players. As we learned in the previous chapter, Creative (www.creative.com) has long included FM radios in its various ZEN MP3 players. And Apple itself has added an FM radio to its sixth generation iPod nano player—but not to any other player in the line.

Why, then, can't you listen to AM or FM radio on any other iPods, or on your iPhone? Apple, I'm sure, will say it's a matter of cost; the pennies that it would cost to add the AM or FM circuitry would push the price up above what the average consumer is willing to pay, blah blah blah. But I don't think that's the case, as they were able to add an FM radio to the moderately priced iPod nano. Why not to any other devices in the line?

If you want to listen to terrestrial radio on your iPhone, you have a couple of choices. Griffin Technology (www.griffintechnology.com) sells the Navigate in-line FM tuner/controller, shown in Figure 28.6, which connects to the dock connector on your iPhone or iPod and adds FM capability. (It also includes a connector to plug in your earbuds.) Or you can install the TuneIn Radio app, discussed previously, and listen to AM and FM stations streamed over the Internet—assuming you have an Internet connection, that is.

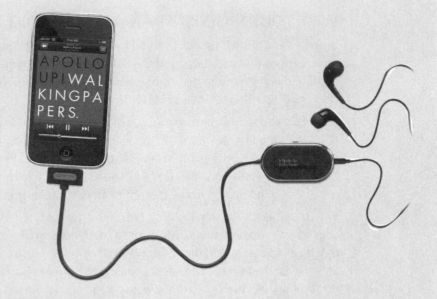

FIGURE 28.6

Griffin's Navigate in-line FM tuner/controller for the iPod/iPhone.

I suppose this really isn't a burning issue, or more people would be complaining about it. After all, many people purchase iPods to escape the tyranny of broadcast radio. Still, there are times and places where AM or FM radio may be your only listening choice; I'd really appreciate it if my iPhone could pick up my local stations, when I want.

Playing Your Portable Music in the Living Room

I don't want to sound like a total snob about digital music. While audiophiles argue about the DAC performance and what file format is best for digital music playback, an equal if not greater number of people are content to store their music libraries on their portable music players and smartphones (re: iPods and iPhones), at a lower (but still acceptable) bitrate. Not everyone has the same amount of gold in their ears, and iPod/iPhone playback is just fine for a lot of folks.

If you count yourself among the portable device-reliant populace, you may still want to play your tunes on the big speakers in your living room. What you need is some way to get the music from your portable device to your home theater or home audio system. You play the tunes on your iPod or iPhone, and listen to them through your system's receiver and speakers.

Fortunately, there are a number of ways to play your iPod, iPhone, or other portable device on your home audio system, and most of them stand well short of breaking the bank. We'll look at the most popular options in this chapter.

29

Connecting Your Device to External Speakers

For many music lovers, the easiest way to share your portable music collection is to connect your portable music player or smartphone to an external speaker of some sort. The simplest, but not necessarily the best, way to do this is to connect an external speaker (via some sort of adapter cable) to your device's earphone-out jack. A more sophisticated connection comes from those external speakers that connect to your device's docking connector; many of these devices also let you operate your iPod or iPhone from the external speaker or remote control.

There are a ton of different types of external speakers you can connect to your iPod, iPhone, or similar portable device. What type you choose depends on your intended use and budget.

Connecting to Powered Speakers

First off, let's look at what exactly I mean when I say *external speaker*. For our purposes, an external speaker is one that is self-powered and has some sort of audio input connection. (The speaker has to be self-powered—that is, have its own built-in power amplifier—since it can't draw power from the iPod.)

What type of device fits this description? Computer speakers, of course. The speakers you connect to your computer are self-powered and connect to a source device via a mini-jack connection—the same type of mini-jack used for the Apple's earphone jack. Which means you can use your existing computer speakers (or any new speakers you purchase) with your iPod.

In addition, studio monitors are also self-powered speakers that work quite well with an iPod or iPhone, thank you very much. I've found you get a lot more bang for your buck with these systems, assuming that you're already in the $200 range or so. If that's too steep for your blood, stick with a lower-priced computer speaker system.

> ♪ ULTIMATELY
> **INTERESTING** Most computer speaker systems actually come with two or three speakers—left, right, and an optional subwoofer. In spite of the multiple speakers, there is typically only one input connector; the other speakers connect to the single main speaker, which then connects to your iPod.

> ♪ ULTIMATELY
> **INTERESTING** Learn more about computer speaker systems and nearfield studio monitors in Chapter 24, "Playing Digital Music on Your Computer." Any of the systems discussed there can also be connected to your iPhone or iPod for playback from the portable device.

The advantage to using computer speakers or studio monitors with your iPod or iPhone is that they're readily available and (at least in the case of computer speakers) relatively low-priced. The main disadvantage is placement; you have to position your iPod or iPhone within a relatively short distance from the speakers, based on the length of the speaker connecting cable. In addition, connecting an iPod to a speaker via its earphone out jack means you still have to control playback via the iPod itself—which might not be that practical, depending on just how short the connecting cable is.

Connecting to a Tabletop Speaker System

Let's be honest. Most computer speakers are functional but not stylish; they simply don't mesh well visually with Apple's design-conscious iPod and iPhone. And, of course, when connecting via your device's headphone jack, you have the issue of control—or lack of it.

A better solution is to utilize a tabletop speaker or speaker system designed especially for iPod or iPhone use. Most of these systems contain a dock of sorts in which you set your portable device; since the iPod or iPhone connects via its docking connector, you can then (in many cases) control the iPod or iPhone via the speaker system's controls or remote control. (The dock also recharges your portable device, in most cases.) Plus, of course, these little puppies look a lot more stylish than your typical computer speaker set.

The most common type of tabletop speaker is a box that contains one or more drivers and a dock for the iPod or iPhone. This may look like a tabletop speaker system, or have more of a boombox-type design. I'm talking about units such as the affordable and compact Altec Lansing Octiv Mini M102 (www.alteclansing.com, $49), shown in Figure 29.1; the functional Logitech S715i (www.logitech.com, $149), shown in Figure 29.2; and the somewhat pricey but trendy Beats by Dr. Dre Beatbox (www.monstercable.com, $399), shown in Figure 29.3. Just insert your iPod or iPhone into the dock and start playing.

FIGURE 29.1
Altec Lansing's Octiv Mini M102 small-footprint iPod speaker system.

FIGURE 29.2
Logitech's S715i iPod speaker system.

FIGURE 29.3

Trendy (and expensive) Beats by Dr. Dre Beatbox iPod speaker system.

On the higher end you have units that connect wirelessly to your iPod or iPhone, using Apple's AirPlay technology. These devices let you keep your iPod/iPhone in your pocket, or control playback from across the living room. Popular units include the JBL OnBeat Air (www.jbl.com, $249), shown in Figure 29.4; the iHome iW1 (www.ihomeaudio.com, $299), shown in Figure 29.5; and the high-end and uniquely styled Bowers & Wilkins Zeppelin Air (www.bowers-wilkins.com, $599), shown in Figure 29.6.

FIGURE 29.4

The JBL OnBeat Air wireless iPod speaker system.

29

FIGURE 29.5

The iPhone iW1 wireless iPod speaker system.

FIGURE 29.6

The high-end B&W Zeppelin Air wireless iPod speaker system.

Connecting Your iPod to Your Home Entertainment System

Of course, even a basic home audio system will sound better than the typical tabletop or bookshelf system. So why wouldn't you want to play your iPod or iPhone through your existing home audio or home theater system?

Well, you probably *do* want to, and you can—with the right connections. Read on to learn how to connect your iPod/iPhone to an audio-only or audio/video home entertainment system.

Connecting via an Adapter Cable

If you only want to play music from your iPod/iPhone (that is, you don't want to play iPod/iPhone videos through your home TV), the easiest and lowest-priced way to go requires nothing more than a simple cable connected to your audio receiver or preamp.

What you need is a way to connect from the single earphone mini-jack on your iPod to the right and left auxiliary audio input jacks on the back of your audio system or receiver. This is typically a Y-cable, with a male mini-jack plug on one end and two male 1/4-inch RCA plugs on the other, like the Monster Cable iCable 1000 (www.monstercable.com) shown in Figure 29.7. Alternatively, you can buy a Y adapter with *female* RCA jacks on the split end, and then connect those jacks to a standard R/L audio cable for connection to an auxiliary input on your audio receiver or preamp.

FIGURE 29.7

Monster Cable's iCable 1000 is a Y-adapter that connects your iPod or iPhone to your audio receiver or preamp.

When connected, power on your iPod/iPhone and your audio system, switch your system's input to Auxiliary, and whatever you're playing on your iPod/iPod will be heard through your home audio system. You still use your iPod/iPhone to control playback, of course.

Connecting via an iPod Dock

A more versatile solution is to use an iPod/iPhone dock to connect to your home audio or home theater system. With this approach, your iPod or iPhone sits in the dock and connects via its bottom-of-unit docking connector, which lets the dock itself (or the accompanying remote control) control playback. The audio outputs on the dock then connect to the auxiliary inputs on your audio receiver or preamp, and the video output (when available) connects to the appropriate audio input.

> **♪ ULTIMATELY USEFUL** You can also use a cable that connects to the dock connector on the bottom of your iPod or iPhone, and then to the right/left audio inputs on your audio receiver or preamp. Some of these cables, such as the official Apple Composite AV Cable (store.apple.com), also include a composite video connection, so you can play iPod/iPhone video on your home theater system.

For example, the Apple Universal Dock (store.apple.com), shown in Figure 29.8, has the requisite iPod docking unit, with outputs for right/left RCA-jack audio and a variety of video connections (dependent on which optional AV adapter you choose). It comes with an Apple Remote to control operation; when connected to an A/V receiver, it displays song info, playlists, and the like on your TV screen. The unit sells for $59, with the various AV adapters extra.

FIGURE 29.8

The official Apple Universal Dock.

In addition, many audio manufacturers also sell their own proprietary iPod/iPhone docks that connect directly to select A/V receivers. Given that these docks may offer different or better functionality when used with a given receiver, you might want to check to see if your receiver's manufacturer offers such a dock.

For example, many Onkyo receivers have inputs for the company's UP-A1 Dock (www.onkyousa.com), shown in Figure 29.9. All you have to do is connect the dock to your Onkyo receiver (there's a special connector on the receiver's rear panel) and then slide your iPod or iPhone into the dock. You can then control your iPod/iPhone with your receiver's remote and view playlist and song information on your TV screen (providing you connect the video output on your receiver to the video input on your TV, of course). It's a relatively elegant solution.

> **ULTIMATELY INTERESTING** Of course, you can also listen to your iPod or other portable music player in your car—and probably do. Most older vehicles don't have such a provision built in, which necessitates adding some sort of third-party solution. Most newer cars have at least an auxiliary audio input, which you can connect to your iPod's headphone output. Some newer models have connections to your iPod's dock connector, and can control iPod playback from the car's audio system console. If you're in the market for a new car, make sure you see what's available—there's some cool interface stuff out there.

29

FIGURE 29.9
The UP-A1 Dock for Onkyo-brand audio/video receivers.

29

WHY *NOT* TO LISTEN TO YOUR PORTABLE MUSIC IN THE LIVING ROOM

At the very start of this chapter, I said I didn't want to come off as a total snob when it comes to digital music. The problem is, I am a bit of snob, especially where audio quality is concerned. Not that I have golden ears; far from it, as I used to be a full-time drummer. But that background as a musician trained me to appreciate superior sound quality. I know how music is supposed to sound, and have trouble set-tling for anything less.

Now, I know there are many folks who enjoy listening to music from their iPods or iPhones over their home audio systems, and think the music sounds just fine, thank you. Personally, listening to compressed music through a quality audio system makes my ears bleed; the better the receiver and speakers, the more I can hear the sonic deficiencies. To each his own, I suppose.

You see, the world of music lovers breaks down into two groups—the average listener and the audiophile. The average listener is satisfied with the compressed digital audio you get from an iPod or iPhone; he can't hear the difference between the compressed version and the original. The audiophile, however, is a more critical listener; he hears the lower bitrate and the truncated frequency response inherent in iPod and iPhone playback, and is appalled.

While audiophiles might (reluctantly) accepted the compromises of compressed audio when listening via earbuds on the go, those com-promises are unacceptable when listening on their home audio sys-tems. These are people who invest thousands of dollars on high-end speakers, high-performance amplifiers, and low-noise pre-amplifiers, and they are unwilling to accept any sonic compromises. Unfortu-nately, compressed audio (in any format—AAC, MP3, or WMA) is a huge compromise.

For that reason, you will never see an audiophile connect an iPod or iPhone directly to a home audio system. The sonic differences are just too noticeable to the trained ear.

What I do, then, is keep two digital music libraries—or rather, two ver-sions of my master library. I have one library, in compressed format, that I use to feed my iPhone and iPods. (Yes, I have multiple iPods. Sue me.) Then I have another library, in lossless format, that I listen to on my main home audio system, and on other devices in other rooms throughout the house. There's no way I could stand to listen to the first, compressed library through my "good" system, so I don't. iPhone and iPod playback are for when I'm on the go, not when I'm sitting on my living room couch.

But that's just me. If music from your iPod or iPhone sounds good enough to you when played on your living room system, then go for it. Everyone's ears are different, and compressed music played through a good sound system might be perfectly acceptable to your ears.

Sharing Your Music

Burning Your Music to a CD or USB Drive

In this section of the book, we look into how you can share your favorite music with your friends. We're going to skip over the whole area of file-sharing websites, because (a) we already talked about them, back in Chapter 12, "Downloading Music from P2P File-Sharing Sites," and (b) they're illegal. Instead, we'll focus on ways to physically, digitally, and socially share your music.

We start, in this chapter, by investigating physical music sharing. Bypassing the obvious (passing a purchased CD to a pal), we'll focus on burning music to compact disc and copying audio files to a USB drive. It may be old school, but it's the school we know—and sometimes love.

Burning Music CDs

Burning tunes to a compact disc is old hat to many music lovers. There's a reason for that; some of us have been doing it for almost two decades.

A Short History of Home Recording

Using some sort of recordable medium to share music dates back to the '70s, '80s, and early '90s, when audiocassettes ruled the world. Before the advent of home audiocassette recording, there really wasn't an affordable way to make a new recording from existing recordings. There never was, for example, a "home wax recording cylinder" back in Edison's days, or "home vinyl record cutting machine" in the '40s or '50s. I suppose that some audiophiles in the '60s and '70s did a bit of music transfer on reel-to-reel tape recorders, but that type of tape deck never really made it big in the mass market, so reel-to-reel tape sharing never became a factor.

It took the invention of the inexpensive recordable audiocassette to put home recording on the map. By the early '70s, audiocassette recorders had hit the mainstream, in terms of both price and penetration, and music lovers every-where learning how to record entire albums or specific tracks onto cassette tapes, and then share those tapes with their friends. There even developed the art of creating mixtapes, with tracks from multiple albums and artists in a kind of primitive playlist format.

Audiocassette recording faded away by the mid-'90s, however, thanks in part to the advent of recordable compact discs. The CD format spun into popular culture in the early 80s, but it took another decade for recordable discs (and computer-based CD burners) became both affordable and commonplace.

Understanding CD Burning

Compact disc technology is getting a little long in the tooth, at least compared with other digital options, but it's still fascinating (to me, at least) how it all works. I mean, we're talking *lasers* here—friggin' lasers!

To create music CDs from your digital music files, you need a recordable CD drive in your PC, CD recording software, and blank recordable discs. Most computers these days come with a CD burner (in most instances, a combina-tion CD/DVD burner), so the hardware part of the equation is ubiquitous. As to the software, it's likely that you already have CD recording software installed on your system, typically as part of the music player app you use. (That's right, you can use the iTunes or Windows Media Player apps to burn CDs.)

As to the discs, know that a recordable CD is about 1.2 millimeters thick, and comprised of multiple layers sandwiched together. The top layer consists of a scratch-resistant coating, on which the disc's label text or graphics can be printed. Next is the recording layer, which is made from a dyed color material. Then, on the bottom, is a clear plastic polycarbonate substrate.

Unlike audiocassette recording, recording music to CD—what we call *burning*—is an all-digital process. You take digital audio files stored on your computer and copy them to a digital compact disc. In the process, the files are converted from their original AAC/FLAC/MP3/WMA format into the compact disc digital audio (CDDA) format used for all commercial CDs.

This digital data is literally burned onto a blank disc. The laser in the CD burner (which is slightly more powerful than the corresponding laser in a read-only drive) is focused through the bottom of the disc onto the recording layer. The laser beam doesn't create pits on the disc, as you find on commercial CDs, but rather bleaches the die where it hits the disc. This changes the transparency of the spot to form a distortion, called a stripe, along the spiral track. These distorted areas in the dye layer reflect less light than the unchanged areas surrounding them, so when a CD player's laser beam reads the newly recorded disc, the beam is scattered by the stripes; only the unchanged areas of the disc are read.

> **ULTIMATELY USEFUL** When shopping for a computer or CD recording drive, you should always look at the drive's write speed. In decoding this specification, a write speed of 1X equals a 150KB per second data transfer rate. If your drive can burn at the 52X theoretical maximum, it's transferring data at 7,800KB (or 7.8MB) per second; a 52X drive, then, can burn a 800MB CD in just under two minutes (102 seconds, to be precise). While it's tempting to burn discs at the fastest possible rate, know that the faster you burn, the more likely it is that errors can get introduced into the process—resulting in faulty or even unreadable discs. For best results, tweak down the speed a tad and give your CD burner a little room to breathe.

Understanding CD Standards and Formats

To make sure that a CD recorded on one system can be played on another, the compact disc industry has established standards for recording different types of data on CD. There are separate standards for audio CDs and for data CDs.

The standard for recording audio data is the Red Book standard. According to the Red Book standard, audio CDs can hold up to 74 minutes of music, plus a table of contents for all the tracks on a disc. (Newer technology has extended this capacity to 80 minutes of music per disc.)

When it comes to blank compact discs, there are two different formats you can use. One format lets you record a disc once; the other format lets you record multiple times, continuously rewriting the disc's contents.

The most common type of blank compact disc is the *recordable CD*, or CD-R. CD-R discs are "write once, read many," in that you can only record a single time, although you can play them back as often as you want. Once you've recorded a CD-R, it's done—you can't go back and re-record over it. (That's the "write once" part of the equation.) If you don't like what you recorded, throw it away and burn a new disc.

ULTIMATELY INTERESTING The standards for recording computer data are the Yellow Book and Orange Book standards. According to these standards, CD-R and CD-RW discs can hold up to 700MB of data.

ULTIMATELY INTERESTING Another reason recordable CDs (in the CD-R format, anyway) became so popular is the cost. You can purchase a bundle of 50 blank CD-R discs for $15 or so, which translates to a cost of just 30 cents per disc. That's a lot lower priced than blank cassettes ever got, and so cheap that if you make a mistake burning a disc, you can afford to throw the bad disc away.

If you want to continuously add data to a CD, or if you want to be able to record over previously recorded material, then you want a *rewriteable CD*, or CD-RW. Rewritable CDs—which typically cost a little more than CD-Rs—let you write over existing data, over and over. In technical parlance, it's a "write many, read many" medium.

You want to use CD-R discs to burn your music CDs. Discs in the CD-R format can be read by most freestanding CD and DVD players, as well as computer CD/DVD drives. The same cannot be said about CD-RW discs, which are pretty much computer-specific—not designed for home audio use.

ULTIMATELY CAUTIOUS Most home and car CD and DVD players cannot read CD-RW discs. For this reason alone, you shouldn't use the CD-RW format for recording audio CDs.

The choices don't end there, however. Not only can you choose between CD-R and CD-RW discs, you can also choose between discs that are specially formatted for audio recording, and those that are best suited for recording computer data. If you're recording an audio CD, you may want to use a blank

CD-R discs that have been designated for audio recording. (As opposed to those designated for data or music.) These discs cost a bit more than plain data CD-Rs, because a portion of the price goes into a royalty fund for musicians and record labels.

Choosing CD Burning Software

To record an audio CD, you need a program that will organize the songs you want to record, and then burn those songs onto a blank CD-R disc. Most music player apps (including iTunes and Windows Media Player) offer CD-burning functionality, although they may not be as full-featured or as easy to use as a separate CD burning program.

For this reason, many serious music lovers prefer to use a standalone program specifically designed for burning audio CDs.

> **♪ ULTIMATELY USEFUL** Everything you do to take care of your normal audio CDs—and a little more—applies to CD-R and CD-RW discs. That's because recordable and rewritable CDs are more susceptible to sunlight, heat, and humidity than normal CDs. (This increased vulnerability is due to the recording layer of the disc, which has to be sensitive enough to be burned by a CD burner's low-powered laser.) To ensure long disc life, avoid scratching the disc surface, or spilling liquids on the disc. Also avoid leaving the CD in direct sunlight, or in hot cars. In addition, while it's okay to print on or label the top of the disc, don't print on the bottom side.

These programs typically offer additional features beyond simple burning, such as creating CD labels and jewel box inserts.

The most popular of these freestanding CD recording programs include:

- **CD Architect** (www.sonycreativesoftware.com, $112)
- **CDBurnerXP** (www.cdburnerxp.se, free)
- **Nero Burning ROM** (www.nero.com, $49)
- **Power2Go** (www.cyberlink.com, $69)
- **Roxio Creator** (www.roxio.com, $99)

What you get from a freestanding burning program over a standard music player program are enhanced error checking (for more reliable burns), the ability to trim tracks (to make them shorter), and easier drag-and-drop arrangement of the tracks you wish to burn.

Before You Burn: Preparing Your Hardware

When you want to burn an audio CD, it helps to do a little preparation ahead of time.

First, know that copying large audio files from your hard drive to a blank CD-R takes a lot of processing power. If the recording is interrupted, for whatever reason, the file being recorded could suffer from data loss—which you'll hear as gaps in the music.

To avoid this sort of data loss, you should make sure that your computer is doing nothing but burning while you're burning. Any other simultaneous activities—using other programs, even running anti-virus software—could cause the copying process to be momentarily interrupted.

So, before you start recording, exit all other open programs. Turn off your anti-virus software, and turn off your system's screen saver. Once the recording starts, you don't want anything interrupting the process.

Before You Burn: Configuring Your Software

On the software side of things, know that most freestanding CD recording programs (and many music player apps) offer several different recording options. You should pick those options that best fit the type of recording you're making. You can typically choose from the following options:

- **Multi-session CDs.** A multi-session CD is one that includes both audio and computer data. You'd use this option if you're mixing normal CD audio with MP3 or WMA files, which happen to be computer data. If you're recording a straight audio CD, you can bypass this option.

- **Track-by-track recording.** When you record track-by-track, the CD burner turns off its laser between tracks. (It's taking this time to read the data for the next track.) This places a standard two-second blank space between each song on your CD. Track-by-track recording is the default mode for most CD recorder programs, because it typically produces the fewest errors.

- **Entire disc recording.** If you want to eliminate the two-second gap between songs, you can opt to record the entire disc at once. This option essentially combines all the songs into one giant file, so that the laser doesn't have to be turned off between tracks.

> **⏱ ULTIMATELY CAUTIOUS** Entire disc recording, since it's copying such a large file, is more prone to errors than track-by-track recording. For must users, track-by-track recording is the better choice.

That's about it for configuration, because whatever format the original file is in (WMA, MP3, or WAV) when it gets copied to CD, it is encoded into the

CDDA format. All music CDs use the CDDA format, so if you're burning an MP3, WMA, or AAC file, your burning program translates it to CDDA before the copy is made.

Even better, you don't have to worry about setting burn quality levels, because all CDDA-format files are encoded at the same bit rate. So you really don't have much configuration to do—other than deciding which songs you want to copy.

Burning an Audio CD

Once your system is ready and your recording software is properly configured, you can start recording. You can record two different types of CDs—one you can play in any audio CD player, and one designed for playback in MP3 players.

To burn a CD playable in all audio CD players, the recording has to adhere to the Red Book standard. That means that the files that get copied to the CD-R disc must first be translated to WAV format, from which they get copied to CD using the industry standard CDDA file format.

The specific instructions for recording a CD differ from program to program, but in general you assemble a playlist of the files you want to burn, insert a blank compact disc into your PC's CD driver, and then click the "burn" button. When you do this, your burning software converts the original AAC/MP3/WMA files to CDDA format and copies them to the blank CD-R disc.

For example, if you want to burn a CD from within iTunes, create a new playlist containing all the songs you want to burn to the CD. (Make sure that your playlist is no more than 80 minutes long, of course.) Now, insert a blank CD-R disc into your PC's CD drive. Select the playlist that contains the songs you want to burn, as shown in Figure 30.1, and make sure that all the songs in the playlist are checked.

When you select **File > Burn Playlist** to Disc, iTunes converts the selected files to CDDA format and copies them to your blank CD. When the entire burning process is done, iTunes displays a message to that effect and ejects the newly burned CD from the disc drive.

The process is similar if you're using Windows Media Player. You start by inserting a blank CD-R disc into your PC's CD drive. Then, from within WMP, click the **Burn** tab, shown in Figure 30.2. Drag the desired tracks, albums, or playlists from the Content pane to the Burn List in the List pane; you can then click and drag items within the Burn List to place them in the desired playback order. When you're ready to burn the CD, click the **Start Burn** button.

FIGURE 30.1

Burning a music CD from iTunes.

FIGURE 30.2

Creating a Burn List with Windows Media Player.

WMP now inspects the files you want to copy, converts them to CDDA format, and copies them to your CD. When the entire burning process is done, WMP displays a message to that effect and ejects the newly burned CD from the disc drive.

Burning an MP3 CD

When you record an audio CD, you're limited to 80 minutes of music. You can fit more music on a CD, however, if you leave the songs in their original digital audio format. For example, a disc full of MP3 files can hold a lot more music—upwards of 200 or more individual songs!

Because you don't have to do any file translation, the process of recording an MP3 CD is both easier and faster than recording an audio CD. You don't even have to use a CD burning or music player app; you can do the copying directly from your computer's operating system.

In essence, all you have to do is insert a blank CD-R data disc in your computer's CD drive. If you're using Windows, open Windows Explorer and navigate to where your music files are stored. Then copy those files to your CD drive. They'll be placed on the CD-R disc in their original audio file formats.

> **ULTIMATELY USEFUL** If you want to make a copy of a CD to another CD, you use a combination of ripping and burning. That is, you rip the files from the original CD to your hard disk (in WAV format) and then burn those files to a second blank CD. Alternatively, you can use a program specifically designed for CD burning, which typically have options for copying entire discs all at once.

> **ULTIMATELY INTERESTING** A so-called MP3 CD doesn't have to contain only MP3 files; it can contain any format audio files—MP3, AAC, WMA, you name it.

> **ULTIMATELY CAUTIOUS** The only caveat with creating an MP3 CD is that you won't be able to play it in some audio CD players. While many home and car CD/DVD players have MP3 CD playback, some don't—so your playback options may be limited.

Burning Music Files to a USB Drive

It used to be that before you'd take a long road trip, you'd burn a few mix CDs with your favorite tunes. When you wanted to listen to music, it was easy enough to slip one of your newly-burned CDs into your car's CD player.

This process is starting to become less popular, if only because some new cars no longer come with CD players. Instead of the formerly ubiquitous in-dash CD player, you now have slots or cables for USB drives. This lets you connect any USB drive directly to your car's audio system; you can then access and play the audio files you've stored on the little memory stick.

> **ULTIMATELY INTERESTING** USB drives, like the one in Figure 30.3, are sometimes called flash drives, memory sticks, and thumb drives. They're really just solid state flash memory stored on a stick with a USB connector on one end.

FIGURE 30.3
A typical USB flash drive, from SanDisk.

Copying music to a USB drive is easy as pie, as you don't have to convert anything; it's assumed that wherever you plug in the drive, it can read the native audio files you've stored there. So all you have to do is copy the selected audio files to the USB drive. There's no additional formatting necessary.

You can then hand the USB drive to a friend for her to listen to, or you can use it yourself to listen to music in another location. For example, you can plug a USB drive into your laptop computer to listen to music when you're away from home, or plug it into your car's USB connector to listen to music while you're driving.

To play back music stored on a USB drive, all you have to do is use whatever music player program you're using (or, if you're

> **ULTIMATELY USEFUL** Some car audio systems make it easy to navigate through multiple subfolders on a USB drive. Others get confused by subfolders. Make sure you read your car's instruction manual to determine the best way to copy and organize audio files on a USB drive for in-car playback.

in your car, your car's audio system navigation) to locate specific files on the drive. Most music player apps (and your car's audio system) will automatically recognize a connected USB drive, as well as file information and ID3 tags, so it should be easy enough to scroll through song titles and artist names as you would on your computer. Find the track you want to listen to, then click play.

WHITHER THE COMPACT DISC?

Compact disc technology has been around for three decades now. It supplanted the then-dominant audiocassette and helped to kill off the vinyl record. It's how a generation or two bought and listened to music.

But the humble compact disc has been in decline for a number of years. Figure 30.4 shows album sales by format from 1973 to 2010; as you can see, after peaking in 2000, CD sales have been on a downward slide since.

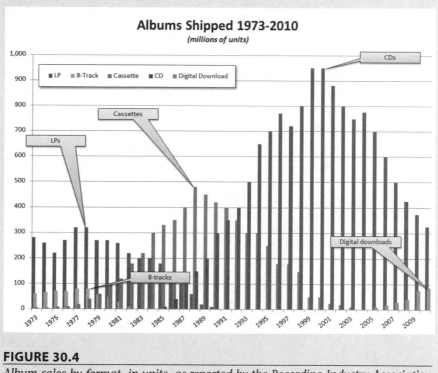

FIGURE 30.4

Album sales by format, in units, as reported by the Recording Industry Association of America (RIAA).

30

More anecdotally, the last CD to sell 40 million copies or more was Shania Twain's *Come On Over*, way back in 1997. (Interestingly, only ten albums in history have sold more than 40 million copies, half of those in the 1970s.) Only one album released this millennium has sold more than 30 million copies, and that was The Beatles' greatest hits album *1*, released in 2000. The biggest-selling album of the past ten years, Adele's *21*, has only sold 20 million albums since its release in 2011; today's typical "blockbuster" album is lucky to break the million-copy level.

So the CD, as a format, is on its way out. But it's far from gone; in 2010, CD sales still outpaced digital album sales (not digital *track* sales, mind you) by about 4 to 1. And even at its lowest level since 1990, today's CD unit sales are higher than the best year (1978) for vinyl LPs.

That doesn't mean, however, that CDs are long for this world. The trends are evident; physical album sales are declining rapidly, while digital sales are on the rise. As to how much longer the humble compact disc will hang on is anybody's guess, it's not going to disappear overnight. And all those CDs you have in your own personal collection don't necessarily lose value just because you (and everybody else) are making more purchases digitally than you used to.

Let us praise, then, the CD, not bury it—at least not yet. It's been a great ride, and there are still a few more miles left in the old thing before the gas runs completely out.

Sharing Your Music Over a Network or Online

I n the previous chapter, we discussed how to share your music physically, via CD or USB drive. In this chapter we leave the physical realm and examine how to share your files digitally—over a network or the Internet.

You actually have a few options for sharing your music digitally, from simple network-based sharing to using email or digital file locker services. We'll look at all of them here.

Sharing Music Over a Network

Whether you're on a home network or a company one, sharing music with other network users is essentially the same process. Assuming that both you and your friend have turned on file sharing and that you've enabled access to the folder where you store your music, sharing a track is as easy as copying a file from one computer to another. All your friend has to do is navigate to your computer on the network, and then to your Music folder; she can then play the track directly from your folder (on her computer, using her own music player app) or copy the file to a location on her computer.

If you don't know how to do all this networking stuff, it's not that hard. Enabling a folder for sharing is typically as easy as right-clicking the folder and selecting **Properties**; when the Properties dialog box appears, select the **Sharing** tab and click the **Share** button. (That's for Windows 7, anyway; the process may be a little different if you're running a different operating system.) If that's too difficult for you, or if you encounter difficulties, call the tech support guy.

The point is, once you enable sharing for your music folder, anyone authorized to do so can access your music over the network. They can make copies of your music files, or just play them where they're at. In fact, multiple users can play the same file simultaneously; that's one of the joys of digital music.

> **ULTIMATELY INTERESTING** This network file sharing is the same technology you use to connect multiple playback devices in your home. Each playback device (computer, network music player, or whatever) connects to your network and accesses the music files stored on your main computer or media server. The individual files are not duplicated on each device, but rather stored centrally and accessed separately.

Sharing Music via Email

Sharing music with other users of your network is easy enough. But what do you do if you want to share a track with a friend who isn't on your network?

One approach is to use email. After all, you can use email to send any file to the chosen recipient, simply by attaching that file to an outgoing message. You can easily send audio files as email attachments.

Easily, that is, until you start considering file size. Depending on the file type and bitrate you use to encode the file, an audio track can get pretty big, byte-wise. A three-minute tune in MP3 format, encoded at 256Kbps, is going to run at least 5MB in size. The same tune in WMA Lossless format will run 20MB or so. Those are pretty big files.

> **ULTIMATELY CAUTIOUS** You'll know you have a problem with sending a file if you receive a "file exceeds limit" message when you try to attach the file to an email message. If your friend can't receive a large attachment you've sent, you'll see the message bounced back to your email inbox.

In fact, those files may be too big to send via email. Most email programs and services have an upper limit on file size; even if you can send the file, your recipient probably has a similar limit on how big a file she can receive.

This means that sending an unadorned audio file as an email attachment probably won't work. You can't even compress the file to send it; ZIP compression doesn't significantly reduce the size of music files. (The file has already been compressed when it was digitally encoded; there's nothing else to compress.)

Bottom line, then, unless you're sending a very short track encoded at a very low bitrate, email probably isn't an option for sharing music. Sorry.

Sharing Music via a Cyberlocker

If email can't handle large audio files, how then can you send tracks to your friends over the Internet?

The answer is in something called a digital file locker service, or *cyberlocker*. This is a site that exists to store and transfer large computer files between groups of users—which makes it perfect for sharing music files.

A digital file locker works almost like a shared folder on your local network. You start by copying a file from your computer to a folder on the digital locker website. You then give access to that shared folder to selected friends (or, in the case of business files, co-workers). Anyone with access to that folder can then access the files within, via the Internet, and copy them to his own PC. The file locker site exists simply to store those files you want to share with others; access to the shared folder is virtually seamless.

Many of these cyberlocker services are free, at least up to a given storage limit. Even if you have to or opt to pay for storage, the price is relatively affordable. In almost all instances, if there's a fee to be paid, it's paid to the party who uploads the files; others sharing the files typically don't pay for access.

Some of the more popular of these digital file lockers include the following:

- **ADrive** (www.adrive.com)
- **Box** (www.box.com)
- **Dropbox** (www.dropbox.com)
- **eSnips** (www.esnips.com)
- **SugarSync** (www.sugarsync.com)
- **Uploadingit** (www.uploadingit.com)

Of these services, I like Dropbox the best because of its ease of use. After you sign up and get everything set up, you see a Dropbox folder on your computer. (You can also access your shared folders from within your browser, as shown in Figure 31.1.) Just drag and drop the files you want to share into this folder, and they're automatically uploaded to Dropbox's site on the web. Files in your Dropbox folder are automatically synched with the shared folder on the web, so there's not much you need to do, other than invite others to join the service and share the contents of selected folders.

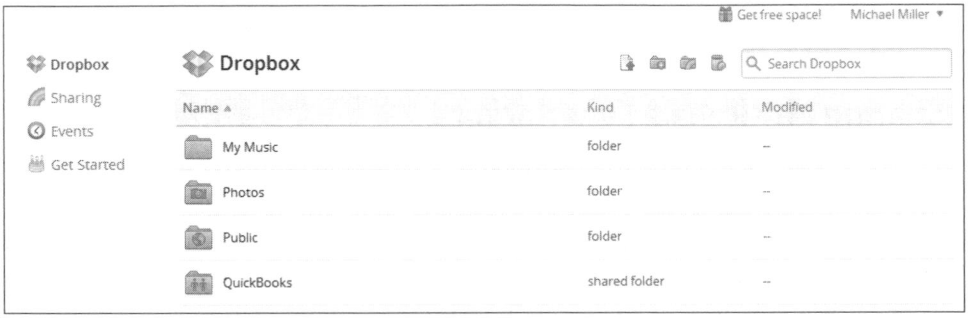

FIGURE 31.1
Sharing folders and files via Dropbox.

What you do, then, is create a shared folder for your music, then upload those music files you want to share. Send out invitations (via Dropbox) to those friends you want to share with, then they can download the shared files from Dropbox to their own computers. It's a fast and easy process.

CYBERLOCKERS VERSUS ILLEGAL FILE SHARING

The one option we don't discuss in this chapter is P2P file-sharing services, including BitTorrent. That's because, as you learned in Chapter 12, "Downloading Music from P2P File-Sharing Sites," these services are not entirely legal. I'm okay with sharing an occasional track with a friend or two, but not with sharing whole albums with the entire Internet. It's the difference between whispering a comment to a friend and shouting a rant from a bullhorn; person-to-person sharing is okay (in moderation), but blasting an album to thousands of people is wholesale theft.

But wait, some of you may be saying, how does a digital file locker service differ from a file-sharing site? They both let you upload music to a central server, and then share that music with others. Sounds pretty similar—at least at first glance.

It's the difference between sharing files privately to a handful of friends and sharing files publicly to anyone and everyone with Internet service. It's private sharing versus public sharing; the former is fine (well, no one's going to arrest you for it, anyway), the latter is blatantly illegal.

That doesn't mean that you can't use digital file lockers in a less legal fashion. I suppose if you managed to invite several thousand "friends" to share a folder on a cyberlocker site you're effectively engaging in the same type of public sharing prevalent on the illegal file-sharing sites. In practice, however, you don't know a thousand people to share a folder with, and most file locker services won't let you send out that many invitations, anyway.

There have been sites that blur the line between cyberlocker and illegal file sharing; Megaupload is one that immediately comes to mind. As you read in Chapter 12, Megaupload tried to pass itself off as a legitimate digital file locker (and many people used it as such), but then facilitated and promoted the ability to share files publicly rather than privately. It's the old private versus public thing; if Megaupload limited its services to private sharing, it probably wouldn't have gotten busted.

Now, some legal beagles out there will point out that even limited private sharing in any fashion is illegal. That may be true; I'm not a lawyer, so don't bust my chops on this one. What I've found, however, is that the authorities (and copyright holders) are much more likely to go after large-scale public activities rather than small-scale private ones. It's one thing, for example, to email someone a quote you found online, and quite another to copy and paste that quote into your own website (or newspaper article or book); the former is sharing something interesting between friends, the latter is plagiarism.

It's the same thing with sharing music. Passing along a few tracks to a handful of friends actually encourages music sales; if a friend likes what she hears, she's likely to go out and purchase the CD or download the track. But posting those same tracks on a public website so they can be downloaded by thousands of users goes beyond simple sharing into the realm of piracy.

In other words, it's okay to share a little— but not too much.

31

Sharing Your Music— Socially

The world is becoming more social, especially online. With the advent of Facebook and other social networks, people are sharing everything they like or dislike with their friends online. (Some people are also sharing their most intimate thoughts, which they should probably reconsider, although that's a topic for another book.)

Why, then, shouldn't you share the music you like with your friends on various social networks? For that matter, why can't you share your favorite tunes with your friends on a given online music service?

The answer to both these questions is you can and maybe you should. Some music services and social networks make it quite easy to share music with your online friends. In most instances, it's a matter of clicking a button to send a link to a song that catches your fancy.

Sharing Music on Facebook

Let's start with the biggest social network out there, Facebook (www.facebook.com). Facebook members share everything, including their favorite music. In fact, they're quite prolific about it, sharing 1.5 billion tunes in the first six months since that option was introduced.

Facebook first offered the ability to share music—via third party services—in September, 2011, as part of its Open Graph protocol. Facebook's stated goal with Open Graph is to let users share content of all types with their online friends, not just the status updates that currently define the social network. It's all a matter of what Facebook calls "frictionless sharing;" every type of content you consume, on any website, is posted on your Facebook Timeline for everyone to see.

This initiative requires the participation of lots of other websites, of course. In the realm of online music, that means getting all the various music services to connect to and play nice with Facebook.

Not surprisingly, many such services have done just that. Each of these sites have their own Facebook app for music sharing; interestingly, some sites let you play their music using another site's app, making the whole system more versatile—and letting your friends who don't belong to your particular service still share your music.

Sharing Music from Another Music Service

To share the music you listen to on Facebook, you have to belong to a music service that connects to Facebook. As of April, 2012, that included the following:

- **Earbits** (www.earbits.com)
- **iHeartRadio** (www.iheart.com)
- **MOG** (www.mog.com)
- **MySpace** (www.myspace.com)
- **Rdio** (www.rdio.com)
- **Rhapsody** (www.rhapsody.com)
- **Saavn** (www.saavn.com)
- **Slacker Radio** (www.slacker.com)
- **Songza** (www.songza.com)
- **Spotify** (www.spotify.com)

If you subscribe to one of these services, you'll need to formally link your account to your Facebook account. You can typically do this from the options or preferences section of the music service, or by logging onto the music service with your Facebook account.

Once you've connected your two accounts (and done any necessary configuration, of course), all the music you listen to will be posted to Facebook. Your friends can then view your favorite tracks via a new Music gadget that appears on your Timeline, as shown in Figure 32.1.

> **ULTIMATELY CAUTIOUS** If you're aghast at the idea of all your Facebook friends seeing everything you listen to online, then all you have to do is *disconnect* the two services. You should be able to do this from your music service's preferences or settings page.

FIGURE 32.1
The Music gadget on a Facebook Timeline.

Viewing Your Friends' Music

Here's a Facebook feature you might not know existed. Facebook has a Music dashboard (actually, a Facebook app) that displays what music your friends are listening to, as well as top songs, recommended pages, and the like. It's actually a nice way to discover new music, as shared by your Facebook friends.

You should see a Music link in the Apps section of the navigation sidebar on the left side of your Facebook home page. If you don't see this link, click the **More** link to view all your apps; Music should be there.

As you can see in Figure 32.2, the center section of the Music dashboard lists playlists and stations recently listened to by your friends on their respective music services. If you belong to the same service, listening to a playlist is as easy as clicking the **Play** button on the graphic (or the title of the playlist) to launch your music service app and start playback. If you don't belong to a given music service, clicking the playlist image or title will prompt you to join the service, launch the app, or whatever action is necessary to listen in.

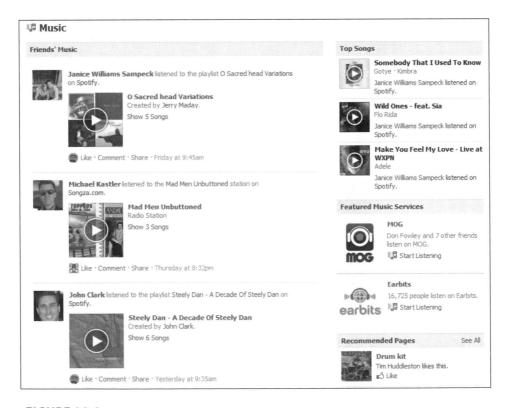

FIGURE 32.2

Facebook's Music dashboard.

Beneath this section is a section for Trending Albums. These are albums that are being listened to a lot by Facebook users. Click to listen to an album—assuming its available on your music service of choice, that is.

> ♪ ULTIMATELY **INTERESTING** If a track, album, or playlist is not available on the music service you've linked to Facebook, you'll be prompted to join the service that does host that music. If it's free, why not?

The right sidebar on the Music dashboard contains several sections. The top section is for Top Songs—those tracks most listened to by your Facebook friends. Click a song title or image to play back the song. (You can do this if the track exists on a music service to which you subscribe; if your service doesn't have the track in its library, you can't listen.)

The Featured Music Services section is kind of an advertisement for a couple of music services that are connected to Facebook. The Recommend Pages section, at the bottom of the sidebar, lists some music-related pages you may want to "like" or subscribe to.

Sharing Music via Live Chat

Related to the Music dashboard is another new Facebook feature that lets you share music in real time with your Facebook friends, via Facebook's live chat feature. In essence, you can hear whatever your friends are listening to (and vice versa), or get a group of friends together to listen to some tunes, with one member of the group serving as the online DJ.

To listen to music via chat, display Facebook's chat sidebar and look for a music note icon next to a friend's name. This indicates that a friend is online, logged onto Facebook, and listening to music. Mouse over the friend's name and click the **Listen With** button. This will launch the player for the music service your friend is using, and you'll hear whatever your friend is listening to.

You can also chat with your friend about the music (or anything else) by starting a normal chat session while listening. Other friends who choose to listen in can also opt to join your chat session, for what then becomes a group chat.

Sharing Links to MP3 Files

Here's another way to share music on Facebook, if you can find a free MP3 version of the song online—and not behind the walls of a music service. If you find said MP3 file on a given website, you can post a link to that file as part of a Facebook status update, and then have that link playable from your friends' news feeds.

ULTIMATELY **USEFUL** One good way to find MP3 files to share is to use an MP3 search engine, like the ones discussed in Chapter 11, "Finding Free Music to Download."

All you have to do is find an MP3 file online (this won't work with other music formats, unfortunately) and then copy the URL for that file. In some instances, that might mean looking for a "download" link and then right-clicking the link and selecting **Copy Link Address** from the pop-up menu.

You then start a new status update on Facebook and paste the URL for the MP3 file into the status update. When you click the **Post** button, this music file is posted to your Facebook news feed, as shown in Figure 32.3. Any of your Facebook friends can then click the **Play** button to listen to the track from within Facebook. Pretty neat, eh?

Lew Archer
Bruce Springsteen: No Surrender (live)

No Surrender Live
By: Bruce Springsteen
No Surrender Live
skitt.net

Like · Comment · Share · 14 seconds ago ·

FIGURE 32.3
Listening to an MP3 file on Facebook.

Sharing Music on Twitter

Facebook is a full featured social network. Twitter isn't. Technically, Twitter is a type of social medium called a *microblog*; as such, it doesn't offer a lot of the apps and sharing you find on Facebook and other social networks.

This means that the only way to share music on Twitter is to tweet about it. Now, you can do this manually, simply by composing a tweet that says something like, "Listening to Steely Dan Aja," or you can include a link to any MP3 file you find online.

ULTIMATELY **USEFUL** Given Twitter's 140-character limit, you'll want to shorten any URL you post by using a URL-shortening site, such as bit.ly.

A better option might be to use one of several third-party services designed specifically for sharing music over Twitter. These services let you search their libraries for specific tracks (or, in some instances, upload tracks from your own library), and then post links to those tracks in your tweets.

The most popular of these services include the following:

- **Song.ly** (www.song.ly)
- **Tinysong** (www.tinysong.com)
- **Tunebirds** (www.tunebirds.com)
- **TweetJamz** (www.tweetjamz.com)
- **Twt.fm** (www.twt.fm)

For example, if you're using Song.ly, all you have to do is enter a song title and then click the **Submit** button. You get a page of search results; find the one you want then click the **Tweet** button. This opens Twitter and creates a new tweet with a shortened URL for the song; post the tweet if you wish.

As you can see in Figure 32.4, the tweet itself looks like any other tweet, with the song title, artist, and clickable URL. Anyone clicking the link is taken to a Song.ly page for this track, like the one in Figure 32.5, where they can choose to listen to it online or buy it from Amazon or iTunes.

FIGURE 32.4

A Song.ly tweet.

FIGURE 32.5

A track page on Song.ly—listen online or purchase a copy.

Sharing Music via Spotify

Spotify (www.spotify.com) is probably the most sharing-enabled music service today. As a social music sharing service, Spotify makes it relatively easy to share music with your friends. You can share to the following:

- Facebook, to either individual friends or to your entire friends list via a status update
- Twitter, to anyone following you on the Twitter service
- Spotify, to anyone you've added to your Spotify People list
- Messenger, to any of your contacts using the Windows Live Messenger instant messaging (IM) service

You can share individual tracks, complete albums, or artists. Given Spotify's close integration with Facebook, and easy ability to tweet the music you're listening to, it's the music service of choice for socially connected music lovers.

> ♪ **ULTIMATELY INTERESTING**   Learn more about Spotify in Chapter 18, "Listening to Music with Spotify."

Sharing to Facebook

Because Spotify and Facebook are linked, the two services make it quite easy for you to share your Spotify music with Facebook users. In fact, there are a number of different ways to do this.

When you find a track, album, or artist you want to share with your Facebook friends, right-click the item and select **Share To**. When the sharing pop-up appears, select the **Facebook** tab, as shown in Figure 32.6. Enter the message you want to accompany this shared item, then click the **Share to Facebook** button.

FIGURE 32.6

Sharing a track from Spotify to Facebook.

The track/album/artist you selected is now posted to Facebook, accompanied by the message you wrote. The post appears on your Facebook profile page and in your friends' news feeds, like the post shown in Figure 32.7. If a friend is already a Spotify member, he or she can click the **Play** button and listen to the track/album/artist from within Facebook. If he isn't a Spotify member, he can click the **Get Spotify** link to sign up for Spotify.

> ♪ ULTIMATELY **INTERESTING** By default, everything you play on Spotify is sent to your Facebook account. (You can change this from Spotify's settings page, if you like.) Not only is every track you play on Spotify is then displayed in your Facebook ticker; the tracks you listen to also contribute to the Music gadget displayed on your Facebook Timeline, which we discussed previously in this chapter.

FIGURE 32.7

A shared Spotify album on Facebook.

Sharing to Twitter

If you have a Twitter account, you can share any selected Spotify track/album/artist as a tweet. All you have to do is right-click the item you want to share and select **Share To**. When the sharing pop-up appears, select the **Twitter** tab. As you can see in Figure 32.8, a link to the item is already entered into the text box, along with the #nowplaying hashtag and a short message. You can accept this message as-is or edit it as you wish. Click the **Share to Twitter** button to tweet the item.

> ♪ ULTIMATELY **INTERESTING** On Twitter, a hashtag is a kind of keyword that other users can use to search for hot topics.

FIGURE 32.8

Tweeting a track from Spotify.

Sharing to Other Spotify Users

When you want to share a track/album/artist with a fellow Spotify member, you simply send a link to that item to that person's Spotify inbox. There are two ways to do this—via the standard Share To dialog box, or by dragging and dropping.

To do it the first way, right-click the item you want to share and select **Share To**. When the sharing pop-up appears, select the **Spotify** tab. Enter the person's name into the **To** box, and an optional message to accompany the link. Click the **Send** button when done.

Alternatively, you can simply navigate to the item you want to share then use your mouse to drag and drop that item onto your friend's name in your People list. When the message pop-up appears, enter an optional message to accompany the link (optional), and then click the **Send** button.

> **ULTIMATELY CAUTIOUS** You can only use the drag-and-drop method with streaming items. You cannot use this method to share tracks imported from and stored on your computer.

Sharing via Windows Live Messenger

Spotify lets you share tracks/albums/artists with any of your friends who happen to be on the Windows Live Messenger IM service. (This presumes, of course, that you also have a Windows Live Messenger account.)

To share music via instant messaging, right-click the item you want to share and select **Share To**. When the sharing pop-up appears, select the **Messenger** tab, enter an accompanying message, then click the **Share to Messenger** button. If you're not currently logged into Messenger, you'll now be prompted to do so.

You'll also be prompted to enter the name of the person you want to share with. Do this (by using the Search Contacts box) and an instant message session now begins, with your link to the Spotify item as your first message.

Sharing to Anyone via Email

You can also share your Spotify music with anyone you communicate with on the Web. It's a simple matter of pasting a link to a track/album/artist into an email, blog post, or web page.

To share a web link to a Spotify item, navigate to and right-click the item you want to share. Select **Copy HTTP Link** from the pop-up menu, then paste the copied link into your email, blog post, or web page.

It's that simple. You can also paste this link into a Facebook or Google+ post, a Twitter tweet, a post to a web-based message forum, or any web-based communications medium.

> **ULTIMATELY USEFUL** Many other music services let you share selected tracks, albums, or artists to Facebook and Twitter. Look for a Facebook or Twitter "share" button on the now playing page; click the item to create a Facebook status update or Twitter tweet with a link back to the currently playing item.

Sharing Music via iTunes Ping

If you're an iTunes user, you have a bit of social sharing built into the iTunes app. That sharing is in the form of Ping, which is Apple's attempt at social networking—with a little not-so-subtle promotion and advertising thrown in for good measure.

You can use Ping to follow your favorite artists, "like" individual tracks and albums, and comment on artists and music. The posts you make are shared with other users who choose to follow you on iTunes.

Ping appears as part of the iTunes sidebar in the iTunes software. As you can see in Figure 32.9, the iTunes sidebar contains information about the currently playing

> **ULTIMATELY INTERESTING** Ping is built into the iTunes app for the iPhone, iPad, and iPod touch, which means you can see artist updates wherever you may happen to be.

> **ULTIMATELY CAUTIOUS** The My Recent Activity section of the iTunes sidebar includes messages from Apple about items for sale in the iTunes Store. Given that these aren't messages from you and have nothing to do with any activity you've engaged in (save for listening to a given artist), this seems like a bit of an overstep between editorial and advertising to me.

item. It also contains, from top to bottom, links to follow this particular artist on Ping and view the artist's profile page, posts from the artist, and your own recent activity regarding this artist.

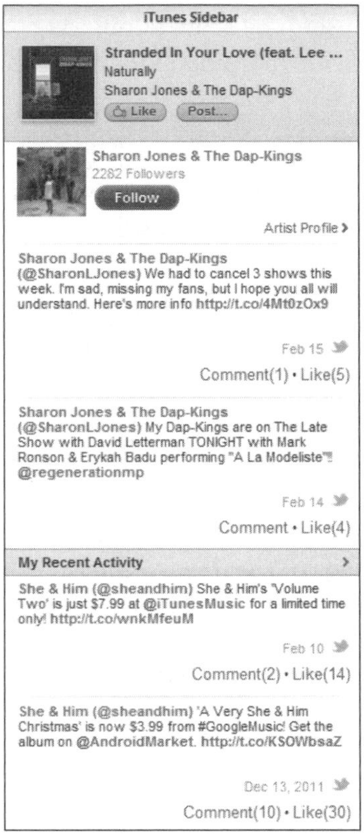

FIGURE 32.9
Viewing Ping social content in the iTunes sidebar.

Posting to Ping

To like or post about a song, album, or artist, click a track in iTunes' main content list. As you can see in Figure 32.10, this displays a **Ping** button; click this button to display a pop-up menu. From here you can click **Like** to "like" the item, or click **Post** to comment on the item. When you click **Post**, iTunes displays the dialog box shown in Figure 32.11; enter your comments into the text box, then click the **Post** button.

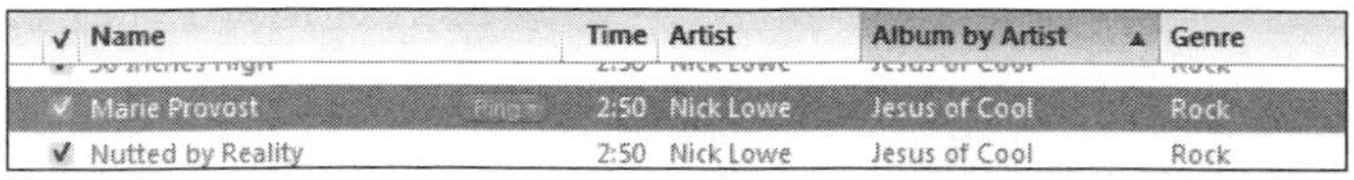

√	Name		Time	Artist	Album by Artist	▲	Genre
√	36 inches High		2:50	Nick Lowe	Jesus of Cool		Rock
√	Marie Provost	Ping	2:50	Nick Lowe	Jesus of Cool		Rock
√	Nutted by Reality		2:50	Nick Lowe	Jesus of Cool		Rock

FIGURE 32.10

Highlight an item and click the Ping button to like or post about an item.

FIGURE 32.11

Posting about an item to Ping.

To follow an artist on Ping, either click **Follow** in the artist section of the iTunes sidebar, or click the **Ping** button for one of this artist's tunes and then select **Follow** from the pop-up menu. If you opt to follow an artist, you'll see posts from that artist in your iTunes sidebar. (To be honest, artist posts on Ping—which of them that are, that is—often mirror that artist's publicly available tweets.)

> **ULTIMATELY CAUTIOUS** You can only post about content that is present in the iTunes Store. If you try to post about an item that iTunes doesn't sell, you'll see a message to that effect. (This is another indication that Ping is more about selling than it is about being social.)

Viewing Your Ping Page

You can view all your recent Ping activity from iTunes' Ping page, shown in Figure 32.12. Just click **Ping** in the Store section of the navigation sidebar (they're really not hiding that selling connection, are they?) to display the Ping page. You can then display selected content by clicking the links in the Ping panel on the right side of the page.

32

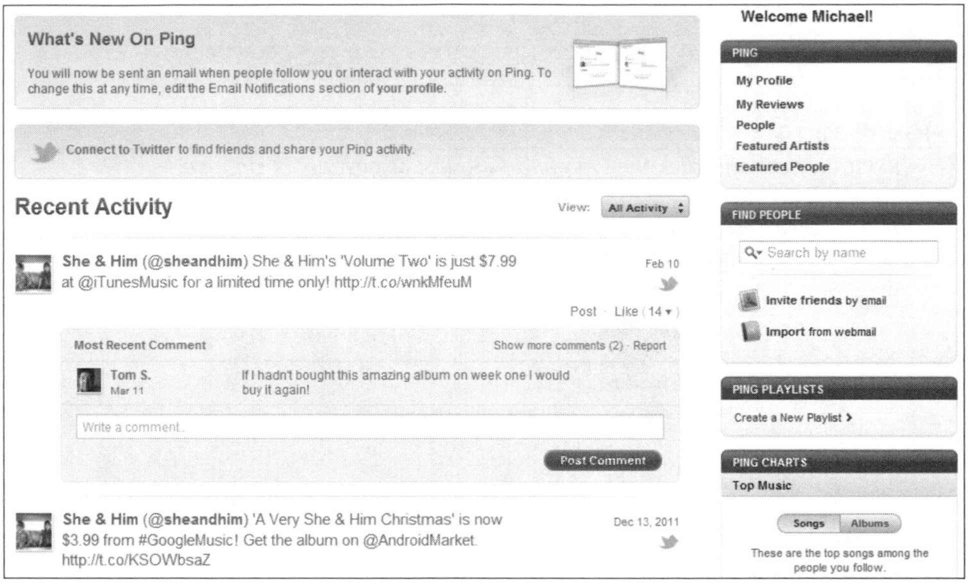

What's New On Ping

You will now be sent an email when people follow you or interact with your activity on Ping. To change this at any time, edit the Email Notifications section of your profile.

Connect to Twitter to find friends and share your Ping activity.

Recent Activity

View: [All Activity ▼]

She & Him (@sheandhim) She & Him's 'Volume Two' is just $7.99 at @iTunesMusic for a limited time only! http://t.co/wnkMfeuM

Feb 10

Post · Like (14 ▼)

Most Recent Comment

Show more comments (2) · Report

Tom S.
Mar 11

If I hadn't bought this amazing album on week one I would buy it again!

Write a comment...

[Post Comment]

She & Him (@sheandhim) 'A Very She & Him Christmas' is now $3.99 from #GoogleMusic! Get the album on @AndroidMarket. http://t.co/KSOWbsaZ

Dec 13, 2011

Welcome Michael!

PING

My Profile
My Reviews
People
Featured Artists
Featured People

FIND PEOPLE

Search by name

Invite friends by email
Import from webmail

PING PLAYLISTS

Create a New Playlist ❯

PING CHARTS

Top Music

[Songs] [Albums]

These are the top songs among the people you follow.

FIGURE 32.12

Viewing your personal Ping page.

Included on the Ping page is a Ping Charts panel, shown in Figure 32.13, which lists the top songs and albums from people you follow. Scroll down to the Concerts panel to view upcoming concerts near you, or to the We Recommend You Follow panel to see what (usually irrelevant) recommendations Ping has for you.

FIGURE 32.13

Viewing your friends' favorite songs in Ping Charts.

Finding Friends to Follow

Finding friends via Ping isn't as easy as it should be. You have to display your Ping page, then go to the Find People panel, shown in Figure 32.14.

FIGURE 32.14

Finding friends on Ping.

From here you can search for friends (useful only if you know their iTunes user names), invite friends via email, or import a friends' list from a webmail service, such as Hotmail. Once you get a list of possible friends, click the **Follow** button to follow a given individual.

I say that finding friends isn't as easy as it could be because there's no way to search or browse for people who share your musical tastes, or who even live close to you. You can only search by user name; you can't search by location or favorite genres. This makes it extremely difficult to find people worth following, in my opinion.

Once you opt to follow a person, you see posts and activity from that person in your Ping activity stream. Most often, this consists of music that person has purchased or listened to, with a button to buy that particular item in the iTunes Store. (I gotta tell you, Ping's constant selling, selling, selling gets me down; it's the antithesis of what social sharing should be about.)

IS SOCIAL SHARING USEFUL OR INTRUSIVE?

The whole social media boom is changing the way our society communicates. Instead of encouraging old fashioned one-to-one communication, whether via face-to-face talk or email, social media lets you broadcast your thoughts and opinions to as many "friends" as you can garner online. It also lets you voyeuristically peep into the inner lives of dozens or hundreds of these "friends," often people you wouldn't give the time of day to, otherwise. It's all about being social and sharing practically everything with practically everybody.

The same goes when you get into the social sharing of your musical tastes. When you sign up to share the music you listen to via Facebook, Twitter, or whichever social network you use, you're exposing your musical tastes to anyone following you on your friends list. They get to see (and hear) what you're listening to, and if you're following them, you get to return the experience.

The question is, do you really want to share all your music with all your online friends? Think about it. Every track you listen to online, put in front of everyone you've ever friended. It that really a good thing? Do you want your old high school girlfriend to know that you're listening to Broadway show tunes? Or your hip colleagues from work seeing that you have a fondness for David Cassidy and the Partridge Family? Or anyone finding out that your most-played track this month was Hanson's "MMMBop?"

I think there are some things that are best left unshared. I don't mind sharing the occasional album or playlist I'm listening to via my Facebook feed, but I really don't want my hundred or so followers to know every song I'm listening to. I'm a firm believer in keeping my private and public lives separate. Yes, it's fun to share a new musical discovery, but I don't want or need my online friends, whomever they might be, to wait breathlessly for the next song I put in the queue, as if it has some sort of mystical importance. Get a life, people. Some things just aren't made to be shared.

32

Discovering New Music with Last.fm and Pandora Radio

There are lots of ways to discover new music online. We'll examine as many as we can in this final section of the book, starting with two of the most popular online music recommendation services—Last.fm and Pandora Radio.

Both of these services have earned their popularity, at least in part, due to their ability to suggest appropriate new music to their subscribers. Yes, you can use both services to listen to the same old stuff you always listen to, but you can also use them to discover new music similar to but different from what you already like.

It's all a matter of looking at what you like (assuming that you actually like what you listen to) and then finding similar tracks and artists. If you like Bob Dylan, for example, you might also like Phil Ochs or even Bon Iver; if you listen to a lot of Boz Scaggs, then Michael McDonald and Steely Dan might also be up your alley.

While most online music services offer some sort of music recommendation functionality, Last.fm and Pandora Radio tend to do it better than the rest—to my ears, anyway. Let's take a look at what both of these services have to offer.

Discovering New Music with Last.fm

Last.fm (www.last.fm) is a streaming music service with an emphasis on music recommendation. (In fact, Last.fm bills itself as a "music recommendation service," and I agree with that assessment.) It can function independently of other music services or work in conjunction with them (and various music player apps, as well) to analyze the music you listen to and recommend other music you might like.

The key to Last.fm's effectiveness is for you to send the service information about all the music you listen to—even on other music services. Last.fm calls this transmittal of music from one service to another *scrobbling*. Its "Audioscrobbler" music recommendation system creates a detailed profile of your musical tastes, and uses your listening history to recommend new music based on your listening habits. It's a terrific way to discover new songs, albums, and artists, based on what you already like to listen to. I can attest that it works very well—and the more music you scrobble, the better it works.

Last.fm's recommendations are totally free, at least in the U.S., the U.K., and Germany. (You have to pay 3 Euros a month outside these countries.) Music is streamed at an acceptable 192Kbps rate. Last.fm offers apps for the iPhone/iPad and Android devices.

> ♪ ULTIMATELY **INTERESTING** Like Spotify, Last.fm is a European import. (It comes from the UK.)

Scrobbling from Other Music Services

While you can use Last.fm as a freestanding (and free) service, it works best if you integrate it with the other music services and music player apps that you use. You can also scrobble music from your iPhone or iPod, which means you can capture all the music you listen to, wherever you may be.

To that end, you can scrobble music from more than 600 partner services, including the following:

- **8Tracks** (www.8tracks.com)
- **AccuRadio** (www.accuradio.com)

- **Audiogalaxy** (www.audiogalaxy.com)
- **Bandcamp** (www.bandcamp.com)
- **Blip.fm** (www.blip.fm)
- **Grooveshark** (www.grooveshark.com)
- **MeeMix** (www.meemix.com)
- **MOG** (www.mog.com)
- **Pandora Radio** (www.pandora.com)
- **Rdio** (www.rdio.com)
- **Slacker Radio** (www.slacker.com)
- **Spotify** (www.spotify.com)

In almost every instance, you have to configure the music service to scrobble to Last.fm; you don't do any configuration within your Last.fm account. Look for the settings or preferences page for your music service to make the connection.

For example, to connect your Spotify and Last.fm accounts, open the Spotify app and select Edit > Preferences. From the Preferences page, go to the Activity Sharing section and check the Scrobble to Last.fm option. You'll need to enter your Last.fm username and password, then you're good to go.

> **ULTIMATELY INTERESTING** You can also connect Last.fm with Facebook. Since Facebook doesn't have audio playback functionality, you're not scrobbling from Facebook, but rather reporting what you listen to on Last.fm to Facebook for display on Timeline.

Scrobbling from PC-Based Music Players

Last.fm will also scrobble directly from a number of music player apps on your computer. There aren't too many players that scrobble natively, however.

> **ULTIMATELY USEFUL** If you're looking for a music player with built-in scrobbling functionality, check out Songbird (www.getsongbird.com).

The preferred approach by many is to install the Last.fm Scrobbler program on your computer. This program will grab everything you listen to on your PC, no matter which music player you use, and scrobble it to the Last.fm service. The Scrobbler app will scrobble music you play on iTunes, Windows Music Player, Media Monkey or any other player app. Go to www.last.fm/download/ to download the application.

33

If you're an iTunes user, you can use a third-party program to scrobble what you play on iTunes. In essence, the scrobbling program sits between iTunes and Last.fm, and sends your iTunes playback info to the recommendation service. Some of the more popular iTunes scribblers include iScrobbler (iscrobbler.soundforge.net) and ScrobblePod (www.mmrr.fi/scrobblepod/).

Investigating Last.fm's Recommendations

There are a few different ways to discover new music on Last.fm. Perhaps the easiest is to investigate Last.fm's recommendations for you. When you log into the Last.fm site, scroll down to the Last.fm recommendations section, shown in Figure 33.1. Here you'll find several types of recommendations, all based on the tracks you've scrobbled to Last.fm:

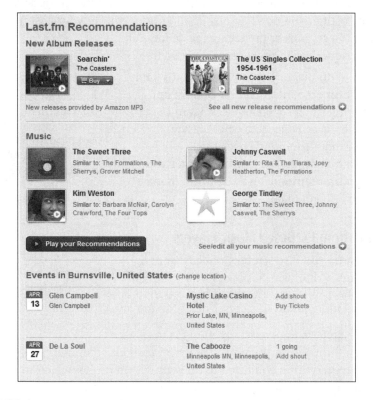

FIGURE 33.1

Viewing an overview of your recommendations.

- **New Album Releases**. These are recently released albums that Last.fm thinks you'll like. Album information is provided by Amazon.com, which explains the **Buy** buttons next to each album; click the button to purchase it from Amazon. By default, Last.fm displays two recommended albums on its home page; click the **See All New Release Recommendations** link to view a full page of new releases you might be interested in.

- **Music**. These are artists that match your listening tastes. Beneath each artist name, Last.fm explains why it recommended that artist, comparing the recommendation to similar artists you've listened to. Click an **artist name** to view a full page about that artist, including featured tracks that you can listen to from the Last.fm website. You can also play an online "radio station" that Last.fm assembles from these artist recommendations, by clicking the **Play Your Recommendations** button.

- **Events**. If any of the artists you've listened to are playing live near you, these concerts will be listed in the Events section on the Last.fm home page.

- **Free Downloads**. If there are any free MP3 downloads available from the artists you've listened to, Last.fm lists them in the Free Downloads section. Click the **Free MP3** button to download a track to your computer.

This box displays only an overview of your total recommendations, however. To view all of Last.fm's recommendations, click the See/Edit All Your Music Recommendations link. This displays the Recommendations page, shown in Figure 33.2. There are three tabs on this page—Music, New Releases, and Free MP3s. Click a tab to view those specific recommendations.

Within the main Music tab, you can filter Last.fm's recommendations by genre by clicking a box (Soul, 60s, Blues, etc.) along the top of the page. Click a given artist to view Last.fm's artist page for that artist; from there you can read more about this performer, play the artist's Last.fm radio station, view albums and tracks by the artist, and even purchase music from that artist.

Creating Radio Stations

You can also discover new music by having Last.fm create a radio station based on a specific artist or genre. Just go to the Last.fm Radio section near the top of the Last.fm home page, as shown in Figure 33.3, enter an artist name or musical genre into the text box, and click the **Play** button.

33

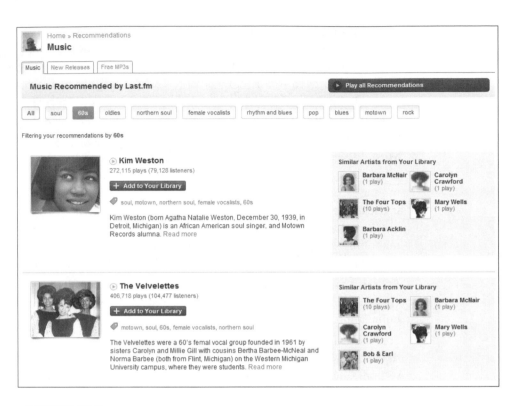

FIGURE 33.2
Viewing all of Last.fm's recommendations.

FIGURE 33.3
Creating a new Last.fm radio station.

33

Last.fm now displays a new page with its own music player, as shown in Figure 33.4, and begins playing back the new station it created for you. Scroll down to the Similar Artists section to see what other artists that Last.fm recommends for you.

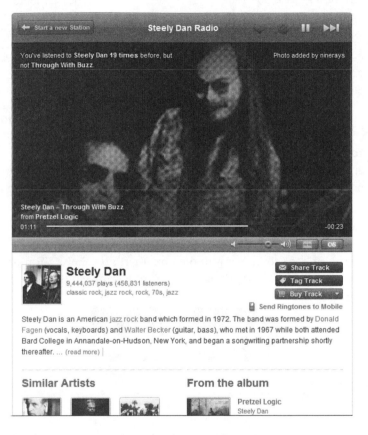

FIGURE 33.4
Listening to a Last.fm radio station.

Discovering New Music with Pandora Radio

Pandora Radio (www.pandora.com) is another popular music recommendation service. It works by playing music similar to song suggestions entered by the user. You can fine-tune the suggestions by voting thumbs up or thumbs down on any given track; your positive and negative feedback affects future suggestions.

Like Last.fm, Pandora is a web-based service. Basic Pandora service is free, although a subscription service is also offered, at $36/year. The free service has ads; the subscription service doesn't.

Pandora's free service streams its audio at 128Kbps—not the best quality available, but probably acceptable for most folks. If you want higher quality audio (192Kbps), go with the paid subscription service.

> ♪ **ULTIMATELY**
> **INTERESTING** Pandora is custodian of the Music Genome Project, which uses more than 400 different musical attributes to describe a piece of music. These 400 attributes are combined into larger groups called focus traits, of which there are 2,000 possible combinations, such as rhythm syncopation, key tonality, vocal harmonies, and the like. Pandora then uses these attributes and focus traits to suggest new music to users.

Creating a New Radio Station

You discover new music on Pandora by entering an artist name, song title, or composer. Pandora then builds an entire real time station based on this single entry.

Here's how it works. Go to the Pandora home page and locate the New Station box, at the top left corner, as shown in Figure 33.5. Enter the name of an artist, song, or composer into the box, then press Enter. (You can also make a selection from the list of suggestions Pandora displays as you type.)

FIGURE 33.5

Creating a new Pandora station.

That's it. Pandora now begins playing the first selection from this station. You can pause and control playback with the transport controls at the top of the page, as shown in Figure 33.6. You also use the thumbs up and thumbs down buttons to "vote" on each track played, as we'll discuss next.

FIGURE 33.6

Controlling playback on Pandora.

Fine-Tuning Your Radio Stations

All the Pandora stations you've created are listed in a sidebar on the left side of the page, as shown in Figure 33.7. Click a station to resume playback.

FIGURE 33.7

Playing a station on Pandora.

The currently playing track is displayed in the middle of the page. You'll see the track's cover art, the name of the track, the artist playing, and the album the track came from. If lyrics for the given track are available, you'll see them under this main information.

There are a number of ways to fine-tune a given Pandora station. You can do the following:

- Click the **Fast Forward** (skip) button in the transport controls to skip the current track. This also tells Pandora you don't like that track.

- Click the **thumbs down** button in the transport controls to tell Pandora you don't like this particular track, and to skip to the next track.

> **ULTIMATELY INTERESTING** You can skip up to 6 tracks per hour per station with Pandora's free service, or up to 12 skips total per day. If you're a paid subscriber, you get an unlimited number of skips per day—but are still limited to six skips per hour per station.

33

- Click the **thumbs up** button in the transport controls to tell Pandora that this track is favorable to you.

- Click **Add Variety** in the left sidebar, directly beneath the name of the station, to display the Add Variety to This Station dialog box, shown in Figure 33.8. Enter the **name** of another artist, track, or composer and Pandora will alter the characteristics of this station to match all the people or songs you've suggested.

> **ULTIMATELY INTERESTING** Two thumbs down to the same artist will ban that artist from the selected station—unless you've previously given that artist a thumbs up. If you don't give any thumb response, Pandora takes that as a positive, but not a strong one.

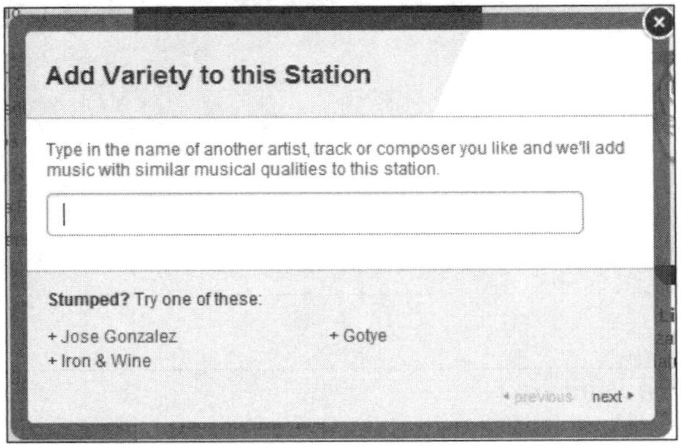

Add Variety to this Station

Type in the name of another artist, track or composer you like and we'll add music with similar musical qualities to this station.

Stumped? Try one of these:

+ Jose Gonzalez   + Gotye
+ Iron & Wine

‹ previous   next ›

FIGURE 33.8

Adding variety to an existing station.

The more effort you put into fine-tuning a station, the more accurate the results. Do a little thumbs upping and downing and you're bound to discover some new music that you really like.

INTEGRATING LAST.FM WITH SPOTIFY

Given Spotify's status as today's hot new music service, I find it interesting how well it integrates with Last.fm, an apparent competitor. The way Spotify does it is smart, in that it doesn't send you to the Last.fm site to get your recommendations; instead, you can view all of Last.fm's suggestions within the Spotify application, via a special Last.fm app.

Once you've connected your Last.fm and Spotify accounts, as discussed previously, you want to install the Last.fm app within Spotify. Once installed, you launch the app by clicking Last.fm in the Apps section of Spotify's navigation pane. As you can see in Figure 33.9, Spotify's Last.fm app consists of four tabs, clickable at the top of the page—Overview, Now Playing, Recommended, and Albums.

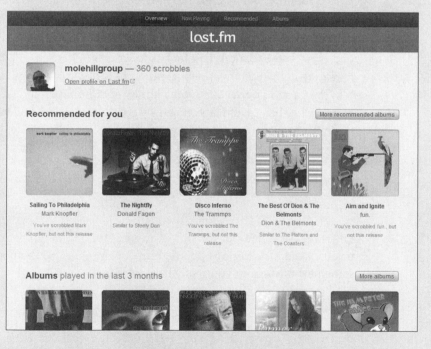

FIGURE 33.9

Viewing personal recommendations in Spotify's Last.fm app.

You use the **Overview** tab to get a quick glance at Last.fm's recommendations. Here you'll find several key sections, including Recommended for You, Albums, Recent Tracks, and Loved Tracks—a good overview of all of Last.fm's various recommendations.

The **Now Playing** tab details the track you're currently listening to on Spotify. Not only do you see information about the track and recording artist, you can also "love" the track (click the **Love Track** button) or create a playlist with similar tracks (click the **Similar Tracks Playlist** button). Similar artists are listed beneath the track/artist description.

The **Recommended** tab lists a dozen albums Last.fm recommends based on your current listening habits. Under each album cover, Last.fm describes why this album was is recommended. Click an album to listen to it now.

Finally, the **Albums** tab lists those full albums you've recently listened to on Spotify. Click the **Add as Playlist** button to add this album as a Spotify playlist.

All that's pretty neat; you never have to leave Spotify to see all the various recommendations Last.fm has for you. But there's also a hidden feature in the Last.fm app for creating new playlists. All you have to do is drag a song from your Spotify library and drop it on the Last.fm title in the sidebar. Last.fm automatically creates a playlist of twenty tracks similar to that song—no typing necessary!

Discovering New Music in the Amazon and iTunes Stores

Not surprisingly, the various online music stores have a vested interest in helping you discover new music. After all, anything new you discover could end up in your shopping cart. The more you discover, the more you're likely to buy.

This is why online music stores are a very good place for you to discover new music. Now, you don't have to buy what you find there, but boy, these places bend over backwards putting new albums and artists in front of you and other potentially paying customers.

With that in mind, in this chapter we'll examine some of the discoverable opportunities in the two largest online music stores—the Amazon MP3 Store and Apple's iTunes Store. If you can't find new stuff there, you can't find it anywhere.

Discovering New Music on Amazon

Let's start with Amazon.com, the world's biggest online retailer. It should come as no surprise that Amazon has a very effective promotional machine oiled up and ready to go—and that machine is particularly effective when it comes to promoting new downloadable music via the Amazon MP3 Store.

What Amazon does best is leverage all the data it collects on its customers. It knows what you've purchased previously and what you've browsed but not yet purchased, and puts that information to good use in suggesting other products in which you might be interested. When this process is applied to music—well, what you end up with are some very appropriate recommendations.

Viewing General Recommendations

The recommendations (for all products) starts on the www.amazon.com home page. Here you'll typically find some sort of promotion at the top of the page, with other recommended products below: More Items to Consider (based on what you've recently viewed), Related to Items You've Viewed, New for You, Inspired by Your Browsing History, and Recommendations for You in various categories. Note that these are, save for that last category, general recommendations from across the Amazon site; depending on what you've been purchasing and browsing, it may include clothing, electronics, and even hair care products. Not very music-specific.

Viewing Music Recommendations

You get your music-specific recommendations when you go directly to the Amazon MP3 Store (mp3.amazon.com). Amazon has a lot of recommendations for you here, including the following:

- **Recommended for You.** These are individual tracks and albums recommended based on your past purchases, as shown in Figure 34.1. To view additional recommendations, click the See More Recommendations link.

- **MP3 Recommendations Based on Your Music.** These are full MP3 albums recommended based on items you've uploaded to the Amazon Cloud Player. This includes items you've purchased, of course, but also items on your computer that you have obtained elsewhere.

FIGURE 34.1

Discover new music recommendations in the Amazon MP3 Store.

■ **Great Deals from Artists on the Rise**. Scroll down a bit and you get into some truly new music—sort of. Yes, these are all new artists that might be worth discovering, but there's a (profit) method behind the madness. You might think these recommendations are hand-picked by some select group of editors or critics, but they're really just paid placements by the artists' record labels. Still, there's some worthy new stuff here, and under each suggestion is a list of similar artists, as shown in Figure 34.2, so you get a feel whether you might like someone or not.

■ **MP3 Recommendations**. Further down the page is a fun little section called MP3 Recommendations. As you can see in Figure 34.3, this section lists a number of individual track recommendations, based on your past purchases, and enables you to preview them before you buy. Just click the **Play** button to listen to a sample of a given track, or click the **track name** to learn more. You can view more tracks by a given artist by clicking the artist name, or click the **Why?** link to discover just why Amazon made this particular recommendation. Finally, if you want to buy a track, click the **Buy MP3** button. I don't know why Amazon didn't put this section higher up on the page; it's probably the most useful thing there, in my opinion.

34

FIGURE 34.2

Discovering new artists—as determined by promotional dollars.

FIGURE 34.3

Previewing new track recommendations.

Now, there's a lot more stuff on the MP3 Store's main page, but it's primarily promotional in nature. For example, you'll typically see 100 $5 MP3 Albums, What's Popular at Amazon MP3, Top Free Albums (worth checking out, but probably nothing worth adding to your collection), and a variety of content tailored to each individual user. There's a Featured in MP3 Store section, which does nothing more than list Amazons' current promotions. Then there are two or three additional sections with content based on what Amazon thinks you like or is trying to promote this month. There's a good reason this stuff is at the very bottom of the page; most of it is purely promotional in nature, with placement determined by how much advertising money a record label ponies up for a given release.

Past that, there's additional discoverable music in the right-hand sidebar. In particular, looks for panes that list best-selling MP3 songs and albums, and one that promotes "movers and shakers" MP3 albums. If your tastes align with what the masses buy, look here.

Bottom line, Amazon makes a lot of recommendations, many of which are decent enough ways to discover new music. Obviously, the more you purchase from Amazon, the more accurate these recommendations will be. Just remember, Amazon is trying to sell you stuff, so there will be promotional announcements scattered throughout the legitimate recommendations. Caveat emptor.

Fine Tuning Amazon's Recommendations

What do you do if Amazon recommends an item that isn't terribly relevant? For example, I often get recommendations based on gifts I've purchased for others—not stuff I'd ever consider buying for myself. Fortunately, Amazon lets you remove irrelevant items, and thus fine-tune your future results.

When you find a bum recommendation, look for and click the **Fix This Recommendation** under the item. This displays the Why is This Recommended for You? window, shown in Figure 34.4, which tells you why Amazon recommended this item. You can then rate the item (from 1 to 5 stars), check the I Own It box, or (this is the relevant one) check the Not Interested box.

Amazon will take your input, either positive or negative, into consideration when making future recommendations. Over time, you should be able to train Amazon to make better recommendations.

34

FIGURE 34.4

Fine tuning Amazon's recommendations.

Discovering New Music on Your Own

Sometimes the best way to discover new music on Amazon is just start clicking around. When you search the MP3 Store for a given artist, for example, you get a list of available tracks, as shown in Figure 34.5. There's a wealth of useful information in this list. You can click a song title to learn more about that song, the artist name to see all the albums from that artist, or an album title to see all the tracks on that album. Even better, you can preview a snippet of any track in the list just by clicking the **Play** button for that track; there's nothing better than actually getting to listen to something new before you decide to buy.

In fact, this preview function is all over the Amazon MP3 Store. (And the main Amazon music section, too.) Open a product page for a given album, and you receive a list of all that album's tracks, as shown in Figure 34.6. You can choose to preview each track individually, or click the **Play All Samples** button to preview all the tracks, one at a time.

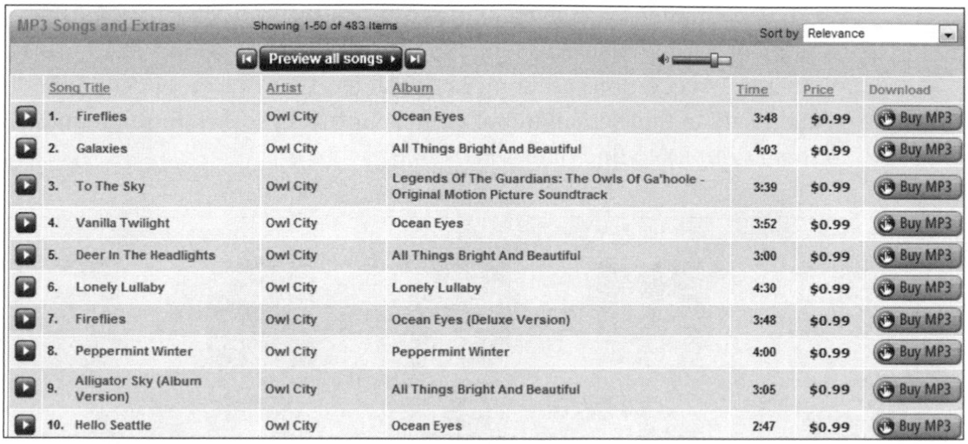

MP3 Songs and Extras		Showing 1-50 of 483 Items					Sort by Relevance
			◄ Preview all songs ► ►		◄ ▬▬▬ ◄		
	Song Title	Artist	Album		Time	Price	Download
►	1. Fireflies	Owl City	Ocean Eyes		3:48	$0.99	Buy MP3
►	2. Galaxies	Owl City	All Things Bright And Beautiful		4:03	$0.99	Buy MP3
►	3. To The Sky	Owl City	Legends Of The Guardians: The Owls Of Ga'hoole - Original Motion Picture Soundtrack		3:39	$0.99	Buy MP3
►	4. Vanilla Twilight	Owl City	Ocean Eyes		3:52	$0.99	Buy MP3
►	5. Deer In The Headlights	Owl City	All Things Bright And Beautiful		3:00	$0.99	Buy MP3
►	6. Lonely Lullaby	Owl City	Lonely Lullaby		4:30	$0.99	Buy MP3
►	7. Fireflies	Owl City	Ocean Eyes (Deluxe Version)		3:48	$0.99	Buy MP3
►	8. Peppermint Winter	Owl City	Peppermint Winter		4:00	$0.99	Buy MP3
►	9. Alligator Sky (Album Version)	Owl City	All Things Bright And Beautiful		3:05	$0.99	Buy MP3
►	10. Hello Seattle	Owl City	Ocean Eyes		2:47	$0.99	Buy MP3

FIGURE 34.5

Previewing music from a selected artist.

MP3 Songs	► Play all samples	◄		
Song Title		Time	Price	
► 1. Falta De Ar		3:59	$0.99	Buy MP3
► 2. Amor De Antigos		2:56	$0.99	Buy MP3
► 3. Asfalto E Sal		2:55	$0.99	Buy MP3
► 4. Retrovisor		3:49	$0.99	Buy MP3
► 5. Teju Na Estrada		0:53	$0.99	Buy MP3
► 6. Contravento		2:40	$0.99	Buy MP3
► 7. Palhaço		2:05	$0.99	Buy MP3
► 8. You Won't Regret It		3:16	$0.99	Buy MP3
► 9. Sereia		0:41	$0.99	Buy MP3
► 10. Baile De Ilusão		3:14	$0.99	Buy MP3
► 11. Fffree		1:06	$0.99	Buy MP3
► 12. Streets Bloom		4:31	$0.99	Buy MP3
► 13. Chegar Em Mim		3:20	$0.99	Buy MP3

FIGURE 34.6

Previewing tracks from an album.

34

When you stumble on a given album or track that you like, look for the Customers Who Viewed This Item Also Viewed section, shown in Figure 34.7. While these suggestions are somewhat influenced by record label promotion, you're likely to find something of interest in this list. Click through and listen to some samples to find out.

Customers Who Viewed This Item Also Viewed

My Head Is An Animal
> Of Monsters And Men
★★★★☆ (20)
MP3 Download
$5.00

Look Around The Corner
(With The Combo Barbaro)
> Quantic & Alice Russell
★★★★★ (1)
MP3 Download
$8.99

Dedicated [+Digital Booklet]
> Wilson Phillips
★★★★★ (21)
MP3 Download
$10.99

Like A Man
> Adam Cohen
MP3 Download
$8.99

That Wasn't Me
> Brandi Carlile
MP3 Download
$1.29

FIGURE 34.7

Discovering music that others have also viewed.

Then, of course, you have Amazon's customer reviews. Customers can rank any item they purchase on a scale of 1 to 5 stars, and that star rating appears at the top of the product page, as shown in Figure 34.8. Scroll down to read individual reviews, like those shown in Figure 34.9, which will give you an indication of what others think about this given album or track. You can opt to view the most helpful reviews, the most recent reviews, or those reviews with a specific star rating (click the rating in the graph at the top of the reviews).

Sigh No More
Mumford & Sons | Format: MP3 Download
★★★★☆ ☑ (446 customer reviews) | 👍 Like (578)

FIGURE 34.8

Viewing an album's overall star rating.

I find Amazon's customer reviews to be one of the best things about the entire Amazon site, and a good way to discover music I might like—or avoid obvious duds. Combine these helpful reviews with the ability to preview just about any track or album available, and you have a combination that I find difficult to beat.

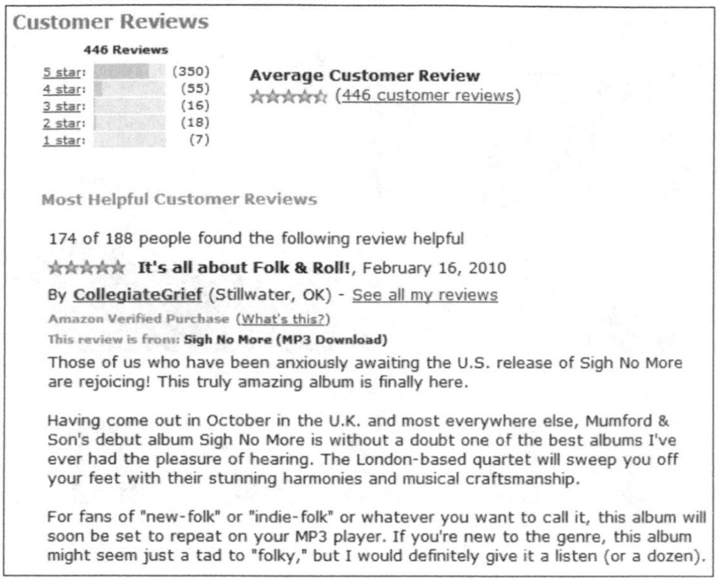

Customer Reviews

446 Reviews

5 star:		(350)
4 star:		(55)
3 star:		(16)
2 star:		(18)
1 star:		(7)

Average Customer Review

★★★★☆ (446 customer reviews)

Most Helpful Customer Reviews

174 of 188 people found the following review helpful

★★★★★ **It's all about Folk & Roll!**, February 16, 2010

By **CollegiateGrief** (Stillwater, OK) - See all my reviews

Amazon Verified Purchase (What's this?)

This review is from: **Sigh No More (MP3 Download)**

Those of us who have been anxiously awaiting the U.S. release of Sigh No More are rejoicing! This truly amazing album is finally here.

Having come out in October in the U.K. and most everywhere else, Mumford & Son's debut album Sigh No More is without a doubt one of the best albums I've ever had the pleasure of hearing. The London-based quartet will sweep you off your feet with their stunning harmonies and musical craftsmanship.

For fans of "new-folk" or "indie-folk" or whatever you want to call it, this album will soon be set to repeat on your MP3 player. If you're new to the genre, this album might seem just a tad to "folky," but I would definitely give it a listen (or a dozen).

FIGURE 34.9

Reading customer reviews.

Discovering New Music on iTunes

Amazon may be the biggest retailer in the known universe, but Apple sells more music downloads. (So there, Jeff Bezos!)

Since a large number of music lovers use the iTunes software and shop in the iTunes Store, iTunes ends up being a good place to discover new music. Apple offers a number of different ways to do so.

What's Interesting (and Promoted) in the Store

The first thing you want to do when you sign into the iTunes Store is click the **Music** tab at the top to go directly to the Music section; otherwise, you're going to have to stumble over movies, TV shows, books, and other stuff that Apple also sells.

What you find on the Music page, shown in Figure 34.10, is somewhat promotional in nature. Okay, almost entirely promotional in nature. But you never know, there might be stuff that's promoted that is also worth checking out.

34

FIGURE 34.10

Discovering promoted music in the iTunes Store.

The very top of the page is a big-assed promotional banner, through which various current promotions rotate. You can bet that it took some big money to get placement here.

Just beneath the big-ass promotional banner is the New & Noteworthy section. You can filter this section by either items new This Week or Recent Hits. In any instance, you're likely to find legitimate new releases here—even if the placement has been paid for.

Next is the What's Hot section. This purports to display iTunes' top-selling items, but I'd bet that there is some promotional consideration for placement here, as well. Call me cynical.

> **ULTIMATELY INTERESTING** Unpromoted new releases are unlikely to show up in the New & Noteworthy section—or anywhere on iTunes, unless you deliberately search for them. Apple, like many retailers, saves its valuable space for those willing to pay for it.

Additional sections follow for various promotions. At the very bottom of the page is a section for New Independent Releases, which, if that's your thing, is worth scrolling down to.

There is some interesting content in the right sidebar as well. I particularly like the iTunes Essentials (click **iTunes Essentials** in the Music Quick Links pane), shown in Figure 34.11. This serves up a hand-picked list of important albums, most of which you probably have but some of which you may have overlooked.

FIGURE 34.11

Viewing iTunes Essentials.

Also interesting are iTunes' Celebrity Playlists (in the More in Music pane), shown in Figure 34.12. These provide some insight into what top music makers are listening to, and that can sometimes be interesting—if you care what Zooey Deschanel, Anthony Bourdain, and their ilk are into, that is.

34

FIGURE 34.12
Discovering celebrity playlists in iTunes.

Previewing New Music

Of course, the iTunes Store has its own preview functionality when you're shopping for new music. Find an album you're interested in and you see that album's track list, as shown in Figure 34.13. Mouse over a track to display the blue **Play** button; click this button to listen to that track.

Scroll further down the page and you see a list of items that Listeners Also Bought, as shown in Figure 34.14. Beneath that are customer ratings and reviews of the selected album. As with Amazon, there's real value in the crowdsourcing of music reviews.

34

	Name			Time	Popularity	Price
▲						
1	Used to Rule the World			4:13	▬▬▬▬	$1.29 BUY ▼
2	Right Down the Line			5:27	▬▬▬▬	FREE ▼
⊙	**Million Miles**			6:21	▬▬▬▬	$1.29 BUY ▼
4	You Can't Fail Me Now			4:15	▬▬▬▬	$1.29 BUY ▼
5	Down to You			3:56	▬▬▬▬	$1.29 BUY ▼
6	Take My Love With You			4:21	▬▬▬▬	$1.29 BUY ▼
7	Not Cause I Wanted To			3:32	▬▬▬▬	$1.29 BUY ▼
8	Ain't Gonna Let You Go			5:58	▬▬▬▬	$1.29 BUY ▼
9	Marriage Made In Hollywood			4:53	▬▬▬▬	$1.29 BUY ▼
10	Split Decision			4:33	▬▬▬▬	$1.29 BUY ▼
11	Standing In the Doorway			5:19	▬▬▬▬	$1.29 BUY ▼
12	God Only Knows			4:26	▬▬▬▬	$1.29 BUY ▼
	Digital Booklet - Slipstream		🗎	–		Album Only ▼

⊙ Preview All   Total: 13 Items

FIGURE 34.13

Previewing music in the iTunes Store.

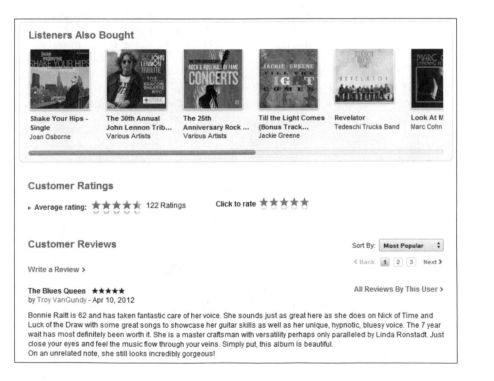

FIGURE 34.14

Viewing what other customers purchased, as well as customer reviews.

34

Getting Genius Recommendations

Given how Apple mixes its iTunes Store with its iTunes music player, it's hard to tell where the store stops and the player starts. With that in mind, it's difficult for me to say whether this next feature is part of the store or part of the player; maybe it's a little bit of both.

I'm talking about Apple's Genius, a kind of automatic playlist/new music recommendation service. It works by creating a playlist based on music similar to a track you've selected; you choose the track from your iTunes music library, and it gets its data and analysis from the iTunes Store. (See my confusion?)

Here's how it works, at least in theory. Display your music library, click a **track** that interests you, then click the **Genius** button in the lower right corner of the iTunes window. Genius will create a new playlist based on what it knows about the track you selected; click **Genius** in the Genius section of the navigation sidebar to see and play that playlist.

> ♪ **ULTIMATELY INTERESTING** Apple also offers Genius Mixes, accessible from the Genius section of the navigation sidebar. These are preselected compilations of tracks from your iTunes library designed for syncing to your iPhone or iPod. They're typically genre-specific, as in Punk Mix, Indie Pop Mix, Urban Crossover Mix, and the like. There's nothing new or discoverable about them; they consist solely of tunes already in your library.

You can also get Genius' recommendations for related music. In this instance, all you have to do is click a track; you'll now see Genius Recommendations at the bottom of the iTunes sidebar, as shown in Figure 34.15.

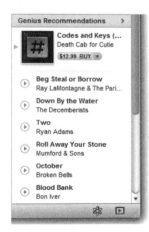

FIGURE 34.15

Viewing Genius recommendations.

View more recommendations by clicking the **Genius Recommendations** link in the iTunes sidebar. As you can see in Figure 34.16, this displays a page with a variety of recommendations based on music (and movies and TV shows) in your iTunes library. You can fine tune these recommendations by voting thumbs up or thumbs down on any recommended track.

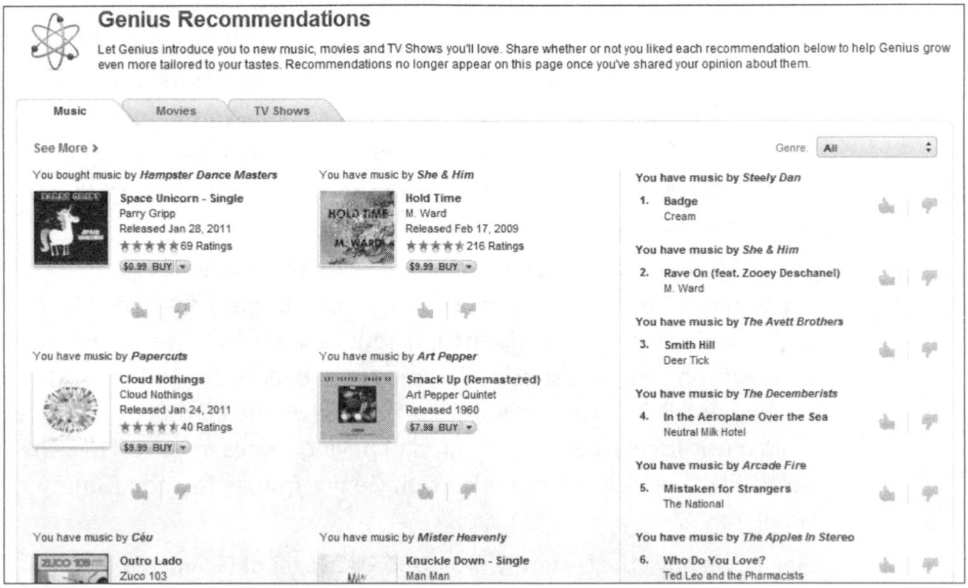

FIGURE 34.16

Viewing iTune's Genius Recommendations page.

Now, you may have noticed that each of these Genius recommendations comes with its own individual **Buy** button. That's because Apple is recommending tracks it has for sale in the iTunes Store. Genius isn't going to recommend something Apple doesn't have for sale, so that's one built-in limitation right there. Also, I'm not sure what criteria Apple uses for its Genius recommendations, but they seem pretty random, at least to me. Still, a recommendation is a recommendation, so take what you can get.

APPLE ISN'T ALWAYS GENIUS

A confession: I don't like Apple's Genius feature. I find it less than genius in many ways and overly promotional in the way it works.

Let's look at its functionality first. One of the big problems I have with Genius is that if you click a track in your library that Apple doesn't have in its online store, it can't generate a Genius playlist. That's probably not a problem for newer releases from current artists (or for any tracks you've purchased directly from iTunes), but if you have a lot of music ripped from CDs and your tastes run older or towards less popular categories (think jazz or classical), then you're likely to run into a lot of cases of Genius brain freeze. And that's annoying.

Speaking of freeze, you may run into performance issues if you try to use Genius with a very large music library. Genius has a tendency to go online to download new information about the tracks in your library, and that can take up a substantial amount of bandwidth and processing power. I've been forced to turn off Genius on the PC that hosts my main music library, because I'm tired of having iTunes freeze on me. (To turn off Genius, select Store > Turn Off Genius from within the iTunes program.)

Finally, we have the blatantly promotional aspect of Genius. Apple really isn't recommending music you might like, but rather recommending products it would like to sell to you. There's a fine line between the two, and, in my opinion, Apple crosses over it. A lot.

In other words, Genius is just another way to serve up somewhat personalized advertising to its customers. It isn't even very good at it, at least in my experience. Yes, Amazon is equally promotional in its recommendations, but it somehow feels less pushy and more relevant. In any case, I find Amazon's recommendations more useful, and I turn off Apple's Genius. Go figure.

34

Discovering New Music via Social Media

Our lives are becoming more social, at least in a super-ficial sense, thanks to the Internet. The various social media—Facebook, Twitter, and so forth—make it extremely easy to share just about anything with just about anybody else online.

There are good and bad aspects about these social media sites, but one of the most beneficial things is how we can use social media to discover new music. It's really a matter of our friends—or people with similar tastes—sharing what they're listening to. There's a good chance that if one of your good friends likes a new band, you'll like that band, too.

Discovering New Music on Facebook

Let's start with the largest social network, Facebook (www.facebook.com). As you've previously discovered, Facebook lets users integrate their online music services with their Facebook activity. The result is that what they're listening to shows up in their news ticker and on their Timeline.

> ♪ **ULTIMATELY INTERESTING** Learn more about Facebook's social music sharing in Chapter 32, "Sharing Your Music—Socially."

To discover new music, you need only be aware of where these new music notices pop up. The news ticker, shown in Figure 35.1, is in the top right corner of your home page, and is updated in real time. (Just like an old fashioned news ticker, natch.) When a friend plays an album or playlist, it shows up in the news ticker with a **Music Note** button; click this button to play what your friend is listening to.

FIGURE 35.1

Discovering what your friends are listening to <u>now</u> in the Facebook news ticker.

You can also find out what your friends are listening to by going to their Timeline. Look for the Music gadget, like the one shown in Figure 35.2, to view recent artists and albums they've played. Click an item to display more information and, if you want, initiate playback.

And, if you know what you're looking for, you're likely to find that your favorite artists have their own Facebook "fan" pages. As you can see in Figure 35.3, an artist page looks a lot like your own Timeline, but customized with some music-specific apps underneath the cover image. You're likely to see information about upcoming tours, new album releases, and the like—and maybe even find some free music to download. Be sure to "like" a given artist page to put their future posts on your own news feed.

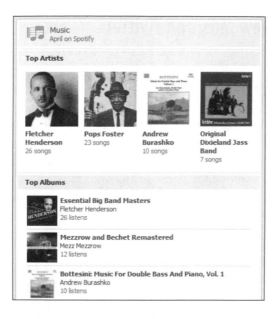

FIGURE 35.2
Viewing your friends' listening habits in the Facebook Timeline.

FIGURE 35.3
James Taylor's artist page on Facebook.

35

Discovering New Music on Twitter

Twitter (www.twitter.com) isn't a social network per se, but rather a microblogging service. That is, people use it to post comments (tweets) to anyone following them, while others read all the tweets posted by the people they follow. There's little direct social interaction.

You can, however, search Twitter for all the tweets that mention specific artists or albums, as well as view trending topics. When it comes to discovering trending new artists and albums, click the #Discover tab then select Browse Categories. Among the various categories listed is the Music category, shown in Figure 35.4. Here you see the most tweeted about artists; mouse over an image to see who that particular artist is.

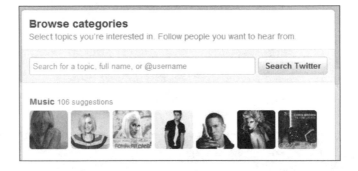

FIGURE 35.4

Browsing trending music tweets on Twitter.

To view all the hot music-related tweets, click the Music head itself. To view all the tweets about a given artist, click that artist's image.

Discovering New Music on MySpace

MySpace (www.myspace.com) used to be the big dog in social networks, but things change. Now Facebook's the largish canine, and MySpace is a fading relic of its past self.

Except that it's been reinvented, to a degree, as a kind of entertainment portal. What you find is that musicians (and other entertainers) are using MySpace to promote their music and connect with their fans.

A quick search for your artist of choice is likely to return that artist's MySpace page, like the one shown in Figure 35.5. Depending on the promotional

35

sophistication of the artist, this page can be either slick as pie or a little more down to earth. (Slick as pie is becoming the norm, however.) Look for free tracks to play online, music videos and concert clips, news about upcoming shows and albums, videos, and messages from the artist. It's really a nice hub for many performers, and a way to learn more about an artist you may be interested in.

FIGURE 35.5
Dar Williams' artist page on MySpace.

There's even more good stuff when you click the Music link at the top of any MySpace page. This displays MySpace's Music portal, shown in Figure 35.6, when you can see what's hot, new releases, music news, and the like. It's a nice place to hang out, especially if your tastes run to newer stuff by younger artists.

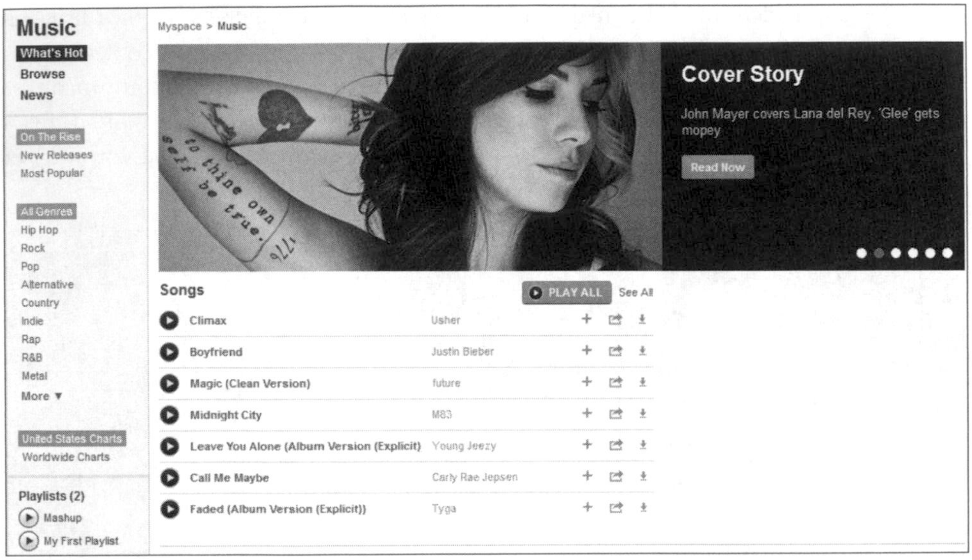

FIGURE 35.6
MySpace's Music portal.

Exploring the Social Aspects of Spotify and Other Music Services

Social networks aren't the only hubs of social activity on the Intertubes. Many online music services are quite social in the way they let their members share music with one another.

Let's look at Spotify as an example, as it's probably the most social of these services. We discussed in Chapter 32 how you can share your Spotify music with others (on Facebook and elsewhere), but Spotify also does a great job of helping you discover new music from your Spotify friends.

First up is the What's New page, or what many consider the Spotify home. Scroll down this page, shown in Figure 35.7, and you see a cover flow-like display of Recommended Albums, based on your recent listening habits. Just beneath this are two lists, Trending Playlists Among Friends and Top Tracks Among Friends. I've found some great stuff by listening to my friends' playlists; just click a playlist title to see and listen to that playlist.

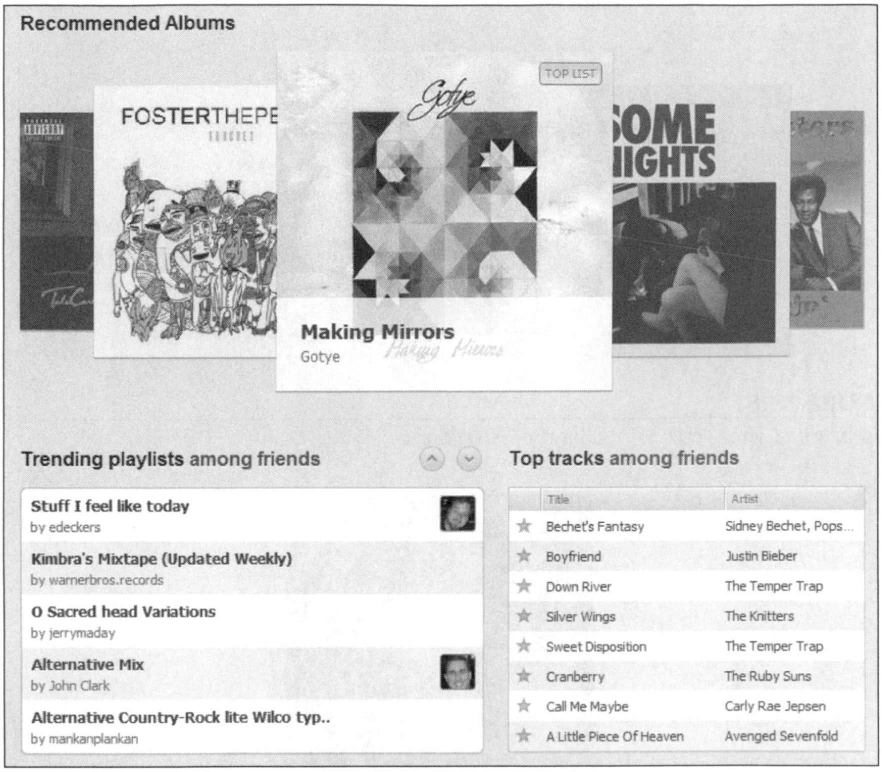

FIGURE 35.7

Viewing recommendations and friends' picks on Spotify.

If you think you share musical tastes with your neighbors, scroll all the way down this page to the Top Playlists Near You and Top Tracks Near You lists, shown in Figure 35.8. I'm not as fond of these lists; they're more interesting in theory than they are useful in practice. I mean, musical taste is seldom geographically defined—at least not at the ZIP code level. I think Spotify offers this only because they can.

More useful is the real-time ticker of what your Spotify friends are listening to, found in the bottom right corner of the Spotify window (and shown in Figure 35.9). Since these are people you've chosen to follow, seeing what they're listening to is often interesting. Again, I've discovered quite a few tracks and artists that I might not otherwise have tried, just because my friends happened to be playing that music at the time.

35

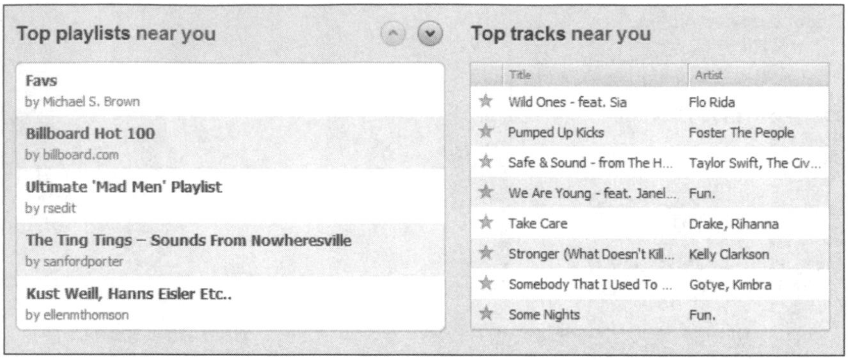

Top playlists near you
Favs
by Michael S. Brown
Billboard Hot 100
by billboard.com
Ultimate 'Mad Men' Playlist
by rsedit
The Ting Tings – Sounds From Nowheresville
by sanfordporter
Kust Weill, Hanns Eisler Etc..
by ellenmthomson
Top tracks near you
Title
Artist
Wild Ones - feat. Sia
Flo Rida
Pumped Up Kicks
Foster The People
Safe & Sound - from The H...
Taylor Swift, The Civ...
We Are Young - feat. Janel...
Fun.
Take Care
Drake, Rihanna
Stronger (What Doesn't Kill...
Kelly Clarkson
Somebody That I Used To ...
Gotye, Kimbra
Some Nights
Fun.

FIGURE 35.8
Discovering what your neighbors are listening to.

John Clark listened to Bodhisattva by Steely Dan
Paul Boger listened to The Moon Is Calling by Nada Surf
Michael Nolan listened to Silver Screen by Beat Connection
Janice Williams Sampeck listened to My Friend by Robbins...
Brian Siemers listened to Now Is The Month Of Maying by Pro...
Jim Logan listened to Married Man

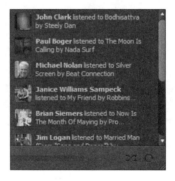

FIGURE 35.9
What your friends are listening to, in real time.

While Spotify is probably the most social of the ilk, other online music services let you discover new music socially. For example, Pandora Radio has a Music Feed feature that lets you follow selected users and view what they listen to with a Facebook-like news feed. As you can see in Figure 35.10, you can play samples of selected tracks, or listen to any stations that your friends have created.

Whichever music service you use, look for that service's social features. You're likely to find several ways to discover new music based on what your friends are listening to.

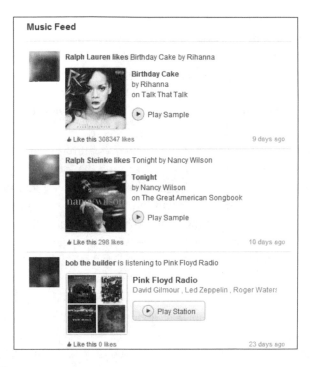

FIGURE 35.10
Viewing your friends' selections in Pandora's Music Feed.

THE MORE THINGS CHANGE...

Throughout my life, I've always been in search of new music. The old stuff's great, I love it and always will, but I remain convinced that there's a lot more truly great stuff out there just waiting for me to find it.

A lot of this new music discovery took place in various record stores over the years. Back in the 1960s, when I was just a wee lad, our local Indianapolis-area Lyric Records stores used to have listening booths in the back. Tell the kid at the counter the name of a particular LP and he fished it out of the cover and handed you the disc, which you then took back to the listening booth and cued up on the turntable. I thought it was terrific that you could listen to an album before you spent your four bucks or so, even if you sometimes ended up getting a pre-listened to album in your bag.

35

This concept of previewing music in the store got more sophisticated in the 1990s, when you started finding CD-based listening stations throughout the retail establishment. Each station had a half dozen or so selections cued up; all you had to do was pop on the headphones, push the **right** button, and you got a nice preview of a given disc.

Previewing an album was just one way to discover new music back then, of course. I can't tell you how many times I got turned onto something new just by hanging around the local record store and listening to what the guy behind the counter was spinning. For example, one hazy afternoon I was cruising the racks at a joint called the Nickel Bag (really!) and was mesmerized by a droning track with lilting vocals that, upon asking, I discovered was Shelleyan Orphan's *Helleborine* album. I bought it and loved it and listen to it still today, and all because some long-haired hippy freak was playing it in the store that day.

Of course, you didn't have to go into a record store to hear about new and interesting stuff. I remember back in my sophomore year of high school having a friend of mine named Lane Williams ask me if I'd heard the new album by Steely Dan. My response ("Who's that Steely Dan guy?") told him that I hadn't, and he proceeded to hip me to *Katy Lied* and several succeeding decades of great music. If Lane were still around today (he passed away a few years ago), I'd thank him for that one.

But that's what friends are for, to share their likes and dislikes and help expand your horizons. If it wasn't for friends and their suggestions I wouldn't have discovered artists as diverse as Marti Jones, Widespread Panic, and Kurt Elling. And I hope I've returned the favor; I know I've recently convinced several friends to listen to British R&B singer James Hunter, and I'm always up to extolling the praises of whichever new discovery I've made recently.

The point is, social music discovery isn't new. We've been sharing and discovering music socially since I don't know when; it's only the medium that's changed. So whether you're listening to a friend's playlist in Spotify or talking about a new album via email or your Twitter feed, it's not all that different from actually talking to a friend about a new release in person. The Internet may make social sharing easier, but it's something we all do, and hopefully will continue to do. If you hear something good, share it with your friends!

Exploring the Best Music Review Sites and Blogs

In this final chapter, we take on the fun but somewhat daunting task of exploring some of the best places to discover new music online. I'm talking about music-related websites and blogs, of which there are more than a few. The challenge is finding which ones offer coverage that is consistently in sync with your personal musical tastes—or that are simply well done, in terms of writing and opinion.

There are lots of different music sites on the web, and it's tough to classify them accurately. Some offer music or equipment reviews, others offer recommendations. Still others aren't technically websites per se, but rather blogs that are posted to regularly by a group of contributors. Still more are online versions of traditional magazines.

36

However you classify them, the sites listed in this chapter are all free and are bound to challenge you, musically, and help you find some great new music to listen to. Read on to see what's out there on the world wide innerwebs.

Exploring Music News and Review Websites

We'll start our tour of music-related websites by focusing on those that clearly focus on music industry news and reviews. Not that other sites mentioned in this chapter don't do this, too, but rather that these sites have news and reviews as their primary focus.

Here's what's out there:

- **All Music** (www.allmusic.com). I've been a fan of the All Music Guide (AMG) for most of my adult life, and a little bit before that. On the surface, AMG is a massive database of information about recorded music; it used to release its information in book format, but now it's available online for all to use, as you can see in Figure 36.1. What you get is a searchable database with information about and reviews of just about every album, song, and artist in recorded history—more than a half-million albums in all, and all with detailed personnel listings.

- **Metacritic** (www.metacritic.com/albums/). This site aggregates reviews from other critics and websites, offering a consensus "metascore" for each item, as shown in Figure 36.2. Users can add their own reviews to the mix, as well.

 ULTIMATELY USEFUL There's also an AMG New Release email newsletter you can sign up for that alerts you to all important new releases on a weekly basis. I must confess that I discover more new albums from the AMG newsletter than I do from any other single source—it's a must-read, IMHO. Sign up for it (and view all new releases) at www.allmusic.com/newreleases/.

ULTIMATELY INTERESTING In addition to its music reviews, Metacritic also offers reviews of movies, TV shows, and videogames.

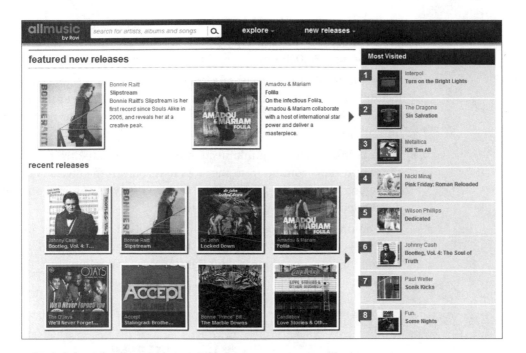

FIGURE 36.1
The All Music website.

FIGURE 36.2
Reading the metareviews on the Metacritic site.

■ **The Music Review** (www.musreview.com). This website is actually a search engine for other reviews online. It searches independent reviews for more than 30,000 artists, or you can browse reviews by genre.

■ **Nashville Music News** (www.musicnewsnashville.com). A great site focusing on country music and the Nashville scene. Includes music news and album reviews, as well as a section specifically for performers and songwriters.

■ **Sputnik Music** (www.sputnikmusic.com). A community-driven review site with reviews coming from the site's users. Given the diverse nature of the user base, you're likely to fine a wide variety of opinions on any given release—which can be a good thing.

■ **Stereogum** (www.stereogum.com). One of the best sites for indie and alternative music news and reviews. As you can see in Figure 36.3, Stereogum does a good job of highlighting new and relatively unknown artists.

FIGURE 36.3

Get your indie music news and reviews from Stereogum.

Discovering Music Blogs

Not all online music reviews are on websites. There are a ton of blogs out there that purport to offer music reviews. Some of these blogs are quite professional in their content, others are just the guy down the street blathering about this or that.

Still, if you're a music lover, it behooves you to seek out some of these music review blogs. Here are the best of the bunch:

- **3hive** (www.3hive.com). Not a review site, per se, but a growing archive of free MP3s from the world of indie and alternative music. A great source for discovering new music.

- **A Blog Supreme** (www.npr.org/blogs/ablogsupreme/). Believe it or not, National Public Radio (NPR) hosts a handful of really interesting and informative genre-specific music blogs. As you can probably tell from the title, this one focuses on jazz, and it's a must-read.

- **Abeano** (www.abeano.com). This is one of the best blogs for new music. It features daily tracks and videos from new artists.

- **The Audiophiliac** (news.cnet.com/audiophiliac/). Not a music blog per se, but a fun little blog focusing on high-end equipment for the digital audiophile, from industry veteran Steve Guttenberg. (No, not that one.)

- **Deceptive Cadence** (www.npr.org/blogs/deceptivecadence/). Another informative NPR blog, this one focusing on classical music.

- **Hear Ya** (www.hearya.com). As shown in Figure 36.4, a music blog focusing on indie artists, including news, reviews, interviews, and free daily downloads.

- **The Hype Machine** (www.hypem.com). This is an interesting one. The Hype Machine scours hundreds of music-related blogs and consolidates what's discussed in a single site. It collects the MP3 links from those blogs so you can click through and listen to the new music being discussed. You can even customize the site to present only news and reviews of the music you're personally interested in.

- **Kings of A&R** (www.kingsofar.com). A great music industry site for discovering new artists.

- **Obscure Sound** (www.obscuresound.com). All manner of indie music news and reviews. You'll also find MP3 downloads, interviews, and the like.

FIGURE 36.4

Indie music news, reviews, and interviews at the Hear Ya blog.

■ **One Track Mind** (www.one-track-mind.com). Another great site for
new artists. Musicians submit their music to the blog for review, in one
of four main genres: Indie, Electronic, Soul, and Hip-Hop. You'll also
find songs posted for free download, which is always a good way to discover something new.

■ **Pitchfork** (www.pitchfork.com). I know, it looks like a website and
smells like a website, but Pitchfork (shown in Figure 36.5) is really a
blog. It's been around since 1995, and features news and reviews from
a multitude of critics. Pitchfork's focus is on independent music, but
also covers a lot of related genres.

FIGURE 36.5

Pitchfork, one of the most popular music blogs in the blogosphere.

■ **PowerPop**

(powerpop.blogspot.com). This is one of my favorite music-related blogs, run by critic Steve Simels, formerly of *Stereo Review* magazine. (I've always loved his famous one-line review of a since-forgotten Doobie Brothers album: "Doobies should be smoked, not heard.") Simels covers the power pop field with his own idiosyncratic approach. This blog isn't as pretty as some of the others (it looks and smells just like the ugly little Blogger blog it is, as you can see in Figure 36.6), but I've always found Simels interesting and funny. It's a definite must read to get your daily dose of the master.

> ♪ **ULTIMATELY INTERESTING**   To tell you how sympatico I am with Mr. Simels, a recent post extolled the virtues of Mark Knopfler's score for the movie *Local Hero*, calling it "classical music, and it deserves to be treated as such, i.e. it should be played at Philharmonic concerts just like any other great opera overture/prelude/intermezzo you could mention." I couldn't agree more; not only is *Local Hero* on my list of top ten (hell, maybe top five) feel good movies, Knopfler's soundtrack matches if not bests his work with Dire Straits and on his own. It really is grand stuff, and it's refreshing to see a top-line critic like Simels recognize it as such.

36

FIGURE 36.6

The utterly unpresupposing PowerPop blog, from the legendary Steve Simels.

Reading Online Music Magazines

Then we have all those music magazines that are evolving from print to digital. Just because they have old school roots doesn't make them any less relevant in this digital age; in fact, some of these are among the best music-related sites on the Internet.

Check out the following:

- **DownBeat** (www.downbeat.com). The premiere jazz mag, shown in Figure 36.7, now online with its news, reviews, and interviews. The site includes a searchable archive of classic articles.

FIGURE 36.7

DownBeat Magazine online, for jazz aficionados.

- **MOJO** (www.mojo4music.com). The online version of the popular U.K. music magazine. Unique in its frequent coverage of classic rock acts, as well as newer artists.

- **NME** (www.nme.com). The venerable *New Musical Express*, online. As you can see in Figure 36.8, this is actually one of the top music sites on the web, period. Tons of news, reviews, videos, blogs, you name it from all segments of the industry.

- **Paste** (www.pastemagazine.com). Music news, reviews, features, and blogs—plus the same for movies, TV, games, and books.

- **Rolling Stone** (www.rollingstone.com). Yeah, RS is still around, and sometimes still relevant. It's online, too.

FIGURE 36.8

One of the best music sites online period, from NME.

■ **Sound and Vision** (www.soundandvisionmag.com). Back in the day it used to be known as *Stereo Review* (and it used to have Steve Simels as its top rock critic). Times change, and we now listen to full-blown home theater systems instead of archaic stereo rigs, but the since rechristened *Sound and Vision* magazine remains a top source of equipment and music reviews.

■ **Spin** (www.spin.com). Music reviews, news, interviews, videos, blogs, you name it. A pretty good site, overall.

■ **Stereophile** (www.stereophile.com). Like *Sound and Vision*, but keeping its old school name and focus. Tons of audiophile equipment reviews, with a handful of music reviews thrown in for good measure.

Using Music Recommendation Sites

There's one more category of website you might find interesting, and that's the music recommendation or discovery site. These sites let you input key data (such as artists or tracks that you like) and spit out additional music or artists you might like. It's a great way to discover new stuff, online.

Here are some music recommendation sites to check out:

- **Music Roamer** (www.musicroamer.com), shown in Figure 36.9
- **Music-Map** (www.music-map.com)
- **TasteKid** (www.tastekid.com)
- **TuneGlue** (audiomap.tuneglue.net)

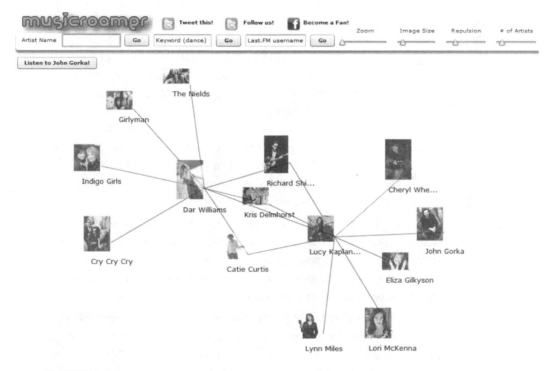

FIGURE 36.9

A web of interconnected artists from Music Roamer. (I started with Dar Williams and went from there...)

36

EVERYONE'S A CRITIC...

Music reviewers and critics have always been harbingers of taste, and the first step for many in discovering new music. Back in the day it was Lester Bangs, Robert Christgau, Dave Marsh, Steve Simels, and the like. Today... well, thanks to the Internet, anybody can be a critic. And that's both good and bad.

If you want to put in your five cents worth about an artist or album today, all you need is a blog, a Facebook page, or a Twitter feed. Anyone can pipe up; in fact, some websites (think Metacritic or even Amazon) encourage individual reviews that they then aggregate into a crowdsourced meta rating.

Unfortunately, it's almost too easy to say that something is the greatest thing in the history of mankind, or that it really sucks, man. (Don't get me started on how web-provided anonymity is contributing to a decline in civil discourse.) In other words, just because someone *can* speak their mind doesn't mean that they *should*. Much of what passes for "criticism" on the web, for both music and otherwise, is mindless self-serving blather. Most web reviewers simply don't have the background and training to offer informed opinion; just because you have an opinion doesn't make it worthwhile to others. The opinion of the cool dude at your local coffeehouse doesn't and shouldn't mean as much as the opinion of an experienced critic.

That's not to say that valid new voices aren't being developed, and quickly, online. The wide wide world of webs is a great training ground; it's certainly easier to post a review on your blog than it is to get a job at a leading music magazine. Some of these budding critics are quite good and will get better with practice. That's great.

It's also not a bad thing to get a feel for the musical zeitgeist, which crowdsourcing does. Yes, one informed critic can speak volumes, but hundreds of less-informed regular folk can also say a lot. If the general opinion is that something stinks, it probably does.

Personally, I like the fact that the Internet hosts so many opinions about so many things. I no longer have to wait for my weekly or monthly music rag of choice to arrive to find out whether a new release is worth buying or not; now I can go online on the day the album is released and find dozens of people voicing their opinions pro or con. You have to apply your own filters, of course, but there's a lot of raw data to go on.

It's the same thing with general information about anything in the digital music realm. Thanks to the Internet, it's a lot easier now than it used to be to find information and opinion about any specific model of equipment, which makes for more informed buying decisions. You can use the Internet to get informed, to see what others are doing, to find step-by-step instructions, and to gain advice from those who came before. It's a true cornucopia of information and opinion, which you can use as you wish.

And that is perhaps one of the big takeaways from this book. Music lovers have benefited from the move to digital, and not just in terms of audio quality and ease of access. The Internet provides various new ways to listen to your favorite music and to discover new music that might become a favorite. The digital revolution is part and parcel of the Internet revolution; to experience everything there is to experience musically today, you have to be online.

Of course, advice is appreciated wherever it comes from, so I hope you've gotten something useful out of this collection of words you're either holding in your hands or reading onscreen. I appreciate the fact that you've spent the time (and money) to read this little book, and hope to hear from some of you in the future. I'll try to keep in touch in my accompanying Ultimate Digital Music Guide blog (ultimatedigitalmusicguide.blogspot.com), so check in there to see what's new—and to add your own comments and opinions.

After all, everyone's a critic, including you. I'm sure there's someone somewhere who's interested in what you're listening to and what you think about it. Maybe someday, thanks to the Internet and all it offers, you'll be as influential as Bangs or Marsh or their old school ilk. Wouldn't it be pretty to think so?

Index